I'm not okay, you're not okay, and that's okay.
~Elisabeth Kübler-Ross, MD

HIGH PRAISE FOR
But You LOOK Just Fine

Finally . . . a first-rate resource to hand to patients or family members of those suffering from depression or an anxiety disorder. A support group in a book! Readers will recognize themselves and find both practical advice and profound inspiration in *But You LOOK Just Fine*. In both words and photographs, the authors profile men and women who live with mood disorders and allow them to reveal their own struggles and coping tools. Readers will recognize and connect with their stories and challenges. A compelling, unique, and important work.

—Sidney Cassell, MD
Physician, Internal Medicine and Rheumatology

This is the first book to literally put a face on depression and anxiety disorders! As a mental health professional for over thirty-one years, I wish this resource had been available long ago. My clients and I would have benefited greatly from *But You LOOK Just Fine*.

Abdulaziz and Sveilich have broken new ground with this realistic portrait of chronic depression, anxiety, post-traumatic stress disorder, obsessive-compulsive disorder, panic disorder, and other mental health challenges. Those who haven't experienced mood disorders will have their eyes opened and will gain a greater understanding and compassion for those who live with these challenges. Those who have lived with mood disorders will recognize their own stories, emotions, trials, and triumphs, and will feel hopeful again.

There is help, there are options, and most importantly, people need to know that they aren't alone. It is amazing how much power there is in the awareness that one is not the only person going through his or her ordeal. Having this awareness in and of itself can lessen the stress of living with these conditions.

Through unique profiles, including words and pictures, the authors show the true story behind the mask of difficult-to-manage mood disorders and allow each voice to be heard. Abdulaziz and Sveilich's gift is not only their writing but also allowing each person to have a voice, their voice, and share a bit about what they deal with on a day-to-day basis.

I highly recommend this book to the general public and especially to those in the mental health community. It is a powerful resource for self help, education, and treatment.

—Nancy Gordon, LCSW

This second installment in the *Just Fine* book series is a wonderful resource for anyone searching for insight into the devastating world of mental illness. Having practiced family medicine for nearly two decades, I have seen the magnitude of suffering caused by these disorders. People often discount the power that these illnesses can have on the human body, and the ripple effect on family and society in general.

Physical symptoms are part and parcel of mental illness but may lead people away from discovering the true cause of their suffering. Our culture's traditional denial of mental disorders as "real" diseases has sadly deprived many patients of appropriate treatments. This latest work in uncovering concealed suffering throws open the closet door and reveals the wide impact of mental illness. More important, however, are the candid profiles of real-life patients and the inspirational work they have done in managing their lives. We all have much to learn in sharing their pain and rejoicing in their perseverance.

—Margaret Elizondo, MD
Family Medicine, Hospice Care and Palliative Medicine Specialist

Between the Diagnostic and Statistical Manual (DSM-IV-TR) and the reality of the lives of our patients, our friends, and ourselves, there has always been a difficult-to-navigate void.

These two authors cross that void fearlessly. Diagnostic criteria are linked to photos and personal statements about the reality behind the pathology. The pathology takes on a human reality. For instance, few therapists and fewer doctors would think to instruct a depressed person to have a few easy-to-prepare meals around. This could mean the difference between health and malnutrition.

This book is a precious contribution.

—Estelle Toby Goldstein, MD
Psychiatrist

"Nobody knows how I feel" and "no one else feels this way" are the most common themes I hear from patients who are struggling with a mood disorder. Sveilich's latest book is here to prove them wrong. Not only does *But You LOOK Just Fine* show these folks they are not alone, the book also offers coping tools, tips, and strategies for symptom management, reminding them that they can make a difference in their own lives.

As a clinical psychologist, I can guide, teach, and support patients on a professional level, but I cannot truly know how they feel. The brave people who have come forward to tell their stories in this book allow patients to say, "That's it. That's exactly how I feel!" and to know that someone understands. I would incorporate *But You LOOK Just Fine* into any treatment plan for patients experiencing a mood disorder and their families.

—Nancy S. Thompson, PhD
Psychologist

If you want to know what it's like to live with a mental illness, you ask the people living with one. Sahar Abdulaziz and Carol Sveilich asked. Prepare to be surprised. Prepared to be enlightened. That's what learning, understanding, and growth are all about. *But You LOOK Just Fine* won't disappoint.

—John McManamy
Author of Living Well with Depression and Bipolar Disorder

This long-overdue book reminds us that the old axiom "Never judge a book by its cover" is true, especially when talking about people with mental illnesses such as depression, anxiety, and the like. They may look just fine, as the book title suggests, but inside they may be struggling with serious challenges that many of us can't even begin to fathom.

As a geriatric social worker, I know I'll be recommending this book to the families and friends of my clients, many of whom have secretly struggled with mental illness for decades. Kudos to Abdulaziz and Sveilich for writing such an important book.

—Lesley Alexander, MSW
Geriatric Specialist

We come into this world unfiltered, pure, and eager. We learn from our families and communities that there are expectations and assumptions about what our lives *should* be. We begin to develop a series of filters and a mask to don as we navigate through life. And if, perchance, we encounter trouble along the way, we develop symptoms and ailments that require an even more complex mask to be woven into that which we already wear.

Soon it seems nearly impossible to remember who we really are—what our true experience is. And those around us have acclimated to the masks we wear and the lies we tell. They are no help to us as we try desperately to disentangle ourselves from the web.

Finally there is a resource for those who have worn that mask, but no longer desire its suffocating fit. *But You LOOK Just Fine* not only provides a wealth of information about the mental disorders and illnesses that those masks often hide, but it also personalizes the material with stories of those who have struggled to live seemingly normal lives, while internally holding onto reality by the skin of their teeth. *But You LOOK Just Fine* gives permission for the masks to be released and shines light on the invisible disabilities that lie beneath, inviting the reader to view these beautiful men and women in their raw truth.

—Sage de Beixedon Breslin, PhD
Psychologist and Author of Lovers and Survivors
and contributor to the Chicken Soup for the Soul *series*

Several of my executive coaching and leadership development clients, including lawyers, also suffer from anxiety and depression. Sveilich's latest book is a tremendous resource to help in the referral process. In the age of social media and transparency, the creative integration of solid information and authentic stories of real people with faces can help people lead much happier and more fulfilling work and personal lives. *But You LOOK Just Fine* connects resilient people facing difficult challenges in a true spirit of collaboration and gratitude.

—Maynard Brusman, PhD
Psychologist and Executive Coach

When I was young and housebound from anxiety, panic attacks, and agoraphobia, I could find no information, nor could any doctor give me a diagnosis to explain what was happening to me. The only thing I knew was that my father, an aunt, and my father's cousin had suffered with similar symptoms for most of their lives.

It is a devastating feeling to believe you are alone in your suffering and think you will never live a "normal" life again. Thankfully Sahar Abdulaziz and Carol Sveilich have gathered up a wealth of information to help you understand these mental conditions. When you read the stories by real people who are suffering just like you, you'll know you are not alone.

—Polly Meyers
Director, Break Free From Anxiety
Moderator, Fear Less-Live More

The word *persona* in Latin means mask. People wear masks for disguise, to avoid recognition, to celebrate. The social mask—the face we hide behind—is often the hardest to take off, especially for those who suffer quietly and invisibly from depression, post-traumatic stress disorder, anxiety, and other mental disorders. *But You LOOK Just Fine* separates the mask from the authentic self behind it.

—Laurel Doud
Author of This Body

Reading the personal stories in Abdulaziz's and Sveilich's new book, and absorbing the struggles and triumphs of those who often suffer in silence behind a facade of being "just fine" reminds one of the therapeutic value of listening deeply on all levels. There is great importance in simply being present in the moment for one another. This is true in the mental health areas and in all health-care settings, but also in our personal contacts of daily life. *But You LOOK Just Fine* will be a valuable reminder of this and a terrific tool for health-care providers.

—Rita Blanchard RN, MSN,
Psychiatric Nurse for forty years

Abdulaziz and Sveilich heard the stories of countless men and women with a variety of concealed mood disorders. They took the stories and wove them into a unique presentation, so others could appreciate the special challenges of looking one way while feeling quite another. They include the hardships these disorders present and useful techniques for dealing with the symptoms.

The authors address each topic from a number of perspectives by including examples of people with depression, anxiety, post-traumatic stress disorder, obsessive-compulsive disorder, and panic disorder. There is a vast divide of acceptance and empathy between hidden and obvious disorders. Through revealing narratives, the authors demonstrate that people find it easier to empathize with those who have visible impairments, but most find it nearly impossible to sympathize with an apparently happy and calm person who complains of unseen symptoms and psychic pain.

This book is a unique resource for those who suffer with mood disorders, those who work with them, and those who love them.

—Diane Dike, PhD
Author and Speaker, Diane Dike has appeared on
Oprah Winfrey's OWN Network

I've heard these heartbreaking stories a thousand times in my career as a doctor specializing in the treatment of anxiety disorders. Because anxiety sufferers tend to be above average in intelligence, it has been my experience that the more education they have, the more likely they are to follow through on treatment, and their outcome tends to be much more positive. *But You LOOK Just Fine* presents a wonderful base of knowledge and lets sufferers know that they are not alone.

—Ron Meyers MA, MS, DC
Co-developer of Break Free from Anxiety
Author and International Speaker

As a health-care worker, *But You LOOK Just Fine* will be an invaluable resource to pass along to our patients. We see a large number of men and women in our practice who show symptoms of depression, anxiety, panic disorder, and other forms of emotional distress. There are too few resources to hand to patients where they can not only see their own stories portrayed, but also view the faces and read the stories of those suffering with similar challenges. There is comfort in numbers and realizing you're not alone in your struggles.

This book is uplifting yet realistic. *But You LOOK Just Fine* offers anything but a "poor-me" approach to living with a mood disorder. It offers hope while revealing realistic accounts of what it is truly like to contend with these daily symptoms and challenges. This is the book that we will gift to many in our practice and will have available to patients in our waiting room.

—Hollie Ketman, LPN
Nurse in Rheumatology for over thirty years

Sufferers of mental illness have a unique struggle. They not only have to cope with symptoms, but they have to cope with the stigma about what the illness may represent in the minds of acquaintances and even family members. Additionally there are many myths and misunderstandings about the various mood disorders.

This unique book personalizes many forms of disorders, removing the veil of suspicion and fear. Behind the veil are human beings with so much to offer—with normal joys, concerns, and strengths. They aren't just their diagnosis, they are so much more. Each one is a whole person.

In this unique book, these individuals are able to share from their heart and mind, providing us with a personalized and valuable viewpoint—their own. The authors truly do supply the reader with a "support group" in book form. Abdulaziz and Sveilich provide a framework for both the sharing of emotions and experiences as well as solid information about various diagnoses. I look forward to recommending this book to both coworkers and clients.

—Julia Terry, LCSW

As a health-care worker, I have seen many patients with major depressive disorders. This disorder affects the young, the middle-aged and the geriatric groups. The different generations have different anxieties and traumas; nevertheless, the end state is equivocal. *But You LOOK Just Fine* offers a realistic presentation of the trials and tribulations of those who suffer with depressive disorders. It enables the reader to empathize and realize they are not alone.

—Mary Jane Strandberg, MSN, ARNP, NP-C

Sociologists talk about the "medicalization of deviance," the process by which deviant acts are transformed from moral issues into medical issues. A recent example is alcoholism, once thought of as a lack of individual discipline and moral backbone, now seen as rooted in genetics. Abdulaziz and Sveilich call our attention to an equally significant and opposite phenomenon, one we might call the normalization (or even trivialization) of illness: when others insist that there is nothing wrong with the sufferer, simply because the condition is not apparent. In both situations, others decide for us what we have or don't have, and how we should feel. And that's precisely why Abdulaziz's and Sveilich's new book and the *Just Fine* series are so important: they demand that we pay attention to the people themselves; it insists that only we know how we feel. And that's also why readers experience the book as liberation.

—Evan Adelson, PhD
Professor of Sociology, Mesa College

But You LOOK Just Fine is an outstanding book! As someone who works in healthcare, I see this as a one-of-a-kind resource. The book features the detailed aspects of a variety of mental disorders coupled with the candid sharing of personal experiences. It may be the only resource available that can truly change and improve the lives of those of us dealing with depression and anxiety disorders.

—Yelena Kipervas, OD
Doctor of Osteopathy

As a registered nurse for thirty-five years, I've found there are many books on the topic of depression and other mental health challenges. This one excels because it delves into the lives of those who actually live with depression, anxiety, post-traumatic stress disorder, and many other mood disorders. We hear the voices of those who know what it is truly like to wrestle with these issues on a daily basis.

Ongoing depression and anxiety disorders are a struggle. Those of us who haven't experienced such a disorder will have their eyes opened, while those who have will feel less alone in their challenges. As a nurse I have seen many people who hurt not only physically, but emotionally as well. They feel terribly alone and hopeless much of the time, like someone who is standing outside looking in, and often terribly isolated. It doesn't have to be that way.

There is hope, there are options, and most importantly, people need to know that they are not alone. It is amazing how knowledge can offer strength when it seems to the sufferers that they are the only ones going through these difficulties. They feel no one understands them, and they oftentimes feel unloved. These issues can cause friends and family members to distance themselves from the sufferer, which only intensifies the feelings of loneliness and hopelessness.

Abdulaziz's and Sveilich's gift of writing and bringing these hidden problems out of darkness and into the light is enhanced further with the use of black-and-white portraits. Each person is allowed to have a voice to share his or her own story and personal coping tools. I highly recommend this book to the medical and mental health community. Share it with your coworkers, put it in your waiting rooms. It gave me a new perspective, and I hope that it will do the same for you.

—Janis Uquillas, RN
Registered Nurse for thirty-six years,
Alternative Health Researcher, Founder: JES Organics

But You LOOK Just Fine is a surprisingly thorough exploration of easily concealed mood and anxiety disorders. It provides insight, knowledge, and hope in the form of suggestions for moving through these often debilitating conditions. The depth of information provided is a perfect blend of clinical language and down-to-earth clarity that can be easily understood by the patient, not just clinicians.

The quotes from the participants are truly helpful. Reading their own candid stories and struggles, as well as learning about their coping tools, is enlightening. I believe this book will help many people gain greater understanding of their condition, greater acceptance of themselves, and the tools to move forward in their lives in a self-supportive way.

—Beverly M. Lubin, MA, MFT

What I find both remarkable and refreshing about the authors and their effort to unmask and confront some of the more insidious emotional disorders that affect and indeed debilitate so many of us, is that they avoid the misuse and even abuse of information that such guides can all too easily promote. *But You LOOK Just Fine* relies on genuine and well-substantiated accounts of the very real struggles we either fail or fear to see in ourselves and others.

—Stephen G. Lincoln
Sociologist and *Criminologist*
Centre for Mental Health and Addiction, Toronto, ON

But You *LOOK* Just Fine

Unmasking Depression, Anxiety,
Post-Traumatic Stress Disorder,
Obsessive-Compulsive Disorder,
Panic Disorder, and
Seasonal Affective Disorder

Sahar Abdulaziz, MS
Carol Sveilich, MA

Please visit the *But You LOOK Just Fine* book-site after you login to Facebook for more coping tips, discussions and resources.
https://www.facebook.com/ButYouLOOKJustFine

Copyright © 2013. Sahar Abdulaziz MS, Carol Sveilich MA
All rights reserved.

ISBN: 1478113995
ISBN-13: 9781478113997

Library of Congress Control Number: 2012911519
CreateSpace Independent Publishing Platform
North Charleston, South Carolina

CONTENTS

FOREWARD — xxi

PREFACE — xxvii
    Carol Shares — xxix
    It Takes a Village — xxxii
    Sahar Shares — xxxiii
    The Hidden Nature of Mood and Anxiety Disorders — xxxvii
    Acknowledgments — xxxix
    About the Portraits and Participants — xli

INTRODUCTION   Why a Book on Easily Concealed Mood and Anxiety Disorders? — xliii

Chapter 1   **PUT ON A HAPPY FACE** — 1
The Misleading Mask of Mood and Anxiety Disorders — 1

    How Do I Look? — 3
    Food for Thought — 5
    The Masquerade — 5
    The Predictability of Unpredictability — 8
    Survivor—Not Just a TV Series — 9
    Suspicious Minds — 10
    The Element of Surprise — 11

Chapter 2:   **ROCK 'N' ROLL** — 15
The Jolt of Depression and Mood Disorders

	The Many Faces of Depression	17
	Depression and Anxiety—What's in a Name?	20
	Coping with a New Diagnosis—Changing the Rules	24
	The Impact of Depression on Self and Others	27
	Validation and Acceptance	29
Chapter 3	**THE INSIDE STORY ON DEPRESSION AND ANXIETY DISORDERS**	33
	What Causes Depression?	36
	Intimacy and Mood and Anxiety Disorders	38
	Mild Mannered or Major Depression— What Do You Have and Why Does It Matter?	40
	Why So SAD? (Seasonal Affective Disorder)	42
	Rock 'n' Rolling with the Baby Blues	44
	Help! How to Assist Someone Who Has a Mood or Anxiety Disorder	45
Chapter 4:	**SNAP OUT OF IT!** *Myths About Depression and Anxiety Disorders*	49 / 49
	Men and Depression	56
	Surviving Depression	60
	Show Me the Money	62
	Screen Time	62
	A Final Note	62
Chapter 5:	**I'M ALL SHOOK UP** *Anxiety: Depression's Close Cousin*	67 / 67
	Generalized Anxiety Disorder (GAD)	69

	Social Anxiety Disorder (Also Known as Social Phobia)	71
	The Blank Face of Phobias	74
	Specific (Simple) Phobias	76
	Treatments for Phobias—EMDR	76
	Pushing the Panic (Disorder) Button	78
	What Is a Panic Attack?	78
	Treatment for Panic Disorder	82
	Agoraphobia	83
	Post-Traumatic Stress Disorder (PTSD)	84
	What Does Trauma Look Like?	86
	The Military and PTSD	91
	PTSD Stemming from Military Life	95
	PTSD—A Family Disorder	96
Chapter 6:	**FLYING SOLO**	101
	The Isolation of Depression and Anxiety Disorders	101
	Isolation and Developing Relationships	104
	The Dating Game	105
	Counteracting Isolation	107
Chapter 7:	**DECIPHERING YOUR DIRECTION**	111
	Types of Therapy	111
	Cognitive Behavioral Therapy (CBT)	111
	Unhelpful Thinking Habits	112
	Art Therapy	116
	Strength in Numbers—Considering Group Therapy and Support	117

Chapter 8:	"MUST" ON THE MIND	125
	Obsessive-Compulsive Disorder	125
	How to Help the Person in Your Life Who Has OCD	132
	Children with OCD-like Behavior	133
	"Normal" Behavior in Children	134
	Cause for Concern	135
Chapter 9:	BRIDGE OVER BUMPY WATER	137
	Additional Treatment and Therapy Protocols	137
	The Benefits of Talk Therapy	137
	More on Cognitive Behavioral Approaches	140
	Online Therapy—Good or Bad Idea?	141
	Treatment Options	143
	New Possibilities on the Treatment Horizon	145
Chapter 10:	EMBRACING A NEW NORMAL	149
	Accepting an Easily Concealed Mood Disorder	150
Chapter 11:	EQUAL OPPORTUNITY DISORDERS	153
	Teens and Senior Citizens with Mood and Anxiety Disorders	153
	Teens and Mental Health	153
	Seniors, Retirement, and Depression	155
Chapter 12:	YES TO SUCCESS	161
	Having Hope While You Cope	161

	Uncovering Good in the Bad	161
	Stages of Acceptance—Going On Despite Grief	162
	Can You Have a Good Day Anyway?	170
	The Worry Window	171
Chapter 13:	USE IT AND LOSE IT	173
	Exercise for Mood and Anxiety Disorders	173
	Stress and Health—Implications of Chronic Stress	178
	What You Can Do To Stay Healthier	179
Chapter 14:	THE UP SIDE OF LIVING WITH DEPRESSION OR AN ANXIETY DISORDER	181
	Lessons Learned from Mood and Anxiety Disorders	188
Chapter 15:	MOOD RIVER	191
	Mind-Body Medicine and Moods	191
Chapter 16:	TRANSCENDING SPIRITUAL PAIN	199
	Spirituality and Other Coping Skills	199
Chapter 17:	THE PAIN CHAIN	207
	The Link Between Chronic Illness, Pain, and Depression	207
Chapter 18:	THE FICKLE NATURE OF BRAIN CHEMISTRY	215
Chapter 19:	TO SHIELD OR REVEAL	219
	The Key to Disclosure	219

Chapter 20:	DEPRESSION AND ANXIETY IN THE WORKPLACE	225
	Employment and Mood Disorders	225
Chapter 21:	HOLD ON	231
	Remaining Hopeful and Cope-ful	231
	Coping with the Difficult Days	232
Chapter 22:	A GLANCE BEHIND THE MASK	241
NOTES		429

FOREWORD

A disability that is not apparent in a person's appearance is no less intrusive, no less painful, no less disturbing than one that can be spotted across the room. And yet many people fail to respect the tremendous impact that the invisible disability has on the human enduring it. For those of us who have suffered in silence and appeared able-bodied and capable to the outside world, who have received looks of disdain or confusion in response to our requests for help, and who have endured mental illness, tragedy, and trauma without community, sometimes without family support, there is finally a sigh of relief. Someone gets it. Someone has finally come forth to reveal our truths, to recognize and acknowledge the reality we have known, until now, alone.

The authors of *But You LOOK Just Fine* provide a wealth of information about the mental disorders that plague so many and are recognized by so few. But anyone can read a textbook or diagnostic manual. What sets *But You LOOK Just Fine* apart from the rest are the tales that are woven through the material, allowing the reader to finally know what it's like for someone to understand what they have been going through, whether for months, years, or even a lifetime. The dozens of men and women who shared their stories so this book could be written for others like them, like us, have brought an end to the isolation so many of us have endured as a result of our attempts to hide our symptoms and disorders. Through these portraits, their dichotomous lives are illuminated. Through their stories, those invisible disabilities are documented in black and white. Through their photographs, their masks are unmasked and memorialized for all to see. There is no more authentic depiction of our struggle.

But You LOOK Just Fine doesn't stop there. The authors don't just expose the challenges of living with mental illness and clinical disorders. They don't just enhance our sense of universality through the presentation of the stories and photos. They tread further into the light by providing solutions. Treatments, interventions, medications, and more innovative protocols are shared for those who are actively seeking recovery and resolution. And for those managing more endogenous, organic, or treatment-resistant disorders, the authors provide tips for coping with it all.

This book may just be the new manual for those suffering in silence, regarded by those around them as *just fine*. It can also be a terrific accompaniment to any therapy or treatment program in use, as it supports and embraces those who have endured their symptoms in isolation. Those who have shared their symptoms, their lives, their stories, and now their faces, become a family of choice for the reader of this book, whose own family may have no understanding of what life is really like for the person who lives with one of these challenging disorders. Through these pages you will find the invitation to finally eliminate the "I'm just fine" mask from your wardrobe and learn a singular truth, perhaps till now hidden: you are not alone.

—*Sage de Beixedon Breslin, PhD*
Licensed Psychologist, Consultant, and Author of *Lovers and Survivors*

Millions of people the world over know the challenge of living with an invisible illness—that feeling of getting dressed, putting on the smile, and acting as if all is right with the world when the feelings on the inside do not match at all.

FOREWORD

Whether one is masking the fatigue and pain of a physical illness such as fibromyalgia, lupus, rheumatoid arthritis, or any number of invisible disorders, or hiding the pain, sadness, and hopelessness of depression, the outside mask is the same—showing the world how you wish you were feeling, not the actual reality of what you are experiencing on the inside. And what happens on those days when the inside reality can no longer be masked? How do we cope and adjust to what ails us?

The authors of *But You LOOK Just Fine* beautifully capture the experiences of real individuals who live with a variety of mood disorders. As is the case with many different mental diagnoses (as well as with numerous "invisible" medical conditions), there's a discrepancy between what the individual is experiencing internally and what the person is displaying externally. Everyone has had a "bad day," when you just don't feel like pasting on the "happy face" and making believe that you don't feel like the world is going to cave in around your ears. Take that one- or two-day feeling and multiply it by 365 days in a row. This can be the experience of someone suffering from a mood disorder, be it depression, anxiety, obsessive-compulsive disorder, post-traumatic stress disorder, or panic disorder.

Ranging from a variety of medical conditions such as chronic fatigue syndrome, irritable bowel syndrome, Crohn's disease, arthritis, and a variety of autoimmune disorders, persons suffering from these types of disorders know well the experience of "looking fine" while "feeling awful" on the inside. Because of this seemingly contradictory duality, persons with chronic illness often suffer in their own personal silence. The simple question of "How are you today?" places the person into a quandary; Do I say how I really feel or do I simply give the perfunctory response of "fine" or "okay" when the true answer is so very different? Do people really want to hear about all of my aches and pains and feelings of sadness about losing my former self?

The authors Sahar Abdulaziz and Carol Sveilich know all of the intricacies of looking one way but feeling another. Both are highly educated, well-trained individuals who both happen to come from helping fields—Sveilich as a counselor at a large university, writer on health topics, and support group facilitator; and Abdulaziz as a counselor and advocate for victims and survivors of domestic violence and sexual abuse. During the course of their lives and careers, it is unlikely that either of them ever entertained tackling the subject of "invisible illness" as a topic for a book. The first successful endeavor arose from Sveilich delving into the world of chronic pain, invisible illness, and how people have learned to cope and survive. The first book in the *Just Fine* series, *JUST FINE: Unmasking Concealed Chronic Illness and Pain*, has been referred to as a "support group in a book"—an accurate representation of the melding of good research combined with true life stories of real individuals who deal with these disorders on a daily basis. Finally having a place to turn to for answers, recommendations, and good, solid support fills a void that previously went unfulfilled.

This new book is full of useful information that details the characteristics and symptoms of mood and anxiety disorders. What this book also provides that other books do not is the fascinating interweaving of individual histories from people who actually live with these disorders. While one can learn about the criteria needed to receive a certain diagnosis, being able to "experience" how, for example, depression impacts one's daily ability to function and the simultaneous internal dialogue that someone with depression lives with provides for a unique and profoundly deep understanding of the anguish and level of challenge encountered as part of the daily struggle to survive.

Depression and anxiety each provide their own unique set of circumstances that can take the joy out of daily living. Coping with the flashbacks and heightened fear reactions that accompany post-traumatic stress disorder are extraordinarily real and debilitating. The horror of having recurrent thoughts intrude into one's mind as one is doing something as simple as trying to get organized to leave the house for work can be life altering to the point of "freezing" the person into a state of complete inaction. Hearing about these disorders from the "inside

FOREWORD

out" is not only invaluable, but it is a brilliant approach to integrating facts with reality. In that each of the authors have their own "invisible illnesses" to cope with, it is likely that their own private experiences have led them to this ingenious pairing as a means of giving readers the best possible picture of living and coping with invisible disorders.

In *But You LOOK Just Fine*, authors Sahar Abdulaziz and Carol Sveilich undertake some of the most pressing issues of our time. Mood disorders impact millions of adults and children on a daily basis in the United States and worldwide. The struggle of living with any one of these mood disorders can totally alter one's existence. As is often the case, an individual can be afflicted with more than one mood disorder at a time. While attempting to cope with the feelings of sadness, isolation, and hopelessness of depression, that same person can simultaneously be trying to deal with high levels of debilitating anxiety that render the person immobile. Over the past forty to fifty years, the stigma of having a mood disorder has begun to lose some of the shame and embarrassment once attached to it. However, even with television bombarding us with commercials for mood stabilizers and medications to help with depression and anxiety, people still shy away from readily acknowledging their conditions. They hesitate to share what it truly feels like to have to "make believe" that all is right with their world when, in fact, the act of sitting up in bed and swinging one's leg to the floor is overwhelming.

Over the past twenty-five years, the number of self-help books and books that attempt to educate the public about mood disorders has grown rapidly. How fortunate for those who already suffer with these challenges that there are now places to turn to for information and assistance about what they are experiencing. In the past, people with "invisible illnesses" had to deal with the lack of information and the feeling that their illness was something they needed to hide or, even worse, feel ashamed of or embarrassed by. Hopefully, with the advancement of research, more information will come to the forefront, and people will be better able to cope with and navigate through these medical conditions. Persons with mood disorders can only be grateful for authors such as Sahar Abdulaziz and Carol Sveilich who have filled a great need by writing *But You LOOK Just Fine*. Readers will enjoy meeting the individuals in the book who were candid and willing to share their personal experiences, coping tools, and journey. The authors' way of intertwining these individual stories with factual information provides the reader with a worthwhile learning *and* supportive experience.

—Shelley Slapion-Foote, PhD
Psychologist for twenty-five years

PREFACE

Just as this book was going to press, the suicide of a former linebacker in the National Football League was headlining the news. Junior Seau was a magnetic and seemingly fearless leader on and off the field. Those who have never known depression couldn't believe how someone who seemed so jubilant, successful, secure in wealth, and with a loving family could consider such a final act. But then they don't know or understand depression. Not "in-a-bad-mood" depressed, but a clinically, chemically imbalanced depressed.

Clinical depression doesn't leave you in your right mind. There are no cool breezes on a warm day. There are no joyful colors or resources to lift you to your feet. Days are gray. A bad day is pitch black. When you are in the grips of depression, rational thought is not part of the package, and this state leaves the rational trigger in the brain switched to the "off" position. A chemical imbalance triggered Junior Seau's thought process in much the same way, bathing him in that same bleak slate of dark hues that depression provides, even after years of bright lights and public glory.

People with depression can't just "snap out of it" or "turn that frown upside down." Depression is a painful and overwhelming state that makes one unable to function or to think clearly or reasonably. Sometimes the chemical changes impact the person in such a way that they cannot fathom facing another day.

Many people suffer alone and in silence because they are scared or ashamed. They feel weak or pitiful. How can a person be incapable of having joy? "Why can't I just have a good time? Why can't I get on with it?" And those in the spotlight, who live under the microscope of public scrutiny, fear being discovered, ridiculed, and shunned should their illness be discovered. So they wear a mask for the public and sometimes even for themselves.

Other people can't fathom how somebody in good physical health, with a decent job, with children who love them, who seems relatively normal and content on the outside, can be terminally unhappy. And when people try to explain it, they often feel pathetic and weak even to themselves, so they suffer quietly.

Junior Seau wasn't just having a bad day or feeling slightly sad when he pointed that gun to his chest. He wasn't being selfish. He wasn't being a coward. He was ill.

We don't know exactly what causes depression, his or anyone else's, but it is a true illness. Whatever the causes, depression still contains the same invasive and debilitating ingredients, and they are sometimes unbearable to endure.

Does it make it easier for others to reach out for help when they see these seemingly macho sports celebrities and alpha-male types such as Seau, Ray Easterling, Dave Duerson, Derek Boogaard, Wade Belak, and Rick Rypien take their own lives? Time will tell. But one thing is for certain: the negative stigma attached to depression must go.

Both authors of *But You LOOK Just Fine* are exceedingly familiar with feeling one way and looking another. They both participate in this charade in their daily lives and for their own individual reasons. It's no wonder that Sahar Abdulaziz and Carol Sveilich are acutely responsive to the uncertainties and unique challenges of concealed mood disorders.

Having a disorder that leaves one's exterior appearance intact, but affects one's inner world in a significant manner is a double-edged sword. On the one hand, the hidden nature of the disorder helps individuals conceal how they really feel, so they can effectively project a healthy, trouble-free demeanor and appearance. To others, this individual may seem calm, cool, and collected. The downside of this, however, is that others may perceive the disorder as less legitimate because the person appears perfectly happy or serene on the outside. Observers cannot fathom how a disorder can be so disruptive on the inside and not reveal itself on the outside. The authors' own challenging experiences led them to unite and create this unique resource on the hidden nature of mood disorders.

Carol Shares

The French writer Gustav Flaubert said that we do not choose our subjects for writing, they choose us. The topic of this book chose both my coauthor and me. We both carry the same gift and burden of feeling one way on the inside while we appear very different on the outside. This can be both a blessing and a curse, depending upon surrounding circumstances.

People sometimes conceal their differences or challenges from others in a multitude of creative ways. That is especially true of those who live with depression, anxiety disorders, post-traumatic stress disorder, obsessive-compulsive disorder, panic disorder, and a variety of other mental disorders. On the inside their stomachs may be churning, their hearts racing, and blood pressure soaring, but on the outside they look perfectly content, happy, and just fine.

There is no mood disorder book on the market that thoroughly addresses this dichotomy of feeling one way on the inside while appearing quite different on the outside. There *should* be such a book, we thought. But how could we literally show this conflict between the inner and outer world? Would people be comfortable sharing what has helped them manage their symptoms and handle their challenges? Would they be willing to share their experiences and emotions in a candid manner while revealing in photographs the pleasing expression and ordinary face they show to the world? Are there numerous methods for treating or coping with these disorders that bring different people varying degrees of success?

The answer to all of these questions is a resounding *yes*. The people profiled in this book had the opportunity and courage to share their stories, which in turn may help countless others uncover their own path to a more contented place.

My own experience in "feeling one way on the inside while appearing another on the outside" is not uncommon, yet at first I felt very much a lone traveler on this all too common journey. It wasn't until 1989 that I noticed my physical health was in decline. At the time I was working as a counselor in a large university and enjoying my daily interactions with the students and faculty. I kept a tidy home, regularly handled numerous tasks throughout the day and juggled difficult responsibilities without letting any of them fall by the wayside. Multitasking was effortless and second nature for me. I had always had what I called "an overactive three-ring circus" mind! However, annoying physical symptoms began to interfere with my daily activities, and they grew increasingly difficult to ignore. The worse these symptoms became, the harder I had to work at minimizing them.

Ultimately I received a diagnosis of several chronic health challenges. I tried to will them away, but that wasn't effective. I tried to live in denial. That worked . . . for several years. On the outside and throughout this struggle, I looked as I always did: perfectly healthy, energetic, carefree, and just fine.

Having my life impacted by a chronic illness and ongoing pain was like having someone come into my orderly home and turn all of the drawers and furniture pieces upside down. My calculated plans for the future were now littered with obstacles. Everything was in chaos. I could not seem to put matters, or myself, back in order. I no longer had resilience. I felt like Humpty Dumpty. All the wise doctors and all my willpower could not put me back together again.

Fatigue and pain filtered in, keeping me from my household chores, social life, and job responsibilities. My mind started to feel as weary as my body. It was no longer clear or capable of functioning at warp speed. I became severely disappointed with myself. My future started to look murky, then gray, then pitch-black.

PREFACE

I woke to days filled with high anxiety, deep sadness, grave disappointment, and feelings of inadequacy. Where was my stamina, confidence, razor-sharp mental capabilities and high-wire act where I could juggle many balls in the air without letting anything fall? My old self, the one in whose skin I had always felt comfortable, had departed. A new self was taking over the old territory, and I had to discover a way to make peace with it. I had to recognize that there was a new set of rules in place. I needed to let go of all previous plans from my old life. I had to embrace a new normal.

I soon learned that living with chronic pain was often accompanied by days wrapped in deep depression and high anxiety. The time had come to seek out some form of support. In searching my hometown for information and support groups, I found few resources. Over the next several months, I decided to take matters into my own hands and plant the seeds of a support group in my community. At the time I had no idea how many other people were living with similar symptoms, challenges, and fears. Feeling isolated and different from the masses around me, I imagined only a handful of people were in the same sorry boat that I found myself sinking in. However, I moved ahead and scheduled the first meeting in my small living room. It quickly grew from a half dozen members to 158!

I eventually wrote a book on the topic of living with an easily concealed illness or physical pain. The book was entitled *JUST FINE: Unmasking Concealed Chronic Illness and Pain.* It became known as "a support group in a book" for those who were not able to leave home easily to attend an in-person support group. It's my greatest hope that this new book on mood and anxiety disorders will become a similar a tool in the mental health community.

A common thread began to emerge from my work with various support services. People with hidden challenges were dealing with two major issues: 1) the actual symptoms of their disorder, and 2) the dichotomy and emotional impact of looking like they *should* be okay but feeling far from it.

Numerous members of these groups expressed the same sentiment on a recurring basis: *we are the healthiest-looking bunch of sick people around!* It was true. We all appeared perfectly healthy, even while dealing with a host of debilitating and chronic symptoms. The disjunction between appearance and inner reality was one of the factors that led to my exploration of concealed chronic disorders, not only with words, but also through photographs.

A frequent topic concerned the frustration of not having these disorders considered significant or valid by friends, coworkers, family members, and even some practitioners in the medical profession. Those with easily concealed symptoms may sometimes begin to doubt their own disorder and diagnoses. Why is this so? When these people catch a reflection of themselves in the mirror, they are able to see for themselves that the crushing fatigue, chronic pain, debilitating mind fog, uncontrollable depression or anxiety, and a host of other challenging symptoms do not necessarily reveal themselves in their outward appearance. Instead the face reflected back at them presents the distinct impression of being just fine.

A person can appear healthy, lively, happy, and on top of his/her game even after years of living with a concealed chronic disability, whether it be a mental disorder, physical illness, or chronic pain. This can become a mixed blessing. Even people who enjoy looking happy and do not want to be perceived as sad, weak, scared, or anxious can begin to doubt or belittle a legitimate mood or anxiety disorder if they themselves are fooled by the outward image they present.

It Takes a Village

We decided to direct this current book specifically to those individuals who live with a mood or anxiety disorder. Our goal is not only to provide the best and most current information on these disorders but also to allow some of those who are afflicted to discuss challenging, common, and recurring issues in a candid manner. *But You LOOK Just Fine* is a book of "show and tell," in which men and women not only reveal the face and expression they share with the world but also let us enter a more intimate world of personal experiences, emotions, and survival. In their own words, we hear what helps them maneuver through their individual obstacle courses of everyday life.

Lao Tzu, a mystic philosopher of ancient China, is best known as the author of the *Tao Te Ching*. He once said:

> *The softest things in the world*
> *May be harder than the hardest.*
> *Soft water can go through the strongest wall.*
> *Knowing this, I know the value of calm.*
> *Knowing this, I know the value of patience.*
> *Knowing this, I know the value of persistence.*

People who live with mood or anxiety disorders know that their most valuable tools are serenity, patience, and persistence. In these pages, they share how these tools assist them, even as these very attributes sometimes elude them.

Sahar Shares

As we move through each new day, we do so with the inherent expectation that most of it will be easily maneuvered. We participate in daily tasks and avoid obstacles almost without thought, just as easily as we open our eyes and take in the morning sunlight. We continue through the day's events and life's hiccups with a minimal amount of distress. We laugh and enjoy that hot cup of tea or coffee, that soft breeze on our face, or a spirited exchange on the phone with a close friend. In private, when we look into the mirror, we see a person who is accomplished, appreciated, or dynamic. When we take a moment to reflect, we honor our dreams, goals, and accomplishments. Life is not a task but a journey.

But wait, I think to myself. This is all wrong! This is how I thought I was supposed to be, but it's not how I really am. Everything is so difficult now. I can't get my brain and body to communicate in the same way any longer. My mind is in a haze. Nothing is easy or fun any longer. Everything is complicated, from opening my eyes in the morning to trying to close them at night to rest. My mind never stops churning, and I don't know where my thoughts are heading from one moment to the next. I am anxious, disoriented, exhausted, and numb. Something monumental has changed inside of me, and I can't wrap my mind around it. I no longer laugh, except when I put on a mask and act as if everything is okay. I still look like the same person to those around me, but I am not the same person. I feel so painfully alone and terribly misunderstood. I feel deeply guilty and horribly ashamed. I want the "old me" back—my old life. I want to be the person I thought I was. What is happening to me?

I recall never feeling quite right since I was about seventeen years old. Before that I never became sick. I distinctly remember earning awards from school for never missing a day. I look back at that time, and I am unable to isolate one single memory of ever having a major cold or the flu. Most, if not all, of my aches and pains I inflicted upon myself due to my natural youthful clumsiness. All my childhood hospital visits resulted from foolish stunts that I pulled, such as running in the house and cracking my head on the TV set, or building a fort in the backyard and having a tool drop on my head. I can even remember falling down while showing off my latest karate move in the kitchen one evening as we were cleaning up from dinner. The term "klutz" certainly applied to me then.

As the years went on, I began to experience physically painful days. Complaining about invisible aches and discomfort wasn't tolerated or encouraged in my family. No one wanted to hear about that. If you hurt you kept it to yourself, unless you were visibly bleeding or one of your limbs was hanging in a cockeyed direction. You went to school, played sports, participated in band, did your chores, and kept your mouth shut. On the outside I looked perfectly fine. My skin glowed. I was always on the go. There weren't any visible signs exhibited to the people who loved me that something terribly wrong was about to take place inside of me.

After many years with an excessive number of bad days and despite a series of misdiagnoses, nothing could have ever prepared me for the day I found out my diagnosis: Crohn's disease. In many ways it came as a relief because there finally was a name for what I had been experiencing. It was real, it was chronic, and there was no cure. It was at this pivotal point in my life that I had to find a way to fully absorb and accept all the new ramifications that came attached to dealing with a very serious chronic illness, including the emotional toll it had already begun to take.

At first it felt rather surreal. I went on a fact-finding mission by searching the Internet and learning all I could from the massive number of websites and books available on the subject. But after a while, everything I read became clinical and repetitive. Nothing I read addressed the indescribable fear and anger I felt inside as I watched myself implode. Nothing I read addressed anything but a list of expected symptoms, an array of different medications and their possible side effects, a few pointers for good nutrition, and a blurb or two about living with the disease. Feeling frustrated, I just told myself that somehow I could find a way to control the pain, make it all go away. I would fix my body by willing myself back to perfect health.

My nights felt endless, and my days were filled with a whole new set of norms. Tasks that were once effortless took longer and demanded additional amounts of my already limited energy. Over the years, as I began to see that my disease was worsening, I also began to become exceedingly frustrated with my physical limitations and with myself, which only drove me to become even more angry and resentful. I didn't like what was happening to me. What had once seemed so simple to accomplish now became so difficult and sometimes nearly impossible. And on top of it all, I still had my family to take care of, to teach, and to nurture. I had several small children at the time of my diagnosis. Their needs didn't just go away because I had a disease. Coupled with feeling ill, I was fraught with guilt about not being able to be the mother I once was. My body decided to change the rules, and I desperately didn't want my children to have a mother whom they would only remember as always being ill and secluded.

The more I ran these thoughts through my head in an endless loop, the angrier and more resentful I became. At first I felt sorry for myself. What exactly did I do to become the recipient of such a disease? How did I get it? Why did I get it? Where did I get it? I had always prided myself on being physically fit, eating well, and never compromising my body with anything remotely dangerous. I ate natural foods, drank healthy teas and lots of water, so what the heck happened?

For many years, I had worked as a hotline worker, counselor, and advocate for victims and survivors of domestic violence and sexual abuse. These individuals were exposed to a constant barrage of traumatic events, which increased the likelihood of them developing a multitude of challenging disorders, or provoking an already pre-existing condition including, but not limited to, post-traumatic stress disorder, anxiety, depression, addictions, dissociative disorders, or even suicide tendencies. The hazardous environment of living as a target of violence, and being physically, emotionally, and spiritually abused, left many clients with a foreboding legacy of life injuries. The majority of physical injuries usually healed in time. However, the mental and emotional disorders that accompanied these injuries threatened their stability and welfare in ways that affected every aspect of their lives and their sense of security. I intuitively understood this conflicting dynamic as a person who, for most of her life, looked physically healthy but on the inside, felt very different. I lived such a life.

From the very young to the very old, from every walk of life, no one is immune to the destruction caused by violence. Constant exposure to life-threatening traumatic events is commonplace in the military as well. During wartime soldiers are exposed to a level of stressors beyond the normal scope of most people's tolerance levels. Soldiers returning home are faced with many challenges, including the heritage of the scars of military combat and the constant threat of daily fears from the battlefield recurring. Post-traumatic stress disorder, flashbacks, anxiety, and depression are widespread, but the stigma against openly seeking help is also prevalent. Not only do soldiers suffer, often alone, but their family members deeply suffer as well.

I remember meeting and observing one young man who had come back from the war. His appearance was similar to when he left home four years earlier, but emotionally he had significantly changed. Before heading overseas he could entertain a room with his colorful stories and keep everyone on the edges of their chairs. Now when we talked, he was incapable of holding his concentration during our exchanges and was apparently also suffering from hypervigilance. His eyes would dart busily around the room as if an ambush were lurking nearby and ready to attack. He was unable to peacefully sleep for long periods of time. He experienced bouts of endless nervous energy and debilitating anxiety and became enraged quickly over minor matters.

I had also discovered that he had become increasingly self-destructive. He would ride his motorcycle over 120 mph on the highway with his hands waving in the air instead of on the handles. Eventually he crashed. Thankfully he lived, but he never sought the needed medical help for post-traumatic stress disorder. He didn't believe that it was a real disorder, nor did he want to be labeled as having any sort of emotional disorder or to be seen as weak. Because he was in denial regarding the seriousness and very existence of his anxiety disorder and the life-threatening danger it was propelling him toward, he wouldn't acknowledge the symptoms he was experiencing or his risky behavior as anything other than wanting to have some fun.

The Hidden Nature of Mood and Anxiety Disorders

Why write a book that compellingly delves into the murky and often misunderstood world of mood and anxiety disorders? Why give voice to the pain behind the exterior mask many of us wear on a daily basis? Martin H. Fischer, a German-born American physician and author, once stated, "If you are physically sick, you can elicit the interest of a battery of physicians; but if you are mentally sick, you are lucky if the janitor comes around."

Many of the current books on various disorders do not address how terrifying and challenging it can feel to be unable to participate in activities, a work life, or ongoing relationships because of symptoms. These books don't focus on those familiar feelings that you've let yourself and others down. They don't examine the long hours spent cocooned in the mind, in the body, sometimes even in the house itself, unable to emerge from the darkness into the light. Sleepless nights. Blurred days. Dreams deferred.

What this book will not do is generate pity. The people profiled in these pages are warriors. They spend countless hours visiting doctors, taking tests, picking up medications, battling insurance companies for coverage, fighting fatigue, and contending with sleep deprivation, appetite changes, increases in pain, and financial adjustments. These types of seemingly endless impediments can cause a person to feel out of control, stressed, hopeless, helpless, and most definitely angry. Anger about all of the "could haves," "would haves," and "should haves" blatantly stares them in the face, almost like a bully teasing and testing his victim.

Coming to terms with a chronic mood disorder is an unrelenting struggle. Learning new coping tools to best deal with difficult situations is not a lesson absorbed overnight. It takes time. This book offers pointers and experiences from those who have already walked this well-worn path. It gives recommendations on how to share the news about your disorder with loved ones, colleagues, or your extended family and friends. The following pages are filled with sound counsel and encouragement about how best to deal with well-meaning individuals who still, out of ignorance or apathy, compound the problem.

But You LOOK Just Fine is an extraordinary journey with many necessary stops along the way. The readers are our valued guests, as well as our partners, in this unique quest toward lifting the veil of cool darkness and sharing the warmth of the light. Light is knowledge, compassion, acceptance, camaraderie, and hope. Welcome.

PREFACE

Acknowledgements

Books are often puzzles made up of words, but also created with time, effort, and heart. We are pleased to be able to express in writing our gratitude to those who have assisted us in making this book possible and who helped us complete the intricate jigsaw puzzle entitled *But You LOOK Just Fine.*

First and foremost, we owe an enormous debt of gratitude to the courageous individuals featured in the last section of this book. They selflessly shared details of the intimate struggles in their own lives and in their own words, in hopes of reaching and benefiting others who may also be battling depression, anxiety, post-traumatic stress disorder, panic disorder, or a host of other mood challenges that are easily concealed but not a comfortable dance partner. The candor and courage of these men and women who shared their coping tools, emotions, and experiences are what bind the pages of this book.

A special note of appreciation to a select and special group of mental health professionals for allowing others to benefit from their knowledge and insights: Gail Saltz, MD; Bejai Higgins, MFT; Kent Bennington, PhD; Sage Breslin, PhD; Shelley Slapion-Foote, PhD; Larry Wampler, PhD; Cassandra Friedman, PhD; Christy Vaughn, LCSW; Lesley Alexander, LCSW; John McManamy, mental health author and journalist; Djamila Abdel Jaleel, LCSW; and Adina Shapiro, LCSW. Also a special thanks to Jason Copping, DC; and Dan Harper, MD.

We'd also like to offer a personal note of appreciation to the early readers of this manuscript for their dear friendship, honest feedback, and keen eyesight. They were and remain our angels and coconspirators in creating this unique resource: Lu Larsen, Becky Platero, Julie Benn, Marianne Regan, Laura Ahmed, Carol Westover, Don Kenney, Beth Krippner, John Butcher, Eileen Ward, and Larry Wampler, PhD. A special thanks to Brad Petersen for his assistance with the photographic and graphic challenges of this book.

A special note of gratitude from Carol Sveilich: During the writing of this book, both of my parents passed away. I'd like to dedicate this book to their memory, and to thank them for the transference of their survival skills and for their sense of humor, which is the fuel that sustains me. I hope that others see their story in its pages and benefit from the shared coping tools and experiences of the brave men and women who appear in the final section of this book. A special thank you to Yao and Sadie, for their carefully crafted purrs and for curling up on my lap during the typing and production of much of this manuscript. And finally, my heartfelt gratitude to Alicia Avila Outcalt for her ever-present support and guidance. She remains wise beyond her years.

A special note of gratitude from Sahar Abdulaziz: Each journey in life manifests both a test and a challenge. During these trying times, when the world's weight feels cumbersome and arduous on my very being, I have been deeply blessed to have the strong shoulders of my husband, Shahid, to lean on, the welcomed coolness of the eyes from my children Tarik, Mustafah, Shadha, Tawfiq, Jehan and Shahid, and the song in my heart given to me by my grandchildren Ariana, Zaidan and Neylan. I have also had my cherished friendships to help keep my spirit recharged and my brother Michael's treasured counsel to reflect upon. Throughout this writing process, my father's genetically imparted tenacity has kept me steadfast, while my faith has kept me honest. I am deeply grateful to all of you who have supported me during this leg of my travels.

PREFACE

About the Portraits and Participants

> *I know the bottom, she said. I know it is with my great taproot;*
> *It is what you fear.*
> *I do not fear it: I have been there.*
>
> —Sylvia Plath

Although there are many good books on the topic of various mood and anxiety disorders, there is an absence of resources that examine an individual's outward appearance and how it runs contrary to the individual's personal pain, symptoms, and inner world. This juxtaposition is the cornerstone of *But You LOOK Just Fine.*

For each person who thought this book would be an excellent vehicle for telling the true tale of concealed mood or anxiety disorders, a dozen more discouraged the project for one explicit reason: they felt that no one would want to reveal his face or her mental disorder in such a public forum, let alone discuss symptoms and challenges in a candid and detailed manner. Much to our delight, the reaction from the community of people who live with concealed symptoms was just the opposite. For many, the interview sessions were cathartic and healing. Each person seemed to gain a great deal of personal insight and growth through involvement with this book, and they all expressed gratitude for the opportunity to participate in such a unique and worthy project.

The uniqueness of *But You LOOK Just Fine* is that the truth about these disorders and their hidden symptoms is revealed through the potent coupling of words and pictures. In the interviews, participants discuss their personal challenges, coping mechanisms, and experiences. Each portrait reveals the person appearing to the outside world: healthy, vibrant, and just fine. However, participants' words reveal the true story and the daily struggle of living with a mood or anxiety disorder.

Although there are many mental health professionals cited in *But You LOOK Just Fine*, this is not a medical book nor should it be used as such.

Rather it is unique in that it explores those individuals whose outsides do not mirror their insides.

All of the individuals profiled in the book are featured with only a first name (or pseudonym) and the first initial of their last name. You will meet John M., who talks about the challenges of the dating world when one has a mood disorder. Mysty D. will convey her first recollections of having depression and what it felt like as a young girl, how it manifested, and how she survived her darkest days. Larry J. will discuss his post-traumatic stress disorder, how it developed during the Vietnam War, and how it impacted his relationships, career, and social life. Keith M. will share moments surrounding his debilitating social anxiety; Janaya G. will talk about her obsessive-compulsive disorder and how it impacts her everyday life; and Don. K. will address how depression and anxiety played a role in his development of alcoholism.

There is a spectrum of emotions that medical tests and medications cannot address or measure. This is where shared human experiences and insights are needed. The power in knowing one is not alone is immense and as necessary as medication or medical treatment. It can keep one's spirits from sinking into a dark place of isolation and despair.

It is the authors' greatest hope that the profiles featured in the second half of the book will help to inspire and educate others, while illuminating the shadows of fear, isolation, and self-doubt that often accompany mental illness.

INTRODUCTION

Why a Book on Easily Concealed Mood and Anxiety Disorders?

> *People want to believe that life is either impossible or easy,*
> *but not that a good life is both difficult and possible.*
>
> — Jean-Paul Sartre

Why write a book about feeling one way—depressed, anxious, panicked—while appearing another way—perfectly composed and pleasant in demeanor?

People are visually oriented for the most part. More often than not, we believe what we see and make character and value judgments based solely on visual perception. But what happens when a person who *appears* happy, content, and just fine to family, friends, and coworkers is quietly suffering from deep depression, panic, or anxiety? Is he taken at his word when he says he is not feeling up to participating in a particular activity, or that he is feeling so panicky or frightened that he can't join the frenzy of activities taking place around him? Or are his reactions misunderstood, discounted, seen as excuses, or interpreted as some character flaw such as laziness or selfishness?

There is frequently a dichotomy between image and reality. Those who feel depressed, anxious, or fearful often appear free of these afflictions. Most of us are guilty of drawing sweeping conclusions based on appearance. Though this is only natural as we assess the abilities, strengths, and flaws of others, it is important to keep in mind just how deceptive appearances can be. A person who uses a walker may appear fragile or helpless but be perfectly capable of shopping, preparing meals, and driving the city streets. Another person who appears fit and able-bodied may be paralyzed by crowds in stores, frightened to walk to the end of the block, or even feel incapable of gathering enough fortitude to prepare a simple meal. Cathy W. expresses a frustration that is typical for a young woman suffering from chronic depression:

> *I try to appear as cheerful as I can to others. This is usually for the benefit of friends who I see socially. I seldom let anyone see how I am truly feeling. Sometimes I just want to scream, 'I'm not okay!' It makes me feel like I'm wearing a mask most of the time, especially when someone asks how I am. I feel so foolish telling others that I'm fine while smiling and making trivial small talk. I know to some degree my depression has affected my friendships; I can feel myself almost resenting friends because they have no clue how depressed I am. How can I be mad at them though? It doesn't show! As a result I feel like a stranger sitting at the table with them, and that only compounds the problem of feeling isolated.*

Having a mood or anxiety disorder often entails a form of psychic pain that is difficult to describe but one that is familiar to those who have plummeted to the depths of despair. This psychic pain not only impacts the way the chronically depressed struggle throughout their day, but it also alters their self-worth and self-image. It colors their vision and changes how they see and experience the world.

It is frequently helpful for people who live with depression and anxiety disorders to hear about other people's stories, trials, struggles, and coping techniques. Doing so not only allows them to learn new coping tools, but it also offers the vital realization that they are not alone in their struggles. Knowing that millions of others live with similar mood challenges offers validation and reassurance. Sharing experiences, feelings, information, and survival skills is invaluable, and it is one of the many reasons this book was written.

All efforts have been expended in the writing of this book to stay as close to the technical and clinical descriptions of mental disorders as possible and to follow details of disorders as laid out in *The Diagnostic and Statistical Manual of Mental Disorders* (DSM). The DSM is published by the American Psychiatric Association, and it provides a common language and standard criteria for the classification of mental disorders.

This book was written for those individuals who may appear problem-free and just fine to others around them but who are nonetheless challenged by debilitating and chronic symptoms. It is a safe place where they can find familiar stories, discover new visions for themselves and their future, and meet new comrades in an ongoing struggle that seems like traversing a combat zone with minefields of exploding highs and burrowed lows. Equally important, this book tells their stories in their own words, so the rest of the world can know and understand the profound challenges that they face each and every day.

CHAPTER 1

PUT ON A HAPPY FACE

The Misleading Mask of Mood and Anxiety Disorders

*God has given you one face,
and you make yourself another.*

—William Shakespeare

"We excel at wearing masks. We fool our friends, our loved ones, our colleagues, even our doctors," says John McManamy, an award-winning mental health journalist and author of *Living Well with Depression and Bipolar Disorder* (HarperCollins 2006). "Deep down inside, however, we are the crying clown, our souls in torment, our psyches in a thousand pieces."

A local newspaper recently featured a full-page story about the suicide of a well-known young man who had appeared on a popular, weekly television series. This handsome thirty-five-year-old man, whose parents owned three long-standing restaurants in Southern California, had been a model citizen. The majority of the citizens around town noticed his pleasing presence and familiar smile. He was truly beloved by his community.

This man, described as an "outwardly vibrant young man," worked as a clothing model for the local stores, managed his parents' restaurants, and had a girlfriend in a seemingly successful relationship. He was "charming, witty, and fun," said his neighbors. He was "the most handsome, polite, friendly person, always with a smile," gushed residents. His friends, customers, and coworkers said he always made everyone else smile because his happiness was contagious.

After his suicide, community members asked themselves how someone so outwardly vibrant and happy-go-lucky could have been suffering secretly and so deeply from severe emotional pain—enough pain to make him want to put a gun to his head. People were horrified, not only because of the loss but also because of the utter shock of this perplexing tragedy that seemed to emerge from nowhere. How could this terrible thing have happened to someone who was so bright, talented, financially secure, handsome, and outwardly happy? On the outside he seemed just fine.

The story brings to mind a poem entitled "Richard Cory," which many children were encouraged to learn in school. It was written by Edwin Arlington Robinson.

> *Whenever Richard Cory went down town,*
> *We people on the pavement looked at him:*
> *He was a gentleman from sole to crown,*
> *Clean favored, and imperially slim.*
>
> *And he was always quietly arrayed,*
> *And he was always human when he talked;*
> *But still he fluttered pulses when he said,*
> *"Good-morning," and he glittered when he walked.*

And he was rich—yes, richer than a king—
And admirably schooled in every grace:
In fine, we thought that he was everything
To make us wish that we were in his place.

So on we worked, and waited for the light,
And went without the meat, and cursed the bread;
And Richard Cory, one calm summer night,
Went home and put a bullet through his head.

To the reader, and to the townspeople presented in the poem, Richard Cory didn't have any visible or conceivable weaknesses or scars until he shockingly took his own life. It could be read as a poem about the wealthy being incredibly miserable despite being surrounded by comfort and luxury; but it could also be read as the story of a man who suffered from debilitating depression that went unseen by others. Richard Cory had everything that a person could want, except for peace of mind and happiness. The voice in the poem envies Richard Cory's wealth without actually comprehending the mental despair that he might be experiencing. And the townspeople, judging only by what they saw, admired him for his healthy bank account and his outward, pleasant demeanor.

Indeed, depression and anxiety disorders don't commonly present to the world a pained face, because those who do suffer are all too astute at wearing many protective masks to shield themselves from this judgmental world—a world that seems to determine what's going on inside a person by what it sees displayed on the outside.

How Do I Look?

What do mental disorders such as depression, anxiety, and post-traumatic stress disorder (PTSD) look like? Simply put, people who struggle with mental disorders look just like you and me.

These disorders often display a misleading mask of contentment, self-assuredness, and inner peace. Because there is frequently no telltale sign of distress, an assortment of internal challenges and chaos can lurk behind the illusion of order and happiness. In short, people who are riddled with panic, despair, and disturbing images often look like everyone else. To the outside world, they appear just fine. Their conflict resides deep within the psyche at a level that is not easily visible or detectable.

Many people who live with these disorders tend to isolate themselves from others. They do so in such a creative fashion that even family members and close friends don't catch on to their deceptive methods. "If I don't fully understand my disorder, how can anyone else?" asks Katy D., a young woman who lives with depression, anxiety, and obsessive-compulsive disorder. "I appear to be a 'normal' person. I struggle daily to do normal things like care for my family and go to the grocery store, but I avoid going out socially. I smile, I laugh, and I listen to the radio in my car, but I also have this anxiety and sadness that is ever-present."

Fame and wealth do not shelter a person from having a mood or anxiety disorder as Dorothy Hamill, the Olympic champion skater, knows all too well. During her career she enjoyed great success and experienced the highs of fame; however, from childhood she moved in and out of the darkness of depression. She also experienced seasonal affective disorder, or SAD. Only in the past few years has Hamill accepted her illness as a chronic condition. She now uses exercise, medication, therapy, and social support to maneuver through the symptoms that used to throw a dark blanket over her days.

Numerous celebrities have braved the stigma of mood or anxiety disorders, and many have come out to reveal their own struggles, success stories, episodes, and treatments. Entertainer Marie Osmond battled depression. Actress and activist Ashley Judd suffered depression and an eating disorder. Writer Anne Rice suffered from depression due to a long-term illness. Actress Brooke Shields struggled with postpartum depression. The long list of clinically depressed celebrities includes actor Owen Wilson, newsman Mike Wallace, and singer Sinead O'Connor. Fame and wealth should never be confused with guaranteed happiness.

Food for Thought

The brain is a physical organ like any other in the human body, and like any other organ, it can be susceptible to disease. As a society we wouldn't ridicule or berate someone with diabetes, heart disease, or a failing kidney. We wouldn't dare joke about such disorders; yet that is exactly how many individuals with depression, anxiety, and other mental disorders are treated, causing them to become increasingly isolated.

Living behind the mask of a mood or anxiety disorder often allows a person to downplay his symptoms. After all there are no telltale signs or visible flaws. By discounting his symptoms or denying the existence of the disorder, the person struggling may delay diagnosis and subsequent treatment. He may fear being judged harshly, especially since there are no outward signs of inner struggles.

The dichotomy of appearing content while feeling awful lies at the heart of this book, and this is why a profile section is featured in the last section. That chapter not only presents informal portraits of men and women who live with mood or anxiety disorders but also encourages them to discuss and share their vast experiences, emotions, and coping strategies as they struggle to manage their symptoms. More importantly this final section allows the reader to see for himself that looks can indeed be deceiving.

The Masquerade

> *The truth is a secret*
> *we often keep from ourselves.*
> —Author Unknown

Most people are visually oriented and tend to believe what they see, rather than consider the less obvious story behind the pleasant smile or cheery demeanor of another. But what happens when the person who *appears* happy and at peace to family, friends, and coworkers is quietly suffering from debilitating depression, a panic disorder, or a phobia, severe anxiety, or obsessive-compulsive disorder? What if he is experiencing dread or disturbing images behind that fragile smile? What if every minute of his day is filled with fear, worry, and the brutal weight of what feels like never-ending depression? Looks can be deceiving, and they frequently are.

Individuals who live with depression, anxiety, post-traumatic stress disorder, panic disorder, seasonal affective disorder, post-partum depression, obsessive-compulsive disorder, and other mental disorders often appear just like their neighbors, friends, and coworkers: perfectly happy, well-adjusted, and calm.

Imagine feeling as emotionally shaky and weak as you would if you were about to speak to a stadium of people peering at you with harsh judgment and wild anticipation. People like Lorna A. don't have to imagine such debilitating and chronic fear. She lives with the ongoing exhaustion and pain of depression and severe anxiety, which caused her career aspirations to plummet. Debilitating depression muddied her thoughts, wreaked havoc with her plans for the future, and interfered with nearly every relationship in her life.

"All of my disorders affect my family life," says Lorna. "I don't have a job that I need to go to, so I should be able to take care of things at home, yet I am unable to do the grocery shopping because of my fear of having panic attacks while standing in a line. Anywhere I need to go where there are people waiting in lines—the post office, the bank, the department of motor vehicles (DMV), the airport—will often trigger a panic attack if I have to stand in a line for any length of time."

A growing segment of the population deals with the profound limitations and challenges associated with hidden mood or anxiety disorders, and their symptoms are not revealed in their appearance. Society is not attuned to the needs of people besieged by easily concealed psychic pain. While many will rush to help someone with an obvious physical challenge, the same Good Samaritans may respond negatively when asked to help or provide special accommodations to someone who looks just fine and doesn't appear to require assistance. Nona L. had to give up the job that she cherished because of the severity of her depression.

> *I know I don't have a career anymore, and all my past hard work and intellectual assets have been reduced to nothing. I am in a state of mind-body meltdown, or 'vocational vacation,' because I can't seem to maintain the work and career I once had. Others don't give me understanding or credit for what I'm going through, and they don't understand why I can't work because I look good. I look just fine. They fail to see what's inside, and that is frustrating for me. Sometimes I become overwhelmed with the pain of my mood disorder. It wears me down and takes a lot of explaining because most people can't relate to being fearful or sad all the time.*

People with mood or anxiety disorders often feel as if they are constantly wrestling with internal fractures, where they feel split into two conflicted halves. One half represents their real emotions, and the other shows a false and superficial ease they feel compelled to project to others. Despite appearing well-adjusted and at peace, people who live with a concealed mood or anxiety disorder may have days, weeks, or months of low self-esteem, limited or no exposure to outside activities, debilitating fatigue, or a host of other chronic symptoms. The ravages of depression and anxiety may test strong-willed individuals, while their enthusiasm for life becomes chronically impacted. Some become too ill or overwhelmed to work. Many are forced to abandon activities and careers that had once been a source of fulfillment and provided them with feelings of self-worth. This dizzying concoction of emotional angst, doubt, sadness, and fear is rarely revealed in their outer presentation.

"It is so much about wearing a mask," says Ruth L. "It takes such an incredible amount of energy to fit in and act 'normal,' whatever that means. But all the while I feel so different on the inside." Some days it's difficult for people with depression and anxiety disorders to put on a mask and act the opposite of how they feel. "I just don't have the energy or desire to act the opposite," says Ruth. "Why bother? Maybe I should just go on strike against wearing a mask!"

The famous portrait photographer Rollie McKenna once said of her photos, "There cannot be one definitive picture, since we human beings have many facets." This statement is certainly true of the photographic portraits that appear in this book. These photos casually but effectively present the disguises normally revealed to the outside world, granting the viewer an intimate accessibility into the illusion displayed through a host of jovial or serene expressions. This, of course, runs contrary to the flood of emotions and the host of highs and lows experienced beneath the surface. The words accompanying the portrait of each participant profiled in the last section of this book reveal what is truly taking place behind the facade.

The Predictability of Unpredictability

Mood disorders often go undiagnosed for years, leaving the person feeling even more depressed, hopeless, and frustrated. Unable to understand why the brain chemistry is no longer balanced properly or why the symptoms persist as they do, the person with the mood disorder continues to feel different and apart. Contrary to popular belief, many people who contend with mood or anxiety disorders do not surrender gracefully to the symptoms, especially if this is a new development and diagnosis and one that did not impact them in the past. They courageously do battle with their symptoms, fears, and dark moods while deeply longing for their previous lives. They fondly recall a time when getting a good night's rest and waking up in the morning with a feeling of calm or joy for life was the norm. They remember easier times that didn't involve a perennial quest for inner peace or a magic pill to cease their unstoppable dark thoughts.

Unpredictability becomes one of the greatest obstacles a person with a mood or anxiety disorder can face. "Most of my clients have conditions where their lives and what they do daily have changed dramatically," says guilt is a wasted emotion, and people who live with chronic depression and anxiety disorders waste a lot of their time on it. They generate heavy doses of culpability and shine the spotlight of blame onto themselves. They feel guilty if they are unable to participate in social activities or work, or they scold themselves if they feel too fatigued to do this or that. They spend an inordinate amount of time obsessing, berating themselves, and generating self-destructive, wide-ranging litanies that chronicle their shortcomings: *I'm no fun to be around; I'm weak; I'm flawed; I don't help with the kids as much as I should; I don't feel as sexual as I should; I'm not earning as much money as I once did; I'm not saving enough money to live on later in life; I'm too moody; I don't do as many chores as my spouse.*

Some have described depression as a dark room with no light switch close at hand. After a while one gives up the hope of trying to find that switch and falls helplessly into a false sense of security, enveloped by the surrounding shadows for long, painful intervals . . . alone. Isolation, dread, and even profound melancholy begin to feel comfortable and familiar.

People are resilient, and those with mood or anxiety disorders can survive nearly anything. But depression and anxiety are insidious; they scramble one's vision, not only of what lies in the future but also of what sits before them in the present moment. These disorders are like a thick fog that distorts a person's view of his own self, of other people, and of the world around him. The disorders trick the brain into believing the worst, even when the best may be waiting right around the next corner.

CHAPTER 2

ROCK 'N' ROLL

The Jolt of Depression and Mood Disorders

*There's no one to beat you,
no one to defeat you,
'cept the thoughts of yourself feeling bad.*

—Bob Dylan, "Ramona"

The extended family of mood and anxiety disorders is too vast to cover in a single volume, so this book focuses primarily on the following: clinical depression, obsessive-compulsive disorder (OCD), social anxiety disorder, specific phobias, post-traumatic stress disorder (PTSD), generalized anxiety disorder (GAD), panic disorder, and seasonal affective disorder (SAD).

Everyone, from every part of the globe, experiences ups and downs in life. This is a fact of life; no one is spared. However, there are times when those "downs" can be life-changing events that make us feel incredibly discouraged and sad about ourselves and life in general. Sometimes these feelings do not last very long. But when despair, anxiety, or mood swings are continual unwelcome companions, it might be more than a fleeting case of the blues or what used to be referred to as "nerves." When a mood shift is a chronic occurrence, it can become "hardwired" into the brain, and then it is likely to become a "new normal." It will continue to operate until treated with counteracting behaviors, ongoing treatment, medication, or a combination of these approaches.

Many times, patients make an appointment to see a therapist, social worker, or psychiatrist and present the professional with a combination of disorders. Clients may be experiencing depression accompanied by anxiety, panic attacks, or phobias. The most common disorders that psychologist Shelley Slapion-Foote sees in her office are those with generalized anxiety disorder (GAD), obsessive-compulsive disorder (OCD), and depression. "Often at least two of these diagnoses are present at the same time in the same client," says Dr. Slapion-Foote. "People who are experiencing free-floating feelings of anxiety, worries, and concerns, and are plagued by the what if's ("what if this goes wrong," "what if this happens to me," "what if I can't handle this," and the list goes on . . .) often experience at least some of the symptoms of OCD. They may have thoughts that repeat and repeat in their head no matter how hard they try to push them away, or they may participate in some type of compulsive thought behavior in an attempt to gain control over those thoughts. Some patients develop physically superstitious behaviors—for example, having to touch every hanger on the right-hand side of the rack of clothes before leaving a store, or having to blow on light switches before touching them because they think there might be a fire inside of them—fearing that if they do not do the behavior, something awful will happen."

This constellation of symptoms often makes these clients feel depressed and concerned that they may be "crazy." Clients dealing with various forms of depressive disorder tend to be tearful, have low self-esteem, or feelings of worthlessness, hopelessness, helplessness, and even wanting to die. "Not that they necessarily want to kill themselves," says

Slapion-Foote, "but they have more a sense of 'nothing is going to get better; I feel awful; I just want to go to sleep and never wake up, so I don't have to feel this way.'"

The Many Faces of Depression

To former talk show host and stand-up comedian Dick Cavett, depression was what he called "the worst agony devised for man." He struggled with it for years, even while appearing on countless television shows and being one of the most recognized figures in Hollywood. There were no telltale signs of his mood disorder. He functioned and looked perfectly content, happy, and calm on the outside. What was his secret to dealing with this debilitating depression? Cavett's response was always "pharmaceuticals, electroconvulsive therapy—and old Danny Kaye movies."

Some describe depression as the loneliest street in the world, murky to the vision, and filled with dim obstacles. Linda N., who is profiled in the second half of this book, says depression feels like being lost in a fog. "It's as if my 'on' button has been switched to 'off.'" Another person describes her bouts of depression as comparable to having a spiritual flu. "It creeps up, and often it's hard to shake off. For me it can last from a few weeks to six months." Cathy W., a young woman with chronic symptoms, describes her depression as a giant weight on her back. "It is very exhausting, like pulling a big rock around with me." Dorothy has lived with her symptoms for more than fifty years: "My depression makes me feel as if I'm trying to walk in a quagmire, and it exhausts me. I can't conjure up any interest in anything at all. When I decide I want to do something or to go somewhere, I really think I want to do it. When the time rolls around, I find I don't want to do it anymore. That's what depression does to me."

Jan. W. has lived with chronic depression and generalized anxiety disorder since childhood, when she was told she was always high-strung and nervous. "Nowadays my depression makes me feel like Alice, falling down the rabbit hole, but with no 'adventure' . . . just darkness," she says.

"My depression convinces me that I am completely alone, that I don't belong, that no one can understand me, and that I am too sensitive," says Nona L. "I get so frustrated with myself and others that I sometimes have this want of getting into a car and driving to nowhere until I find peace. I daydream about going away to places where no one knows me and finding peace in those places."

Strangely enough, the darkness and fears of depression and anxiety disorders can settle around us, acting as a familiar cavern of comfort. We know it. It knows us. We can even refer to it as our normal state. It's a part of our lives, like an unpleasant but recognizable family member who is not easily dismissed.

Roberta has lived with chronic depression for most of her life. Looking back on her teen years, she knew something was "wrong" but didn't quite know what it was or how to fix it. Since there was not much to compare it to, depression and anxiety became Roberta's *normal*. Shame and fear became constant yet comfortable companions. Her instinct told her to keep her disorder a secret and paint on a mask plastered with a bright, cheery smile. That way no one would ever have to know.

Meanwhile, behind the facade of pleasantness, there was a constant, negative voice spinning lies that Roberta believed: "I'm a complete fraud. If they knew who I really was, they would never want to talk to me, hire me, or spend time with me. Everything I have came about through sheer chance. It's not because of anything good that I did. Soon people will find out what a fake and basket case I am, and they will want me out of their lives. Then I will live alone until I die." Such are the constant messages heard over and over again by individuals when they are experiencing depression, anxiety, or feelings of unworthiness.

People who live with depression and anxiety often wake up to fear. It may not be the sort of fear that roars like a lion or knocks one over the head like a heavy brick, but it is a distant bell that can get louder as the day goes on. It can overpower normal everyday sounds and influence every decision one makes throughout the day.

What helped Roberta cope with these episodes of depression and anxiety? "Medication altered or rebalanced my brain chemistry. Yoga helped. Using some cognitive therapy, or what I call 'reality checks,' helped enormously. I often ask myself, am I labeling this accurately? Am I overemphasizing the direness of the situation or fortune-telling the future before it's even here? I have a tendency to do that." In addition her regular therapy sessions and some mindfulness meditation practices help keep Roberta anchored in the real world and remove her from a future that hasn't happened and a past that she cannot change. Staying in the moment is her saving grace.

We are not only living in interesting times; we are living in a fortunate era. We now know a great deal about the symptoms of depression and how profound they can be. The brain is an instrument that can be used for great success. For those with significant mood or anxiety disorders, however, the brain can also create destruction or anguish in personal and professional life.

Think of depression as a multi-headed beast. It can manifest with a variety of symptoms including anxiety, despair, panic, insomnia, fatigue, and/or restlessness. The degrees of depression can range from mild melancholy to suicidal thoughts. Depression is not a one-size-fits-all illness. It can wear many hats and produce a multitude of symptoms. Additionally each individual reacts to depression and brain chemistry changes in a very personal and unique way. No two people have identical symptoms or responses to specific treatments.

Depression can result in feeling sad and worthless, being unable to sleep at night, and barely having the energy to muddle through the day. Depression can leave people feeling unfocused, indecisive, and forgetful. They can feel uncomfortable in their own skin or trapped in negative thought loops playing inside their head. Being plagued with anxiety, ruminating over one's mental state, and worrying that the depression will never end are also common.

Since depression and anxiety are hidden, others liken it to a horrible secret that can't possibly be revealed; however, to publicly declare it a mental disorder is to fully recognize it is an illness like any other. Doctors parallel depression and other mental disorders with such illnesses as diabetes because they are chronic disorders that are managed by medication and other treatment. Yet many men and women, young and old, suffer through depression and other mental disorders in silence and shame. They dread being stigmatized. They fear being thought of as less capable. They are frightened of being seen as worthless in the eyes of society.[1] As Alexa Ray Joel, the daughter of Billy Joel and Christie Brinkley put it, "When you're that depressed, you don't feel like anybody is going to understand."

The reality is that discussing one's own mood or anxiety disorder can be enormously cathartic because it informs one in a very concrete way that others share in and deal with similar symptoms. Suddenly people come up and share stories about their own bouts with depression. No, a depressed person certainly is not alone. In 2010, between 13 and 14 million Americans reported suffering from depression, and those were merely the reported cases.

Depression and Anxiety—What's in a Name?

The preferred term for a severe depression is mood disorder or major affective disorder. This diagnosis can include many forms of depression, including dysthymic disorder, cyclothymic disorder, manic-depressive disorder, and similar mood disturbances. Many mood disorders have been proven to have a genetic factor, which, when combined with prolonged stress caused by any traumatic or nerve-racking situation, can *evolve* into a major affective disorder. Adults with a traumatic memory from childhood, such as rape or abuse, and those who are constantly exposed to stress from ongoing mental or physical trauma are especially susceptible to developing major depression. The theory is that prolonged stress and sadness exhaust the neurohormones in the brain, such as serotonin and norepinephrine. Such depletion, along with a genetic predisposition, can produce a major depression.

Being depressed can mean a person spends the entire day in bed and still does not feel rested. It can mean one has an inability to care about the future. Depression can be as seductive as a skilled lover or as crafty as a salesman beckoning customers to sell them on a wrap of gray flannel for warmth and reassurance. It allows one to think that there is no other way to look at or live in the world. It fools its victims and then, little by little, takes bites out of their hours and days.

Being told to keep one's chin up or pull the self up by one's own bootstraps when depression sets in has no benefit. Unfortunately, many people in our culture are conditioned to heed such adages, particularly men. An unofficial Marine slogan states "Pain is weakness leaving the body." As a result, veterans who are experiencing depression or anxiety may not report their symptoms or seek treatment. "When Humpty Dumpty broke," says Stefan P., "there was no way he was going to will himself well. Well, I can't will myself out of this depression and anxiety disorder. Believe me, I've tried."

However, many people with mood or anxiety disorders do try to "will" themselves out of their symptoms. Though positive self-talk can be greatly beneficial to those who suffer with mild anxiety or depression, such "willfulness" alone, without professional treatment, typically will not work for most individuals with moderate to severe symptoms.

One person shared that she used a form of cognitive therapy that was useful to her during times of anxiety and mild depression. "I was able to 'will' myself to be less anxious, less shy, and less depressed." When she became anxious, she would do a lot of "self-talk" that replaced negative "what if" scenarios with a different set of directives: "For instance, if I had to enter a room with people I didn't know, I used self-talk to ask myself 'What's the worst thing that can happen? Will you die? Will you turn into a pile of ashes?' Without feeling as if I was being rational and using my brain, the answer was a resounding 'No!' You won't die; you'll feel a little uncomfortable, but you'll get over it."

Karen A. also uses self-talk to calm some of her symptoms of depression and anxiety. "I don't try to cure myself because I can't. I use self-talk though. I will tell myself that I am a good person and that I am someone worth respecting, being liked, loved, and trusted. Most times this works; sometimes it doesn't."

By applying this type of thinking in a variety of settings, Karen found her anxiety reduced significantly, which then made her feel more secure and confident. That reduced her shyness and allowed her to function more effectively. "I had the opportunity to find out that people actually liked me and that I had a good sense of humor!" Being more successful in interacting with the external world, in turn, lessened her depression, because it's really hard to beat yourself up on a regular basis when people are enjoying your company and laughing at your jokes. Human beings are not to be underestimated.

People are not born in a depressed or anxious state. Babies do not emerge from the womb sad about their future, trying to control their environment by obsessively washing their tiny hands over and over, or compulsively straightening their crib. Waves of depression and anxiety can start to wash over any one of us at any age. Some mood or anxiety disorders result from an experience—for example, those who develop post-traumatic stress disorder as a result of a disturbing event or something that took place in their early environment. Other mood or anxiety disorders can come about because of a gradual shift in brain chemistry that can take place over a long period of time.

People who live with depression, anxiety, or other mental disorders often do not accept their diagnosis easily, especially if it comes later in life after they have experienced years of being asymptomatic. They valiantly do battle with these destructive dragons, even if they do not ultimately slay them. They often yearn for their previous life when they were free of trauma, panic, and psychological pain. They fondly recall a time when the sun shining on their faces felt uplifting, when a trip out of the house or to a neighborhood store didn't feel like a climb up Mount Everest. They recall times when they weren't flooded with unreasonable fears and fright. They remember when nighttime was a time of peaceful slumber, when they didn't wrestle with the dark or with disturbing images. They remember easier times that didn't involve a constant juggling act of medications to help soothe or combat symptoms. They miss earlier days when travel was not fraught with unpredictable emotions and riddled with anxiety.

"At the risk of being overly simplistic," says Kent Bennington, a medical and family psychologist, "and keeping in mind the complex causes and expressions of mood and anxiety disorders, it may help to picture depression and anxiety along a continuum of arousal, with extreme anxiety (terror) at one end and extreme depression (deadness) at the other. Back-and-forth movement along this continuum can be rapid or slow and a person can become stuck in one place." Bennington continues to explain that the middle of the continuum quickly disappears when overwhelming, terrifying experiences offer no escape other than retreat into the safety of being underwhelmed (i.e., depressed), leaving the two poles, anxiety and depression, virtually face-to-face.

"Given the absence of a comfortable middle range where life can feel more normal, one initially feels more anxious as he becomes less depressed or experiences more depression as he becomes less anxious," says Bennington. "It's important at that point in the recovery process for the patient to understand that he or she may have to choose between deadening withdrawal or heightened anxiety, with anxiety lying in the direction of greater aliveness. Ideally over time, and with the help of psychotherapy and/or medication, the continuum elongates and the mid-range of the continuum is reestablished, offering a greater sense of normalcy."

At some point, most people who live with mood or anxiety disorders stop trying to cure themselves or fight the disorder. Instead they work toward a peaceful coexistence with their mood fluctuations and challenges. The kicking and screaming stage may end and give way to a truce of sorts. This can be the start of a new and different form of existence that is not only livable, but also brings about a certain sense of comfort.

Coping with a New Diagnosis—Changing the Rules

> *I like living. I have sometimes been wildly,*
> *despairingly, acutely miserable,*
> *racked with sorrow, but through it all*
> *I still know that just to be alive is a grand thing.*
>
> —Agatha Christie

Sometimes a disorder seems to materialize from out of nowhere, and then remains a constant companion. A difficult situation may bring on the first episode. After that point the mood challenge becomes chronic.

People who suddenly face an onslaught of symptoms from a mood or anxiety disorder may feel severed from their past. They are flung like an arrow from a familiar setting into unknown terrain. Feelings of dread, waves of anxiety, bouts of sadness, and peaks of panic can fill every minute of the day. They are the sort of symptoms one wants to shake off like a chill. But symptoms of a disorder, to paraphrase Welsh poet Dylan Thomas, often "do not go gentle into that good night."

Nona L.'s depression makes her feel sad and unenergetic, as though she just wants to sleep the day away. "I'm unable to complete tasks. Sometimes I get very upset with myself about it, and sometimes I accept it and move on. If I push myself through my depression to accomplish something, I end up so exhausted in the end—both mentally and physically. I get into self-blame and feel so unfit and terribly helpless. I've lost all the knowledge, and I can't remember even simple tasks. I forget a lot, and I always say the wrong words. I know the answer, but . . . I can't remember!" Nona has to read and reread things, and she still finds she doesn't absorb what she is reading. "It's the same with watching television. If I'm watching the news on TV, I don't seem to absorb it. When I am driving, I have lapses of memory for direction. My listening skills have gotten weak as well."

Nona L. used to be a high-powered manager in the information technology field. She was industrious and creative; she believed in doing the impossible and winning. She enjoyed travel, theater, cooking, reading, teaching, and writing. Now depression has taken over and displaced all of those interests in her life. "My depression leaves me with the belief that I'm all alone, that I don't belong, that no one can understand me, and that I'm extra sensitive. I'm much too sensitive to everything."

Nona L. often feels helpless due to her depression. "I do not know if my current existence and mood are real or just a bad dream that one day I will wake from and be smiling—without the current anxiety, fear, and pain. Then I have to tell myself it's not a dream, and I have to accept my depression as a way of being in my journey of life."

To see Nona L. one would not know she is depressed, anxious, or experiencing any sort of negative emotion. "I tell myself that no one deserves a sad face. I dress up and tell myself that I am lucky to know that I have a problem with depression. I equip myself with awareness, acceptance, and gratitude, telling myself that we all have our challenges, and this is mine. I can take care of it, even if it is terribly painful at times."

People who live with a depression or anxiety disorder face an overwhelming range of challenges as they wrestle with bad feelings and a negative self-image. They must assign new roles to family members and to themselves. They must learn a new set of rules for their everyday lives—rules that involve simplification, rationing out their energy for the most important daily tasks, and pacing themselves through the ups and downs of their symptoms. They discover that they must refresh and embrace their spirituality in a new way, one that releases the angst they feel toward their condition, even if the lift is temporary. They must somehow learn to accept all of the emotions surrounding their new limitations and challenges. But first they have to learn what those limitations are.

"I live with depression, panic attacks, and post-traumatic stress disorder," says Rachel W., whose anxiety disorder came on after an auto accident at age twenty-three. "It makes me feel as if it takes much more energy to do 'normal,' daily life activities. I have to continually fight for the right, for sanity, and for assurance that the parenting choices I'm making are the right ones for my children."

"I feel like I'm wearing a mask most of the time, especially if someone asks how I am," says Cathy W., who lives with chronic depression. "I feel like an idiot telling them I am fine, while smiling and making trivial small talk. I know to some degree that my depression impacts my friendships; I feel resentment . . . almost anger at friends when they have no clue how depressed I truly am. I feel like they are in some sort of delusional state! How fair is that? It's not. They can't *see* my depression, but it's real, and it's severe."

Adina Shapiro is a licensed clinical social worker and professor at the Virginia Commonwealth University School of Social Work. She specializes in treating clinical depression, general anxiety disorders, and eating disorders in her busy practice. "I see many patients with these disorders. Very often, patients aren't even aware that they are depressed when they first come in. They may complain of vague symptoms such as sleep difficulties, general unhappiness, irritability (a frequent, underpublicized symptom of depression), ennui (feeling lost or directionless in their lives), and blame directed at some external source. Since people often think of depression as a more 'dramatic' illness, evidenced by frequent crying and suicidal thoughts, they don't consider that some whom they meet may be depressed. Labeling the disorder for them is very helpful as it helps them feel reassured that they have something treatable."

There is a difference between reactive depression (in reaction to a loss, for example) and "endogenous" depression, which is deeper. The latter would include someone who has been mildly depressed his whole life and tends to interpret things in a negative way. Either form is treatable. Dr. Shapiro doesn't jump to medication first when she is working with patients. "I try to work with them on underlying causes and help them to make the changes in their lives that allow them to feel more empowered and optimistic. A full-blown depression, which I also often see, includes people with crying spells, appetite changes, suicidal thoughts or plans, and general decreased functioning. They may have difficulty working, concentrating, and/or being social. People around them complain that they are not present emotionally."

Sometimes depression doesn't get better, despite medications and therapy or a combination of the two. This is often referred to as treatment-resistant depression. Symptoms such as feeling hopeless, being disinterested in activities, and experiencing sadness persist despite treatment. Sometimes symptoms improve, only to keep coming back. Treatment-resistant depression can range from mild to severe and generally requires trying a number of approaches to find out if one thing, or a combination of therapies, can be discovered to effectively quiet the symptoms. Dr. Cassandra Friedman, a psychologist, finds that resistant depression is the most difficult form of depression to treat. "There often is no rhyme or reason to depressed patients, and they do not take kindly to medications. Sometimes there is a need to try different medications or a combination of medications, along with ECT (electroconvulsive therapy) to break down the depressive episode."

The Impact of Depression on Self and Others

Whether a disabling mood or anxiety disorder hits quite abruptly, or simply crawls leisurely at a snail's pace into one's path, slowly and methodically disassembling a person's existing lifestyle and routine, it is devastating to the person and to those around the person. What was once taken for granted and easily accomplished is now a constant stream of uphill battles and obstacles. Responsibilities in relationships may need to be modified, lifestyles may have to be altered, and moods may fluctuate more frequently. Friends and family members who have been available in the past may slowly pull away. They see the same person before them, but something has changed, and they are not comfortable with that. Some will stand by the afflicted person; others may retreat out of fear and misunderstanding. Unfortunately the latter outcome is common.

Cathy W.'s depression forces her to stay away from social events. "With close friends, I just feel like I have to hide it because I can't expect them to 'fix' it. It can be frustrating though, because I so want to be able to let them know how I am feeling; however, I think they would get so sick of hearing it! Most of the time I feel like I am not honest with my friends; therefore I am not really a true friend at all. I feel like a mere stranger with them, and that only compounds the problem."

Mood and anxiety disorders can have a huge impact on relationships in general and on family life in particular. Changes in the ability to function commonly cause resentment among family members, especially if prolonged. A general sense of helplessness can prevail, leading to more anger and resentment, thereby enforcing a vicious interpersonal cycle of frustration and deeper depression. "It is very important to establish open communication between family members and to allow the 'tough' conversations to take place," says therapist Adina Shapiro. "Family members can commonly feel blamed for the patient's illness, partly in reaction to the frustration and helplessness that they feel. Withdrawal—emotional, physical, and sexual—can reinforce distance and cut off family members, which can be a hard cycle to break."

Depression has impacted Lisa A.'s family life as well as her friendships. She becomes irritable and very withdrawn from her usual activities when her depressive episodes become more severe. "There are days that it is extremely hard for me to pull myself out of bed. My friends and family have had a very hard time adjusting to the ups and downs of my depression. When I am withdrawn because of increased periods of depression, my husband has to increase his activity and workload within the family. At one time this caused resentment. We have learned through the last five years of marriage, however, how to cope and communicate more effectively through these low periods."

There will always be those who are threatened by mental illness or fearful of anyone who is "different," because that difference reinforces their own feelings of helplessness; however, new acquaintances may understand the importance of support and take on crucial and supportive roles. Eventually a few significant relationships may develop from within support groups or from people who secretly share some of the same symptoms. Old friendships may shift, and family relationships may become strained, or they may become richer and more defined.

"My low points can be hard on my close friends," says Rachel W., who lives with depression and post-traumatic stress disorder. "Acquaintances probably don't understand why it's a bit of a push-pull at times. When I'm up, I socialize a lot; but when I'm down, I really close down."

Having to relearn how to live one's life is not an easy chore, but it is a worthy goal to strive for. What makes it more difficult for others in the case of mood or anxiety disorders is that the person with the disorder looks just the same as ever. Nothing on the outside has changed. Only the inner world has shifted, and that can be confusing for family members, friends, and coworkers. Others see the same person on the outside, and they cannot fathom why or how things have changed so dramatically on the inside.

Those who live with easily concealed mood or anxiety disorders must learn to educate family and friends about their symptoms and daily challenges. It is not a disease process that can be handled well in isolation. The person with the disorder must be able to openly communicate their needs and wants without feeling guilt or a sense of being a burden. Clear communication is difficult, even under the best of circumstances; but even more so with the challenges of living with depression, post-traumatic stress disorder, or anxiety. Having such a disorder can be a full-time job with numerous responsibilities. No wonder fatigue and depression are part of most mental disorders.

Validation and Acceptance

Some people are diagnosed after they have endured many months or years of perplexing symptoms. This new medical name for their condition and suffering may give way to a sense of relief. Why would they feel such liberation? There is finally an anchor to which they can ground their worries, fears, and anxieties. This anchor is called validation. People tend to be more frightened when they have very little knowledge or information about their condition. Once a diagnosis is reached, treatment options can be discussed and approached. Solutions can be raised. The light at the end of the tunnel can come into view.

Sometimes, however, the person with the mood or anxiety disorder has his own doubts about whether his condition is real or valid because he sees the same face in the mirror . . . and that face appears to be just fine. Adding fuel to the fire, many of these types of disorders escape proper diagnosis for months, and sometimes years, because of their hidden nature.

While some people may feel relief with a diagnosis, others may experience a kind of personal crisis. It may feel like a harsh slap in the face and bring feelings of overwhelming anxiety and panic. The newly diagnosed person may wonder how to cope with all of the symptoms and the adjustments that appear to be needed. However, instead of asking, "What if I cannot cope?," a better question might be "How *can* I cope?" How does one regain a sense of self-worth and accomplishment when a mood disorder makes it difficult to perform the numerous chores and routine tasks that were once easily achieved?

Often people with an ongoing but easily concealed mood or anxiety disorder must learn to become their own best allies. They need to grieve the loss of things they can no longer easily manage and locate activities that remain doable. This important first step in the healing process takes place in the psyche. It's called acceptance—acceptance of the cards one has been dealt, acceptance of the ebb and flow of symptoms, acceptance of an unplanned turn of events that has arrived nonetheless.

The onset of a mental illness is the beginning of a new adventure that often involves the loss of many familiar aspects of one's previous life. Goals, control, flexibility, energy, and independence can all be affected. Sometimes people will begin falling into an emotional crisis because they do not feel they have a future. "I worry about the future," shared one young woman who has suffered with chronic depression most of her life. "What if I'm still in this horrible emotional place when I'm in my seventies and eighties? Maybe by then someone will have come up with a vaccination for depression and anxiety. Wouldn't that be nice? Maybe a patch one can put on once a week to keep the demons from coming through the door." Often people have to restate their faith in a better future as *Tomorrow may be easier. If not, there is always the next day.*

Learning to live with a mood or anxiety disorder must begin by educating oneself about the disorder, gradually rearranging priorities, becoming more realistic, and recognizing new limitations, as well as setting new attainable goals and developing new strengths. Accepting oneself as having a mix of strengths and weaknesses becomes a vital life lesson for those who live with chronic mood or anxiety disorders.

None of us likes to be labeled or referred to as having a particular disorder, whether it is phobic, obsessive-compulsive, or clinically depressed. We really have to ask, "What are diagnoses anyway?" Are these truly "templates of psychopathology, perfect truths, or more likely, a woven web of guesses?" says psychologist Kent Bennington. "Although the intent of diagnoses is to improve understanding enough to provide appropriate treatment to remove or reduce the troubling, distressing symptoms that cause the patient to seek treatment in the first place, the reality is that diagnoses can be misleading and result in misunderstanding, and sometimes in years of little or no progress."

"By whose authority," Dr. Bennington asks, "does the patient accept a diagnosis? Most often it's the examining doctor or therapist." But does the diagnosis provide useful information? Does it serve a purpose beyond satisfying a third-party payer on the patient's insurance coverage who will not reimburse the provider without it? Bennington suggests that each of us is so highly individualized genetically, biochemically, psychologically and behaviorally that formalized diagnostic systems can, at best, only scratch the surface of our emotional histories, makeup, and functioning. "So if by 'coming to terms with' means 'accepting as true,' then I should hope patients would be strong enough and differentiated enough to find out what the label means—to remember the sign is not the thing it signified, and with their therapist's help, to sort out how this label applies to them and how it does not, and why this label is necessary."

When a patient is in a depressed or anxious state, it is often challenging to sort out the entire diagnosis and treatment picture because cognitive function is not always at its best. Doctors owe it to their patients to explain to them that this is a diagnosis and treatment approach for our consideration, yours and mine, and we are hoping that it "fits" well enough to help us to help you. "This sets the stage," says Bennington, "for a relationship in which the therapist and patient are journeying forth together in the service of a common goal."

Nobody wants to be alone in sadness, and no one wants to be alone in happiness. It's important to note that there are more resources today for those with mental disorders than ever before. The Internet offers community support groups and online chat rooms that may focus on a particular disorder or challenge. Support and education for conditions such as depression, phobias, obsessive-compulsive disorder, panic attacks, postpartum depression, post-traumatic stress disorder, and many others are available online day or night.

Additionally there are therapists who specialize in effectively treating many disorders with newer, non-medicinal techniques or techniques that are used in conjunction with medications. There are numerous resources on the horizon and much to explore when sorting through the coping tools and treatments for depression and anxiety disorders. Learning how to manage symptoms is crucial, but learning how to adapt to them is equally essential.

CHAPTER 3

THE INSIDE STORY ON DEPRESSION AND ANXIETY DISORDERS

*Courage doesn't always roar.
Sometimes courage is the quiet voice
at the end of the day saying,
"I will try again tomorrow."*

—Mary Anne Radmacher

Most of us are familiar with the definition of depression. It is a mood disorder that causes one to feel sad or hopeless for an extended period of time. More than just a bout of "the blues" or temporary feelings of grief or low energy, depression can have a significant impact on one's enjoyment of life, work, health, and the people in one's life. It can linger for weeks, months, years, or a lifetime.

People who live with clinical depression are unable to take pleasure in activities that were once enjoyable because of the chronic nature of their disorder. Depression often makes each and every action laborious. Those experiencing the disorder may or may not notice the changes, as they can be subtle at first and more pronounced later.

As previously mentioned, some of the physical and mental problems often experienced with depression include sleep problems, change in appetite, inability to concentrate, memory problems, and aches and pains. People who suffer from this disorder often feel worthless, helpless, and hopeless about their ability to make things right in their lives. They sometimes welcome sleep and experience their waking life as a living nightmare. It is difficult to feel productive when mentally and physically depleted.

People with depression may be reluctant to seek help because they feel that the disorder is a sign of personal weakness or a character flaw, or that they should be able to "pull out of it" on their own. If they were just feeling sad, that might be the case. However, depression is not just feeling sad. It defies simple labels. Ironically many people do not seek help for depression because they are . . . well . . . too depressed. In some cases they are in a state where they cannot determine that it is depression that is causing their severe misery. Depression can be based primarily on biochemical components brought on by a drop in serotonin levels. Sleep deprivation and anxiety merely add fuel to the fire, stoking an already precarious situation.

Some people have summed up depression as spending all day in bed and still not getting a good rest! They experience disturbed sleep patterns, sleeping either too much or not enough, and consistently feel exhausted. The brain's electrical activity can be measured during sleep by an electroencephalogram (EEG). EEG recordings of depressed individuals taken during sleep show a clearly abnormal pattern with decreased rapid eye movement (REM) latency. REM is a normal stage of sleep characterized by the rapid and random movements of the eyes.

It's important to note that depression impacts everyone quite differently with no set pattern or predictable disease process. Some feel down for extended periods of time; for others, the feelings of depression come and go. For people like Nona L., who has lived with depression, anxiety, phobias, and panic disorder for twenty years, "symptoms come and go except my sadness. It is always there. I blame myself for everything and feel unfit to accomplish anything. I feel helpless against depression."

People with short episodes of mild depression may still be able to hold employment, care for their families, and take care of daily activities. In severe cases, however, depression can cause people to become incapable of communicating, unable to do routine activities or work, or may even bring on thoughts of suicide. The spectrum of depression, as the saying goes, is as deep as the ocean and as wide as the sky.

Depression seems to tag along with most mental disorders. It is good friends with anxiety, pals with panic and post-traumatic stress disorder, and is a close cousin to a host of other anxiety disorders. The rational question becomes "Who *wouldn't* be depressed dealing with such persistent and debilitating symptoms and mood challenges?" Therefore depression is a reasonable response to what is happening to a person who lives with any form of mental disorder or mental pain. A great number of changes and challenges must be contended with. As a result, most people would feel discouraged and experience some degree of depression if they had to try to both manage their mental health and navigate insurance systems that sometimes seem to be at odds with their needs.

Sadly, most people who live with a chronic mental illness and are in the midst of suffering are not able to think proactively; yet they are often left to seek out mental health resources on their own. It is incredibly hard to be resourceful when one is physically and psychologically challenged. Antidepressants are often prescribed to assist with fatigue, but seldom is a health advocate added to the treatment plan to provide assistance in making phone calls, being persistent with follow-up, and doing all that is needed to overcome the frustration of dealing with the health insurance "merry-go-round."

Many people feel as though their life is put on hold while they contend with symptoms of depression and anxiety. Having to jump through the necessary hoops in order to obtain proper treatments and understanding can compound people's feelings of depression, separateness, and vulnerability.

In the previous book, *JUST FINE: Unmasking Concealed Chronic Illness and Pain,* depression was compared to being buried under an extraordinarily heavy blanket from which one cannot emerge. The poet John Keats once wrote of depression:

> *I am in that temper*
> *that if I were under water,*
> *I would scarcely kick to come to the top.*

Depression can lead to a loss of physical mobility, cognitive functioning, and social connections, and can generate other lifestyle changes. When a person experiences some form of psychic pain all the time, an incredible amount of energy is used to move through the necessarily daily chores or simply exist from one minute to the next. The pleasure of living can easily become lost in the fog of depression.

"I don't often make plans with others anymore," Lorna A. tells me. "I never know when I am going to be feeling well enough to go somewhere. I have to force myself sometimes to go to lunch with friends. I am now home almost all the time. I have become something of a hermit."

Frequently depression can leave a person feeling unwanted and unlovable even though he appears worthy, pleasant, and perfectly presentable to the outside world. The person may believe he is of no use to others or to this world. He may feel that his deep suffering is a sign that he deserves to be punished. Sometimes a person can become angry in a spiritual sense and rail at God or at the universe. A deep depression is often a general loss of faith in those things once seen as important and fulfilling.

What Causes Depression?

Depression may be triggered by stressful life events, physical illness, certain drugs or medications, or inherited traits. Often people who live with chronic illness or ongoing physical pain experience chronic depression and/or anxiety as an unwelcome "side dish" to their illness. Although the causes of depression are not entirely understood, we know it is linked to an imbalance in brain chemistry. Once the imbalance is corrected, symptoms of depression can improve greatly.

Some studies have revealed that if you have a "first-degree relative" (parent, child, or sibling) who is dysthymic or depressed, there is a 20 to 25 percent chance that you too will be dysthymic or depressed. If your ancestry is one-quarter or more Celtic, Irish, Scandinavian, Native American, Welsh, or Scottish, chances are you've lived with lower-than-normal serotonin levels from birth. Research from Dr. Mirko Disic of McGill University found that on average, women have significantly lower levels of the neurotransmitter serotonin than men—about one third less. Perhaps this is why women are diagnosed with depression more frequently than men.

No one is capable of controlling his genetic inheritance, and a tendency toward any illness, including a low mood or anxiety disorder, doesn't mean one is simply stuck with it. It merely means one has to adjust and customize treatment to deal with the body's individual requirements. So remember, while you didn't inherit a low mood, you did inherit a greater propensity to develop a genetic tendency and thus, a greater risk of suffering from low moods. You also inherited a greater-than-average risk of needing treatment. Not only is depression not your fault, it is not something that you created. You cannot be blamed in any way, shape, or form for this illness.

Lorna A. lives with both depression and panic disorder. "Most people who don't really know me think I am a very laid-back person because I hold a lot of the anxiety inside. It is easy to hide it. It seems other people think that depression and anxiety are easy to get rid of just by changing one's attitude about things, but sometimes that does not work. I can hear people say, 'Just snap out of it!' I even wonder myself why that isn't easy to do. For me it takes medication as well as love and support from my family and friends. And then there are times that all of these things simply do not prevent my having a panic attack or period of depression."

No matter how hard they try to snap out of it, people with depression often feel as though they are falling into a gloomy and dark abyss with no jagged surfaces to grab hold of. And if these jagged surfaces suddenly appear, the person in a clinical depression might not have the strength or will to reach for them or even recognize their existence or availability. Depression and other mental disorders can be all-consuming, and the disorders don't necessarily leave a lot of room for proactive action, namely, the ability to reach out for help.

Intimacy and Mood and Anxiety Disorders

"Intimacy? Sex drive? Alien concepts!" laughs Jan W., who has suffered with unrelenting depression since childhood. "The medications pretty much kill any desire I have for physical intimacy, much to my partner's unhappiness. Sometimes I can get past it but usually not. It's not a subject I'm comfortable talking about either with my therapist or my partner."

Relationships and sexual activities often suffer when people are depressed or highly anxious, as [these disorders] compromise the ability to relate intimately to others. "A depressed person is unlikely to experience sexual desire or interest, and the anxious person, even if interested, may very well be driven by the need to feel safe, valued, reassured, and tranquilized," says psychologist Kent Bennington. "Erectile dysfunction is commonly associated with anxious and/or depressed states. Some people use sexual contact to deaden emotional pain, and some use sex to avoid intimacy. Who's to say either is wrong on occasion? The problem arises when the needful, avoidant, or disinterested partner cannot sustain feelings of aliveness and contact, and cannot organize and maintain a satisfying and loving relationship over time. When someone is depressed or anxious, it's very difficult for that person even to hear the other person, much less to be emotionally supportive or responsive." Additionally medications such as antidepressants play havoc with sex drive. So there is really a two-fold problem: 1) depression and/or anxiety can lessen the sex drive to nearly zero, and 2) the medications interfere with the sex drive.

"My disorders play a role in my sex drive or lack thereof," says Marty W., who lives with depression and obsessive-compulsive disorder. "When I feel very depressed, the last thing on my mind is sex. My medication also has a major impact on my sex drive. If I wait until my libido increases, however, I might never have sex again! Even though the desire is not there, I like the closeness and the feel of another person's body close to mine."

Inevitably, when a man or woman is feeling anxious, depressed, misunderstood, isolated, or not listened to, desire to engage in sexual activity diminishes. When someone is worried about possibly losing sanity, or if anxiety is dominating the mind, it seems impossible to think of anything else. There is very little thought or energy left for being intimate. "If the person is taking medications for depression, many of these drugs have the side effect of reducing sex drive when intimacy is already lowered in the first place," states psychologist Shelley Slapion-Foote. "Partners often don't understand why their partner is no longer interested in sex when they had been prior in the relationship. This leads to arguments, misunderstandings, and hurt feelings. It is important that couples discuss this aspect of their relationship in a safe and secure setting, such as with a psychologist or with a mental health specialist." If each person is able to comprehend that one partner is not physically or psychologically in a space to engage in intimate relationships, rather than having either feel less desirable, both partners will be helped. As the anxiety and depression begin to lift, the partners can make plans for specific times to reintegrate the waning intimacy back into their relationship.

Mild Mannered or Major Depression—What Do You Have and Why Does It Matter?

Anyone diagnosed with "major," "clinical," or even "chronic" depression should understand that these are generally different terms for the same condition.

Depression caused by a chemical imbalance in the brain is known as clinical depression (also known as chronic or major depression) and differs from reactive depression. Reactive or normal depression, which most people feel at one time or another, is often activated by a situation or an event that one reacts to with strong emotions, such as the death of a loved one, the breakup of a relationship, or the loss of a home or job. This type of depression is psychological because the depressed person is emotionally "reacting" directly to something that has happened.

A reactive or normal depression will usually go away on its own within a few days to a few weeks. The person may require or benefit from some talk therapy, but in most cases the reacting person will move on, find another job, grieve, and adjust to the loss or crisis. Long-term symptoms and a progression of symptoms will not arise or dominate because of one single event.

Clinical depression is a coat of a different color. It is normally triggered by a chemical imbalance in the brain. This is a biological disorder of the brain, but it has psychological symptoms. This type of depression need not be the result of a stressful or upsetting event. Often these changes to brain chemistry appear seemingly out of nowhere.

What makes clinical depression all the more confusing for people is that events and circumstances can trigger a bout of clinical depression instead of reactive or situational forms of depression. In this case the loss of a home or job, or the death of a loved one might cause a person to become depressed in the reactive manner, but then the reactive depression triggers a chemical reaction in the brain that turns this reactive depression into a chemical (clinical) depression. At this point the person who has a predisposition to chemical depression finds himself or herself unable to overcome the depression that was initially triggered by an unpleasant event.

It is easy to confuse these two forms of depression. People suffering with what appears to be a reactive depression later find out that their depression is, in fact, caused by a chemical imbalance in the brain. Yet the reason they did not understand earlier was due to their lack of knowledge about depression. If they look back, they may discover that they were indeed depressed in their teens or early twenties, and the more current event simply deepened the already existing clinical depression.

An important fact that people often don't understand is that clinical depression is a *biological* disorder. While there are psychological symptoms that result from these biological, chemical imbalances in the brain, the true cause of the suffering related to these disorders is physiological, not psychological. This means that to treat these disorders one needs to balance the brain chemistry. With balanced brain chemistry, debilitating symptoms can ease. And while it can sometimes be difficult to find the right treatment to balance brain chemicals, this is an important distinction for family, friends, and society to understand about people who suffer with depression.

Let's compare depression to another biological disorder: diabetes. Diabetes is a chemical imbalance in the pancreas. This biological disorder also has psychological symptoms, some quite similar to depression, yet no one confuses it with a psychological illness. Instead the psychological symptoms are perceived for what they are—symptomatic results of a physiological (biological) imbalance.

Depression is treatable. If clinical depression were just a character or personality flaw, it would be a psychological issue. Psychological issues require counseling, sometimes leading to months or years of therapy. But depression is physiological (as in physical). Clinical depression is a chemical imbalance in one of the organs—the brain. The patient simply has a biological, biochemical disorder that causes some form of mental impairment.

Not all depression is severe. A chemical depression called dysthymia is basically a mild chemical depression. The symptoms never reach such severe depths that the individuals with dysthymia cannot have successful relationships, or work and function in daily life. However, the dysthymic person may be impacted by a constant low-level depression that fuels a lack of motivation, limits ability to concentrate, and causes fatigue, over-sensitivity, loss of confidence, and lower self-esteem. Dysthymia may be less disabling than clinical depression, but it can also impact relationships, careers, and enjoyment of life.

"Sometimes it takes much more effort to do what seems normal—get up, get ready, get out of the house with the children, engage in suburban parental banter, which is part of life for a stay-at-home mom with young kids," says Rachel W. "Before having kids I could hibernate and get a lot of good reading done. Now I have to get back out there each day."

Why So SAD? (Seasonal Affective Disorder)

Animals react to the changing seasons with changes in mood, metabolism, and behavior. Humans are the same. Most people find they eat and sleep slightly more in winter, and dislike the dark mornings and short days. For some individuals, however, symptoms are severe enough to disrupt their lives and cause considerable distress. These people may be suffering from seasonal affective disorder (SAD).

"My seasonal affective disorder, and all that goes with it, makes me feel as if someone pulled a gray blanket over my world," says J.A., an educator, writer, and counselor who lives in the state of Washington where the skies are often gray for long stretches at a time. "When I'm dealing with SAD, I don't feel like being as social, and I really need to push myself out the door. I become unproductive. Working a lot out of my home makes matters worse because I sometimes will find it easier to stay in bed longer and sit in front of the TV when I should be working."

SAD is a type of winter depression that affects an estimated half million people every year, usually between September and April but particularly during December, January, and February in the northern hemisphere. SAD is not a psychosomatic or imaginary illness. It is a real disorder and affects people's lives in a multitude of ways.

"I am very aware of my symptoms being problematic," says J.A. "Others rarely, if ever, notice that I'm suffering. But it's upsetting because I realize what is happening with SAD, and I can't have an impact on it. My symptoms make me more and more reclusive." One thing does have an impact on J.A.'s symptoms: the end of winter! Another effective therapy that helps J.A. and others deal with SAD is light therapy.

Depression can affect circadian cycles or biorhythms. Many animals, including humans, have circadian "clocks" in our brains that regulate physical and behavioral functions on a twenty-four-hour basis. The clock helps control sleep and wake patterns, hormones, body temperature, mood, digestion, and other functions. There is growing evidence that some individuals' circadian clocks are quite sensitive to the amount of sunlight they are exposed to each day. During the winter, when the daylight hours are shortest, these people develop depressive symptoms. During the summer, when daylight hours increase, their depressive symptoms resolve. Individuals with SAD can sometimes be helped with exposure to light from a special "light box" during the winter months. Light treatment sometimes may be able to reverse or improve this kind of depression.

Fred H. lives with clinical depression in addition to SAD. "I have had surges where I make progress followed by periods when I slip backwards. With seasonal affective disorder, I usually lose weight during warmer months and then gain it back during the winter. I may exercise for as much as eight or nine months per year, and then I stop during the winter. It would be wonderful to have a good year. I want to think that, between my own efforts and the help I get from a psychologist and psychiatrist, it will happen. I'm working on getting a light box to help me with this fall and winter."

SAD impacts people in various ways. Some men and women have sleep problems that cause them to oversleep, which leaves them feeling weary and fatigued. Others cannot get out of bed, or they overeat and have carbohydrate cravings. Still others feel so depressed with feelings of despair, guilt, and anxiety that normal tasks become frustrating and overwhelming. They avoid company, lose libido, feel tired, and have physical symptoms such as joint pain and stomach problems. As mentioned, symptoms seem to be at their worst in the darkest months because the problem stems from the lack of bright light in winter. Researchers have found that in addition to bright light, which positively impacts brain chemistry, large dosages of vitamin D also can help. Vitamin D is in great part produced from exposure to sunlight.

Rock 'n' Rolling with the Baby Blues

The birth of a new baby can be a joyous event, but that's not always so for the new mother who is plagued by debilitating mood swings. What is common is for a new mother to feel overjoyed one minute and be crying the next. These feelings are often called the baby blues. They tend to ease up a couple of weeks after giving birth. But sometimes there is a more serious problem—an illness called postpartum depression (PPD), which causes more significant symptoms than the baby blues. It also tends to last longer.

Some symptoms of PPD include feeling hopeless, worthless, or guilty; lacking energy; crying endlessly; being unable to think clearly or make decisions; having problems with appetite and sleeping; showing no interest in the baby; having thoughts about harming oneself or the baby; and feeling unable to cope or like life isn't worth living.

Actress Brooke Shields does not shy away from honestly talking about her trials and experiences with PPD after the birth of her daughter. When "crippling depression" ripped through her world, she was devastated. In her memoir, *Down Came the Rain*, Brooke describes in candid detail just how painful a journey PPD was. "My profound detachment made me suffer unbearably, and I believed I had nowhere to turn. I remember looking out of the bedroom window and envisioning myself jumping. I concluded that it wouldn't be too effective because we weren't high enough. This upset me even more. The frightening part was that my thoughts were extremely rational. They made clear sense to me. It felt like an appealing option to erase myself from this life. What would stop me from acting on any of these thoughts? I needed and wanted a way out. My mind was full of visions of escape, and these constantly overshadowed thoughts about my miraculous baby girl."

The stigma attached to those suffering from mood disorders, PPD included, makes many women frightened or ashamed to seek the mental health assistance they so desperately need and deserve. Brooke's words also convey how devastatingly dangerous PPD can become if left untreated. "During what was becoming one of the darkest points in my life, I sat holding my newborn and could not avoid the image of her flying through the air and hitting the wall in front of me. I had no desire to hurt my baby and didn't see myself as the one throwing her, thank God, but the wall morphed into a video game, and in it her little body smacked the surface and slid down onto the floor. I was horrified, and although I knew deep in my soul that I would not harm her, the image all but destroyed me."[2]

Help! How to Assist Someone Who Has a Mood or Anxiety Disorder

If a friend or family member is living with depression or another mental disorder, the question often becomes "How can I best assist?"

"I'm not sure that anyone can really understand what deep depression is like unless they have suffered from it themselves," one woman with clinical depression told me when I asked her what people do not understand about this disorder. "There is a lack of understanding of just how crippling depression and panic can be. It doesn't work for me to just be told to get over it and that things will be better tomorrow. While I appreciate it when others attempt to be sympathetic with me, I think I would appreciate it more if they just told me to let them know if they can help in some way. I don't like it when they try to suggest some way to 'cure' me!"

- **Acknowledge that the depression the person is experiencing is an illness, just as diabetes or cancer are medical conditions.** Depression is not brought on by personal weakness, which is unfortunately still a common belief. Brain chemistry is impacted. It is not something the person with the disorder chooses; it chooses the person. Unfortunately many people who experience clinical depression feel a sense of shame or denial about it, which is why it is so important to realize that they simply can't "snap out of it" at will.
- **Realize that isolation is often a symptom of depression.** A friend or family member may be "hiding out" in a sense. He or she may not be communicating as much as usual or may be housebound and unable to go out very often. Since part of a depression and anxiety disorder is not wanting to go out, it's useful to make your presence known in that person's life in a regular way. They need connection with others, and it's vital that you seek them out, visit, call, or reach out in some other manner.
- **Persistence pays off.** When people are deep in depression, their verbal skills are not quite up to par. Therefore an in-person visit with them is always best. It's necessary to be persistent, even though it may not be easy to be around someone who is depressed. Remaining a constant in their life is the best way that you can support them during the difficult times. If they pull away, don't take it personally. Recognize that it's part of the illness.
- **Protect yourself while remaining present.** Some people fear getting too deeply involved with a depressed person. They feel the depression, anxiety, or panic will rub off on them, so they steer clear. Remember that you can sit with them, talk to them, watch TV with them, or simply spend time with them without feeling what they feel or how much they feel.
- **You can only do what you can do.** Helping someone who is depressed is sometimes challenging and frustrating. You may want the person to seek help when the individual is not willing

to accept help. You may try to socialize with the person, but they keep shutting you out. It's important to recognize you can help, but you can't *make* someone seek treatment or feel better.

- **Don't be afraid to ask.** One of the biggest myths about depression is that a caring person should never ask someone if that individual is contemplating suicide. On the contrary, it is important to ask and to take it seriously if the answer is affirmative. In fact, asking someone about whether or not they are suicidal can provide a measure of relief to them and open the door for treatment. If they are contemplating suicide, offer to help. Find them a mental health professional immediately, or drive them to the emergency room for an intervention.

- **Urge the depressed person to seek assistance.** If you know someone who is not necessarily severely depressed but still struggling, urge that person to seek counseling. Let your friend or family member know that you are aware that there are a number of treatment options, and that feeling as depressed as the person feels doesn't have to be constant in his/her life. You can offer to drive or accompany the person to an appointment and sit in the waiting room among the outdated magazines. You can also let them know that you're on their side.

CHAPTER 4

SNAP OUT OF IT!

Myths About Depression and Anxiety Disorders

Depression is like any other medical illness. It is caused by the interaction of biological and environmental influences, but it manifests in psychological as well as physical symptoms. In spite of the prevalence of depression and anxiety disorders in contemporary society, many myths and misconceptions are associated with the disorders—so many, in fact, that it's difficult to know where to start.

Perhaps the most common myth is this: If someone can't snap out of either a depression or an anxiety disorder, it means the person is weak or has a character flaw.

"A few people in my life have told me to 'just relax' or 'calm down,' and that makes me furious sometimes," says Jenni P., a gifted writer and website founder. "It is just not that simple with anxiety. Observers don't seem to understand that, of anything in the world, what I would often most like to do is relax and calm down, and yet my body and mind fight me. So such solutions are incredibly frustrating to hear."

Another woman, Jannine P., says she will never forget her oldest sister telling her to just snap out of it. "She told me to get over whatever it was I thought I had. My family never really understood what was going on or cared to know. Other people have said to me that it's just a phase."

Being told to simply snap out of it by someone who has not experienced a significant level of depression is like telling someone in a wheelchair to walk again, or insisting that someone with liver disease simply get over it. Depression can run so deep and be so damaging that sheer will and dogged determination are not the weapons that will deliver someone from such a hellish place.

"I had a girlfriend come to my house one day and jerk back my draperies in her cheerful demeanor," says Dorothy F. "She told me to get up and get over it! I resented the hell out of that."

Some people who do not suffer from mood disorders have a difficult time wrapping their mind around depression, anxiety, post-traumatic stress disorder, panic disorder, and how these disorders can impact behavior and outlook. "It is so much easier to place the blame on the person rather than to learn about the actual 'mechanisms' that are causing the external behaviors in the first place," says Dr. Shelley Slapion-Foote. "It's the kind of thing that, unless people have walked in the depressed or anxious person's shoes, they really cannot appreciate the pain and the energy that is drained just by daily living."

Ironically, it is often the person who is most fearful of depression and anxiety who demands that those in psychic pain simply pull themselves up by their bootstraps and march on, toughen up, and rise above it. They are so terrified of these states themselves that they "require" the person with depression or anxiety to magically and quickly "will" themselves out of the disorder. If they see that the person in pain cannot do that, it simply adds to their own fear and level of personal discomfort.

"Patients routinely attempt to will themselves out of their symptoms or mood," says Dr. Larry Wampler, a therapist and author of the book *The Sacred Dance: Spiritual Opportunities of Marriage.* "Despite all the media discussion on mood disorders being a legitimate medical condition, many people still harbor the misconception that depression is somehow a character flaw, curable by willpower, positive thinking, or plain old 'bucking up.'"

"Among the reasons for this misconception," adds Dr. Wampler, "is simple semantic confusion. The same word 'depression' is used to describe the medical condition and the 'normal' mood slump that everyone experiences in response to setbacks in life such as denting a new car, breaking a leg, getting fired, or having the same fight with your spouse for the tenth time. We feel sad, discouraged, demoralized, and inadequate; we're tempted to judge ourselves, retreat into our shell, avoid our friends, and give up trying. We might say we feel 'depressed.' But that's not what clinical depression is."

"Sometimes I feel as if I am not taken seriously by my friends and family regarding my depression and anxiety," says Lesa H. "I get the 'Oh, just get over it!' response from them, and this makes me feel like my emotions are not valid. I think they also try to push me sometimes into things I am not capable of dealing with, but they think it is helping me. In fact, it does the opposite. It brings on a panic attack when they pressure me into an uncomfortable situation."

A myth that many people believe is that if a person is depressed, there has to be an external factor bothering him or her. The fact is that outside factors are not always necessary to make a person depressed. We now know that chemical changes in the brain can lead to depression without any external precipitating factor.

Depression is not a personal failing. Depression is an illness and a chemical imbalance. It is not something that is chosen; it is something that simply exists. That is not to say that one cannot make efforts toward proper treatment and improvement. That's not only possible; in most cases it is advisable. However, despite overwhelming scientific evidence to the contrary, some people still believe that anxiety, depression, and other psychological disorders are chosen and must be "all in your head."

It is often difficult to open up to others about depression, anxiety, learning disabilities, phobias, and other forms of mental disorders.

It makes it even harder to admit to the lesser condition of being dysthymic (shy or timid, just slightly depressed) because dysthymia is not considered life-threatening. Additionally many people take on the added pressure and stress that this is somehow of their own doing or their own fault. If they weren't so "weak," they could and would simply snap out of it. Not so!

Mood levels have biochemical (physical) origins. That has been proven by the fact that low moods can be successfully overcome with purely physical interventions such as medication or nutrition. If mental disorders, whether depression, anxiety, obsessive-compulsive disorder, or comparable conditions, were indeed "all in your head," how could a mood-elevating diet or antidepressant drug make you feel better?

When you try to confront a challenge while the brain chemistry is off-balance, you are already beginning at a disadvantage because everything will be perceived as more difficult and complicated than it actually is. Once the proper chemical balance is achieved in the brain, your entire outlook can change, not only on small issues and problems but also on the world in general. With a proper balance of chemicals, you may be easily able to handle personal conflicts and challenges, and have the strength to work with and resolve seemingly impossible situations.

What about the myth that you can simply will or psych the self into a bolder, more confident personality? There is a huge motivational industry in place via CDs, books, and seminars: how to easily overcome a problem in just ten-easy-steps. Simply attend this seminar and turn your life around in one weekend! With such hopes and expectations in mind, you may have spent hundreds of dollars on similar promises and perhaps gained some valuable insights that were short-lived, while others have stayed with you for a long time. Chances are, however, most of what was heard, learned, and read didn't produce the promised results. As a result you may have believed this failure to be due to a personal weakness, that it was somehow your fault. Perhaps you blamed yourself for not studying hard enough, for not listening to the recordings often enough, for not putting the principles into practice with dedication and fervor.

How easy it would be to simply will yourself into a personality without doubt or fear, where confidence was abundant and sadness a distant dream. "Sometimes I have daydreams and little fantasies about me being this confident young girl who just does what she wants, when she wants, and nothing bothers her. She doesn't have an anxiety or social disorder, and she can go out and have fun and not worry about being nervous or anxious. I would really like to be this girl," says Lesa H. "I would just like to be myself, have fun, and feel unguarded."

There are motivational speakers who may truly inspire you and infuse you with new and potent ideas. They may make you feel motivated and hopeful. If you walk out of the seminar feeling terrifically optimistic for a while, or listen to a CD series and feel hopeful, this is a good thing. It proves to you, if nothing else, that feeling "up" is a viable state and an attainable one. When you have a good run of success, meaning no significant episodes in your mood or anxiety disorder for at least six months, a tremendous feeling of hope follows.

Another common myth is that depression only happens when something bad transpires in a person's life, such as the death of a family member, losing a job, or a serious relationship breakup. The truth of the matter is that depression can occur even when life is going quite well. The fact is that things going amiss in life can ignite depression, but that ignition is not always the precursor to a depressive episode. Depression can often be associated with an imbalance in brain chemistry, which has nothing to do with tragic life events.

Yet another myth is the idea that if one is willing to wait it out, depression will simply dissipate. While this can sometimes happen with a mild depression, it is unlikely with a moderate depression or a chronic anxiety disorder, which might not simply go away. If left untreated, the disorder can last for months or even years, and it can worsen over time.

Let's keep the myths coming, shall we? There are dozens of them floating about. How about this one? Antidepressants turn one into a different person. Many would argue with this and say that antidepressants can actually make one feel more like him- or herself once again.

Other myths include the thinking that depression is a problem of the Western industrialized world and not of developing countries. The fact is depression affects people in all cultures around the world. However, what is true is that "sadness," particularly in old age, is considered "normal" in some countries and not a disease to be treated by a doctor. This thinking is, in fact, another myth.

Still another myth is that even if depression is an illness, there's nothing to be done about it. After all it can't be treated the way other diseases can be treated. In fact depression is a treatable disorder and causes suffering on a worldwide scale, at any age, and in all ethnic groups. The burden of depression and other disorders has been underestimated in the past. Currently, out of the ten leading causes of suffering worldwide, five are psychiatric conditions, including depression. By 2020 depression will be the second-largest cause of suffering, next only to heart disease.

Myth-busters continue with a common one about alcohol: drinking booze lifts one's spirits. Wrong. Alcohol is actually a depressant and may, in fact, worsen depression. Not only do the effects of alcohol wear off, but that so-called high will require yet another drink, and another, and another. This self-medicating treatment can lead to physical addiction. There are no solutions in a bottle, certainly not for depression.

What about the myth that drugs used for treating depressions are addictive? Actually antidepressants are not addictive or habit forming. When depression is in remission, the drugs can be slowly tapered off and stopped. It is best to have this supervised by a doctor.

Another myth relates to economics. Poor people often suffer from depression because they don't make enough money. Is that true? Look around you. Look at the news on TV, in newspapers and magazines. Many wealthy and famous people such as Ted Turner, Rosie O'Donnell, and Donny Osmond have been known to suffer from depression, anxiety, sleep disorder, bipolar disorder, or panic disorder. Though low socioeconomic status may be a contributing factor for depression, this and anxiety disorders can and do affect people across all socioeconomic levels.

Psychiatrist Gail Saltz says the first important step is to realize that depression is a medical condition. "More than half of this country still believes that depression is due to personal weakness as opposed to understanding that it's an illness," Dr. Saltz says. "Treat the illness, and those people can be like anyone else."

Dr. Wampler has been a psychologist in Southern California for more than twenty-five years. He earned his PhD in psychology from Vanderbilt University. When he was an undergraduate in the early 1970s, he worked on a research team studying depression from a behavioral perspective. At that time the field was dominated by Martin Seligman's exciting new theory, "Learned Helplessness." That notion proposed that depression might just be a bad habit, arising out of a mistaken lesson that "what I do doesn't really matter." The resulting passivity makes it a self-fulfilling prophecy leading to depression. "It predicted that depressed people would feel better if only we could prompt them to stop thinking and talking in such negative patterns," says Wampler with a slight grin, "which would lead to better social relations and other constructive action." Wrong!

A final myth that is worthy of discussion is the power of positive speech. Depressed patients were recruited for a treatment program aiming to instill positive speech. "Understandably enough, people who are depressed tend to complain a lot when they consult a therapist. They describe their unhappy feelings and physical pains. They recount their problems in life. They express a pessimistic outlook. They appeal for help." Wampler's job was to watch therapy sessions from behind a one-way mirror and code these "negative" statements and their "positive" counterparts. "We hoped to demonstrate a reduction of negative speech and an increase in positive speech, to be followed by improvement on independent measures of depression."

"The researcher-therapist would listen politely for a while," says Wampler. "Then he or she would explain to the patient how we believed this kind of talk only made the problem worse, by driving away potential friends. Henceforth, we would try to help them change their speech patterns. Subsequent sessions were divided into periods of 'free talk,' when the patient could say whatever he wanted, and 'positive talk,' when no negative statement would be allowed. If the patient complained or expressed unhappiness during the latter segment, the therapist would interrupt and firmly correct him."

"In some very mild cases of depression, this naïve intervention was marginally successful in changing the way the patient talked. But even then it had little impact on the symptoms of depression. In more serious cases, the treatment was completely ineffective, bordering on abuse. I vividly recall one poor soul, a man in his forties, suffering from a major depressive episode. His face was drawn in pain; he continually wrung his hands. The relentless demand for positive talk was more like torture for him, sometimes bringing him to tears. It was painful for me to observe. He was clearly unable to comply. Trying to make him do so was like prodding a cow to fly."

This type of primitive research occurred at a time before the advent of committees to protect human subjects. It would not be approved today. However, it provided clear proof to Wampler and others that in cases of serious depression, appeals to willpower, whether from friends, family, therapists, or the patients themselves, are "completely ineffective" and, in many cases, downright inhumane.

As one man with depression shared with us during the writing of this book, ". . . sometimes when I see the signs that I'm slipping, such as eating more or becoming more isolative, I'm not always able to do anything to intervene and help myself up and out. It's especially heartbreaking to know I'm beginning to go deeper into my actions and to be unable to stop it."

Men and Depression

Although depression affects men as well as women, mental health professionals see far fewer men with depression than women. Why? Just as men are less likely to ask for directions on the road, they are less likely to ask for help with their depression and anxiety.

Compared with women, men tend to be more concerned with appearing to be successful, strong, competitive, and powerful. Most men don't like to admit that they feel fragile or vulnerable, and so they are less likely to talk about their feelings with their friends, loved ones, or doctors. This is just one of the reasons why they often will not ask for help when they become depressed.

Men often feel that they should rely only on themselves and that it is somehow weak to have to depend on someone else, even for a short time. Additionally men have difficulty recognizing the symptoms of depression. Men may be more willing to report irritability, fatigue, loss of interest in work or hobbies, and sleep disturbances rather than feelings of sadness, worthlessness, and excessive guilt, which are commonly associated with depression in women. As a result four times as many men as women die by suicide, even though women make more suicide attempts during their lives.

Let's face it, even in this day and age, depression is often viewed as a predominantly female affliction. But this may be because the condition is often overlooked and misunderstood with respect to men. Depression is difficult, if not impossible, to see. It is a secret sadness in many ways. What usually does present itself on the surface, particularly with men, is the "evidence" of depression or the defenses used to hide it.

We see it in the covering up of these feelings of deep sadness with substance abuse, or it may manifest with outbursts of anger and rage, or in isolating behavior. Self-medication may include drinking, taking street drugs, or the inappropriate use of prescription drugs, womanizing, and even watching excessive amounts of television or movies. Some forms of self-medication are tolerated or even encouraged by our culture, so it is hard to get across to men that what they are doing is numbing rather than stabilizing the depression.

As previously mentioned, depression in men can also affect sexual libido and performance. The problem becomes convoluted and complicated with men because they are often unwilling to admit any problems dealing with their sexuality. Many mistakenly feel that the problems they are experiencing are related to their manhood, when, in fact, they are caused by a medical problem such as clinical depression. Depression in men may have other serious consequences.

In a Veteran's Administration twin study, investigators looked at the onset of heart disease in depressed participants between 1993 and 2005. Men with depression in 1992 were twice as likely to develop heart disease in the ensuing years, compared to men with no history of depression.

Unfortunately for men as well as for their partners, men see a greater disconnect between clinical depression and what is commonly classified as a "legitimate" medical issue. For instance, when one breaks a bone, the condition clearly requires medical treatment. But if one's mood is persistently bad, he is responsible for it on his own, from a male point of view, due to a lack of understanding of the mechanics of depression. Women may be more inclined to research and understand depression because emotions are seen as their domain, whereas men are more likely to understand what a torn ACL means for a football player's career. Talking about feelings is also seen as something that women do, while men focus on that which is concretely fixable.

"Depression equals vulnerability, shame, and lack of functioning. That takes away the man's masculinity, and for men, that takes away the sense of self," says William Pollack, PhD, the author of *Real Boys: Rescuing Our Sons from the Myths of Boyhood*. In the American ethos, Pollack says, "a man who's vulnerable is not even a man any more . . . It's the equivalent of being psychologically castrated."

It is important to mention that this type of reactive behavior is not necessarily written in stone, and thinking about emotions and talking about them can be an acquired skill. Men need to learn that they too can benefit from therapy when they gain more knowledge about mood or anxiety disorders, and when they realize it is certainly *not* feminizing to learn this sort of skill.

Many men still come from the John Wayne school of thought: "It's only a flesh wound." That's how some men deal with it. "It's not real. I can lick it." Depression is thought of as a weakness and something to get over. There's still something disgraceful about it, even in today's society. A real man—a John Wayne type—would simply "get over it." Many men react to depression by getting involved in a dangerous activity that takes their complete attention away from self, such as mountain climbing or skydiving.

Clinicians historically have viewed the lower rates of depression among men as a response to their having some natural protective ability that women lack. The fact is that the disorder likely manifests differently and has been overlooked. If a man becomes immersed in mountaineering or skydiving, perhaps he doesn't *seem* depressed. The use of drugs and alcohol is a more typical male response and diagnostically clouds the issue. Irritability is also more likely to be a male sign of depression, but it's not always screened for by clinicians.

A man who divorces his wife, starts spending money, and begins to drink more has historically been labeled as having a "midlife crisis," when his behavior is more likely indicative of a midlife depression.

Many men complain of the physical symptoms of depression such as sleep troubles, fatigue, headaches, or stomach distress without ever discerning their psychological source. Compared with women suffering from depression, depressed men are more likely to behave recklessly, drive fast, drink heavily or take drugs, or seek out confrontation. Instead of acting as if they are filled with self-doubt, depressed men might bully and bluster and accuse those around them of failing them.

The often-untold story of depression is the effect it has on the partners of those who suffer from the illness. Depression frequently buries the emotions of the person who is not suffering from the disease. The "healthy" partner becomes the caretaker, the rock who stands strong while the dark, unpredictable moods of the depressed partner ebb and flow. There is no room for the other person to express personal sadness, frustrations, or loneliness. Since the partner is not the one suffering from a debilitating illness, he or she becomes cut off from a less intense, though no less real, emotional experience.

The result is that partners of people with depression often fall into a trap. They become angry because normal-but-unexpressed emotions, such as sadness or nervousness, gradually morph into anger.

The partners may shut down or become martyrs because eventually they feel so full of anger that it's all they've got. The partners can't fix the depression, so they resign themselves to it. The best course is for couples and family members to be educated and treated for depression together.

Compounding the problem for men is their sexual functioning becoming compromised. This can lead to negative self-assessments that further exacerbate depression. (The exception: Some men become more sexual in what is thought to be an attempt to help themselves feel better.)

There is a cultural belief that men are supposed to be in control, successful. Men should not only be self-reliant and in control of their emotions, but also in control of all things in their lives. To admit depression may be seen as an affront to this. To make matters worse, it is something within the man himself that he cannot rein in. It is faceless, nameless, and not as easily understood as other chronic health problems. Understanding it, let alone controlling it, is foreign to the male psyche, particularly if we acknowledge that men aren't often raised to be emotionally literate.

Upon recognizing their problem for what it is, men should take heart in knowing that 80 percent of people who seek help can experience improvement of symptoms or, in male-speak, the illness can be "fixed."

Surviving Depression

People who live with depression can watch endless reruns on television, let the bills pile up, and function on too much or too little sleep for days on end. These are not skills you'd want to list on any resume, but they are reality.

There are some who live with chronic depression who become expert at making accommodations for it. They learn quite quickly that their cognitive skills may give out during low periods. As a result, they develop ways of keeping track of things the short-term memory doesn't seem equipped to deal with. They become gifted at keeping lists of "to do" items so that they don't get off track. Another helpful coping trick is to create a notebook of important information. When we are sinking into a bout of depression, strangers are not the people we call on for assistance or a sympathetic ear. That's why keeping a notebook of important information is a must.

- The notebook should contain names and numbers of friends and mental health-care providers who know the situation and are aware of the pitfalls and cycles of your moods.
- Tell others about your notebook of key contact people and then keep the numbers of your friends and mental health-care provider handy.
- Preparing this notebook and making contact with someone close to you regarding its whereabouts is something you want to do *before* you sink into a severe episode of depression. When one is in a depressive episode, it is sometimes difficult to think clearly enough to even bring the notebook out of the drawer or remember where it was placed. Therefore establish this plan before your next episode.
- A list of medications and dosages that have worked well, and those that have not, is excellent information to keep in the notebook.
- Your pharmacy's phone number with a copy of your insurance card or payment method is also something you'll want to have readily available in the notebook.

The "survival" notebook may also contain:

- A basic shopping list of groceries with items that can be circled. The list can be given to a family member or friend who has offered to do the grocery shopping for you.
- A list of easy-to-prepare meals that don't take a great deal of skill or time to complete. Also keep a few clipped easy-to-make recipes

- A few menus from favorite take-out places and a list of favorite grocery stores that deliver.
- A list of household chores that need completing and how to accomplish them successfully.
- Pets need extra care too, so make sure to include any numbers or information necessary for their care/safety, including your veterinarian's number in case of emergency.

Show Me the Money

Having an electronic banking system set up on your computer is a good way for people with mental disorders to stay on top of their finances. It's often easier to hit a few keys on the online billing page in order to pay monthly bills than to write checks and place stamped bills in the mail.

Screen Time

People who live with severe depression often can focus on computer tasks when all else seems unmanageable. It seems odd, but this has been proven time and time again. When people with depression cannot seem to function in the outside world, managing a small-scale world on the small screen is still feasible. Watching television also seems like a much more manageable pastime and can help a person who is suffering with a mood or anxiety disorder get through a rough patch with minimal effort.

A Final Note

Sticky Post-It Notes rule! To have notes all over the bathroom and kitchen walls with simple instructions is often a wonderful survival skill that can be helpful when you start sinking into the cognitive confusion that often accompanies depression.

"When I can't keep track of what I need to do, I plaster yellow sticky notes all over my house," says Don K. "They remind me of what I need to accomplish that hour or that day. I don't know what I'd do without them."

"I have to do whatever I can to not let the anxiety and fear get overstimulated," says Stefan C., who has lived with severe depression and anxiety for close to fifty years. "This has meant watching TV and working on the computer. I have to keep busy all the time; otherwise the worry starts to grow, which in turn activates the anxiety, which eventually causes the volcano of fear to erupt. I am mostly homebound and have to keep myself from worrying by doing computer work or watching TV programs."

When one is faced with a significant bout of depression, Dr. Wampler strongly suggests to first honor those unhappy feelings, console ourselves, and reach out to friends for support if you are able to do so. "We also need to screen our thoughts or do so as best we can." Often it is difficult to do this when we're in the midst of a particularly bad episode of depression. However, it's important to attempt to catch our thoughts to see if we are overgeneralizing ("I *never* do anything right"); projecting current misery into the future ("I'll *never* recover from this," "I'm going to be out of work *forever*," "I'll end up homeless," "I'll die alone in the streets."); or wallow indefinitely in our pain ("I feel sooo miserable. I can't stand this."). The tools of cognitive therapy can assist people in correcting these invalid, paralyzing thoughts.

Dr. Wampler also reminds us that it's vital to forgive ourselves for however we might have contributed to our misfortune, humbly accepting our human limitations, and attempting to learn from the errors of our ways. We all make mistakes. That's how we learn and grow.

Last but not least, it's essential to devise a plan and work to remedy the situation as best we can. We naturally admire those who can do all of these things. "They tend to be upbeat and optimistic, whatever their circumstances," says Wampler. "We're inspired by stories of people who overcome misfortune to achieve big goals. We attribute it to their character and rightly aspire to be like them. That's fine, but we should also partly credit their genetic programming, specifically their physiological capacity to maintain a good supply of neurotransmitters, even in the midst of adversity." (Neurotransmitters, such as serotonin, norepinephrine, and dopamine, are chemical messengers in the brain.)

Human beings, he reminds us, vary considerably in this capacity. "At the high end are people like Christopher Reeve, who persevered with hope and good humor despite a devastating paralysis." Most of us are in the middle. At the low end of the spectrum are people whose baseline supply of neurotransmitters is naturally low. "Even in normal circumstances," reports Wampler, "they tend to be glum and pessimistic with low energy. What's worse, their neurotransmitters are vulnerable to going into a downward spiral. This is clinical depression, a medical condition based in the brain chemistry." It can be triggered by a misfortune—divorce, losing a loved one, or being let go from a job—but it also commonly occurs on its own internal cycle without regard to life events. Sometimes it's seasonal, such as with seasonal affective disorder (SAD)."

Fred H. has lived with depression since his teenage years. "Doubting myself is dangerous, and unfortunately it's often part and parcel of being depressed. It's frustrating to think about undertaking something that requires sustained effort and then to doubt my ability to stick with it. At my worst I may avoid taking things on because I worry that I'll end up quitting."

With clinical depression it is difficult, if not impossible, to pull one's self out of a deep episode of depression no matter how hard one tries. It is cruel and cold-hearted for society to fault individuals or label them as having weak characters because they cannot do so. It is a matter of brain chemistry—not a character flaw or weakness. Unfortunately, since self-judgment is one of the biological symptoms of clinical depression, those who live with the disorder are inclined to fault themselves for being "weak" or "lazy" or lacking in willpower. They can benefit somewhat from systematically striving to apply cognitive therapy and to rephrase negative or self-defeating thoughts. "But for them it's like swimming upstream against a strong current," adds Wampler. "No matter how hard they try to correct their discouraging thoughts, maintain a good attitude, and be proactive, they remain clinically depressed. Everything looks bleak. They simply hurt—emotionally and often physically. They may have trouble getting out of bed in the morning, let alone going on job interviews or taking other constructive action."

Some of the coping tools that assist individuals with depression are cognitive therapy, medication treatment, talk therapy, relaxation techniques, and a host of other therapies that will be discussed further in various sections of this book—and by the participants themselves. Becoming prepared before a down cycle begins can help to maintain one's emotional balance and daily life without veering too far off the pathway. It can help maintain relationships, employment, and daily challenges.

Therapist Adina Shapiro believes in a combination of techniques. "Certainly talk therapy as a foundation, coupled with medication when symptoms are severe enough. I teach patients relaxation and mindfulness techniques in which they are encouraged to pay attention to their feelings and use them as information about what needs fixing in their lives, rather than as a problem that needs to be eliminated." In talk therapy, Shapiro focuses on the thought patterns that often keep patients' depression going.

Often challenges with fear and anxiety can make leaving the home extremely difficult. One way to deal with this problem is to write letters, join online support groups, and make frequent phone calls to those who offer the greatest comfort level. Nonverbal techniques such as creating artwork, doing simple dance movements or yoga in the comfort of one's home, or playing a musical instrument can also counteract feelings of isolation. "Listening to music sometimes will help my mood," says Jan W. "If I can focus enough to do some yoga postures, that too can help." Sometimes a simple craft project or a wild dance in the living room, accompanied by flailing arms and sweeping movements, can work wonders toward counteracting some of the most desperate and hopeless feelings.

CHAPTER 5

I'M ALL SHOOK UP

Anxiety: Depression's Close Cousin

> *Worry is a misuse
> of the imagination.*
>
> —Dan Zadra

According to psychologist and anxiety specialist Robert Leahy, the average high school student today seems to suffer from the same degree of anxiety symptoms as the average psychiatric patient in the early 1950s. Even though fear is our most essential emotional protective gift from Mother Nature, our collective internal security system has gone haywire. And unfortunately a verbal directive such as "just calm down" or "please relax yourself" can actually make a person feel more anxious.

Why is anxiety on the rise? After all we live in a time when fewer immediate legitimate threats lie in wait. In prehistoric times our ancestors were constantly concerned about where their next meal would come from. Living on the edge, they were terrorized by wild animals that could literally rip them to shreds. But when was the last time you had a close encounter with a roaring lion or a growling bear other than at the local zoo?

We now live in times with massive stores jam-packed with aisles of every food and convenience item we can imagine; our automobiles are put through multiple crash tests; our fellow passengers are X-rayed and patted down by airport security; our medical centers and hospitals are state of the art. We are safer and more secure than at any other time in history, yet it seems modernity has neither brought us calm nor true security. Instead it has somehow put us out of touch with how to manage our worst fears and distressing anxieties. Technology, meant to bring people closer, has put people at a distance, even though it allows individuals to communicate and reach across the globe in record time. It seems to have put us out of touch with the warm touch of one another and the comfort of an embrace.

Sometimes reactions to outside dangers or perceived dangers are useful and quite natural. Our brains are wired to accept this information about possible pending danger and to take action out of self-protection. However, when the situation is overwhelming, occurs frequently, interferes with daily life, or is recognized to be irrational, it may be an anxiety disorder. It is a sense of not being in control of anxiety, even when information that logically counteracts it is present and available.

"My anxiety disorder can sometimes feel like it's controlling me rather than my controlling it or having control over it," says Lesa H., who lives with generalized anxiety disorder, social anxiety, and frequent panic attacks. "When I am clear-minded and not experiencing an attack, I understand that the things I go through when I'm in an attack are very real, yet extremely illogical. This frustrates me because I can't see this while I'm having the attack. The attack itself seems to cloud my judgment and any logical thought. I seem to dig a hole deeper and deeper for myself and then find it very hard to calm down and get out of it, and I spiral down further the longer the attack goes on."

Anxiety, like its cousin depression, is also a multi-headed beast that manifests in many forms. Some of the different forms of anxiety include generalized anxiety disorder (GAD), obsessive-compulsive disorder (OCD), panic disorder, post-traumatic stress disorder (PTSD), social phobia (or social anxiety), and specific phobias.

Generalized Anxiety Disorder—GAD

Physicians are becoming more aware that anxiety disorders must be treated because long-term consequences are profound. The impact of anxiety on stress-exacerbated medical illnesses and the immune system is now accepted in the medical community. That's why the "coming out" of mental disorders among celebrities is useful. It shakes off the stigma that once existed and propels people to seek treatment.

Anxiety can also have a strong genetic component. If a parent suffered panic attacks, the child can learn those responses. If a family member responds well or poorly to a particular medication, or if side effects are a huge problem, genetics suggest that the same will be true for a relative.

Generalized anxiety disorder, or GAD, is characterized by persistent, excessive, and unrealistic worry about everyday things. This worry goes on every day and possibly all day. People with GAD feel their worrying is beyond their control and can't be turned off. They often expect the worst, even when there is no good reason for concern. Their excessive worrying is often about health, family, money, or work. This worry is hard to control and is present on more days than it is absent. The unrelenting worry interferes with everyday living and can affect all areas of life, including social, work, and family. Physical symptoms of GAD can include fatigue, restlessness, difficulty sleeping, muscle tension, irritability, gastrointestinal discomfort or diarrhea, and edginess.

The ADAA (Anxiety Disorders Association of America) promotes the message that up to 90 percent of those affected by anxiety disorders can be effectively treated. Cognitive behavioral therapy or psychosocial intervention may be more effective than medication in the longer term because individuals with anxiety disorders actually learn to desensitize themselves. Taking a horizontal position on a psychotherapist's couch has been replaced with short treatments that may number as few as four to twelve sessions. The key in these sessions is identifying self-defeating beliefs, negative thinking, and the amplification of danger. These examinations and realizations hold the promise of success because unhealthy, unrealistic, and unrelenting dark thoughts can stick to the psyche like glue. Learning to recognize and detach from them on a regular basis is a successful treatment for anxiety disorders.

Stefan P. lives with an anxiety disorder but copes with it by managing his activities. Medications have helped Stefan P. so he is "okay as long as I live a life of isolation and never do anything anyone else takes for granted. The medications that came on the market about fifteen years ago are much more effective than the older tricyclic medicines that hardly helped me at all. The doctor had me altering my medicines all the time, and none of them really helped significantly after a while. I was fortunate to have a very intuitive and psycho-pharmacologically savvy psychiatrist who noticed that my primary problem was anxiety and not depression. Once he started me on the anti-anxiety medications, I slowly got better, but it took about four years. I was mostly homebound and had to keep myself from worrying all the time."

Having to go on and off medications in order to find the correct one and the right dosage is a trying experience for most people. "Being so heavily medicated keeps my symptoms in check, but it often feels like a dark cloud is hanging over my head," says Stefan P. "It can feel like it's ready to rain symptoms at any moment if the dosage shifts into the wrong zone."

Social Anxiety Disorder (Also Known as Social Phobia)

> *You can't stay in the corner of the forest*
> *waiting for others to come to you.*
> *You have to go to them sometimes.*
>
> —from: Winnie the Pooh

Social anxiety disorder, or social phobia, is characterized by an intense fear of self-embarrassment and being scrutinized and judged by others in social or performance situations. Some people with social anxiety disorder literally feel sick from fear in seemingly nonthreatening situations, such as ordering food in a restaurant, signing one's name in public, or making a phone call. Though they recognize that the fear is excessive and unreasonable, people with social phobias feel powerless against their anxiety. They are terrified they will act in a way that will be embarrassing or humiliating. The anxiety can interfere significantly with daily routines, occupational performance, or social life. It can make it difficult to complete school, participate in interviews, obtain or maintain a job, and to create and maintain friendships and romantic partnerships.

Robin T. also tends to feel very alone. Her social anxiety has caused a severe impact on her social life and on the person she felt she was before the symptoms intensified. Robin says, "I've isolated myself from everyone. I don't go out at all. I have no desire to see anyone. More than anything, I wonder where that person is that I was before."

Janaya G.'s primary symptoms of social anxiety include being in public places and having to interact with others. "I often rehearse what I'm going to say to the checkout person in a store before I approach that worker; I often feel awkward and nervous. I also avoid eye contact with others, and I even struggle with going out with friends. I spend a lot of time isolating myself from others."

Most people who suffer with social anxiety do not share their symptoms or the nature of their disorder with those around them. Sandi H. hasn't opened up to many of her friends about her difficulty with anxiety. Like many people who suffer from social anxiety and other mental disorders, it is often difficult to do so. "I often wear a 'mask,' look my best on the outside by wearing makeup, dress nicely, and do my hair; this way I can hide the pain that I am feeling inside."

Lesa H. has suffered for five years with social anxiety and panic attacks. She also tries to mask her feelings. "Sometimes I try to bottle up my feelings, and I try to appear overly cheerful; but I find that it's only a matter of time before it all hits me, and I come crashing down very quickly with an attack. Self-doubt and the feeling that others are forming opinions of me bring some of my anxiety attacks on. In my mind I go through an analysis of the situation that I'm in, and I find the best and worst possible outcomes and try to think about them logically. It's almost a matter of brainwashing myself into thinking that everything is fine so that I don't have an anxiety attack."

People with social anxiety are often perceived by others as being too quiet, shy or withdrawn, disinterested, and unfriendly. They *want* to behave comfortably and effortlessly around crowds and want to make friends and be involved in social interactions, but they are often stopped in their tracks by fear and severe anxiety when they attempt to do so.

Emily M., who is a therapist herself, works very hard to be proactive with her symptoms. She has been accused of being an introvert in social and occupational situations despite her best efforts to appear what she calls socially normal. "My introversion is misunderstood as aloofness," she says. Emily has dealt with her own symptoms of depression and social anxiety for twenty-five years. She realizes very well that this disorder has left her feeling socially disconnected. "I isolate from friends and family. I get angry and saddened. I get envious of happy people."

Larry J. limits those he allows into his world when he is in a severe state of anxiety—out of self-preservation. "I am isolated from most of the outside world. I have at the most three people whom I consider my friends. I have many acquaintances, but for the most part, I just cope with the help of my wife, my friends, and my doctors."

"I often feel like I'm trapped in a cage that I built myself," says Claudia G. "I can see others going about their lives, and I want to take part in joyous society, but I can't figure out how to open the door. Sometimes I get a taste of what it's like to be a part of that world, but something always seems to push me back inside. There is a sense of security and familiarity in this cage, but it comes at a great cost."

Julie P. becomes exhausted and frazzled from having to work all day, but at the same time she appears as if everything around and inside of her is sailing along effortlessly; she looks stress-free and just fine. "It takes so much for me to create a front and pretend to be normal that it just drains me." She had difficulty working full time because it depleted her energy to pretend to be what she wasn't feeling for so many hours of each day. "I just cannot relax around others, especially those whom I do not know well." For Julie, it became too stressful to keep up a facade of being just fine. "I try to pretend that everything is okay and that nothing 'gets' to me, when, in fact, *everything* gets to me! I have a low-stress threshold."

Social anxiety is usually accompanied by low self-esteem. Larry J. has been affected by these problems since returning from Vietnam in 1968. He was only twenty-five years old at the time. The symptoms have impacted his career and work. "My feelings of aggression and worthlessness were causing me problems in my work as a contractor. I was always feeling that I was not performing at my best, even though I received many compliments on my work. I prided myself on being a perfectionist, and regardless of what I had accomplished, I just did not assimilate my achievements into my feeling of well-being. Many people tried to make me realize all the good I had accomplished in my life, but I always measure my successes by my failures."

Lesa H., a young student, feels that having a social anxiety disorder plays a large role when planning any type of outing. "There are some things that I cannot do socially with friends. I cannot walk into a crowded venue alone, nor can I go somewhere unfamiliar when I'm alone. Large crowds make me edgy, and I feel I have to really try to keep myself from having an attack." Lesa realizes that this disorder has had a large impact on her family life as well. "My mother has to take a lot of time from her work when I am going through bad patches to help me along. She has had to take time off work to accompany me to some places so that I don't feel so alone."

Social phobia, which seems to accompany other anxiety disorders or depression, affects about 15 million American adults. Men and women are equally likely to develop the disorder, which usually begins in childhood or early adolescence. There has been some evidence that genetic factors are involved in the development of social anxiety. Many people who live with social phobia tend to develop substance abuse problems in an attempt to self-medicate their anxiety.

The Blank Face of Phobias

A phobia is an excessive or unreasonable fear of an object, situation, or place. Phobias are quite common and often take root in childhood for no apparent reason. Other times they spring from traumatic events or develop from an attempt to make sense of unexpected and intense feelings of anxiety or panic.

Simple phobias are fears of specific things such as insects, infections, or even flying. Agoraphobia is a fear of being in places where one feels trapped or unable to get help, such as in crowds, on a bus or in a car, or standing in a line. It is basically an anxiety that ignites from being in places or situations from which escape might be difficult (or embarrassing). A social phobia is a marked fear of social or performance situations.

When the phobic person actually encounters, or even anticipates, being in the presence of the feared object or situation, immediate anxiety can be triggered. The physical symptoms of anxiety may include shortness of breath, sweating, a racing heart, chest or abdominal discomfort, trembling, and similar reactions. The emotional component involves an intense fear and may include feelings of losing control, embarrassing oneself, or passing out.

Most people who experience phobias try to escape or avoid the feared situation wherever possible. This may be fairly easy if the feared object is rarely encountered (such as snakes) and avoidance will not greatly restrict the person's life. At other times avoiding the feared situation (in the case of agoraphobia, social phobia) is not easily done. After all we live in a world filled with people and places. Having a fear of such things can limit anyone's life significantly, and trying to escape or avoid a feared object or situation can escalate and make the feelings of dread and terror even more pronounced.

In some situations regarding phobias, the person may have specific thoughts that contribute some threat to the feared situation. This is particularly true for social phobia, in which there is often a fear of being negatively evaluated by others; and for agoraphobia, in which there may be a fear of passing out or dying with no one around to help; and of having a panic attack, where one fears making a fool of oneself in the presence of other people.

"My symptoms only occur if there is a trigger," says Lesa H. "For example, I can be happy and confident, but as soon as I am in a crowd of people, I become nervous and anxious and begin to doubt myself. I feel the sweating coming on, the tightness of breath, and have to fight to control my symptoms. Sometimes I can control some of the symptoms; however, I find that once out of the situation, it all comes tumbling down like a load of bricks, and I have an anxiety attack just as a release mechanism of all that stress.

"Most people don't understand that the fears and anxiety I feel are genuine and that the impact they have on me is significant," she says. "People who have never experienced such sensations find it difficult to understand, especially when my attacks are brought on by things that they may comfortably partake in every day."

With some phobias there may be accompanying frightening thoughts ("I'm trapped and can't get out of here"; "This plane might crash"). However, with other phobias it is more difficult to identify any specific thoughts that could be associated with the anxiety. For example, it is unlikely that a person who is spider-phobic is afraid of making a fool of himself in the presence of the spider. With these phobias the cause seems to be explained more as a conditioned (learned) anxiety response, which has become associated with the feared object.

Specific (Simple) Phobias

Specific phobias are characterized by strong, irrational, and involuntary fear reactions to a particular object, place, or situation. They may involve feelings of being trapped and not being able to leave. These fear reactions lead people to dread confronting common, everyday situations, or to avoid them altogether, even though they logically know there isn't any real threat of danger. The fear doesn't make any sense, but nothing seems to be able to stop it. When confronted with the feared situation, someone with a phobia may even have a panic attack—the abrupt onset of intense fear or terror in which individuals feel as if they are losing control.

Phobias can disrupt daily routines, limit work efficiency, reduce one's self-esteem, and place a strain on relationships, since individuals will do whatever they can to avoid the uncomfortable and often terrifying feelings of phobic anxiety. While some phobias develop in childhood, most seem to come out of the blue, usually arising in adolescence or early adulthood. They typically have a sudden onset, occurring in situations that previously did not cause any discomfort or anxiety. Common phobias include fear of animals, insects, heights, thunder, driving, flying in airplanes, public transportation, dental or medical procedures, and elevators.

Treatments for Phobias—EMDR

Eye Movement Desensitization and Reprocessing (EMDR) is a method of psychotherapy that is an effective treatment for some cases of phobias, trauma, and psychological stress. Psychologist Francine Shapiro made the chance observation that eye movements could reduce the intensity of disturbing thoughts under certain conditions. Dr. Shapiro studied this effect, and in 1989 she reported the success of using EMDR to treat victims of trauma in the *Journal of Traumatic Stress*. Since then EMDR has developed and evolved through the contributions of therapists and researchers throughout the world.

No one knows exactly how any form of psychotherapy works neurobiologically in the brain. What we do know is that when a person is extremely upset, his brain cannot process information as it does ordinarily. One moment becomes frozen in time, and even remembering that trauma may feel as bad as going through it initially. The images and feelings haven't been altered. Such traumatic memories can have a lasting negative impact that interferes with the way a person sees the world and relates to others.

What actually happens during a typical EMDR session? It is not unusual for a therapist to guide the client to a problem emotion or event during the treatment. As thoughts and feelings rise to the surface, the therapist works with the client to verbally redirect their eye movement (or use a tapping technique if the eye movement is too difficult for the client to manage). This back-and-forth eye movement or tapping is an important part of the treatment. As these eye movements are re-directed, the negative emotions are thought to be released. The directed pattern of eye movements continue until the unwanted feelings and emotional trauma are neutralized and the troubling event is re-associated with positive thoughts about oneself, such as "I now realize I wasn't to blame for that event."

The theory is that EMDR can have a direct effect on the way the brain processes information. Normal information processing is resumed following a successful EMDR session, and the person no longer relives the same images, sounds, and feelings connected to the traumatic event. The person may still remember what happened, but it is less upsetting to him. Many types of therapy have similar goals. However, EMDR appears to be similar to what occurs naturally during dreaming or rapid eye movement (REM) sleep. Therefore EMDR is often thought to be a physiologically based therapy that assists the individual in seeing disturbing bits and pieces of a disturbing past situation or event in a new, less distressing way. To date approximately twenty controlled studies have investigated the effects of EMDR. These studies have consistently found that EMDR effectively decreases or even eliminates the symptoms of post-traumatic stress for the majority of clients. Clients often report improvement in other associated symptoms such as anxiety, so this sort of technique is often explored by therapists with clients who have panic attacks, severe grief issues, disturbing memories, phobias, pain disorders, eating disorders, performance anxiety, addiction, experience of sexual or physical abuse, or personality disorder.

Pushing the Panic (Disorder) Button

> *It is dangerous business going out your front door.*
> —J.R.R. Tolkien

Claudia G., knows when she is about to have a panic attack, so she tries to use a preemptive strike to get through it in public. "When I am in a public place, and I start to get anxious and panicky, I try to cover it up because of the fear of being noticed and looking like a freak. For example, if I'm in a store, I'll pick up an item and look at it really closely and concentrate on it until the feeling starts to subside. Sometimes I leave the place altogether. When friends invite me to go out with them, I usually accept, and then I make up an excuse at the last minute so that I can pull out of it. It has put a lot of strain on relationships I've had, and I've lost good friends and potential relationships as a result."

What Is a Panic Attack?

A panic attack is an overwhelming mental and physical experience in which one feels a sense of dread and doom. Such an attack is normally a swift and unforeseen period of intense fear or discomfort. It often strikes without warning—seemingly out of the blue. Your heart begins to pound hard in your chest or it starts to race. You may feel some dizziness or a bit nauseated. You may think, "I'm dying! I have got to get out of here and fast!" It may be difficult to catch your breath or to breathe normally. You may experience feelings of terror or have chest pains; you may feel tingling or numbness, or experience a feeling of unreality or loss of control.

Panic attacks can certainly be terrifying. They can strike when you are away from home or in the comfort of your own room. They can be experienced while you're trying to fall asleep, operating a vehicle, shopping in a store, or riding in an elevator.

There is a difference between anxiety and panic attacks. Although panic attacks commonly occur in all the different types of anxiety disorders, the difference lies in the duration and intensity of the symptoms. Panic attacks are episodes of intense fear that last only a short while. On the other hand, anxiety comes on more gradually, is less intense, and lasts longer.

It may sound surprising, but panic attacks are quite common. *The Merck Manual* reports that panic attacks occur in more than one-third of adults each year. You may experience an isolated panic attack and yet be otherwise perfectly happy and healthy. However, many people experience panic attacks as part of another disorder, such as social phobia, generalized anxiety disorder, or major depressive disorder.

Not everyone who experiences panic attacks will develop a panic disorder; many people have one attack but never seem to have another. For those who do have ongoing panic attacks, the disorder can become extremely disabling if left untreated.

Panic disorder is often accompanied by other conditions, such as depression and sometimes alcoholism, and may initiate phobias, which can develop in places or situations where panic attacks have occurred. For example, if a panic attack strikes while one is riding in an airplane or on an elevator, the person may develop a fear of flying or elevators and perhaps start avoiding them.

When Nona L. feels a panic attack coming on, she feels as if her heart is falling from its original place in her chest. "I get so weak and shaky; my legs feel weak, and I almost collapse and have to sit down. It's so weird!"

Panic disorder strikes between three and six million Americans and is twice as common in women as in men. It can appear at any age, in children or in the elderly, but most often it begins in young adulthood. The American Academy of Family Physicians reports that panic disorders usually develop in the late teens and in the twenties. They rarely develop after the age of thirty-five. Once the attacks develop, panic disorder tends to be a chronic condition. The frequency and intensity of the panic attacks tend to wax and wane over time. However, the sooner the person gets treatment, the better the outcome will be.

Some people's lives become so restricted that they avoid everyday outings to stores or driving in cars. In severe cases they won't even leave the house. They begin to avoid any situation in which they fear a panic attack will occur. When an individual's life becomes so significantly limited and controlled by the disorder, as happens in about one-third of all cases of panic disorder, the condition is called agoraphobia. It's interesting to note that a tendency toward panic disorder and agoraphobia runs in families. The good news is early treatment of panic disorder can often stop the progression to agoraphobia.

Linda N.'s panic attacks manifest as feeling shaky. She cannot sleep or eat and can barely swallow. "I felt I was dying and was basically just waiting for it to happen. I just wanted to be Linda again, but I feared that she was gone and this horrible, terrified, panicked person had taken her place. With the help of medication and a diagnosis, I slowly came back to life. I still have a dread and fear that the panic attacks will return though. I worry that my medications are not as effective as they once were. I don't like the idea of having to 'maintain' my condition. I just want it to go away."

When Lorna A. starts to have a panic attack, she feels like she is not connected. "I almost don't remember how I got wherever I am, and so

I am startled to realize that I am in a situation with people with whom I should be interacting. I start to get very shaky and lightheaded and feel as though I have to get out of the situation immediately or I will pass out. I am not able to stand in a line without being afraid that I will have a panic attack, and of course, the more fear I feel about having one, the more likely it becomes that I actually will."

If you have panic disorder, ongoing episodes can certainly take an emotional toll. The memory of the intense fear and terror that you felt during the attacks can negatively impact your self-confidence and cause serious disruption to your everyday life.

Typical symptoms of panic disorder include:

- **Anticipatory anxiety** — Instead of feeling relaxed and like yourself in between panic attacks, you feel anxious and tense. This anxiety resembles that of generalized anxiety disorder (GAD) and stems from a fear of having future panic attacks. This "fear of fear" can present itself for long spans of time and become very disabling.
- **Phobic avoidance** — You begin to avoid certain situations or environments. This avoidance may be based on the belief that a situation caused a previous panic attack. Or you may avoid places where escape would be difficult or help would be unavailable if you had a panic attack.

As previously mentioned, some people who experience panic disorders try to self-medicate with alcohol or drugs. They feel the substances will quiet their anxiety and fears. The National Mental Health Association reports that 30 percent of people with panic disorder use alcohol and 17 percent use drugs in an attempt to control or deflect their symptoms. Unfortunately these attempts to self-medicate almost always make matters worse. Additionally a large percentage (some reports say 20 percent) of those with panic disorder attempt suicide.

Treatment for Panic Disorder

How you deal with your own anxiety disorder often arises from how you and your physician or practitioner conceptualize what you are struggling with. If your practitioner believes the problem is solely biological, driven by problems with brain chemistry and no outside source, then your only treatment suggestions will likely be those that will improve brain chemistry.

Biological treatments for panic attacks in the form of medications can begin with the older tricyclic anti-depressant medications, such as Elavil and Tofranil, which raise brain norepinephrine levels. During the waiting period before these medications start to work, tranquilizers are often prescribed. They may include Xanax, Klonopin, Ativan, or Valium. This group of medications, called benzodiazepines, can and does cause tolerance, meaning that if you take them regularly, their effectiveness will drop, and you will require a higher dosage. While many people prefer a non-medicinal approach to treatment, anti-depressant medications have a long, successful history in alleviating panic attacks.

Sometimes anxiety disorders seem to appear out of the blue. Others find that anxiety has been a close companion since childhood and has worsened over time. There are those who have anxiety brought on by an "existential crisis" of sorts—a time when they lose their bearings, sense of purpose and/or direction, or their connection to the world and others. It is vital to explore all issues related to anxiety and panic before turning to a quick-fix approach, whether it is with over-the-counter supplements or traditional medications.

If you and your practitioner determine that what you are experiencing is an existential crisis of sorts, medication or powerful supplements will not fill the void of a life in search of meaning. It is important to first explore any immediate causes of conflict, such as family dynamics or work stress, because extreme conflict can precipitate anxiety and panic. If there are practical ways to resolve the conflict, it's important to try those first before moving on to other methods.

Guided imagery can be helpful because of its power to go deep into the subconscious mind, using the mind-body connection—not just the mind. It's a gentle but powerful technique that focuses and directs the imagination. Guided imagery normally involves being verbally guided with visualization and direct suggestion using imagery, story-telling and metaphor. If you decide to pursue guided imagery, hypnosis, or the like, do your research. Not all practitioners of alternative treatments are created equal; some have decades of experience, and some have mere hours. For example, someone with a weekend certificate in hypnotherapy is not qualified to assist you in diagnosing your true problem.

Various forms of meditation also can serve as useful anti-anxiety treatments. Mantra meditation works for almost everyone. It is quick to learn and apply. Basically you choose one word, or mantra (sound), and repeat it over and over in a seated position with eyes closed. Focusing on the breath will also help most people but is not quite as easy as mantra meditation. Mindfulness, both as a meditation technique and as a way of being in the world, will assist in moving the physical body out of the mind.

People who live with panic disorder or generalized anxiety disorder are trapped in the prison of their thoughts. In order to calm and tame your mind, you need to observe it as an outsider would observe a movie. That is what meditation teaches us to do—to watch our thoughts flicker in and out of our mind and detach from them in the process. Meditation and yoga, both good practices for an overactive, panic-ridden mind, dampen the "fight or flight" impulse, which aids in calming and healing the body and then the mind.

Agoraphobia

Agoraphobia is translated as "fear of the marketplace." It was traditionally thought to involve a fear of public places and open spaces. However, it is now believed that agoraphobia develops as a complication of panic attacks. If you have agoraphobia, you are afraid of having a panic attack in a situation where escape would be difficult or embarrassing. You are also afraid of having a panic attack where you wouldn't be able to get help. Because of these fears, you may begin to avoid crowded places such as shopping malls or sports arenas. You may also avoid planes, cars, or other forms of travel. In more severe cases, you might only feel safe at home.

If you have agoraphobia, you might avoid going anywhere without the company of a "safe" person—someone you feel will provide control of the situation or give you control back "just in case" it is needed. Some people with agoraphobia avoid physical exercise or exertion because they believe it might trigger a panic attack.

Post-Traumatic Stress Disorder (PTSD)

*I have learned now
that while those who speak about one's miseries
usually hurt,
those who keep silence hurt more.*

—C.S. Lewis

Post-traumatic stress disorder, or PTSD, consists of common symptoms displayed by survivors of combat, serious accident, or natural or man-made disaster; by witnesses to the violent death of others; and by the victims of torture, terrorism, rape, abuse, or other crimes. All these events fall outside the range of "normal" human experience and leave the individual with delayed or protracted intrusive responses, which can be so debilitating that they prevent normal day-to-day life.

A specific trigger or stimulus causes PTSD. Those with this disorder usually have persistent anxiety accompanied by nightmares, flashbacks, or difficulty relating to other people. They experience feelings of numbness, irritation, or agitation.

The extent of PTSD varies from person to person. PTSD can occur while in an abusive relationship or after it has ended. PTSD can last only a short time, or it can remain for years. In any case, it is advisable to seek a counselor or therapist for help in coming to terms with the events that have led to PTSD and to explore ways to either lessen them or their impact.

Even if you did not suffer bodily harm during a hurricane, war, or the terror attack on 9/11, traumatic stress of seeing disturbing images or living through various upsets and ordeals can cause physical effects as well.

People who are repeatedly exposed to life or death situations such as emergency room nurses and doctors, emergency medical technicians, police officers, fire fighters, rescue squad workers and medical personnel on burn wards or trauma units where stress levels and mortality rates are high, all witness trauma. Anyone who has experienced these types of events has experienced a shock and, even if he ultimately escapes danger, may feel as if life "just isn't the same anymore."

Birth parents who have lost custody of their children usually suffer from depression, and the children separated from their parents usually exhibit symptoms of PTSD, reports Djamila Abdel Jaleel, a caseworker who works with families in crisis. Support groups are typically useful in these situations. "These groups give the client the feeling of not being alone in the situation. Members of the group can empathize and then encourage their peers to move on."

People may experience a variety of reactions to trauma, many of which are understandable and sometimes short-lived. They may or may not develop PTSD. Those who do develop PTSD experience trauma along with intense fear, helplessness, or horror, and then they develop intrusive symptoms such as frequent, disturbing nightmares or flashbacks to the event. Most people who have PTSD have symptoms that get in the way of normal life and last longer than a month.

"My symptoms come and go," says Rachel W. who lives with PTSD. "The toughest, most recent episode was when my child reached the age I was when I was molested. It triggered an extreme amount of anxiety, nightmares, and insomnia. [My family] act as if they need to deny me in order to not admit that all the secrecy and hiding was detrimental. I truly believe that although they acted according to their best ability and knowledge at the time, it was very likely the secrecy and hiding caused me more long-term damage than the actual molestation."

What Does Trauma Look Like?

Trauma can bud from issues of abandonment, neglect, and physical or sexual abuse. Other traumas might include shock stemming from accidents, violence, surgeries, and other events that are overwhelming to the psyche. Accumulated hurts or injuries of childhood can also fall into the trauma category.

Tom Butz, PhD, offers a very good explanation of how people are different from animals when it comes to trauma. He suggests that to successfully navigate a traumatic event, humans must respond either by resisting and overcoming a threat ("fight"), or by avoiding and getting away from a particular threat ("flight"). If we are unable to accomplish either of these options, a third state is entered that is common to all animals: we freeze. Unlike our animal friends, however, the frozen state of heightened autonomic arousal or anxiety may become chronic over time. Although animals in the wild can literally and figuratively shake off their threats, we humans have the distinct ability to become frozen in our distress. In PTSD and panic disorder, chronic symptoms such as hyper-vigilance, sleep disturbances, anxiety, isolation, depression, and addictive behavior can remain stuck and are not easily shaken off.

No one can deny that the late George Carlin, comedian and great observer of life, had a way of dismantling words and human behavior and putting them all back together again in enlightening, blunt, and often shocking ways. He declared his own war on euphemisms: "I don't like euphemistic language, words that shade the truth. American English is packed with euphemisms, because Americans have trouble dealing with reality; and in order to shield themselves from it, they use soft language. And it gets worse with every generation."

As an example, Carlin described the evolution of that "condition in combat that occurs when a soldier is completely stressed out and is on the verge of nervous collapse." In World War I, the condition was known as "shell shock. Simple, honest, direct language. Two syllables."

By the time World War II rolled around, it was called battle fatigue. The term made the condition sound like a minor discomfort. Fatigue is a far less powerful word than shock. During the Korean War, the authorities came up with the expression "operational exhaustion." Carlin said of this label, "The phrase was up to eight syllables now, and any last traces of humanity had been completely squeezed out of it. It was absolutely sterile: operational exhaustion. Like something that could happen to your car."

Then he continued, "We got into Vietnam, and thanks to the deceptions surrounding that war, it's no surprise that the very same condition was referred to as 'post-traumatic stress disorder' . . . I'll bet if they had still been calling it 'shell shock,' some of those Vietnam veterans might have received the attention they needed."

In this one memorable routine, Carlin described how the labels for soldiers' psychological problems changed during the course of the major wars of the twentieth century: from "shell shock" to "battle fatigue" to "operational exhaustion" and then "post-traumatic stress disorder." Yet these disorders remain one and the same. All are significant and can present enormous challenges.

It bears repeating that PTSD impacts not only soldiers in war, but also men, women, or children of any age who have been exposed to a major traumatic event such as a physical attack, or who have witnessed a disturbing event. These events include robbery, rape, a natural disaster, or a serious accident. Events such as Hurricane Katrina and the terror attack of 9/11 would certainly qualify as disturbing events, as would military service in any war. The suffering resulting from these events has enabled researchers to gain new insights about how best to treat PTSD. Additionally the mere diagnosis of a serious disease can trigger PTSD in some people. Children who have experienced severe trauma, such as war, a natural disaster, physical or sexual abuse, or the death of a parent, are also inclined toward PTSD.

The worrisome combination of nightmares, flashbacks, anger, and depression that plagues people with PTSD is a devastating condition to live with. It is also overwhelming for the family and friends of the person with PTSD, and can wreak havoc on intimate relationships. In fact epidemiological evidence points to PTSD as one of the mental health conditions most likely to lead to personal and interpersonal relationship problems. Among the common problems therapists find: individuals with PTSD not wanting to attend family or social events for fear they'll be "cornered" by an unforeseen person or circumstance; not sleeping in the same beds as their spouses because of nightmares; inciting relationship conflict due to excess anger and irritability; and over-managing their children's behavior because of unrealistic fears about their safety.

The current treatments developed by psychologists for PTSD include:

- **Prolonged-exposure therapy.** In this type of treatment, a therapist guides the client to recall traumatic memories in a controlled fashion so that the client eventually regains mastery of his thoughts and feelings around the incident. While exposing people to the very events that caused their trauma may seem counterintuitive, it is done in a gradual, controlled, and repeated manner, until the person can evaluate his current circumstances realistically and understand that he can safely return to the activities he has been avoiding in his daily life.
- **Cognitive-processing therapy.** This is a form of cognitive behavioral therapy (CBT) used to treat PTSD and rape victims. Practitioners work with clients who hold false beliefs that the world is no longer safe or that they are incompetent because they have "let" a terrible event happen to them. This treatment places great emphasis on cognitive strategies to help people alter erroneous thinking that has emerged from the event.
- **Stress-inoculation training.** This is another form of CBT, in which practitioners teach clients such techniques as breathing, muscle relaxation, and positive self-talk to help manage and reduce anxiety.
- **Other forms of cognitive therapy.** These include cognitive restructuring, which is a set of techniques for becoming more

aware of our thoughts and for modifying them when they are distorted or are not useful.
- **Eye-movement desensitization and reprocessing.** In this treatment, also known as EMDR, the therapist guides clients through simple techniques, such as eye movements or tapping on the palms of the hand, at the same time they are recounting traumatic events. Psychologist Kent Bennington uses EMDR as an effective intervention treatment with PTSD patients. It's not clear how EMDR works, and, for that reason, it's somewhat controversial. However, EMDR therapy's efficacy is supported by research, according to Dartmouth University psychologist Paula P. Schnurr, deputy executive director of the National Center for PTSD.
- **Medications.** Selective serotonin reuptake inhibitors (SSRIs) are being used with success in many cases. Two in particular, paroxetine (Paxil) and sertaline (Zoloft), have been approved by the Food and Drug Administration for use in treating PTSD. Other medications may be useful in treating PTSD as well, particularly when the person has additional disorders such as depression, anxiety, or psychosis.

The promising prolonged-exposure therapy and cognitive-processing therapy are at the forefront of treating PTSD right now, especially in the population of combat veterans.

At the same time, other researchers are experimenting with add-ons to these proven treatments to increase their effectiveness. Some are looking at how virtual reality might enhance the effects of prolonged-exposure therapy. In virtual reality a client experiences 3-D imagery, sounds, and sometimes smells that correspond with a traumatic event. Virtual reality puts the patient in a greater state of sensation and experience, increasing the likelihood of a positive response to treatment.

Some psychologists are starting to think about ways to treat PTSD when it is accompanied by other psychiatric and health conditions. Psychologist John Otis, of Boston University and the Veterans

Administration in Boston, is testing an integrated treatment that aims to alleviate symptoms of both PTSD and chronic pain in veterans of the wars in Vietnam, the Persian Gulf, Iraq, and Afghanistan. The treatment combines aspects of cognitive- processing therapy for trauma and cognitive behavioral therapy for chronic pain.

"We think these two conditions may interact in some psychological way that makes them more severe and challenging to treat," Dr. Otis says. In particular he and others presume that "anxiety sensitivity"—fear of experiencing one's anxiety-related symptoms—may increase the odds that certain individuals with PTSD have more problems than others.

While the study is not yet finished at this writing, results are encouraging. Further Dr. Otis says, "Many of the veterans who are getting the integrated treatment are experiencing partial or complete remission of both kinds of symptoms."

There is an ongoing debate about whether medications should be used to dampen an emotional memory. In some cases of PTSD, propranolol (or Inderal), a drug originally developed for hypertension, has been found to quiet or prevent PTSD if taken soon after a stressful event. It may even decrease the symptoms decades later if taken while a patient is undergoing regular therapy sessions.

Propranolol works by blocking the flow of adrenaline whose release assists in solidifying memories. However, such treatments are still considered controversial and in some cases may reduce pleasant memories as well as unpleasant ones. Will such therapy erase happy thoughts along with the emotions born of trauma, such as fear and anxiety? And if this medication effectively erases unpleasant memories, can it also potentially erase shame for taking part in unethical or violent behavior?

Some therapists feel it is a crude method that is not yet fully understood and that to proceed with experimental treatments would be foolish. Instead they favor a personal one-on-one process where insights can be gained between therapist and patient.

On the other hand, an argument can be made in favor of this treatment. One may look at the countless men and women who are willing to do anything to be rid of the psychological pain that goes hand-in-hand with PTSD. After all, medications in the benzodiazepine family, such as Valium, Ativan, and Klonopin, are given to soften the impact of emotional distress and experiences. Cognitive therapy is offered to help people reprogram their painful emotions. Is the taking of a medication such as propranolol so different?

It is clear that much more research is needed on treatment options for PTSD. The prevalence of coexisting psychiatric disorders such as depression, anxiety, substance abuse, and personality disorders increases according to the severity of a person's PTSD symptoms. There is still more to learn, but sizeable steps have been taken in developing effective treatments that will assist veterans and others suffering from PTSD. Hopefully those impacted by combat stress and other forms of trauma will be able to reach out for care in the not-so-distant future without feeling ashamed or discouraged.

Those who live with post-traumatic stress disorder look like everyone else. There is no visible sign of their disorder. Their fears, anxiety, and feelings of separateness do not manifest in their outward appearance. The disturbing images that play in the mind do not necessarily translate to one's facial expression or exterior demeanor. To the unsuspecting crowd, and even to family members and friends, they *look* just fine.

The Military and PTSD

We are living in turbulent times. People are being called into roles and action in ways that are contrary to the gentler side of the human spirit. The mind, as the human storehouse of memories, is constructed to accept information, determine its importance, compartmentalize it, and file it away until needed. Some information, however, is completely and utterly buried so deep that the brain never expects to have to retrieve it. Other information the brain takes in is so painful, so explicitly graphic and explosive that it should have been put in the "Do Not Enter" file.

However, for some inexplicable reason, it wavers slightly below the surface, vulnerable to the slightest trigger or memory to retrieve it and set off an avalanche of emotional and physical responses.

How an individual will respond to these memories and past horrific experiences cannot always be predicted. How each person will fare after responding is also unpredictable. What causes one person to suffer from PTSD while another person is able to function and appear more normal is unknown. What is most predictable is that many people do suffer, and more will continue to suffer from this disorder; they all need help.

A perfect example of this can be seen in the reactions of soldiers returning home from war. No individual can be absolutely certain about exactly what they have had to experience or witness and at what level of intensity or duration. All of what they have seen, been exposed to, and repeatedly had to do to survive can never be truly conveyed in words. In stressful situations the human mind, whose very job it is to protect the body it inhabits, begins to malfunction. Positive thoughts are replaced with negative or catastrophic thoughts, very often without any realization by the brain that this is happening. Whether realized or not, the reaction a person has will depend on the level of stress endured during the traumatic event.

PTSD is not a "weak person's disease," as many have often incorrectly assumed, and it can literally attack the strongest individual if the circumstances are right and the trauma is sufficiently significant. Nothing can adequately prepare a person to defend himself emotionally from the shock and remnants of certain traumatic experiences. More often than not, without help, many of these people will suffer deeply and for extended periods. And all the while, as this inner emotional war is raging, on the outside and to the rest of the visual world these returning soldiers look just fine and, perhaps, better than fine. They appear to be self-assured, disciplined, and extremely fit on the outside even while dealing with a psychological concoction of dread, fear, and nightmares on the inside.

The stigma attached to having any debilitating emotional disorder such as PTSD, especially among military personnel, makes it difficult to reconnect appropriately to the everyday stressors of life, particularly when knowing the next emotional trigger can come from anywhere at any time. An already high stress level combines with an even stronger negative reaction to feelings of shame, and the unresolved symptoms continue to fester. PTSD does not have a specific time frame in which to manifest after a disturbing occurrence or series of events takes place. An episode can occur days, weeks, months, or even years after the trauma occurred.

Some will feel depressed or very sad, while others will feel angry or consumed with guilt. Some people will try to cope with these symptoms by shutting down, becoming introverted and emotionally closed to those they care about; while others will go to the opposite extreme, becoming workaholics in an attempt to keep the emotional turmoil and bad memories at bay. Some may choose to start using alcohol or drugs to numb the pain in an attempt to make the bad memories and nightmares cease. Unfortunately there are no quick fixes for the pain of PTSD. If not treated properly, it won't get better on its own. It may, in fact, become more rooted and disruptive in the individual's life.

Help is available. PTSD is very treatable, but finding a trusted doctor or counselor and feeling comfortable communicating with that practitioner is absolutely critical for the treatment to work effectively. Cognitive behavioral therapy isn't easy, since talking about traumatic events can be extremely difficult, but cognitive behavioral therapy has had wide success in treating PTSD. Talk therapy helps the individual to work out verbally with the counselor or doctor the emotional backlash from the traumatic event and begin replacing those negative thoughts with mutually developed positive strategies.

When therapy alone isn't enough, a patient may also be prescribed an antidepressant that will biochemically help lift the depression or sadness that accompanies PTSD. In most cases treatment can run from three to six months, in some cases even longer. However, the earlier the treatment begins, the greater the chance for success and the sooner the patient will begin to experience feelings of health and well-being.

It's undoubtedly a vicious cycle but one that can be interrupted and dismantled if help is made available and sought out. While more studies are needed to help health professionals treat veterans with PTSD, intervention needs to be tailored to meet the specific needs of the individual. Coping strategies can be developed to empower a person with treatment choices that will integrate the returning warrior back into a more normal lifestyle while recapturing what was lost at that pivotal period of time.

People with PTSD may develop other problems, such as alcohol and drug abuse. Drinking or using drugs to self-medicate the symptoms is a common, yet unhealthy, way of coping with upsetting events. One may drink too much or use drugs to numb the self, to help to forget, or as a way to deal with difficult thoughts, feelings, and memories related to the traumatic events or experiences. If a loved one begins to experience substance abuse, one should try to get the person to see a health-care provider for treatment of the underlying cause of drinking or drug use.

Trauma can be connected with anger in many ways. After a trauma one might think that what happened was unfair or unjust. The person might not understand why the event happened or how it happened. These thoughts can result in intense anger. Although anger is a natural and healthy emotion, intense feelings of anger and aggressive behavior can create problems with family, friends, or coworkers. If the PTSD patient becomes violent when angry, the situation becomes even worse. Violence can lead to people being injured, and there may be legal consequences as well as feelings of guilt that will have to be dealt with.

PTSD also often causes employment problems. This can be related to difficulty concentrating at the workplace or on work-related projects, or to problems interacting with others. There may be episodes of uncontrolled outbursts or anger, and the patient may feel alienated from others. The individual may find it difficult to work with others, to make decisions, or to work on projects that require these skills.

PTSD Stemming from Military Life

Although it was once inadequately understood or discussed, post-traumatic stress disorder is turning up on the public's radar more and more as the numbers of Iraq and Afghanistan war veterans seek treatment for the illness.

According to a Rand Corporation study in April 2008, approximately one out of seven service members have returned from deployments with symptoms of PTSD. The Department of Veterans Affairs reported about a 70 percent jump in veterans seeking treatment for PTSD in the twelve months before June 2007 and an additional 50 percent rise in the nine months following. Unfortunately, despite all of the public focus, myths about PTSD continue to persist.

One myth is that the disorder is purely psychological. In fact it is a biologically based condition pushing the body's stress-response system into overdrive. Still, being diagnosed with PTSD has a stigma associated with it. What does one say to friends and even family when there are no visible signs of a disability? The person hasn't lost a limb in battle, yet he isn't the same person who left for deployment.

There is often a distrust of what cannot be seen. Not readily visible are the feelings of social alienation and anger, suicidal thoughts, and overall feelings of distrust. The festering, unseen wounds of trauma from combat or serving in the military are real. Some disabled PTSD veterans hide from society by living in remote places. Frequently their relationships suffer, and their job history is often erratic.

Although treatment offers many people relief from symptoms, most Americans with PTSD wait an average of twelve years before seeking treatment. Many shrug off symptoms on their own or with the help of friends. Because PTSD can impair so much of a person's life, mental health experts are concerned about the impact on young soldiers returning from war.

A study by psychologist Joseph Boscarino of the Geisinger Health System in Danville, Pennsylvania, shows that Vietnam veterans with PTSD, but without heart disease in their mid-thirties, were twice as likely as veterans without PTSD to die of heart disease by their fifties.

That's equal to the greater heart attack risk from smoking two to three packs of cigarettes a day for more than twenty years.

Although the military screens today's troops for PTSD, which wasn't done during the Vietnam era, about half of recent veterans with PTSD symptoms haven't sought treatment.

The likelihood of developing drug or alcohol abuse is accelerated the longer someone has PTSD. Sexual problems in veterans with traumatic stress are another concern. Combat troops with PTSD are far more likely than other men to have erection difficulties. The causes may be biological or emotional, or both.

PTSD—A Family Disorder

The entire family is profoundly affected when any family member experiences psychological trauma and suffers from PTSD. Some traumas are directly experienced by only one family member, but other family members may experience shock, fear, anger, and pain in their unique ways simply because they care about and are connected to the survivor.

Living with an individual who has PTSD does not automatically cause PTSD in others, but it can produce "vicarious" or "secondary" traumatization. Whether family members live together or apart, are in contact often or rarely, feel close or are emotionally distant from one another, PTSD can affect each member of the family in several ways. Family members may feel hurt, alienated, frustrated, or discouraged if the person with the disorder loses interest in the family or intimate activities, or becomes easily angered, emotionally isolated, or detached.

Even if the trauma occurred decades ago, survivors may act—and thus family members may feel—as if the trauma never stopped. They may feel as if they're living in a war zone or disaster area if the survivor is excessively tense, on guard, easily startled, or enraged. They may find themselves avoiding activities or people and becoming isolated from friends. They may feel that no one could possibly understand the situation.

PTSD frequently causes relationship problems, including divorce and violence. These problems can be fueled by PTSD-related anger, violence, or emotional distancing. Significant others may come to feel that dialogue and teamwork are impossible. It becomes difficult to build trust. There may also be a lack of interest in socializing or an absence of enjoyment in activities that were once pleasurable.

Caring friends and family may discover that the survivor is incapable of having a simple discussion about plans and decisions for the future, because he or she feels there is no future to look forward to. In some cases the survivor has difficulty listening and concentrating without becoming distracted, tense, or anxious; in other cases, the individual may become angry, overly suspicious or hypervigilant toward family members or toward others. Those suffering from PTSD may find it very difficult, if not impossible, to discuss personal or family problems, and they can become controlling, demanding, overprotective, or unreasonably anxious and fearful about problems, envisioning them as potentially terrible catastrophes.

In families where one parent is suffering from PTSD, the other parent may compensate by becoming overly involved in their children's lives because of loneliness and a need for positive emotional feedback, or from the feeling that the mate can't be counted on as a reliable and responsible parent. For the survivor, this "discounting" of participation as a co-parent can be attributed to his expressed feelings of hypervigilance and guilt that may be carried over from past traumatic experiences involving children. The partner may feel the need to be the sole caregiver to their children if the survivor is uninvolved with the family. This situation can also arise when the PTSD individual is overly critical, angry, or even abusive, often due to trauma-related anxiety or guilt.

Family members may find their sleep disrupted by the trauma survivor's sleep problems—reluctance to sleep at night, restlessness while sleeping, severe nightmares, or episodes of violent "sleepwalking." Loved ones also often find themselves afraid to go to sleep, having terrifying nightmares, or having difficulty getting a full and restful night's sleep, as if they are reliving the survivor's trauma themselves.

Ordinary activities such as going shopping, to a movie, or for a drive in the family car may feel like a reliving of past trauma if the activities trigger flashbacks or memories of the traumatic event for the survivor. The survivor may go into "survival mode" or on "automatic pilot" suddenly and without explanation, shutting down emotionally, becoming pressured and angry, or going away abruptly, leaving family members in shock, and feeling stranded, helpless, and worried.

Trauma survivors with PTSD often struggle with intense anger or rage. They can have difficulty coping with an impulse to lash out verbally or physically, especially if their trauma involved physical abuse or assault, war, domestic or community violence, or being humiliated, shamed, or betrayed by people they needed to trust. Family members can feel frightened of and betrayed by the survivor, despite feeling love and concern.

When suicide is a danger, family members face unavoidable strains: worry ("How can I know if suicide is going to happen, and what can I do to prevent it?"); guilt ("Am I doing something to make him feel so terrible, and should I be doing something to make him feel better?"); grief ("I have to prepare myself every day for losing her/him. In many ways I have to live my life as if she's already gone."); and anger ("How can he be so selfish and uncaring?"). Trauma survivors with PTSD are more inclined to contemplate and attempt suicide than people who have not experienced trauma or are not suffering from PTSD. For the family there is good and bad news in this respect. The good news is that very few trauma survivors, even those with PTSD, actually attempt or complete suicide. The bad news is that family members often must deal with a survivor who feels sufficiently discouraged, depressed, and burdened with such self-blame and self-loathing that he or she seriously and frequently contemplates suicide.

What can families of trauma survivors with PTSD do to care for themselves and for the survivors?

- Continue to learn more about PTSD by attending classes, viewing films, or reading books.

- Encourage but don't pressure the survivor to seek counseling from a PTSD specialist.
- Seek personal, child, couples, or family counseling if troubled by "secondary" trauma reactions such as anxiety, fear, anger, addiction, or problems with school, work or intimacy.
- Take classes on stress and anger management, couples communication, or parenting.
- Stay involved in positive relationships, in productive work and education, and with enjoyable pastimes.

Note: If physical, verbal, or sexual violence is occurring, family members such as spouses, children, or elders must be protected from harm.

Many trauma survivors do not experience PTSD, and many couples, families, or friendships with an individual who has PTSD do not experience severe relational problems. Successful intimate or close relationships require:

- Creating a personal support network to cope with PTSD, while maintaining or rebuilding family and friend relationships with dedication, perseverance, hard work, and commitment.
- Sharing feelings honestly and openly with an attitude of respect and compassion.
- Continual practice to strengthen cooperative problem solving and communication.
- Infusions of playfulness, spontaneity, relaxation, and mutual enjoyment.
- Timeliness of treatment to help with PTSD. Even brief treatment can be effective.

CHAPTER 6

FLYING SOLO

The Isolation of Depression and Anxiety Disorders

*Things do not pass for what they are,
but for what they seem.
Most things are judged by their jackets.*

—Baltasar Gracian

One of the most difficult symptoms to deal with during a depressive episode is feeling disconnected from reality. This feeling causes individuals to retreat deeper into their own worlds. They become isolated from their loved ones and friends, and the loneliness tends to intensify the depression.

Doing new things terrified Tracy L. who suffered from social anxiety and panic disorder. She was afraid of doing something to embarrass herself: "I felt like I stuck out like a sore thumb and that everyone was always watching me." Tracy didn't like to be outside her comfort zone for long periods of time, and as a result a great deal of the time she remained where she felt most comfortable and secure: at home.

Many patients of psychologist Shelley Slapion-Foote experience isolation with their disorders, be it depression or anxiety. "When someone is feeling poorly, the last thing they want to do is to be with others. The depressed patient is feeling like they have nothing of value to offer anyone and tend to isolate themselves away from family and friends. Persons affected keep work relationships to a bare minimum, and they spend much of their time 'in their heads,' thinking about their troubles and how awful they feel. They think that no other person would even want to associate with them because they feel as if they have nothing to offer. They lose their sense of humor and they tend to think of themselves as useless or losers."

The person who experiences anxiety tends to shy away from others for a slightly different reason, however. "When someone is anxious," says Dr. Slapion-Foote, "they become very focused on the thoughts and feelings that make them anxious. These thoughts and feelings tend to make them feel even more anxious, and they seek out isolation so that their chances of 'making fools out of themselves' are minimized. They believe that the isolation somehow insulates them from their feelings of anxiety, which, of course, it does not." Isolation merely allows the anxious person more time to run negative thoughts around inside their head and ruminate, which in turns leads to more anxiety.

Individuals with these types of disorders do not normally seek out support groups because of their own fears, depression, and their reluctance to be in contact with others. Some may seek out information online, which is much less threatening and doesn't require face-to-face interaction with others. "The most advantageous services to help these populations," according to Slapion-Foote, "appear to be individual therapy with a psychologist who is highly trained in cognitive behavioral techniques and relaxation techniques, and who has a good working relationship with a psychiatrist, neurologist, or primary care physician."

"My last episode, or what I call 'crash,' came on a weekend," says Jan W., who lives with chronic depression and anxiety. "I had stopped talking to anyone, and I was crying all the time. I decided to shut myself in the bedroom and start cleaning out my closet. I had piles of clothes and shoes all around me. A few minutes later, my partner found me lying on the bathroom floor, crying hysterically and saying, 'I couldn't do it; I just couldn't do it!' I had no memory of how I got to the bathroom or even of the crying jag."

One thing to set in place to help symptoms from worsening is to be in contact with one or two people several times a week. This can be someone to call or e-mail (whatever feels most comfortable), someone who can share a movie or simply join in watching TV. An anxious person does not have to share every emotion with this person, but he or she should be someone who will be there when and if needed.

There will be times when an anxious or depressed person just wants to shut out the world and be alone with the self and with private thoughts. There is nothing wrong with that. Many people who live with depression and anxiety disorders want to be alone in a quiet room as often as possible. However, every effort should be made to keep this reaction from becoming a daily or regular habit. Schedule short seclusions once or twice a week, but remember to maintain a sense of balance in daily life.

When one chooses to go into private space for a while, it's useful to do it in a way that is helpful rather than hurtful. For instance, instead of just staring at the TV screen for hours or lying in bed obsessing about perceived problems, try to do crossword puzzles or other mind puzzles, draw or to paint, play a musical instrument, journal thoughts, or write a story. Keep it nice and light. In this way isolation doesn't become a period of deep introspection resulting in agonizing over concerns and difficulties, ruminating about the past, worrying about the future, or beating up on oneself. Harness tranquility and calm but not the anguish that can accompany a depressive episode. It is this anguish that can eat away at the soul, as Robin D., one of the book participants profiled, expressed so beautifully in her poem "A Day in the Life of Loneliness":

> *I'll be your friend, if you let me,*
> *Think of me as a dark shadow hanging over you.*
> *I'll bring you down a peg or two,*
> *Let me show you how unworthy you are,*
> *And perhaps you will consider wallowing in self-pity.*
> *For I am your friend, Loneliness,*
> *And I can take you to the depth of depression and despair,*
> *And leave you gasping for air.*

Isolation is a part of depression, but there are ways to work with those feelings in a productive way rather than giving in to the shadows of melancholy.

Isolation and Developing Relationships

When one looks happy and calm yet cannot participate in activities such as trips, movies, or taking a short walk with friends because of the severity of symptoms, explaining why is sometimes difficult and tiring. People with depression or anxiety disorders grow weary of explaining why they cannot do this or that. Some people feel that others expect too much from them and that they are letting them down in some way if they can't keep up.

One of the things that seems desperately unfair to those who live with mood or anxiety disorders is the impact on friendships and romantic relationships. Many people with depression and anxiety disorders have difficulty not only maintaining established friendships, but also in making new friends, because their symptoms keep them from being continually active and socially involved.

"I don't have friends. People don't come over to my house. It's a habit of keeping people at arm's length. I guess I believe it protects me. The friends I have had whom I let know about my illness have not remained my friends," says Katy D., a young woman who suffers with depression, anxiety, and obsessive-compulsive disorder. "The best way to describe my family and my illness is toleration—not empathy or understanding. While my parents think I should have faith and have a positive attitude, I believe they feel it is something I can just 'get over' by sheer will. My husband wants to know very little about it. He feels helpless when he cannot 'fix' the situation, so I hide my mood problems now. I don't want to be a burden."

Since the symptoms are for the most part invisible, there is often fear of skepticism and distrust on the part of others. Many people don't tell new acquaintances (or even old friends) about their depression, anxiety, panic attacks, or obsessive-compulsive or post-traumatic stress disorder symptoms. Since their friends, family, or coworkers cannot actually "see" the disorder or symptoms, why would they believe they are real? That is often the thinking on the part of the person who has the mood or anxiety disorder. There is also a great deal of shame involved in simply admitting to a mood or anxiety disorder. Will they think I am "less than," "weak," or "inadequate" because I have this disorder? Many people don't understand that depression and anxiety disorders arise from an imbalance of chemicals in the brain. Some know it but don't believe it or accept it as true. Those suffering from a disorder may feel they don't have the stamina to keep up with new activities and relationships, so they step back from potential friendships and dating partners. As a result they spend more time alone, and fall into a deeper state of isolation.

The Dating Game

Every one of us is a flawed being. That's what makes us human. For some, flaws manifest in the psychological arena. We may have panic attacks or become scared of heights. We may be painfully shy, distrustful, or suffer from bouts of depression. For others the difficulty is physical. We may have an illness or condition that we feel sets us apart from the rest of the world and leaves us feeling different from the masses.

The reality is most people feel they have one thing, or many things, to hide from the world. This notion comes into play in relationships and romance. We try to present an ideal being to our mate for as long as possible. This is not always the best route to take, although it doesn't mean that one should spring a mood or anxiety disorder on a new partner during the first date.

Sometimes trying to be as up front as much and as quickly as possible is a good idea. However, in most cases it is probably best not to talk about having a debilitating mood or anxiety disorder on the first couple of dates, or to include every detail of personal distress until one senses strong feelings for this new person and wants to continue the relationship.

If you get to a stage at which you think you may want to spend a significant amount of time with a new and special person in your life, let him or her know you have something to discuss. Try to share your story with confidence and matter-of-fact conversation, not with pessimism and shame.

Talk to the person you care about in a place where you feel safe and will not be interrupted. Let the new person know you are nervous about talking about your issue so the listener is not flippant in response. Then take a chance and tell your emerging friend what you are ready to disclose. It can be a wonderful talk because many people are surprisingly considerate. Some may even share a secret or two about themselves with you! Perhaps your listener might have experienced personal feelings of depression or anxiety, or have had a family member who suffered with obsessive-compulsive disorder or post-traumatic stress disorder. You won't know unless you bring up your own issue, but knowing when to raise that issue is a crucial and individual decision.

You may feel that the person you are dating will "freak out" if told about your mood challenges. The most important component before disclosure is to be comfortable with your own situation and with your mood or anxiety disorder. What may be required for you is time, self-examination, patience, or perhaps even some counseling sessions geared specifically toward becoming comfortable and accepting of your depression or anxiety disorder, especially if this is a new diagnosis. Being comfortable in your own skin, no matter what you consider to be a personal flaw, is an extraordinarily worthy goal. It is only then that you can present your symptoms and diagnosis to your partners, family members, friends, or coworkers in a matter-of-fact and confident manner.

Counteracting Isolation

> *We're afraid to be alone,*
> *Everybody's got to have a home.*
> *Isolation.*
>
> —John Lennon

Living with a mental disorder, whether it is depression, anxiety, or panic disorder, can remove one from society and everyday life, and lead one to set up housekeeping in some lonely, darkened corner. Those with ongoing depression or anxiety disorders often do not have the energy to seek the help they need from mental health professionals. They hibernate at home and isolate themselves from family, friends, and the outside world. Unfortunately they often beat themselves up about their shortcomings, and they focus more on what they can't do than on what they can do. They sometimes lose faith in the mental health system, where there are no guarantees or clear-cut tests to determine what will help their symptoms.

It's easy to give in to the feelings of being different or less than, or simply wanting to avoid those unpleasant emotions such as fear and nervousness. However, these very feelings are symptoms of mood or anxiety disorders, not reality. There is nothing inherently wrong with solitude. Sometimes it's good to get away, do some self-reflection, and sort things out without impact and influence from the peanut gallery. But isolation in large dosages is often not good for us, especially if we are already feeling different from the masses. Feelings of separateness and loneliness are often side dishes to depression and anxiety disorders.

Exercise can seem overwhelming and unrealistic to someone who lives with a chronic depressive disorder, because the fatigue that often accompanies depression can be debilitating. Therefore exercise seems like an activity that is not doable. However, exercise doesn't necessarily mean jogging around the track or swimming laps. It can be simply taking the stairs and walking more frequently over the course of weeks and months. In other words, it can literally and figuratively mean taking small steps instead of giant steps. It's important to realize that fatigue may be something that the mind has conjured to tell you that your body is not capable of achieving, or even beginning, an exercise regime because you're simply too weak or weary.

When people experience social anxiety, they often have to take extra steps and make special efforts to join activities that involve other people. Even if it is extraordinarily challenging, people who live with social anxiety, depression, and other isolating disorders need to make an effort to interact with others. Finding easy, low-key ways to do this is a good start. One woman started by joining a local support group for her particular mood challenge. It wasn't easy for her, but after the initial agony of forcing herself to attend meetings, she slowly got to know the other members and eventually became one of the group facilitators. Now going to meetings is something she not only doesn't dread but an experience she looks forward to. Here is a place where she feels accepted and knows she can be herself.

A man who had severe social anxiety was also an artist. His effort to get involved with others began by joining a local artists' group. He found that attending a group with a set purpose diffused the social anxiety he experienced because there was a set agenda and topic. He didn't have to make small talk with a drink in his hand. Last year he organized a new artists' group, and he has been invited to address other groups about Internet art marketing. He could not have imagined himself doing this just a short time ago. Helping other artists has not only been gratifying for him, but has also helped get him out of the house and out of isolation.

If you are finding yourself isolated and housebound, it is sometimes useful to think about groups you might join based on your knowledge and interests. Did you always want to learn how to paint or to speak Spanish? Taking an adult class at your community college is a great way to meet people in a stress-free environment.

Volunteering is another extraordinary way to meet other people and to use your skills while setting your own hours. However you choose to break your existing isolation, start small and give yourself time to adjust. Don't expect to feel comfortable at your first meeting. It may take some effort, but the struggle to push yourself a bit beyond your comfort level may eventually be worth its weight in gold.

CHAPTER 7

DECIPHERING YOUR DIRECTION

Types of Therapy

Cognitive Behavioral Therapy (CBT)

Cognitive behavioral therapy (CBT) is the most researched psychotherapy modality for anxiety and panic disorders. Cognitive behavioral approaches teach patients to view panic situations differently and demonstrate ways to reduce anxiety. For example, they may be taught to use breathing techniques to refocus their attention should a panic situation arise. Another technique used in CBT, called exposure therapy, can often help alleviate the phobias that may result from panic disorder. In exposure therapy, people are very slowly exposed to the fearful situation until they become desensitized to it.

Some of the items taught in CBT might include paying attention to all-or-nothing thoughts or statements and the use of the words "always" and "never." By replacing these thoughts with more realistic ones and with positive expectations, we can retrain our mind to see the same situation more clearly and, therefore quite differently. CBT teaches techniques for temporarily stopping a runaway mind. It also teaches one to examine the unrealistic notion of perfectionism. A drive for perfection can easily cause anxiety, irritability, anger, and depression. The reality is there is no such thing as perfection. CBT can help us see that with repetitive and practical exercises and by studying common situations and circumstances.

Over time, people tend to get into unhelpful thinking habits. This is especially true of those who suffer with depression or an anxiety disorder. CBT helps people identify these negative or unrealistic thinking styles so that they can be noticed, challenged, and altered. Carol Vivyan, a cognitive behavioral psychotherapist, believes that everyday situations and automatic thoughts can be viewed in new and more helpful ways with practice and retraining. By challenging negative or all-or-nothing thinking, CBT helps people breakout of the vicious cycle of negative thinking, feeling and behavior. The idea is to alter the way you feel over time by changing or challenging your thoughts.

The first chart reveals the most common unhelpful thinking habits. Once a person can identify their most common unhelpful thinking styles, they can begin to notice them, catch them, and see the situation in a more useful and realistic light.

Unhelpful Thinking Habits

Once you can identify your unhelpful thinking styles, you can start to notice and challenge them, resulting in seeing the situation in a different, more realistic way. How many of the following automatic distorted thinking habits ring true for you? View the second chart for useful replacements.

Mental Filter Mental filters are present. We notice only what the filter wants or allows us to notice, and we dismiss anything that doesn't "fit". It's akin to looking through gloomy or dark glasses that only catch the negative stuff, while anything more positive or realistic is dismissed.	**Judgments** Making evaluations or judgments about events, ourselves, others, or the world, rather than describing what we actually see and have evidence for.
Mind-Reading Mind-reading is when we assume we know what others are thinking (usually about us).	**Emotional Reasoning** Making assumptions based on emotions. "I feel bad so I must be bad!" "I feel anxious so I must be in danger!"
Prediction Believing we know what's going to happen in the future.	**Mountains and Molehills** Exaggerating the risk of danger, or the negatives. Minimizing the odds of how things are likely to turn out, or minimizing positives.
Compare and Despair Seeing only the good and positive aspects in others, and comparing ourselves negatively against them.	**Catastrophizing** Imagining and believing that only the worst possible thing will happen.
Critical Self Putting ourselves down, self-criticizing, blaming ourselves for events or situations that are not (totally) our responsibility.	**Black and White Thinking** Believing that something or someone can be only good or bad, right or wrong, rather than anything in-between (shades of grey).
Shoulds and Musts Thinking or saying "I should" (or shouldn't) and "I must", puts pressure on ourselves, and sets up unrealistic expectations.	**Memories** Current situations and events can trigger upsetting memories, leading us to believe that the danger is here and now, rather than in the past, causing us distress right now.

This second chart reveals common unhelpful thinking habits and suggests more balanced, realistic and positive thoughts to replace them.

Finding Alternative Thoughts

Unhelpful Thinking Habit	Alternative more balanced thought
Mental Filter	*Am I only noticing the bad stuff? Am I filtering out the positives? Am I wearing "gloomy specs"? What would be more realistic?*
Mind-Reading	*Am I assuming I know what others are thinking? What's the evidence? Those are my own thoughts, not theirs. Is there another, more balanced way of looking at it?*
Prediction	*Am I thinking I can predict the future? How likely is it that my prediction will actually happen?*
Compare & Despair	*Am I doing that "compare & despair" thing? What would be a more balanced and helpful way of looking at it?*
Critical Self	*There I go, that internal bully is at it again! Would most people who really know me say these things about me? Is this something that I am totally responsible for thinking/believing?*
Shoulds and Musts	*Am I putting more pressure on myself, setting up expectations of myself that are almost impossible? What would be more realistic?*
Judgments	*I'm making an evaluation about the situation or person. It's how I make sense of the world, but that doesn't mean my judgments are always right or helpful. Is there another perspective?*
Emotional Reasoning	*Just because it feels bad, doesn't necessarily mean it is bad. My feelings are just a reaction to my thoughts – and thoughts are just automatic brain reflexes.*
Mountains and Molehills	*Am I exaggerating the risk of danger? Or am I exaggerating the negative and minimizing the positives? How would someone else see it? What's the bigger picture?*
Catastrophizing	*Well, thinking that the worst possible thing will definitely happen isn't really helpful right now. What's most likely to happen?*
Black and White Thinking	*Things aren't totally white or totally black – there are shades for grey. Where is this current situation on the spectrum?*
Memories	*This is just a reminder of the past. That was then, and this is now. Even though this memory makes me <u>feel</u> upset, it's not <u>actually</u> happening again right now.*

For additional information on CBT, visit website: www.get.gg

CBT is generally viewed as one of the most effective forms of psychotherapy for treating panic attacks, panic disorder, and agoraphobia. Since it centers on changing the thinking patterns, it can help a person develop better ways of coping with fears. The first aspect of treatment for panic disorder and agoraphobia typically involves education. The individual learns about the nature of anxiety and the fight-or-flight response experienced during a panic attack. The client is educated on the sensations and feelings surrounding panic attacks, and is assured that what is being felt is normal and that they are not going crazy. Simply knowing more about the disorder can go a long way toward relieving distress. A client is also taught to identify and evaluate the "automatic thoughts" occurring during a panic attack. Many of these thoughts are irrational and exaggerate the danger of the situation. Clients are taught to take the power away from these thoughts and to learn to think in new, more realistic and productive ways.

Another aspect of CBT involves teaching a person how to control breathing. The person may first be asked to hyperventilate. Hyperventilation brings on many sensations such as lightheadedness and tightness of the chest that may occur during a panic attack. By learning to control breathing, people can develop coping skills that can be used to calm themselves when they begin to feel those familiar anxious and panicky thoughts and feelings.

An important part of CBT is determining where negative self-talk is coming from. Whose voice is it that speaks so negatively through you and about you? Is it your mother, father, brother, spouse, or kids from your past teasing you on the schoolyard? In addition to discovering the source of these negative messages, there is a need to halt automatic negative thinking. CBT teaches techniques for controlling a runaway mind flooded with negative thoughts, by focusing on what is calming and positive.

In addition to CBT techniques and medications, other psychotherapy approaches that are sometimes suggested include family therapy, cognitive behavioral group therapy, relaxation, and stress relief techniques such as the "relaxation response," taught by Dr. Herbert Benson (*Timeless Healing*), mindfulness meditation, tai chi exercises, and many others.

Some people find the greatest relief from panic disorder symptoms when they take certain prescription medications or keep their medications handy "just in case." Often just having the medication in a pocket or purse is enough to put the person at ease. Like CBT, medications can help to prevent panic attacks or reduce their frequency and severity.

Art Therapy

Professionals sometimes introduce art therapy, the therapeutic use of creating art, to those who experience illness or trauma. It is based on the belief that the creative process involved in artistic self-expression helps people resolve conflicts and inner difficulties, reduce stress, increase self-esteem and self-awareness, and achieve insight into what makes them do what they do, or feel as they feel. Through the process of creating art, people can increase awareness of their emotions; cope with stress, symptoms, and traumatic experiences; and sometimes strengthen their cognitive abilities.

Art therapists are professionals trained in both art and therapy. They are often found in settings such as mental health and rehabilitation facilities, or in private practice. Art therapists are knowledgeable about human development; psychological theories; clinical practice; spiritual, multicultural, and artistic traditions; and the healing potential of art. They use art in assessment, treatment, and research. This approach to therapy is often useful to those who have difficulty putting their feelings into words. A traumatic event often sends one into a state of disbelief, shock, or turmoil. The process of creating art can unwind these feelings and associated emotions while helping people understand their way of thinking and their inner selves.

Any medium can be used in art therapy, including collage, paintings, photography, drawings, or cutouts. A clinician usually guides a client in how to make a piece of art that reflects a particular emotion or perhaps expresses what happened that day. The clients are often encouraged to discuss what the creative work means to them once it's complete.

Marvi Lacar, a photojournalist living in New York, used her camera to capture the hidden grief and misery of her own depression. Rather than write an article or story to express her emotions when her father passed away in 2008, Lacar utilized her photographs to act as a visual diary of depression. These photographs of inner conflict and pain reflected her own world of deep despair and hurt—a world that is often left hidden and indescribable.

During the worst days of Lacar's depression, she spent countless hours sleeping and was unable to feel anything but numbness. "This must be what it feels like to be dead, but I'm not dead."

Benjamin Lowy, Marvi Lacar's husband, is a photojournalist and no stranger to mood disorders himself. After documenting wars, Lowy suffered from post-traumatic stress disorder. Having his own experience with PTSD helped him make it clear to his wife that she could not beat depression on her own. "You just can't snap out of it," he told her. He also made it clear that "depression wasn't a state of mind but an illness."

Lowy not only helped his wife recover but also worked and encouraged her to document her experiences and thoughts into photographs. Lacar let her photographs speak for her when she could no longer trust herself to make words out of her feelings.[3]

It is thought that creating artwork of any type acts as an effective tool by capturing a problem on paper, which sends it to an external source, thereby making it easier to deal with. Producing such a work of art can also give people a better sense of control and confidence about themselves. Most importantly, this expression allows the emotions to come out into the open. Perhaps we can all benefit from this approach, no matter how large or small the conflict or emotion, by learning something from our artwork about our emotions, our conflicts, and ourselves.

Strength in Numbers—Considering Group Therapy and Support

Most talk therapy involves one-on-one meetings with a psychotherapist, but other arrangements can be helpful, too, depending on the needs of the person and the severity of the disorder.

Group therapy. This involves a small group of people meeting in regular sessions with a therapist. Interacting with others and hearing their problems can support your efforts to change and reduce your sense of isolation. Group therapy can be particularly helpful for people with social anxiety, depression, or phobias about social settings, because it provides a safe place to practice and gather supportive feedback from others. A group may be organized around a single topic, such as anxiety, depression, or a medical condition, or it may be concerned with more general issues. Inherent in the structure is the understanding that most people cope with similar problems.

Before joining a group, you will likely be interviewed by the therapist and may be asked to commit to a certain number of sessions. It is usually helpful to attend group therapy in combination with individual sessions.

Family therapy. This involves family members only and is usually focused on specific problem solving. It can help families correct miscommunication, change dysfunctional patterns of blame, or adjust to altered circumstances, such as to a family member with a mood or anxiety disorder or a chronic illness. Family therapy may be especially helpful when an individual's psychological problem affects other members of the family.

Support groups—the kindness of strangers. Support groups are usually organized around a particular mood or anxiety disorder such as depression, panic disorder, anxiety, divorce, or recovery from addiction. A professional does not always lead the group, and the sessions are not a form of psychotherapy, but they can be extremely helpful for individuals or families confronting certain circumstances. Like group therapy, support groups may be time-limited or ongoing.

Some people feel their parents, siblings, coworkers, family members, or even good friends don't "get it" or cannot accept the patient's disorder. Nor can they comprehend the symptoms one has to contend with. One way to cope is to make friends with others who truly understand the challenges you are dealing with on a day-to-day basis.

People in pain and discomfort often seek out others who are suffering with similar symptoms in order to validate their own. Validation and support can be found in support groups or simply by connecting with one or two other individuals who live with chronic symptoms. Although the person may have a slightly different disorder or severity of symptoms, such an individual has the ability to be empathetic, encouraging, and to provide a great source of support.

"Support groups are crucial to my recovery," says James C. "To be among like-minded people who do not judge or shame me offers me a safe haven to discuss the pain of anxiety and OCD." James also believes that the person with the disorder is sometimes the last one to see their own progress. Other people in the group may be able to point out what is not apparent to the person who lives with depression, OCD, or anxiety. "There is nothing in this world that is more nurturing than being with people who believe in you and can alert you to your own progress."

If a support group is not available in your area, there are online support groups that focus on individuals who live with your particular mood or anxiety disorder. Companionship, strength, and comfort can often be found in such groups of like-minded and caring people.

A support group is a living entity of camaraderie that never wavers. Most groups offer their members a contact list to utilize between meetings. If you are having a particularly difficult day, have a question about how to cope, or simply want a laugh or a little companionship, reaching out to someone you know to be supportive can be very helpful.

It's important to remember that each support group has a personality of its own. If you find a group is too focused on complaints and not enough on coping techniques, information, and general support of its members, find another group. Not all support groups are created equal!

A few people are not able to benefit from a support group. There are various reasons for this, from social anxiety to having previous experiences that might not have been favorable. "I do not attend groups because I am too empathetic," says Katy D., a young woman who lives with anxiety and depression. "I tend to try to 'save' people by taking on their problems, whether it's to avoid the reality of my own disorders, or I just like to take the focus off of myself."

For other people, however, there is much to be gained in a support group setting. As strange as it may seem, some individuals feel their friendship circle actually expands after a diagnosis of depression, anxiety, or any other mental challenge. Les is a woman who regularly attends a support group. She was unable to continue her full-time career as a graphic designer because of her depression and anxiety. Les shared with the group that she probably had more friends now because she had more time for friends. She went on to say that she would not have met, befriended, and grown close to the special people in her support group had she not developed this disorder in the first place, and most assuredly, would not have done so outside of her work environment.

Hypnosis. Hypnosis has been recognized by the American Medical Association since 1958 as a form of treatment and is one of several non-medication approaches that ease or cure panic disorder in some individuals. Research has legitimized the use of hypnosis in psychologists' offices and medical facilities as a complement to standard therapies, and more patients are turning to hypnosis as an alternative to more invasive treatments or drugs.

A study published in *Proceedings of the National Academics* showed that people under hypnosis demonstrated less activity in the part of the brain called the anterior cingulated cortex, an area linked to decision-making, than did people who weren't hypnotized. Dr. Stephanie Buehler, a psychologist in Irvine, California, says that she can put patients under hypnosis and desensitize them to the entire process of getting on an airplane, the plane taking off, the patients being afraid of the flight, the plane landing, and the patients exiting. She claims to teach them, under hypnosis, to go from something they are afraid of to a safe place inside. She teaches them to feel a sense of control and relaxation. While clients are under hypnosis, she feels that the usual defenses can be resolved so that people are receptive to suggestions and more capable of incorporating them.

At Children's Hospital of Orange County in Orange, California, nurses and psychologists help children manage anxiety and pain using self-hypnosis techniques. They do this not as a substitute for pain medications but as a way of helping the medications work better. Children tend to be easier to hypnotize. Three out of four adults can be hypnotized; the length of time the effects of hypnosis last varies. Self-hypnosis using the Lamaze method has been around a long time. It helps women manage the pain experienced during childbirth.

When patients undergo hypnosis with a psychologist and learn self-hypnosis, they are acquiring tools that can be used as needed and that will help them regain control of their lives. However, not everyone is susceptible to hypnosis. According to David Spiegel, a prominent hypnosis researcher and associate chairman of the Department of Psychiatry and Behavioral Science at Stanford University, there is now evidence that genetic factors play a role in the ability to be hypnotized. "Some people have a certain variant of the gene involved in making the neurotransmitter dopamine." (Reminder: Neurotransmitters are chemical messengers in the brain.)

It is thought that hypnosis can strengthen the effect of the mind on the body by changing the way a person perceives sensations. The technique helps narrow the focus of attention so the symptoms of a panic attack don't overwhelm individuals, and they can mentally and then physically relax.

In addition to hypnosis, other nondrug therapies that may (or may not, depending on whom you ask) work for panic attacks include "tapping," or Thought Field Therapy (TFT), and, as previously mentioned, cognitive behavioral therapy (CBT). There are always new therapies arising to assist with panic disorder. How about laughing panic away? Some people do, and Steven Sultanoff, a clinical psychologist in Irvine, California, and past president of the American Association for Therapeutic Humor, says it works. Dr. Sultanoff uses humor visualization with his panic attack patients, asking them to see themselves in a situation where they've laughed uncontrollably. When panic symptoms arise, the patients go back to that image of themselves laughing. "Humor replaces the distressing emotions of a panic attack," says Sultanoff, "and if the humor leads to outright laughter, it changes the physiological responses of the attack as well." When you're anxious, he explains, your serum cortisol, or stress hormone, level rises; laughter is believed to reduce the cortisol levels.

Other therapists encourage the use of what is now known as energy psychology, specifically Thought Field Therapy (TFT). This involves the tapping of acupuncture (or acupressure) points and can be taught so that a person can do it himself. In this therapy, it is said that each thought we have produces an energy field, which triggers a chemical change in the body. This chemical change produces behavior changes and bodily sensations, such as a racing heart, sweaty palms, dilating eyes, and shortness of breath. We then associate these bodily reactions with sensations such as fear, anxiety, and panic.

While talk therapy can help you to comprehend why you have panic reactions, and medications can change the chemicals in your brain and body, energy psychology like TFT deals with the energy field related to the thought. By tapping specific acupuncture points in a specific order, you can discharge a negative energy with the specific thought, such as a fear of flying, heights, or falling asleep. Some feel that tapping on these acupressure points corresponds to the adrenal glands, which control the stress responses.

Many therapists, however, prefer to use a desensitization approach to treat panic disorder. In this form of therapy, the patient may be asked to imagine himself in a situation that normally causes him to feel panic; sitting in a plane or standing on a high ladder are two common scenarios. The therapist tells the person to hold that image for thirty seconds. The amount of time increases each time the person repeats the exercise. While the patient imagines the scene, the therapist advises that the patient should think of the worst-case scenario, and the therapist poses "what if" questions. What if you panic when you're on a ladder? You can always climb down from the ladder. What if you feel faint in the airplane? The flight attendant will help you. There's always an answer to "what if" questions. What desensitization offers is a psychological safety net, where the person learns to face the fear and not feel as though it's the "end of the world" if they go through the experience.

CHAPTER 8

"MUST" ON THE MIND

Obsessive-Compulsive Disorder

Anything worth doing is worth overdoing.
—Mick Jagger

The statistics shift by the minute, but it is thought that seven million Americans live with an anxiety disorder called obsessive-compulsive disorder (OCD). This disorder is typified by intrusive worrisome thoughts (obsessions) and repetitive rituals (compulsions) that are aimed at freeing the affected individual of those thoughts. Some people obsess about hurting others, some focus on contamination and germs, and still others concentrate on symmetry.

One of the common themes that runs through this disorder seems to be that of being "certain" of matters, whether they are the germs on our hands, the proper cooking of food, our uncertainty that we unplugged all the electrical cords before leaving the house, or that we have removed all the dust from the corners of the room. Are we clean? Is our house clean?

Has everything been done correctly and thoroughly? Is everything safe? The person with OCD must know this beyond a shadow of a doubt before he can relax.

Janaya G. is a woman who has an obsession with time. "I feel the need to start or stop doing activities at the beginning of an hour or on the half-hour (like brushing my teeth at exactly 11 p.m. or watching TV from 2:30 p.m. until 3:00 p.m.). I do certain things in sets of threes (three bites of food before taking a drink; rinsing my mouth out and spitting in sets of threes). I also have intrusive, obsessive thoughts about deep issues like death, questioning reality, and my own existence. My psychiatrist has referred to this as deep end-of-the-ocean thinking."

OCD is sometimes known as the "disease of doubt." The patient often knows that his or her obsessive thoughts and ritualized actions are irrational. In other words, they make no logical sense. Yet he may still worry that the fears may be true, unstoppable and unpreventable. In the end, the rituals end up being a controlling force in the person's life.

Performing these so-called rituals provides only temporary relief, and not performing them increases anxiety. Others live in terror that they will accidentally do something wrong, such as harm someone, blurt out an improper statement, or throw something out by mistake.

If lack of certainty is a common challenge, then warding off uncertainty is a common quest. For some it means checking and rechecking everything around them in the name of safety, or scrubbing hands to make certain they are germ-free. It may mean arranging various items in order to make sure there is symmetry, or repeating actions to assure themselves that everything is in perfect order.

Obsessions are ideas, images, and impulses that run through a person's mind over and over again. For example, if people are obsessed with germs or dirt, they may develop a compulsion to rigorously and repeatedly clean their hands. If they develop an obsession with intruders, they may lock and relock their doors many times before going to bed. Being afraid of social embarrassment may prompt people with OCD to comb their hair compulsively in front of a mirror in an attempt to get it just right or perfectly coiffed. Sometimes they get stuck at the mirror and can't move away from it. Performing such rituals is not pleasurable. At best it produces temporary relief from the anxiety created by obsessive thoughts.

A person with OCD doesn't want to have these thoughts and finds them disturbing, but he can't manage or control them. Sometimes these thoughts just come once in a while and are only mildly annoying. Other times a person who has OCD will have these types of thoughts on a continual basis.

The following are some common obsessions:

- Fear of dirt or germs.
- Disgust with bodily waste or fluids.
- Thinking about certain sounds, images, words, or numbers all the time.
- Concern with order, symmetry (balance), and exactness.
- Worry that a task has been done poorly, even when the person knows this is not true.
- Fear of thinking evil or sinful thoughts.
- Fear of harming a family member or friend.

The following are some common compulsions:

- Cleaning and grooming, such as washing hands, showering, or brushing teeth over and over again.
- Checking drawers, door locks, and appliances to be sure they are shut, locked, or turned off.
- Repeating actions such as going in and out of a door, sitting down and getting up from a chair, or touching certain objects several times.
- Ordering and arranging items in certain ways.
- Counting over and over to a certain number.

- Saving newspapers, mail, or containers when they are no longer needed.

For many years OCD was thought to be a rare disorder, but that's no longer the case. About one out of every forty people will experience OCD at some time in their lives, and the disorder seems to affect men and women equally.

The cause of OCD has not yet been found. Many researchers believe that it may be inherited. If one person in a family has OCD, there is a 25 percent chance that another family member will also have the condition. Stress and other psychological factors may also contribute to the development of OCD.

Additional research suggests that chemicals in the brain that carry messages from one nerve cell to another may cause OCD. One of these chemicals, serotonin, helps to keep people from repeating the same behaviors over and over again. A person who has OCD may not have enough serotonin. Some researchers think that OCD develops when the brain produces too much or too little of some particular neurotransmitter. In such a case, nerve messages cannot travel smoothly from one part of the brain to another. They may begin to recycle—that is, to travel again and again across the same set of nerves. This constant repetition of nerve messages might be responsible for the repetitive behavior characteristic of compulsions.

Many people who have OCD can function better when they take medications that increase the amount of serotonin in their brain. People who have OCD often have other forms of anxiety, such as phobias or panic attacks. People who live with OCD may have accompanying depression, an eating disorder, or a learning disorder such as dyslexia.

Individuals with OCD have both obsessions and compulsions, but some may experience only one or the other. This disorder has the potential of impacting one's life to a great degree or to a very small degree. Each individual's symptoms and the degree of impact on life are unique. Some are terribly troubled by their obsessions. Some are not troubled, but their family members and partners are terribly inconvenienced or bothered by their loved one's behavior. Still others are barely impacted by their disorder, and neither are the people around them. Like most mental disorders, the spectrum is a wide one, with one end being extraordinarily troublesome and the other being barely noticeable.

Since OCD cannot be seen with the eye, it falls into the realm of easily concealed disorders. People may assume the behavior of someone with OCD simply reflects the traits of laziness, lack of willpower, bad parenting, or trauma. Assumptions like these lead to blame and guilt. The reality is OCD behaviors that are irritating and demanding are actually symptoms of the condition. People with OCD feel they have little or no control over their anxiety disorder, and often feel frustrated and distressed about their need to act compulsively. When family members and friends are more informed about OCD, it is often easier to be supportive and understanding. Says Linda C.:

> "I think my anxiety over the various symptoms and illnesses/bad days affects my husband and grown children. I think they both understand certain habits that I have always had, such as being late due to my obsessions, fatigue and pain, my confused state of mind, and my lack of short-term memory at times. I can't recall the number of times they have said, 'Mom, we just told you that!' My husband, on the other hand, does treat me in a different light, and I feel some comfort from him. It took some time, but bringing him along to my doctor visits has helped. It was more believable for him to hear it from the 'horse's mouth' rather than from me. Taking a family member along on a doctor's visit is very helpful."

There are resources available that can help resolve misunderstandings and alleviate some of the distress surrounding this disorder. These include books, videos, Internet websites, and news groups. The Internet offers support groups and information about specific aspects of OCD, such as hoarding, obsessive thinking, and hyper-responsibility. Community resources such as telephone help-lines and support groups are also available.

OCD can impact people's employment and career in other challenging ways. Lorna A. was diagnosed with OCD just a couple of years ago, but she has suffered much longer; she was forced by the disease's symptoms to leave her job. She gets frustrated when she finds herself unable to complete tasks or jobs that used to come so easily to her. More importantly, the changes have impacted her family's finances, forcing them to move to a less expensive neighborhood and to closely watch their spending habits. She explained it was difficult for her to locate a job where she would not have to interact directly with others. Eventually she was able to do graphic design for a while and then began to work at a hospital where she learned to use computers and hospital information systems. Lorna says, "I was a systems analyst for over twenty years before I had to quit working altogether. My job included meeting and training the users, and that often led to panic attacks. Often I had to cancel training sessions or meetings because of my disorder. I have not worked for the past three years. I held a job that I loved, but I just couldn't do it anymore. I miss my job and the sense of self-worth I got from it. My self-esteem has gone way down since I stopped working."

In an article titled "Strategies for Coping with OCD in the Workplace," Donna Gillet, a rehabilitation specialist, and Michael McKee, a clinical psychologist, reveal that it is difficult for a person with OCD to determine the balance between a desire to pursue a specific profession and a desire to return to a minimum level of functioning. When obsessions revolve around contamination fears, health-related jobs may be avoided, and counting compulsions may make the ability to perform accounting tasks nearly impossible. It is difficult and painful, but sometimes necessary, to make the decision to abandon a beloved job or career because of the potential for serious symptoms to be reactivated.[4]

How then can people with symptoms of OCD manage in the workplace? Once on the job, the person must decide how to address his symptoms. A decision must be made to disclose or not to disclose the condition to others, including supervisors. The prospective employee needs to assess how much extra help, if any, will be needed to learn and perform the job.

Severe OCD symptoms can cause the worker to be a perfectionist in his or her work to such an extent that it is impossible to complete job responsibilities and various tasks. They may read and reread material to make certain it is perfect. They may fail to submit assignments and jobs at work because they fear it's not precise. They may take a long time to complete tasks, or not complete them at all because of the need to be flawless in their efforts.

Some people who live with OCD suffer from an obsession with the order of objects. The first thing they do when they come home from work is to check objects in the room. If something has been moved around, it can be quite upsetting. Their distress may lead them to insult family members. The person with an object obsession may suffer from the need to place objects in "order," even in other people's homes, which can lead couples to stop socializing with friends or attending parties. Soon their lives become reclusive due to the obsessive nature of the person with OCD.

It can be difficult, demanding, and exhausting to live with a person who has OCD. Family members and friends may become deeply involved in the person's rituals and may have to assume responsibility for a large number of activities that the person with OCD is unable to undertake.

Many times family members will attempt to accommodate OCD symptoms, which can place an added stress on family relationships. Spouses and parents of adults with OCD report a significant impact on family functioning as well as increased stress. A national survey conducted by Harris Interactive for the Anxiety Disorders Association of America (ADAA) stated that more than half of adults with untreated obsessive OCD reported that their condition had a negative impact on important relationships at work, at home, and in their personal lives.

The person with OCD often feels helpless and is convinced that others do not even want to attempt to understand his or her disorder. For instance, the person with OCD can feel cheated or offended when friends, spouse, or family members accidently ignore their personal rules about the best way to function. The "rules" are often a main focus within a relationship or family.

In the case of a married couple, the non-OCD person is often compelled to assist the OCD partner by accommodating his illogical practices of cleaning and straightening, and other compulsive rituals. The partner is often "pushed into a corner" and made to do anything that lessens the symptoms for his loved one because he doesn't want to rock the boat. A person with OCD often needs family support, particularly while dealing with compulsions. However, this makes the person with OCD feel guilty for disrupting his loved ones' lives in such a vital way.

OCD and relationships is a much-debated topic. Many couples and families use it as a real or imagined excuse for breaking up their relationships and family. However, there are many persons who live together, taking OCD on as a partnered challenge.

How to Help the Person in Your Life Who Has OCD

If your loved one, friend, or coworker has OCD, it's necessary to communicate clearly that you understand the difference between the symptoms of OCD and the person. For instance, you can say to him, "I know this is not you; this is your OCD." This will help to diminish the person's feelings of guilt and low self-worth, and thereby reduce his levels of stress and anxiety.

Encourage the person to talk about his symptoms. Tell him you want to know more about how the disorder impacts his days, and how you can be more supportive. Do not discuss the logic of OCD with someone who has it! Most people who live with OCD realize that their obsessions and compulsions are extreme, unnecessary, and illogical. To remind them of this can only make them feel defensive.

Encourage the person you care about to seek professional help. OCD is generally not a condition that will go away without treatment. Perhaps you can offer to assist in locating an experienced therapist or to go with the person to the first appointment. After all, if the OCD has involved you, other family members, or friends extensively in rituals and avoidance behavior, you will need to know the best ways to modify your involvement so that the treatment can be as effective as possible.

Encourage discussion about OCD as a common and treatable anxiety condition that is nothing to be ashamed of.

Acknowledge improvements, however small, and suggest the person reward himself for any progress made. Try to be patient and maintain a non-judgmental attitude. This will encourage the person to focus his efforts on slow and steady improvements. If he gives up on treatment after it begins, remind him of the strides that have already been made. Progress, not perfection, is the goal!

In some cases people with OCD may be reluctant to seek professional assistance for their disorder. They may fear the stigma associated with mental illness or be concerned that they will discover they are more disturbed than originally thought. They may also be wary of having to give up their compulsions. Often people with OCD feel that their personal rituals are necessary to their survival. They may be fearful of "failing" treatment or therapy. They may have fears about medications. What if they don't work? What if nothing works? They will feel like even more of a failure!

It's important to encourage the person with OCD to look for treatment with a professional who is experienced in treating the disorder using evidence-based approaches. Anxiety about treatment may worsen if the person with OCD is exposed to an incompetent or inappropriate treatment service. Most importantly, you might want to stress that knowing when to seek help is actually a sign of strength, not weakness.

Children with OCD-like Behavior

When is OCD-like behavior in children a "red flag" that something significant is taking place and when is it just normal behavior? Sometimes it's difficult to distinguish because symptoms aren't always clear and consistent.

For any mother who has watched her four-year-old daughter open and shut the same drawer or door for an hour, it's not too difficult to understand the worry that can accompany such behavior. Is your child developing obsessive-compulsive disorder? This is of special concern to people who have the disorder or have someone in their family who exhibits symptoms of OCD.

While OCD can be diagnosed in children as young as four years old, much of repetitive behavior is normal in children who are simply attempting to exert control in their lives. It is often helpful to have a guide to refer to concerning what is considered normal and what may be considered worrisome when it comes to OCD.

"Normal" Behavior in Children

- Ages two to three: It is common for kids this age to be extremely rigid about rituals like bath and bedtime.
- Ages three to five: Repetition is typical for this age group. For instance, a child might want to read the same book, watch the same DVD, or build up and then knock down the same structure over and over again.
- Ages five to six: Rules become extremely important, especially in terms of games.
- Ages six to twelve: Children in this age group are often superstitious and prone to hoarding certain items or collecting a particular thing.
- Preteens and teens: This is when children become obsessed with shows such as *High School Musical* or ones with teen stars. Admit it. You had a crush on a teen idol or star in your day, didn't you? David Cassidy? Madonna? John, Paul, George, or Ringo? The

Monkees? The Jackson Five? Farrah Fawcett? Diana Ross? It's completely normal.

Cause for Concern

If the behavior is dramatic, persistent, and distressing, a parent should become a bit concerned about OCD. If a child is stopped from repetitive behavior, it is normal for the child to cry and become visibly upset. However, if there is a meltdown that lasts for hours, that's not necessarily normal behavior.

If the child won't touch dirt, play with messy items such as paints and chalk, throw away garbage, or feels that "If I don't close this door six times, harm will come to someone," that is distressing behavior that may need examination. At that point it might be best to contact a pediatrician for younger children, or go directly to a child psychologist for older children.

CHAPTER 9

BRIDGE OVER BUMPY WATER

Additional Treatment and Therapy Protocols

*Whenever someone sorrows, I do not say, "forget it,"
or "it will pass," or "it could be worse"
...all of which deny the integrity of the painful experience.
But I say, to the contrary, "It is worse than you may allow yourself to think.
Delve into the depth. Stay with the feeling.
Think of it as a precious source of knowledge and guidance.
Then and only then will you be ready to face it
and be transformed in the process."*

—Peter Koestenbaum

The Benefits of Talk Therapy

Another name for talk therapy is psychotherapy. This sort of therapy usually addresses upsetting symptoms and emotions using psychological techniques rather than (or in addition to) medication treatments. There are many forms of psychotherapy, but the two most popular are psychodynamic therapy and cognitive behavioral therapy.

Although psychotherapy is the foundation of psychological treatment, the initial suggestion can raise some issues and concerns on the part of the person considering or being asked to seek professional help. Are my family members and friends sick of hearing my problems? Does my physician think I'm nuts? Can talking really help me? Would medicine work better than simply sitting down and talking to a mental health professional? How do I find the right therapist to talk to?

Just as the treadmill, aerobic classes, and the exercise bike can all help achieve fitness, many types of therapy can help one understand the self better, change behavior that is not serving well, and relieve difficult and troubling symptoms. A patient may do better with one type than with another or find that a blended approach, drawn from different schools of psychotherapy, suits the situation best. Regular participation in the process is more important than the type of approach chosen.

"At the simplest level, talk therapy can increase medication compliance and enhance treatment outcomes through supportive interventions and problem-solving assistance, thereby increasing control over how we respond to whatever situations we've gotten into," says psychologist Kent Bennington. "Talk therapy can help us reframe symptoms within a larger perspective, clarify the challenges, and shape them into manageable, bite-size pieces leading to consideration of alternative courses of thought and action."

Therapist Adina Shapiro regularly employs talk therapy in her practice. She feels it's as important as medication in treating a variety of mood or anxiety disorders. "Studies have shown that a combination of talk therapy and medication is much more effective than medication alone. I always cringe when I hear about people getting diagnosed with depression and being handed pills without any plans for talk therapy to understand what initiated and sustains their illness," says Shapiro. While she feels that those who have long-standing depression or bipolar disorder may need to be on medication for long periods, they also need to understand their mood disorders, develop coping mechanisms for dealing with those disorders, and learn to reinforce their own strength.

"The form of psychotherapy I practice combines traditional psychodynamic psychotherapy, in which I work with people on the relationship between their histories and their current lives, with cognitive behavioral therapy, which focuses on thought and behavioral patterns that can keep a person stuck." Essentially Shapiro helps her patients identify their internal schemas, which are messages they have received throughout their lives that keep them in a negative frame of mind and tap into their strengths. "These schemas are often reinforced by internalized family relationships; in other words, messages we received growing up about ourselves stay with us without our awareness—messages like 'I'll never amount to anything,' or 'I'm so ugly,' that we have assumed to be true without questioning the stories we tell ourselves."

"There are many, many effective ways of doing talk therapy with people, and I use different techniques with different people," says Shapiro. "This is not a one-size-fits-all practice. For example, one woman I worked with who had anorexia and severe body image issues needed a combination of traditional therapy with guided imagery and some sessions with her father in order to challenge and change her negative self-talk. She was also on medication but told me that the talk therapy was invaluable."

Janaya G. struggled with eating disorders most of her young life. Anorexia nervosa and bulimia nervosa are often accompanied by depression and various anxiety disorders, and Janaya wasn't spared these challenges. "Mental illness has nothing to do with intelligence," says Janaya. "When I was treated for my eating disorder in mental health institutions, I participated in programs with patients who were doctors, lawyers, and professors. They were all highly intelligent people struggling with similar issues that seem so silly to others. How can intelligent people have such a warped view of reality? I believe that intelligence can be a person's worst enemy when dealing with a mental illness because an intelligent person has an ability to rationalize disordered thoughts and behaviors."

Shapiro also encourages her patients to try whatever techniques they feel might help them in their recovery, such as guided imagery, meditation techniques, alternative practices such as acupuncture, as well as consulting traditional physicians. "I help people to identify what they gravitate to and what they think may help." While some of her patients may sneer at alternative treatments, others seek and embrace them. It's important for all people to move toward a path that feels right, to one they feel will be most useful to them in their particular set of circumstances.

Some therapists employ only one approach or technique, but many incorporate bits and pieces from many different therapeutic approaches. Christy Vaughn, a licensed clinical social worker, often suggests that her clients use a combination of relaxation techniques (such as visualization and breathing) and cognitive therapy (such as relabeling distorted thoughts) for treatment of anxiety. "Moreover, since the main general trigger to negative mood symptoms is stress, any form of stress management is helpful, such as exercise, yoga, massage, and meditation. If the clients are experiencing severely disabling or dangerous symptoms (such as feeling suicidal) then I recommend adjunctive medication management."

The most important elements in any type of therapy situation are trust and the ability to internalize suggestions for new and innovative ways of looking at challenges and dealing with symptoms. Such elements can lead to new ways of alleviating feelings of isolation and alienation. Psychotherapy can help a person to see the meaning in his struggle and to help him accept the mental illness as one part of the self, but not *the* main part of the self. A person may have an illness, but no person is his illness.

More on Cognitive Behavioral Approaches

Cognitive behavioral therapy (CBT) is less focused on the underpinnings of feelings; instead it emphasizes how to change the thoughts and behaviors that are causing problems right now. CBT is often used to alter difficult behaviors such as procrastination or phobias, and it can also help address conditions such as depression and anxiety. David Burns, MD, is a leader in cognitive behavioral therapy methods. He has written several successful books and workbooks geared at practitioners as well as at patients who live with chronic depression, anxiety, phobias, or panic disorder. His books and recordings provide powerful techniques and step-by-step exercises that help individuals cope with the full range of everyday challenges and symptoms.

Cognitive behavioral therapists believe that one can change feelings by changing thoughts and actions. For example, a person may have patterns of distorted thinking such as excessive self-criticism or guilt, always anticipating the worst, or attributing unpleasant motives to others. Such feelings may make him or her vulnerable to feeling bad. CBT teaches the person to recognize these patterns as they emerge and to alter them. The "behavior" part refers to learning more productive responses to distressing circumstances or feelings, such as relaxing and breathing deeply instead of hyperventilating when in an anxiety-provoking situation.

Online Therapy—Good or Bad Idea?

People spend a great deal of free time online doing shopping rather than driving to the mall. They may join groups of like-minded people to share their views on politics, hobbies, or interests. In the same vein, online support groups for various psychological disorders are very popular now. People with depression will seek out a support group or message board for those struggling with the same issues. Those who suffer from SAD, phobias, PTSD, or anxiety will also seek out information and support on such sites.

The computer universe has evolved in such a way that even psychotherapy is now available online. However, those who want to access actual therapy sessions via the Internet should know there are reasons why this may not be a good idea. Unlike personal contact, in which what is expressed cannot be taken back once it is spoken, using the Internet and reviewing a "presentation" in written form is helpful when someone wants to create a certain impression. But this approach goes against what psychotherapy is about. The spontaneous outpouring of feelings is more effective when experienced in person.

Therapy is an intimate and interactive form of communication. Therapists are highly trained to observe body language, vocal intonations, and even the most fleeting of facial expressions. There are many nonverbal signals that can only be gathered in person. When the therapist is in cyberspace, the client cannot see and feel the compassion or sense the proper presentation of information that is personally intended, nor can the therapist observe those feelings and information properly.

Another serious consideration is confidentiality, which can always be compromised when we are dealing with online communication. Not only people who don't know the client, but also the client's own family may fall upon private interactions and may misunderstand them or take them out of context.

Nevertheless some people prefer anonymity. They don't want the therapist to put a name to a face. E-mailing and texting feels comfortable for those accustomed to the medium, and they feel they express themselves best in this manner. But what are they truly expressing? What are they choosing to omit?

Are there any advantages to online therapy? Some therapists feel that online therapy is a good "starter therapy" for people not comfortable or familiar with face-to-face therapy. It is felt that certain individuals are more likely to be more candid in written communication than in verbal communication. People may try out therapy first online and then begin in-person therapy when they are more comfortable with disclosure and interactions. Online therapy also allows therapy to be more readily available to people in remote areas, and it may work for patients who need a specialist in a particular area such as phobias.

Insurance coverage rarely includes Internet counseling. Individuals normally have to pay an up-front fee with a credit card, and sessions can run anywhere from $80 to $200 on average.

Online therapy is certainly not appropriate for patients diagnosed with significant mood disorders, and in general, mental health professional associations do not approve of Internet therapy. It is also worth mentioning that at the current time no laws or guidelines exist for such counseling practices.

Treatment Options

Anxiety disorders can be treated with psychotherapy, medication, or both. CBT is the most common treatment for phobias (irrational fears of certain objects or situations). If someone has generalized anxiety or obsessive-compulsive disorder, CBT can help the client learn to respond differently in situations that cause anxiety. A combination of psychotherapeutic approaches is required to help people with post-traumatic stress disorder (PTSD) to come to terms with their trauma, losses, and painful memories.

Either talk therapy or medication can be used to treat mild to moderate depression, but combining them may be particularly effective. For example, researchers at the University of Pittsburgh School of Medicine found that when depressed people, age sixty and older received psychotherapy along with an antidepressant, they were symptom-free longer. Their quality of life and social interactions improved more than those of patients receiving either treatment alone.

Lisa A. knows without a doubt that she would spend most of her days in bed either sleeping or crying if she didn't take antidepressant medication for her mood disorder. "Some people look down upon others for taking antidepressants. But, for me, I cannot see ever living my life without being on medication. It has saved my quality of life. Medication has been a true lifesaver."

Lorna A. found that there were times she felt she could do well without medication. When she ceased taking her prescribed medication, however, she had difficulties. "Stopping my medication is a dangerous thought for me. I have tried it before, and I got so low and disconnected that it took a considerable amount of time to get back to feeling 'normal' once I went back on."

Recent research comparing before-and-after brain scans of people being treated for depression suggests that medication and psychotherapy counter depression in different ways.[5] Among people receiving CBT, PET scans showed increased blood flow in the limbic, or "emotional," system and decreased activity in certain "thinking" areas of the brain. Subjects who took antidepressants showed different changes in the same brain regions. This may help explain why individual responses to treatment vary so much.

After diagnosing depression, a primary care doctor is more likely to prescribe an antidepressant, and a psychiatrist is more likely to recommend psychotherapy and an antidepressant. (Note: A psychiatrist is also more likely to prescribe the antidepressant at the appropriate dose for the patient and to monitor that patient accordingly.) Patient preferences should be considered. If the primary care physician prescribes an antidepressant, the patient can request a referral for psychotherapy or wait to see his response to the medication, which may help encourage more effective participation in talk therapy.

A psychiatrist may provide psychotherapy and prescribe medication, but most psychotherapists cannot prescribe drugs. If a patient is seeing a non-MD psychotherapist, he or she may recommend that the patient ask his physician about a prescription for an antidepressant. In that case it's important for the therapist and the prescribing physician to collaborate on providing the best care for the patient.

For seasonal affective disorder, the standard approach is regular exposure to bright light. But new research indicates that CBT may work just as well by helping patients revise their negative thoughts about the lack of light and learn ways to cope with winter darkness.

New Possibilities on the Treatment Horizon

> *Fairy tales are more than true;*
> *not because they tell us that dragons exist,*
> *but because they tell us that dragons can be beaten.*
>
> —G.K. Chesterton

There are millions of people living with depression and anxiety who are helped tremendously by a treatment approach of medications and therapy. However, there are others who either do not respond well or prefer to find a different route of treatment.

Therapeutic recreation is one way that people with mood or anxiety disorders can benefit both mentally and physically through stimulation and movement. Therapeutic recreation may include the creative arts, music therapy, equestrian therapy, and other physical activities such as swimming and tennis.

The Nintendo Wii gaming system is a new addition to therapeutic recreation. It is a great supplement to traditional therapeutic recreation because the system is so intuitive and easy to use, even for those with severe depression and other debilitating disorders. People of any age or with any amount of video game experience can enjoy it. Sports games such as tennis, ping-pong, billiards, boxing, and bowling, have been beneficial for all ages, whether for teens or for elderly patients with severe depression.

Therapists report that the Wii has helped spark interest in leisure activity in depressed people and has been helpful to those with anxiety disorders. There is another development in our brave new world that takes existing technology and utilizes it in innovative and exciting ways. A pacemaker can regulate a heartbeat that's out of whack. Picture in your mind a pacemaker-type device that jolts the brain and effectively regulates mood circuits, which can potentially ease deep depression. Deep brain stimulation (DBS) does just that. It has the potential to improve both severe depression and obsessive-compulsive disorder. With this type of stimulating approach, the abnormal signals to the brain that cause depression may be regulated. In early studies those treated with DBS also had improvement in both short-term memory and quality of life.

This new treatment for those with psychiatric disorders involves implanting a device whose charge has to be adjusted and fine-tuned by a psychiatrist for deep-brain stimulation. Surgeons place tiny implantable electrodes into certain nodes of the brain that are believed to be malfunctioning.

This form of treatment would not be considered for those with mild or occasional depression but rather for those suffering from chronic major depression, when all other treatment approaches including psychotherapy, medications, and electroconvulsive therapy have failed.

According to the American Association of Neurological Surgeons, DBS has been used in the past two decades to treat Parkinson's disease, multiple sclerosis, and other pain disorders or tremors. Using such a treatment for OCD or major depression would be an off-label use of this device.

Of course the idea of using an electrical jolt to shock away depression isn't new. Electroconvulsive therapy (ECT) has been used for decades. However, DBS treatment would be more selective than ECT, does not produce seizures as does ECT, and does not have the same memory and cognitive side effects. DBS could be a promising treatment option not only for severe depression but also for a host of other disorders, such as Alzheimer's and morbid obesity.

Experimental treatments with magnetic stimulation are now attracting researchers' attention. Repetitive transcranial magnetic stimulation (TMS) uses real magnetic fields to induce changes in brain function. There's some evidence that it may make nerve-cell connections more efficient and modify how regions of the brain actually work together to regulate mood.

TMS was developed around 1986 by neurologists studying brain function. TMS is a cousin of ECT, commonly referred to as "shock treatment." Unlike ECT, however, TMS does not require anesthesia. Rather it is localized, and its side effects have been mild (headaches or scalp discomfort). The FDA is still deciding whether repetitive TMS should join antidepressants and ECT as approved treatments for depression. The results thus far have been promising, but there is further research to focus on before TMS becomes readily available.[6]

CHAPTER 10

EMBRACING A NEW NORMAL

*Nobody realizes that some people
expend tremendous energy
merely to be normal.*

—Albert Camus

Some people live a good part of their life without a mood or anxiety disorder, when suddenly—BAM! Depression, anxiety, post-traumatic stress disorder, or another mental disorder suddenly emerges and adjustments need to be made. Daily routines and common daily rituals must be rerouted and reexamined. The old way of doing things now must be replaced with a new normal—a new way of being in the world.

"In some ways, it's easier to live with the known symptoms of my depression and anxiety disorders," says Jan W. "Isn't there a saying that goes, 'Better the devil you know than the devil you don't?' Waking up symptom-free from what I've been living with all these years, well . . . it would probably send me to the ER in a panic!"

People who live with a concealed mood or anxiety disorder often need to revise their own expectations of themselves. They must learn to redefine their notion of achievement because the old definitions cannot be relied upon to offer a sense of feeling worthwhile or skilled. They must learn to develop a new normal. By redefining what makes a good day or a worthy accomplishment, they can learn to appreciate their own uniqueness and embrace their depression or other disorder as just one part of who they are.

Dr. Jason Copping says a certain percentage of his patients get a payoff of sorts from their mood or anxiety disorder and are not inspired to truly get better. They feel comfortable in their new normal that may include dark days, heightened fear, and lack of social contact. Their new normal has become an old friend, a cozy and familiar blanket of comfort. They perceive it to be the essence of who they truly are.

When certain people begin to experience an improvement in their symptoms, whether through medication, talk therapy, or another useful treatment, they sometimes have trouble adjusting to a symptom-free existence. In other words, they have difficulty adjusting to a new regulated mood (or new normal) and actually feeling good, happy, and free of anxiety. "They are so used to their identity being wrapped up in being the 'sick one,' they need to adjust to their new role," says Dr. Cassandra Friedman.

Accepting an Easily Concealed Mood Disorder

Adjusting to a mood or anxiety disorder impacts a person's internal and external life in a multitude of ways. People who live with a concealed mood or anxiety disorder must embrace it in a way that releases the angst they feel about the change it has brought to their lives, even if the release is temporary. They face an overwhelming range of challenges as they wrestle with guilt and self-blame. Depression and anxiety disorders become a family affair in that they have a tremendous impact on family and relationship dynamics. "Any time one has a chronic issue, the condition becomes a family affair, bringing about anger and exhaustion," says Friedman. Persons with a mood or anxiety disorder must now assign new roles to family members and to themselves. They must learn a new set of rules for their everyday life, one that involves simplification, rationing out their energy for the most important daily tasks, and pacing themselves through the ups and downs of their moods. They must somehow learn to accept all of the emotions surrounding their new limitations and challenges.

At some point people who live with depression, PTSD, panic disorder, anxiety, or other mental challenges stop trying to cure themselves or fight the disorder and instead work toward a peaceful coexistence with it. This isn't especially difficult to do because in most cases they appear perfectly fine. It is what lies just beneath the surface that tells the true story.

While many who suffer with easily concealed mood or anxiety disorders struggle to maintain a degree of normalcy in their lives, if the malady does not affect the person's outside appearance, that person has the opportunity to keep "the beast" hidden from others. We all want to buy into the image of happiness, peace, and mental stability, and we want others to buy into our illusion of having those sought-after characteristics. For some, putting symptoms on the back burner and ignoring them is an expression of denial; for others, it is a survival mechanism.

There is an ongoing dichotomy between image and reality. The line between who *appears* disabled and who *is* disabled is a ragged one. Most of us are guilty of drawing sweeping conclusions based on appearances. Though this is only natural as we assess someone's abilities, it is important to realize just how deceiving looks can be. Someone in a wheelchair may be perfectly capable of grocery shopping, cooking, and driving the city streets, whereas another who appears fit and able-bodied may have trouble walking to the mailbox or gathering enough stamina to prepare a simple meal because of a mental disorder.

Having a mood or anxiety disorder, whether ongoing or new, changes not only how one does things but also who one is. In the face of an extraordinary mental challenge, some have an easier time than others honing in on the strength and wisdom necessary to reinvent a worthy life. In all cases we hope that as the former self and previous way of being in the world falls away, a new way of carrying on and embracing life will arise.

CHAPTER 11

EQUAL OPPORTUNITY DISORDERS

Teens and Senior Citizens with Mood and Anxiety Disorders

Teens and Mental Health

There are so many myths circulating about how to best approach teens who experience depression that it's rather mind-boggling. For instance, many parents assume that teens are naturally moody, and that's just the way they are. It's a phase. They will surely grow out of it. But according to the National Institute of Mental Health, up to 8 percent of adolescents experience clinical depression. When depression in teens goes unaddressed, it can interrupt important learning and social development. That is why it is vital for parents to learn to distinguish between typical moodiness in teens and non-typical behavior that could point toward clinical depression.

Another myth is that depressed kids are always loners or *appear* depressed. The fact is that depression can impact popular teens and perfectionists as well as quiet, withdrawn teens. Depressed teens feel alone even when they are not alone, and even when they are popular, on the honor roll, a top football player, or serving as class president or lead cheerleader. Depression, after all, wears the mask of normalcy. These teens can appear well adjusted and happy-go-lucky to those around them, even to family members.

Another common myth is that depression isn't inherited, when, in fact, it does run in families. If a teen has depression, it is likely that one or more parents may also have depression. Data shows that when a mother gets treatment for her depression, her child often gets better, so it's important for other family members to get treatment for themselves if warranted.

Many parents believe that resuming normal routines helps depressed kids recover and feel better quickly. However, if a teen is clinically depressed, everyday activities can seem overwhelming and too massive to contend with. That's why parents should attempt to make reasonable accommodations rather than simply push the child to maintain his usual routine. Depression is twice as prevalent in teenage girls as boys, and that may have something to do with the different ways boys and girls react to stress.

Many parents throw up their hands in frustration or fear. They feel there is nothing they can do to impact their child's behavior or depression. However, it's important to remember when dealing with a depressed child that one should pick one's battles. Taking away privileges from a depressed or anxious teen may lead to more symptoms. It is imperative to have the teen take responsibility for his behavior but not to punish him for the way he feels. Teens, for the most part, long to be normal and accepted by their peers. So if they are not allowed to do those things that they normally do, they begin to feel alienated. Of course parents should never drop all expectations of the teen; that action would not be productive. This can be a fine tightrope to walk, so consulting a therapist is often a good idea.

If you are a teen and your friend is showing significant signs of depression, just listening and being supportive can be very helpful.

Encouraging your friend to talk about his or her feelings is important. Letting him or her know you understand their feelings is an excellent starting point. At the same time, it's important to take care of yourself and let the appropriate adult know about your concerns for your friend. Also, strongly consider giving your friend the number of a 24-hour Crisis Hotline.

While celebrities with mental health problems are given massive media attention, the number of teens seeking mental health treatment has nearly doubled in the last couple of years. Why? Teens become fans of these celebrities as they follow their fashionable and youthful indiscretions, downfalls, and fumbles. They live vicariously through the idols' errors. Teens see their heroes as cool and want to be like them, even if it's just a fantasy. Looking up to a celebrity removes youth from their small world of homework, school, sports, and chores. Many teens regard their lives as dull and routine. They see fame and fortune as the ultimate prize, and they see the seemingly exciting lives of attractive but troubled celebrities as appealing. It is not outlandish to say that mental disorders are fashionable. With all the substance abuse and suicide attempts in Hollywood, our youth have cast their eyes in that direction and are following their favorite stars' actions with great interest and reverence.

Seniors, Retirement, and Depression

Depression in the senior population is often viewed as a normal part of aging. The difficult changes that many elderly individuals face—such as the death of a spouse or medical problems—can lead to depression, especially in those who do not have a strong support system of family and friends. Other factors that can contribute or lead to depression include isolation and loneliness caused by living alone; having a dwindling circle of friends; undergoing a move; experiencing a reduced sense of purpose related to job loss, illness, or physical limitations; and sensing fears of dying, health issues and financial challenges. It's easy to see that the combination of an inability to pay for medications and treatment, an inability to get out and seek help, growing feelings of loneliness and isolation, perceived abandonment by children, and the loss of friends who are passing away or ill could contribute to depression among the elderly.

Some people find themselves experiencing clinical depression, an anxiety disorder, post-traumatic stress disorder, or other significant mood shifts for the first time when they reach this senior stage, and their life has shifted out of the career and work setting and out of their usual home and family environment. Adjusting to a new disorder impacts a person's internal and external life in a multitude of ways, sending routine and common daily rituals out the window and replacing them with a new way of functioning and being in the world.

However, depression is not a normal or necessary part of aging. In fact most seniors are satisfied with their lives despite the challenges of growing old. Unfortunately depression is the most common mood disorder that social worker and geriatric care specialist Lesley Alexander sees in her practice. "Senior citizens must deal with a great deal of loss, whether it be loss of job, income, home, spouse, driver's license, or independence; and that loss can lead to varying degrees and periods of depression. In older adults depression can often be mistaken for dementia." The symptoms that often show in seniors are lethargy or confusion. Seniors can stop eating or have an increase in physical challenges, including heart problems. "They may have problems sleeping and may just 'give up,' so that they aren't motivated to do anything," adds Alexander. "They may also stop taking care of their personal hygiene." Depression in the elderly can often be treated effectively. But according to the February 2009 issue of the *Harvard Mental Health Letter,* it can be challenging not to mistake its signs for symptoms of another medical disorder.

Seniors will often try to or believe they can "will" themselves out of their symptoms and go that route rather than take medication or pursue therapy. "Two of my clients," says Alexander, "made attempts at going to a senior center as a way to prove to me that they were not depressed. One client went only once, and another went two or three times, but that was it. Each one ended up isolated again at home."

Alexander feels antidepressants or anti-anxiety medications are good potential treatments for some seniors. "I currently have a 92-year old female client in hospice who has been struggling with depression for quite a while. She used to cry all the time and talk about her wish to die so she could just get it over with. She was initially reluctant to try medication, but after my continued gentle pushing, she agreed to begin a trial of antidepressants. After a few weeks on medication, she was able to say she felt better, and she was aware that her improvement was due to the medication. She no longer talks about wanting to die (even though she knows she will sooner rather than later), and her crying episodes have stopped. Support groups would be extremely beneficial for seniors. Unfortunately there are very few such groups for seniors who are depressed or anxious."

Left untreated, depression not only prevents older adults from enjoying life as they live it, but the illness also takes a heavy toll on health, increasing the likelihood of placement in a nursing home, disability, and death. Suicide risk also increases with age; white men over age eighty-five have the highest suicide rate in the United States.

We are now finding that middle-aged men and women are more likely to retire early from their jobs if they are depressed. A study conducted in forty-eight states followed nearly three thousand adults between the ages of fifty-three and fifty-eight and tracked them every two years between 1994 and 2002 for mental health and labor force status changes. It was found that middle-aged men who experience the ongoing symptoms of depression are more likely to retire from their jobs at an early date, and retirement-aged women often do the same, even if the depression they experience is mild.

What does this tell us? It seems that illness, whether mental or physical, pushes individuals to consider retirement before they truly need to do so, or before they otherwise would want to do so. Ironically those who retire early because of depression often find that their loss of income becomes problematic, causing more stress and depression to ensue. This stress can have a far-reaching and damaging impact on health or in qualifying for medical care.

Although some seniors with depression develop classic symptoms such as persistent sadness and despair, others may seek help for less typical symptoms such as fatigue, tremors, heart palpitations, or vomiting. People may also report significant cognitive problems such as not being able to concentrate well or recall things. It's not entirely clear why symptoms of depression in seniors may differ from those in younger adults. Coexisting medical problems, medication side effects, and the natural aging process may all be contributing factors.

How can we help a senior family member who is dealing with depression? The very nature of depression interferes with people's ability to seek help. It zaps their energy and self-esteem. For depressed seniors raised in a time when mental illness was highly stigmatized and often misunderstood, it can be even more difficult, especially if they don't believe depression is a real illness. They are often too ashamed or proud to seek or request assistance, or they may fear becoming a burden to their families.

If a senior citizen you care about is depressed, you can make a difference by offering to listen to your loved one with compassion and patience. Don't criticize the feelings expressed. Instead point out hopeful realities that might be present. You might also want to help the individual seek out an accurate diagnosis and appropriate treatment. Help him locate a good practitioner, accompany the senior to appointments, and offer support by just being there. Often that's the best medicine of all.

Another thing you might consider doing is getting the elder out of the house and giving him some positive mental stimulation by being around other people and events. Invite the senior to a movie or museum or to something they can easily attend and enjoy. Help the aging person with shopping and suggest some healthy items and alternatives. Cook for the elder or prepare meals in advance if you are able to do so. Schedule regular outings, or if the elder lives some distance away, call every week on a particular day and time to simply chat. You'd be surprised at how much positive anticipation those phone calls generate.

As people age, there are particular conditions and illnesses that impact brain chemistry which can bring on depression. These illnesses include heart attacks or heart disease, Parkinson's disease, stroke, and Alzheimer's. Many medications also have depression as a side effect. Steroids, painkillers, hormones, and arthritis medications are just some of these. It's no wonder that depression is such a significant and common problem for so many as the symptoms of the disorder can come from a wide range of sources.

The loss of mental sharpness is sometimes just a normal sign of old age, but it could also be a sign of depression or dementia, both of which are common in the elderly. Since depression and dementia share many similar symptoms including memory problems, sluggish speech and movements, and low motivation, it can often be difficult to tell the two apart. One difference that can help distinguish between the two: the depressed individual may worry or notice personal memory problems or decline in cognitive function. Most people with dementia will not seem to care. The person with depression will know the correct time, date, and current location. The person with dementia will be confused, disoriented, and lost in familiar places. There are other differences that only a mental health professional can help determine; therefore it is important to seek out early care.

Unfortunately many primary care doctors do not identify depression in senior populations. They may briefly discuss the issue in office visits but only in passing. More often than not, the patient does not bring it up for reasons of stigma, denial, or simply the apathy produced by the depression itself. However, this suffering among seniors is something that we must all learn to recognize. Depression in this population is a significant public health concern for both men and women. It increases not only hospitalizations but also morbidity.

CHAPTER 12

YES TO SUCCESS

Having Hope While You Cope

Uncovering Good in the Bad

Many people with chronic mood symptoms and mental pain find pleasures in the simple things in life, the sorts of tasks and interests that got lost in the shuffle of a frantic day when they were just trying to hold their heads above water. In the slower pace that comes from a managed life, the birds outside are singing a more noticeable song, the rain is falling in patterns that were missed in the hustle and bustle of the days that came before, and sitting to sip some tea is a soothing respite for a body that is hurting and a mind that is trying desperately to cope. A new pair of eyes is beginning to awaken to see a fresh way of functioning in this very different mental landscape. A chronic mood or anxiety disorder can lead us back to this simplicity and the enjoyment of life's little pleasures.

"Writing about my illness and related behaviors has played a very strong role in my healing and recovery," says John M. "Writing allows me to come to terms with my past, gives meaning to my present, and gives me the courage to face the future with hope."

"I always tell myself it could be a lot worse," says Marilyn M. "I have learned to accept this new lifestyle. I grieved for my old life and then put it away. Very few people have a perfect lifestyle; some are better than mine, and some are worse. I always try to keep that at the forefront of my mind."

Stages of Acceptance: Going On Despite Grief

> *Acceptance, submission, surrender—*
> *whatever one chooses to call it,*
> *this mental shift may be the master key*
> *that unlocks healing.*
>
> —Dr. Andrew Weil

Feeling constant psychic or physical pain, or living with a concoction of debilitating feelings of dread, depression, or anxiety is not on anyone's wish list. It's important to recognize that grief is a natural response to these unwelcome visitors. The nature of an ongoing depression or anxiety disorder is that the person can be in one state of mind one day and feel that is "normal," only to be catapulted back to very opposite symptoms the next day.

While some people experience their mood or anxiety disorder from an early age, many people who live with depression or an anxiety disorder grieve their former self—the one that didn't experience such debilitating symptoms. They recall days that weren't riddled with fear, sadness, and uncertainty.

Dr. Elisabeth Kübler-Ross delineates the five stages of grief following a serious loss: 1) denial and isolation, 2) anger, 3) bargaining, 4) depression, and 5) acceptance. These are the same stages that characterize the aftermath of a diagnosis of a serious mental illness. There are losses of functionality and of one's previous way of living and existing day to day.

In the first stage, denial, people tend to reject the idea that their mood or anxiety disorder is a part of their permanent reality. They may avoid therapy appointments and refuse treatments because they cannot believe what is happening to them. They may withdraw from long-standing social contacts. This stage may last from a few hours to a few years.

"I find myself denying or doubting my diagnoses. Of course I do. No one wants to be told they have a mental illness; no one wants to hear they are disabled," says Karen A., who suffers from generalized anxiety disorder and social anxiety, panic disorder, depression, and post-traumatic stress disorder. "When I was diagnosed with anxiety disorders, I thought that meant I was crazy. As a result I didn't tell anyone. I tried to struggle in a marriage for twenty-eight years, yet I always doubted my feelings and thoughts. But I believe everyone has to go through a stage of denial before accepting any traumatic event in life. I feel others doubt my illness. I appear to be well, level-headed, jolly, and I look okay on the outside. How frustrating it is to be surrounded by others who don't understand the illness of depression."

Pamela D. pushed herself beyond her own emotional limits because of her denial about her mental disorders. "I have often tried to run away from my symptoms and problems. Now I realize that I was in denial. It isn't possible to run away from these things, any more than someone with cancer can run away from that diagnosis. I blamed myself for a very long time and was angry because of the things I knew I was being held back from because of my disorders. This simply furthered the cycle of self-loathing and depression, however."

To get stuck in the denial stage not only taxes the mind and body but also makes it difficult to reach the acceptance stage and move forward. When others urge a person to look on the bright side or suggest various ways to minimize psychological turmoil, the individual on this emotional roller coaster may feel great pressure to hide or deny feelings or emotions. What may result is a lengthy and increasingly complex healing and acceptance process.

The second stage, anger, may find the grieving person furious at therapists, psychiatrists, the world, his God, or at himself for letting the depression, anxiety, or other symptom strike him or get the better of him, despite the fact that there was likely nothing he could have done to prevent it. People in this stage may feel like they are failures or are weak human beings for allowing their moods to make them feel more vulnerable and create upheaval in their lives. They may begin to resent those around them who do not seem to struggle with the same dark moments or anxious hours. For example, one person may think to himself: "How dare I get depressed when my sister-in-law, who is such a miserable and complaining so-and-so, lives worry-free?" Or "How could I find myself in such a deep depression when I exercise, always treat others well, and seldom complain?"

When people get stuck in the anger phase of the grief process, they can become annoyed and be at odds with everyone and everything. "I've paced myself and kept stress at bay. I worshipped according to the practices of my religion. I took good care of my family. It just is not fair!" They view the people around them as if they are living happy, carefree lives.

Sometimes people with mood or anxiety disorders resent those who tell them what to do to pull themselves out of their "blue mood," or inform them what antidepressant to try or which supplement to take, which meditation or yoga practice to attempt to "cure" themselves or to feel better. This can bring up feelings of resentment and irritation. However, if people remain at this stage, bitterness can displace what is left of their energy, and anger can begin to eclipse their remaining enjoyment of life.

In the bargaining stage, there is a trade, a deal, a bartering that takes place. This juncture is very much like a huge swap meet where one comes to exchange his depression, panic, or anxiety for anything else that might be on the table. Take this dark mood away, and I will smile at every stranger in the street forevermore. Remove this anxiety, and I will call my mother every Sunday. I promise! Is it a deal? Usually it is not.

During the bargaining stage, a newly diagnosed person may try to effect reconciliation with his mood or anxiety disorder through an offer to exchange something for relief, or to make a deal for something in return. "If I only stop isolating myself on weekends and meditate daily, I will be able to manage my moods." This sense of extraordinary bargaining power and unrealistic control might suggest other solutions, such as the decisions to become charitable or more devout.

Bargaining moves the grieving, angry person to make deals with God. Desperate to preclude another bad bout with depression or anxiety disorder, those in the bargaining phase try to become better human beings. If I help others who have this disorder, it will surely alleviate my own symptoms. If I do this, will it take away my anxiety or fear? What if I were a kinder person? Would God make my disorder go away? What if I changed the way I treat people? Will God remove this imbalance from my brain chemistry? What if I try to be more patient with my kids? Will I score enough points to get out of this prison of discomfort and despair? Give me a "Get Out of Jail Free" card!

The next stage is significant depression, the phase marked by numbness, melancholy, or a profound sense of psychological exhaustion that merely compresses and pushes down the anger bubbling just below the surface. People who are able to retain employment while depressed may find that they simply can no longer engage in their work. They may present themselves to the world as they always have, with the same wardrobe, makeup and smile, but they are not mentally in attendance. Those suffering from depression often function on autopilot. They move through their daily chores and responsibilities, but their hearts and souls are not in their work. Their thoughts are a million miles away.

By working through grief and loss, men and women with mental health challenges move forward into a new life. They learn to reduce stress by lowering their expectations; by generating new, more attainable goals; and by minimizing or reprioritizing the must-do tasks in order to get through the day, the morning, or the hour. Sound decision-making and the successful completion of chores and simple activities often translate to the greatest sense of well-being.

One thing people find helpful is to write a letter to their depression or anxiety symptoms or to the disorder itself, as if they were appealing to a friend or relative. Here is one example:

> Dear Phobia: I know you are with me to serve a purpose, even if I cannot see it now. I accept that, but I want you to know that I will continue to seek out and obtain treatments that will help me feel better and deal with these challenges you present.

Instead of feeling trapped, boxed in, and helpless, some people are able to locate a community support group for their particular mood or anxiety disorder, whether it be a depression group, anxiety seminar, or cognitive therapy session for dealing with panic disorder. There they find solace, comfort, inspiration, and knowledge.

Why are groups so useful for those with mood or anxiety disorders? People with mood or anxiety disorders, particularly anxiety and depression, tend to isolate and not discuss their inner demons. However, it is often helpful to ask others who are in the same situation how they have coped. People in groups often discuss not only what they have gone through, but also how they have successfully dealt with difficult situations and times. Sometimes simply knowing that you are not the only one plagued with particular symptoms is healing in itself. Individual therapy is also very helpful; it can provide a fresh perspective, an alternate look at the disorder and symptoms, and it can enable an individual to value life in new ways.

Support groups remind us that we're not alone and that compassionate assistance is available, despite and amidst our suffering. "This is especially the case when family support is unavailable," says Dr. Larry Wampler. "Other people's stories give hope for improvement and inspiration to persevere in treatment even, for example, if an initial medication provides no relief. Patients can also garner practical tips and coping strategies that may be very useful." The only risk for groups is that they can sometimes be construed as substitutes for professional help, but professional help is vital for depression.

Supportive therapy that focuses on destigmatizing depression or anxiety disorders, and offers information and explanations for why certain symptoms creep up or why particular things happen, is crucial. Being able to share feelings with others who are going through similar experiences or having similar symptoms is invaluable. Just having someone who can say to you, "I know you feel awful, so why don't you take some time out, lie down, take a hot bath, and take care of yourself right now? It will be all right," can make all the difference in how one perceives his own mood or anxiety disorder. "There is no judgment, no suggestion of 'faking' or 'imagining it all' because all group members are going through the same things that each one is enduring," says Dr. Shelley Slapion-Foote.

The final stage is acceptance. During this period the sadness, anger, and mourning for the way things used to be, or could have been, taper off. Acceptance means agreeing to make peace with the mood or anxiety disorder without struggling to wrestle it to the ground or push it out the door. Acceptance means finding genuine peace without allowing envy or anger to become frequent intruders.

Acceptance is not easy to achieve. The person who reaches this final stage decides to take ownership of the situation without a demand for reciprocity. Acceptance means coming to terms with the anxiety, depression, or another disorder. It means that life, though changed, will go on. And it means that despite the limitations and symptoms, there is no need to run from, disguise, or exchange this new life for something else. The individual who accepts a mood or anxiety disorder realizes that he cannot escape his reality. He can either live in harmony with it or its occasional flare-ups, or find treatment for it. Thus, finally there is peace.

Sometimes a person who has arrived at acceptance may regress to one of Dr. Kübler-Ross's earlier stages through the surprise of another severe episode of the existing depression or anxiety, or through the acquisition of a new and accompanying disorder. This period is often characterized by a variety of conflicting and powerful emotions including sorrow, loneliness, and shame. Such potent feelings are very stressful and counterproductive.

Barbara, who lives with severe depression accompanied by anxiety, finds that denial serves an important and useful purpose. She does not want to fully acknowledge that she is disabled because she wants to be "normal." Since she appears perfectly balanced and steady, she can even deceive herself. Having an easily concealed mood or anxiety disorder makes it much more difficult for the person to emotionally and psychologically accept his own disorder. Furthermore, people who tell the suffering person that he looks great or just fine contribute to this inner conflict. After all how can there truly be something wrong if no one else can see it? Such disorders are not only easily concealed from those in the outside world, but they also have the insidious ability to mask their existence to those suffering from the disorder themselves. It is difficult, if not impossible, to contend with something one can't see or be aware of.

To summarize, Dr. Kübler-Ross's stages of grief apply to the person with a mood or anxiety disorder in this manner: the person with depression or anxiety first tries to ignore it, then struggle against it, try to make a deal with it, experience the depth of it, and finally accept it. Some people ignore their symptoms until they become so persistent that ignoring the issues becomes impossible. Finally the individual who has a chronic mood or anxiety disorder has to work through, not around, the reality of the mental condition.

There is no preordained schedule for moving through the various stages of grief and acceptance. Often the stages overlap. It's important to remember that grief is as unique as the individual who is experiencing it. One person may skip a step while another person may add a new one. However, most people begin their journey of acceptance with feelings of denial.

"Being on Social Security disability and having such a severe mood disorder was never going to happen to me," thought Louise G. "I still think I will get rid of it somehow." People who are newly diagnosed with a mood or anxiety disorder are not prepared to deal with the loss of their previous mental health. They may begin to doubt the doctors, the conclusions and diagnoses, and the seriousness of the diagnosis. A common response is to shield themselves from thoughts about the impact of a particular diagnosis or a label they have associated with their disorder. Filing these worries away and putting them on a shelf for another day is much easier. "It took me six years to accept my diagnosis," reports Louise. She found herself stuck in the denial stage and set up camp there for a while. "It was extremely difficult to reconfigure my life and alter my responsibilities because of this mood disorder."

People often use their denial to derive strength. Many people who live with depression or anxiety disorders tend to be very stoical at times and put their disorder on the back burner. They ignore the symptoms and downplay the impact it has on their day. It is their way of coping. The symptoms of these disorders are masterful at flying under the radar and can often be difficult to grasp.

Sometimes friends, relatives, and even mental health professionals will try to convince a person not to feel sorry for himself. It's easy for them to offer this advice because, after all, the suffering person looks just fine to them—happy and healthy, with no visibly apparent anxiety, fear, rage, or other disturbing symptoms. But most people can benefit from a period of irritation about their situation if a pity party doesn't last for too long. The trick is to lament and vent anger but not let the anger become consuming. Get it over with, pick yourself up, dust yourself off, and get on with the business of living and making peace with the biochemical changes that have occurred.

You have heard it said that knowledge is power. When a person acquires information about his mood or anxiety disorder, the need for denial and anger often dissipates. This puts the person and his emotions back in the driver's seat. To become an active participant in one's own treatment is a powerful and healing tool. Therefore seeking out assistance from support groups, one-on-one therapy sessions, seminars, or simply reading more about a particular disorder is going to serve the person with the mood or anxiety disorder well.

The effects of a mood or anxiety disorder are profound. As with any major life shift, there is a search for meaning. Why did I develop this anxiety or depression disorder in the first place? Why is it happening at this time in my life? Is there a rhyme or reason to its presenting itself right now, or did I simply develop a mood or anxiety disorder like so many millions of others? It is often useful to discuss these issues with a mental health provider such as a therapist or social worker. You may not come to any earthshaking conclusions, but it often helps to talk over these issues and get them out on the table before moving forward.

Most people eventually reconcile themselves to their mood or anxiety disorder. They tolerate its intrusion into their lives. They manage the symptoms and modify their time as needed. In order to maintain some level of peace, they learn to hold the hand of anxiety and depression or other accompanying challenges—not because they want to but because they must befriend their symptoms and create peace of mind, both literally and figuratively.

An intrusive mood or anxiety disorder leads one to feel out of control. The embarrassment of the inability to perform as well as in the past, or the lack of productivity in their new life can lead some people to a new way of defining who they are. Many individuals find positive aspects in their mood or anxiety disorders, such as being special or unusual among the masses but in a good way. After all who wants to be like everyone else? People learn to embrace their good days and tolerate the frustrating ones. As their daily regimen changes, they learn to catch the rhythm of a new set of rules. Eventually an updated self can emerge from this new way of being. Embracing that new self can be the biggest success imaginable.

Can You Have a Good Day Anyway?

How do people live a full life despite living with significant depression or anxiety? Those who live with an easily concealed mood or anxiety disorder may have to relearn how to have a good day. They may have to teach themselves how to be at peace and redefine what feeling fine truly means. They may need to challenge previous notions of what faith and spirituality are and the roles they can play in these new lives. They may need to learn how to laugh again.

In many ways individuals with mood or anxiety disorders are given a chance for a new and different life. They have to learn to take care of themselves with a gentle touch and to modify activities so that they are more reasonable and realistic. Roles in the family may wiggle about. Some family members and friends may initially resist new roles and responsibilities because they liked things just the way they were. The person appears the same, so why can't everything remain the way it used to be?

The person with the mood disorder may appear the same as they used to when they did not struggle with chronic or more significant symptoms; however, priorities may have to be adjusted and limitations must be taken into consideration. For example, if one cannot partake in active outdoor activities as easily as before because of depression or anxiety, why not keep the mind active by using a computer? Write about feelings, or start a novel. Express yourself through art. Pick up those felt pens or watercolor paints you once dabbled with in school, and attack the paper with whatever energy and ability you have. Many people, because of their mood or anxiety disorder, discover the gifts of hidden talents. Try to focus on what can be accomplished, not on what cannot be accomplished.

The Worry Window

Bejai Higgins is a therapist who recommends a "window of worry hour" to many of her clients who live with anxiety and depression. Since many of her clients have serious issues to worry about, she never attempts to tell them not to worry. That is not only unproductive but it's also not possible to get a result from such a command. What she does suggest is that they go ahead and worry, but "instead of doing it in bits and pieces throughout the day, try to concentrate on it to make it more efficient. This also leaves the rest of the day relatively worry-free!"

This window of worry hour can be any hour of the day. The person is instructed to do nothing during that designated time period but worry, even using lists if he forgets what items in his life to worry about. Nothing else is allowed to be included—be it TV, family members or friends and their problems, music, work—nothing! "The important part is that if you think of a worry at some other time of the day, you cannot stop to worry about it then; you must make note of it and put it aside until the next window of worry." Higgins notes that this takes some practice, but the practice starts working in a week or so.

When you get to your window of worry hour, look over the items on your worry list and ask some questions about it. Is it within your direct control? Maybe only part of it is under your control. If part of it is under someone else's control, can you contact them and request an action that would help you?

"Separate out the part that is under your control, and ask some more questions," says Higgins. "Is there an action that I can take now that would reduce this worry? If yes, take it. If yes but not now, schedule the action so that you do not forget it. If you need more information to answer the questions above, make an action item to acquire that information."

Go through each item on your worry list, analyzing degrees of control and possible actions. "If you go through this exercise for each worry, your subconscious will realize that you are not trying to avoid the issue, and it will stop pushing it to the front of your mind all the time," Higgins says. "If you suffer from anxiety, it cannot hurt to set aside an hour a day to try this technique. Give it a good try for a week, and see if you are less frazzled at times other than that one hour you allow for a focus of worry."

CHAPTER 13

USE IT AND LOSE IT

Exercise for Mood and Anxiety Disorders

When you are living with depression or an anxiety disorder, exercising may be the last thing you think of or manage to do. Finding the energy and motivation to go to the gym or even go for a walk around the block can seem overwhelming. After all melancholy and fatigue are trademarks of depression.

Depression can often make it difficult to roll out of bed, let alone put on some running shoes or suit up for the health club. However, staying active is as vital to emotional well-being as it is to physical health. Exercise isn't a cure for depression or anxiety, but the psychological and physical benefits it offers can sometimes improve mental health symptoms. If nothing else, increased physical activity is a positive strategy to help manage the symptoms of anxiety and depression. Exercise isn't meant to replace medical treatment of depression or anxiety, but it can certainly help lighten some of the symptoms if done in combination with regular treatment.

Research suggests that it may take at least thirty minutes of exercise a day for at least three to five days a week to significantly improve depression symptoms. However, smaller amounts of time, such as ten to fifteen minutes of activity, can improve mood in the short term. Starting with small amounts of time is often easier for people who are suffering from these disorders.

Just how exercise reduces symptoms of depression and anxiety isn't fully understood. Some evidence suggests that exercise raises the levels of certain mood-enhancing neurotransmitters in the brain. Exercise may also boost feel-good endorphins, release muscle tension, improve sleep, and reduce levels of the stress hormone cortisol. In addition, exercise increases body temperature, which can have a calming effect. All of these changes in the mind and body can reduce feelings of anxiety, irritability, sadness, stress, fatigue, anger, self-doubt, and hopelessness.

Even if there were no scientific evidence that exercise alleviated symptoms of depression and anxiety, logic would seem to argue that exercise could build confidence by providing a sense of accomplishment. We all know that meeting challenges or goals, even if they are small ones, can boost self-confidence. Exercise can also make one feel more confident about physical appearance and provide a sense of value.

What else can exercise do for a person who is suffering with a mood or anxiety disorder? It has already been discussed that depression and anxiety disorders can easily lead to isolation, which in turn can feed the symptoms. Exercise sometimes gives a person a chance to meet others, even if it's just to exchange a smile with them as you walk or run down a street where you live or work out in the gym.

Exercise is also a healthy distraction! If you isolate yourself indoors, it is easy to ruminate about yourself and how bad and worthless you might feel. This can make your symptoms or episode of depression or anxiety last longer. Exercising can shift the focus away from your inner self and unhealthy thoughts to something more productive. To motivate yourself change the way you think about exercise. Instead of telling yourself that movement and exercise will leave you with achy muscles and fatigue, remind yourself that most people feel better after moderate exercise and have more energy, positivity, and optimism. They are not more fatigued; they feel invigorated.

Doing something active to help manage your mood or anxiety disorder is a productive coping strategy. Trying your best to feel better by escaping and isolating yourself from others, or simply hoping your symptoms will go away, is not as useful as the simple act of moving your body and getting your heart pumping.

Research studies prove it. According to a 2007 study at Northwestern University, researchers saw symptom scores dramatically improve when a group of thirty-two women with moderate depression finished a three-month program of exercise. An additional study at the University of California, San Diego, found that overweight women who began a regular exercise program significantly lowered their scores on a standard test for depression. Additional research points to the same benefits for men. These results are worth consideration by anyone having trouble putting feet to the pavement.

You may not only feel a lessening of depression, but you may experience a boost in overall energy and self-esteem. If you are inactive, set your sights on walking briskly for twenty to thirty minutes at least three days a week. Once you get into the swing of things, increase that to five days a week. That's enough to give you most of the health benefits associated with physical activity. If you do well with that, incorporate another sport that is of particular interest to you and that you find relaxing or energizing, such as swimming, yoga, cycling, or aerobics.

It's important to first identify what activity or exercise you enjoy doing. That will help you stick with it. Do you enjoy taking walks and looking at the flowers and yards around your neighborhood? Do you like seeing other people working out around you? Do you like to run along the beach, bike to the store, or walk around the mall and window shop? All of these are productive ways to get your body moving and your heart pumping. Many people find listening to an MP3 player with their favorite music or audio book a nice addition to or inspiration for their exercise routine.

Set reasonable goals for yourself. You do not have to walk five days a week for an hour a day when you begin. What's reasonable to you? Is ten minutes possible today? How about twenty minutes two or three times a week? Start where you can. Tailor your plan to fit your realistic abilities right now. Exercise should be something you look forward to doing, not merely something you feel you ought to do. Think of it as a therapy session—something that will be a tool to act on your brain chemistry, even if it's barely perceivable.

Examine some of the things that might discourage you from exercising. If you feel intimidated by others or are self-conscious, for instance, you may want to exercise in the privacy of your own home. If you stick to goals better with a partner, find someone to work out with, or ask your spouse, sibling, or a good friend to go with you the first few times. If you don't have extra money to spend on a gym membership or special equipment for your home, do something simple that's cost-free: walk. It's one of the best exercises.

People who live with depression are particularly likely to feel shame over what they perceive as failure. Give yourself a big pat on the back for every step in the right direction, no matter how small. If you skip exercise one day, it doesn't mean you're a failure of some sort and you might as well give up. Everyone goes off schedule at some point, no matter how good his intentions are, even if he doesn't suffer from the struggles of a mental disorder. Think of that old expression and chant it to yourself: "Get back on the horse!" You'll be glad you did.

Remember exercise can help to relieve tension, stress, sadness, and anxiety. Several studies have conclusively shown that regular exercise has a "tranquilizer effect" that decreases anxiety. By not only exercising but also *exorcising* your excess negative emotions and increasing adrenaline through physical activity, you can enter a more relaxed state of being from which to deal with the issues and conflicts that are causing your anxiety. Exercise is one of the best coping mechanisms to combat anxiety and stress.

Please note that exercise can sometimes offer only a short-term fix for anxiety. The relaxation induced by exercise lasts for only four hours or so, and the anxiety returns to its previous level within twenty-four hours. Therefore, if you are suffering from chronic anxiety, you will need to exercise nearly every day to see an effect. If you become anxious during the day, you may want to exercise first thing in the morning. On the other hand, if you suffer from insomnia, you may want to exercise in the late afternoon. Beware that exercising too late in the day may make it difficult for you to fall asleep.

Studies are inconclusive when looking at whether you need vigorous exercise to reduce anxiety. Some studies suggest that exercise should be fairly intense, but not exhausting, to best elicit the tranquilizer effect. Other researchers have found that light exercise, such as walking or swimming, decreases anxiety just as effectively as vigorous jogging does. Sports such as tennis, handball, golf, and biking have also been shown to help people relax. Again, choose an exercise that works best for you.

If you suffer from the physical symptoms of anxiety such as excess sweating, gastrointestinal distress, or a racing heart, you are likely to benefit from physical exercise. However, if your anxiety is caused by psychological causes—excess worry and ruminating, difficulty concentrating, or intrusive thoughts—you may find great relief from calming exercises such as yoga, tai chi, or chi gong, and mental exercises such as guided imagery, meditation, or self-hypnosis.

Start any exercise program gradually, and check with your family physician before beginning any regime to make certain you are in good physical health. If you exercise regularly, but depression or anxiety symptoms still interfere with your daily living, seek professional help. Exercise isn't meant to replace medical treatment of depression or anxiety.

Some people begin feeling so elated when they begin an exercise routine that they decide to wean themselves off their medications, often without informing their therapist or psychiatrist. This is unwise. Any regular exercise program can kick in feelings of not only joy and energy but also euphoria and clarity that are sometimes addicting and misleading, and can leave one with a sense of power over one's mood or anxiety disorder. It's best to let your health practitioner monitor any alterations in medication dosages, even if you are feeling better with exercise.

The benefits of regular physical activity are clear. Study after study has shown that exercise increases longevity while decreasing morbidity and mortality from a host of diseases. It also alters the brain chemistry, which alleviates symptoms of depression and anxiety. Someone once said that if exercise were a pill, it would be the most powerful medication known to mankind. The only problem is that it is difficult to inspire individuals to take that pill every day. Inactivity should be considered a destructive state or at least one that can lead to a host of diseases.

Don't forget to include sexual activity as part of your physical activity. Orgasm is a great release of muscular and emotional tension. Like other forms of physical activity, make sure it is fun, varied, and not stressful.

Stress and Health: Implications of Chronic Stress

Stress can exacerbate an existing physical illness as well as any mental disorder. When faced with chronic stress and an over-activated autonomic nervous system, people begin to see physical symptoms. The first symptoms, such as chronic headaches and increased susceptibility to colds, are relatively mild. With more exposure to chronic stress, however, more serious health problems may develop. These stress-influenced conditions include:

- Depression
- Diabetes
- Hair loss
- Heart disease
- Hyperthyroidism
- Obesity
- Obsessive-compulsive or anxiety disorder

- Sexual dysfunction
- Tooth and gum disease
- Ulcers

In fact it has been estimated that as many as 90 percent of doctor visits are for symptoms that are at least partially stress-related.

What You Can Do To Stay Healthier

To keep stress, especially chronic stress, from damaging your health, it's important to be sure that your body does not experience excessive states of this physiological arousal. There are three important ways to do this:

Learn Tension-Taming Techniques. Certain techniques can activate your body's relaxation response, putting your body in a calm state. These techniques, including meditation, yoga, deep breathing exercises, journaling and positive imagery, can be learned easily and practiced when you're under stress, helping you feel better relatively quickly.

Prevent Excess Stress. Some acute stress is unavoidable, but much of the episodic acute stress and chronic stress that we experience, and the type of stress that damages our health, can be avoided or minimized with the use of organization techniques, time management, relationship skills, and other healthy lifestyle choices.

Seeking Professional Help. Sometimes stress becomes so great that people develop stress-related disorders or need the help of medications, herbal treatments, or the aid of a professional. If you experience excessive anxiety or symptoms of depression, find yourself engaging in unhealthy or compulsive behaviors, or have a general feeling that you need help, talk to your doctor or a health-care professional. There is help available, and you can start feeling better and more in control of your life soon.

Whatever your situation, stress need not damage your physical health.[7]

CHAPTER 14

THE UP SIDE OF LIVING WITH DEPRESSION OR AN ANXIETY DISORDER

Is there an upside to being down? Are these disorders connected to creativity?

Some people may fall off their chairs when they read the title of this chapter. After all how is it possible that there are advantages to living with a mood or anxiety disorder? Yet many well-respected individuals from all walks of life, from creative types to deep-thinkers, would say that their work was a byproduct of their particular mental disorder.

Some of our most exceptional and imaginative people, from artists to business professionals to politicians, have lived with depression or some form of mental disorder. Well-known writers such as Ernest Hemingway, Tennessee Williams, Virginia Woolf, Herman Hesse, William Faulkner, and numerous others attempted suicide or were hospitalized in a psychiatric facility or asylum. Many famous poets, including Emily Dickinson, Sylvia Plath, Edgar Allan Poe, T.S. Eliot, Ezra Pound, Robert Lowell, and Anne Sexton, suffered with mood or anxiety disorders. Artists such as Paul Gauguin, Georgia O'Keeffe,

Vincent van Gogh, and Jackson Pollock were hospitalized at some point for mood or anxiety disorders. Composers and musicians can also be added to the long list of creative people whose lives were affected by mental disorders.

Actors and comedians who suffer or suffered from clinical depression or other mental disorders include Carrie Fisher, Dick Cavett, Jim Carrey, Vivien Leigh, Martin Lawrence, Ned Beatty, Linda Hamilton, Burgess Meredith, Ben Stiller, Heather Locklear, Patty Duke, and Jonathan Winters. Do you have all day? The list is lengthy.

In the early 1990s, Larry King hosted a one-hour show with guest Mike Wallace of the TV show *60 Minutes*. During the discussion Wallace addressed his own battles with clinical depression. As it turned out, that show had more viewer reaction than any previous Larry King show. There were many depressed people in America who related intensely to Wallace's story.

Celebrities can play a role in helping depressed people: when someone like news journalist Mike Wallace or writer William Styron acknowledges that he struggles with the disorder, it is easier for others to feel less stigmatized about receiving a diagnosis of depression. The general public is often surprised to learn that celebrities suffer with mental disorders such as depression or that they check themselves into rehab for an anxiety disorder. Why? Because to the people around them and to society at large, the celebrities appear just fine. In fact they seem to be high-functioning individuals who have achieved great success and happiness.

Mood or anxiety disorders can feature both good and bad characteristics. However, before taking action to deal with one of these disorders, it's vital to come to acceptance of it. Only then can one hope to turn some negative aspect of the disorder into a positive criterion.

Some people who live with mood or anxiety disorders discount their brainstorms before they have a chance to fully surface and become something beneficial. The negative thinking that surrounds depression and anxiety can put a quick stop to a brilliant concept before it has a chance to emerge.

Eric G. Wilson, the author of *Against Happiness: In Praise of Melancholy,* maintains that there is a critical need for sadness to exist and be recognized rather than run from or stamped out. Over time Wilson came to realize he was prone to depressive moods, and he has made peace with his downhearted state. It took him some time to do so, however. He read a plethora of books on how to become more content with the self and with one's own life. He tried smiling more. He tried to become more active, to get out of the house and away from his sadness. He finally became disgusted with these feeble attempts to be something he was not and decided instead to embrace his inner gloom. In his book he calls on others to do the same.

Wilson makes a point of saying that he is not romanticizing clinical depression, which he truly believes is a condition that should be treated. But his concern lies in the plethora of medications used to treat what he calls "mild to moderate sadness." He worries that in overmedicating conditions, our culture may become less vital and creative and certainly less interesting.

Melancholy, he argues, prompts people to think about themselves and the world in which they live in a more thoughtful and profound manner. Wilson urges others to get to know their partners, their families, and friends who live with depression and encourages them to embrace the darkness of their souls as well as the light. "Only then can you know that person."

It can be argued, however, that not all great artists or pioneers were depressive or even melancholy; therefore not all mood-altered individuals were or will be groundbreaking inventors or great contributors to society. Yet there is a scientifically proven relationship between brilliance and depression and between gloom and greatness, which suggests that a large number of our cultural groundbreakers have found their originality in their despondent moods.

Why is this? Melancholia seems to ram itself against the comfort of conformity in society. It thrives in unchartered territory. It forces us to reexamine our relationship to the world, granting us new vision and insight, and it energizes our mind.

Wilson points out in *Against Happiness* that the world can remain boring, familiar, repetitive, and habitual much of the time. Then along comes what Keats calls the "melancholy fit," and suddenly life becomes new and appealing again. New possibilities emerge.[8]

With all this said, it's equally important to consider that the highly glamorized belief that mood or anxiety disorders somehow heighten the creative genius among artists, writers and musicians might be a bit off the mark. We may hold this image partly because we romanticize the idea of artistic inspiration. For some, creative expression can be a way of making an intolerable situation (such as feelings of depression, melancholy and anxiety) more acceptable, or such expression can be a tool for diffusing its power.

It's certainly true that some forms of emotional distress *are* more common among artists, musicians, and writers. Serious depression strikes artists ten times more often than it does the general population. The link, however, is not creativity. Artists are more likely to be self-reflective, to ponder, to obsess, and to examine themselves or their lives in a detailed fashion. That thinking style, as opposed to creativity itself, is a hallmark of depression.

Evidence that madness does nothing to heighten creative genius comes from a study done by psychologist Robert Weisberg. He meticulously studied the creative output, along with the letters and medical records, of composer Robert Schumann, who was known to endure bouts of manic depression that drove him to attempt suicide.

Schumann wrote a great deal of music during his manic intervals. But quantity is one thing, and quality is another. There's more at stake than simply producing unique products; truly creative people must have the ability to tell a good idea from a bad one. Weisberg found that Schumann's compositional output indeed multiplied during his manic years, but the quality of his efforts did not change. When mania struck,

Schumann wrote more great pieces, but he turned out more ordinary ones too. Mania "jacks up the energy level," Dr. Weisberg points out, "but it doesn't give the person access to ideas that he or she wouldn't have had otherwise."

"Mild to moderate depression is part of my temperament, my personality," says John McManamy, a mental health journalist and author. "It is a part of who I am. If my energy is down, my thoughts tend to be very dark, but the key difference is I thrive in this state. My neurons are working with me or perhaps me with my neurons.

McManamy is the author of *Living Well with Depression and Bipolar Disorder: What Your Doctor Doesn't Tell You That You Need to Know*. He was diagnosed with bipolar disorder in 1999 at age forty-nine following a suicidal depression and a lifetime of denial.

"Here's the fallacy," he says. "If you are undergoing major or minor clinical depression right now, all those around you, including your psychiatrist, assume your brain will eventually boot back up to 'normal.' But if depression is a true part of your personality, you may already be imprisoned in your own version of 'normal.' There is no pill for changing one's personality, and heaven help us if medicine ever came up with one. Nor do we necessarily want to change our personalities. Far more productive is focusing on our strengths and virtues. My dual tendencies to think deeply and get depressed are so intertwined that it serves no useful purpose for me to try to separate the two. Whole new worlds open up to me. My life is far richer and more meaningful on account of it."

The world we reside in is full of good things to enjoy and be in awe of. At the same time, it is also a place of terror, devastation, stress, and sadness. The darker emotions of grief, panic, and sadness are seen as unwelcome guests. We all suffer from these emotions or from the ailments that stem from denying or deadening ourselves to them.

Each successive generation seems to emerge more depressed than the one before it. Millions more men and women will be diagnosed with phobias or anxiety disorders in the decades to come. Sleep disorders too are on the rise. Children are being diagnosed at younger ages and in increasing numbers. Mental disorders, which were once reserved entirely for adults, are now being applied to children. Diagnoses seem to have mushroomed.

If that's the bad news, what's the good news? It's that emotions themselves offer us a means of individual growth, learning, and healing. Painful emotions are a power to be reckoned with, and most people do, at some point in their lives, experience turbulence and mood challenges. The fact is great suffering can open the mind and the heart to otherwise unexplored gifts and realizations. Each mood or emotion has its own kind of wisdom or peril. Each has its purpose and its gift of transformation. Given half a chance, dark moments can move a person from grief to gratitude, from fear to surrender, and from hopelessness to optimism. What better way to appreciate the good stretches of time than to have lived through and survived the dark periods?

It is not the swings of mood that dampen our days the most, but in many cases it is the fear of those swings. We avoid, deny, or medicate them. We judge ourselves harshly, and we live in shame because of our threatening and murky thoughts. We shun them, and we run as fast as we can from the thoughts rather than concentrating on them. Artists, on the other hand, sometimes focus on the dark corners of their psyche. They pull them out, examine them, and release them to a canvas, a page, or a musical instrument. Emotions don't always mean there is something "wrong" with us. They can simply mean that we are alive, that we are feeling our lives and trying to contend with a stressful world or difficult circumstances. Depression and anxiety serve a purpose. Pain can sometimes be nature's way of drawing one's focus to an area of one's life that is in need of attention, care, or concern.

Fear is the emotion that seems to be shelved or looked at with shame more than other emotions, especially for men. However, fear is and always has been critical to our survival, both individually and as a species. It urges us to protect ourselves. Fear is the adrenaline surge of "fight or flight" that moves us to act. The trick is to maintain awareness in the midst of this powerful emotion, to allow this emotion to move through us, and to allow ourselves to feel vulnerable.

Sadness too has its uses. When we see something in ourselves that we cannot bear to accept, despair makes us face ourselves rather than look away. It gives us an opportunity to create meaning from pain. Experiencing sadness and other difficult emotions helps us to toughen our resilience.

We are told that it is abnormal to feel hopelessness or depression for more than two weeks at a time, regardless of events in our lives. "Contact a physician if your symptoms last longer than X amount of time." But anyone who has ever experienced depression or anxiety knows that coping with these mood disorders requires a great deal of time and stamina. They sometimes require scrutiny and space before they move on.

All of us, at one time or another and to one degree or another, experience the pain of being alive and being humanly connected to others. We can use the power of our most fear-provoking emotions for the purpose of healing not only ourselves but also the community of others who live with mood or anxiety disorders. Emotions are universal. Feeling and healing together is necessary, and these disorders can lead us to closeness with others who we have not yet experienced and would not have experienced without the gift of our highs and lows.

Experiencing our own crises and parade of emotions can help turn up our "radar" to catch the frequency of pain and suffering in others. It can prompt us to reach out to their cries when and if we are capable of doing so. Sometimes growth or healing arises when we find that we have something to give to others who are living with the same challenges. Each of us is a work in progress, and each of us has the ability to process the healing and lessen the pain in ourselves by reaching out to others in similar situations.

As Nicholas Cage's character says in the film *Moonstruck*, "We're not here to make things perfect. Snowflakes are perfect. The stars are perfect. Not us." Life can hurt. Serotonin can jump up and down without our permission. We are not in this life to be free of pain but to be moved and ultimately changed by it.

Lessons Learned from Mood and Anxiety Disorders

> *You don't throw a whole life away just because it's banged up a little.*
>
> —Chris Cooper as Tom Smith in *Seabiscuit*

To say that those who suffer are glad they developed a mood or anxiety disorder because it taught them more about themselves, about human nature, and about learning to appreciate the good in life is quite a rationalization. To find meaning in one of the most difficult circumstances in one's life doesn't necessarily make it a festive occasion worthy of celebration. Let's put away the party hats and balloons. Yet, more often than not, such struggles beget tremendous insight and ultimate contentment. People who effectively deal with their disorder discover what they are truly capable of, where their strength lies, that they can endure and survive, and most importantly that they have self-worth. This self-knowledge has the potential to fundamentally enrich lives.

One woman shared with us that her anxiety disorder forced her to slow down, which allowed her to truly experience her home life and examine her friendships more closely. She now does crafts out of her home and sells them on the Internet. She works in the garden and thoroughly enjoys it. She has created a beautiful and quaint home on the inside and out, where she enjoys having company visit. She has found a way to make lemonade out of lemons, as the saying goes, by exploring and expressing herself with more creative activities and interests.

Some people find they have more time for self-reflection and for a deeper spiritual life. Others find they are much more empathetic to other people and their problems, whatever they might be. One man reported that in the long run, having his disorder had forced him to look at his life more philosophically and less as a series of superficial work-related achievements. He had a greater appreciation of the magnificence of the world and the simple pleasures of family life.

Grappling to accept a diagnosis of clinical depression or another ongoing mental disorder, many people confront for the first time the sobering reality of their human limitations. "This is typically more difficult to accept with a mental disorder than with a physical malady," says Dr. Wampler, "perhaps because we identify even more strongly with our minds than with our bodies. Even if medication results in complete remission of symptoms, it's very humbling to realize that all our vaunted powers of intelligence and willpower can be derailed by a shortage of certain chemicals in the brain." However, this self-knowledge is accompanied by a major emotional and spiritual benefit: opening the door to discovery that we are no less worthy of care and love despite our limitations, despite a bit of funky brain chemistry.

We are all human. We have our frailties and moments when we are not feeling our best, when we are not emotionally resilient. It is not only okay but also healthy to share these shortcomings with one another. One of the most important lessons one can learn from a severe mood or anxiety disorder is that sometimes life's challenges cannot be overcome by sheer will but must be adjusted to.

CHAPTER 15

MOOD RIVER

Mind-Body Medicine and Moods

We find ourselves in an innovative era in which traditional practitioners are sometimes the ones to suggest complementary treatments or alternative care to their clients. One reason for this is that some mood or anxiety disorders with unrelenting symptoms are difficult to treat. Additionally there is now well-documented evidence to justify the increasingly widespread use of alternative medicines and complementary treatment approaches for both psychiatric and physical symptoms within Western populations.

"I am intellectually very curious," says TV talk show host Montel Williams. "I open my mind to all approaches to health: conventional medicine, nontraditional and alternative therapies, acupuncture, and Eastern medicine."[9] "Previously, I had been on various antidepressant medicines to cope with the depressive episodes that my physical pain made worse," says Williams, whose depression was brought on by living with the pain and other symptoms of multiple sclerosis. He felt that a newly adapted eating regime helped his symptoms of depression.

"I felt that my ebbs and flows were softer, that the emotional swings were not as severe, and that I didn't go into such deep spirals of depression. I felt the need for less medicine. The bad feelings were further and further apart."[10]

Some people simply do not handle well the side effects of medications, and some people do not like to take medications. Others reject the suggestion that they will have to be filling prescriptions for a long period of time, perhaps doing so for a lifetime. They choose to set out on the adventure alone, without the assistance of medication. "More often they misconstrue the prospect of disordered brain chemistry as an indication that they are somehow defective," says Dr. Wampler. This to them feels unacceptable. "In these cases I provide cognitive therapy, with attention to gently challenging their unwarranted refusal to accept humbling human limitations. Usually they come to understand that the physiological 'defect' underlying depression is no more personally shameful than a diagnosis of diabetes or any other medical condition."

Wampler also points out that a significant number of people who are successfully treated with medication return a year or more later, complaining of a relapse. "Upon inquiry they report that after a few months, they were feeling completely normal, so they went off the medication, counting themselves as cured. A few months after that, they fell back into depression. But the onset is so gradual and insidious that they forget that the medication was a crucial element of their prior recovery. For many people it's hard to come to terms with the fact that they have a chronic condition that may require lifelong medication."

While it's true that medication can have an enormous impact on moderate to severe depression, Wampler also points out that, upon the resumption of medication at the prior dosage, the depression doesn't always resolve. "For unknown reasons, a higher dose or a different antidepressant may be required the second time around."

Lesa H. has attempted some self-help methods that have been successful for her. "I have used a meditation and imagery method in which I close my eyes and focus on calm, deep breathing and picture a window with curtains of any color I may like at that time; and outside that window is me, and I'm wherever I want to be that is safe, fun, happy, and I am all three of these things. I focus on what 'me' outside the window is doing and what I am feeling, and I try to feel the same safe, fun, and happy thoughts wherever I am. This method I find to be very helpful."

Some traditionally trained practitioners offer treatment options that combine traditional psychiatric medications with complementary or alternative treatments. The new generation of trained therapists and psychiatrists is often more open and accepting of combined approaches such as biofeedback techniques, acupuncture, meditation, or herbal supplementation. Some alternative or holistic treatments involve mental or spiritual efforts. Meditation, relaxation, guided imagery, and hypnosis are but a few of these approaches. Scientists believe that the brain's ability to change physiologically through natural, self-produced chemicals is extraordinary.

Historically the existence of mind/body interactions was considered nonsensical by many traditional physicians who exclusively practiced Western medicine. However, there is a growing recognition that unconventional medications and treatments work well for a certain percentage of patients who participate in medical studies in which they are unknowingly given drugs with no medicinal value. This reaction, known as the placebo response, is thought to be a result of the power of suggestion, which can result in actual physiological changes. Ironically the very scientific methods utilized by conventional Western medicine in the testing of medications have provided the best scientific support for the existence and power of the mind/body connection. Given the proper environment, the brain produces powerful chemicals and medicine, able and willing to connect to and heal the body despite the absence of traditional medical treatments. As writer Norman Cousins wisely pointed out, "The placebo is the doctor that resides within."

Dan Harper, MD, used to be a traditional medical physician, but now he combines nutritional and supplemental therapies with conventional Western medicine. He sees a large number of patients in his practice who present with depression, anxiety, and other mental disorders. "There are many different biochemical pathways that can go wrong, all of which can be helped or corrected by natural as well as pharmaceutical methods." Dr. Harper feels that many environmental and genetic factors may play a role in the dysfunction of brain chemistry and in mood or anxiety disorders, but their effects can often be corrected by lifestyle changes, detoxification of the digestive system, and correct nutritional supplementation.

Dr. Jason Copping is a chiropractor and nutritional counselor who assists his patients with treatment through nutritional supplements. "I'm not thrilled with the current diagnoses that are floating around out there. Patients with anxiety often come in to tell me they have been diagnosed with depression or a variety of severe mood disorders."

The most common symptoms Dr. Copping sees in his office are fatigue, inability to sleep, exhaustion during the day, and muscle tightness. "Some people can't leave their homes as they have such severe anxiety or full-blown panic attacks."

He believes that many of these disorders are caused by vitamin and mineral deficiencies. "The most common element missing is calcium. Even if patients are on a calcium supplement, they can still present with low calcium because most of the store-bought calcium, if it is not food-based, is useless."

According to Copping, the cause of these vitamin and mineral deficiencies is the high intake of refined foods and sugars. "Every one of my patients with depression and/or anxiety has sugar every day; some of them have it with every meal. My most successful case was a person who came in with the label of 'crazy person.' She couldn't hold a conversation, let alone a job. She had sugar after every meal. I asked her to try to do one meal a day without sugar, but it was too difficult for her. So we approached a shift in her diet very gradually. We slowly weaned her down from the high sugar intake she was used to. Her personality completely altered. She now holds down a good job and speaks normally. We have accomplished moving 95 percent of the sugar out of her body, and it has made a tremendous difference."

At the same time that Copping asks his patients to make dietary changes, he gradually introduces food-grade nutritional supplements that replace what they are missing. "You can't go from an imperfect diet to a perfect diet overnight. Slow changes—that's the key. We slowly take out the bad dietary items, like soda, bread, and sugary desserts and replace them with good food choices—proteins, vegetables, and fruit. At the same time, we are adding supplements."

Copping feels that the most important elements missing in a person who is experiencing depression or anxiety are calcium, essential fatty acids, potassium, and B-complex (not separate B-vitamins). B vitamins in nature appear in a complete formula and are not found in isolation. That is how Copping feels we need to reintroduce them to the body.

"What the general public doesn't understand is that much of depression and anxiety, as well as other disorders, are caused by vitamin deficiencies. Everyone has a unique personality, but things such as daily stress deplete the vitamins and minerals from the body. We are often told that we have depression or anxiety or whatever because there is something wrong with us. Something is broken inside that needs to be fixed. It should help people to understand that many of the symptoms they are experiencing are caused by vitamin deficiencies. Many people have developed an intolerance to processed foods. Their bodies can't take them in anymore, and when they try to, dysfunction occurs. It is not their fault. And when I say vitamins, I'm not talking about the vitamins you buy in the drugstore but rather food-grade products that don't separate out the vitamins [from the other compounds]."

But aren't grains and whole wheat good for us? Copping says that wheat in this country is not only processed but also sits in silos for close to four years before heading to the grocery shelves. To keep it from going rancid, it is sprayed with substances containing mercury to preserve it and to kill the rats and such that run over it. "It's basically a poison. When people think they are wheat intolerant, it's likely that they are chemical intolerant instead."

Copping's patients do better on a steady diet of protein, vegetables, and fruit. "It's almost miraculous how their moods turn around. Some people do fine on dairy [products] such as raw milk, but not on pasteurized milk products, which tend to create mucus. Yogurt too is still processed as well as full of sugar. It's hard to get around that unless you make your own, which is labor intensive . . . and not too delicious!"

Mental health professionals who treat depression and anxiety disorders see the public's demand for such approaches and are conscious of the heightened awareness about them. More and more, clients opt for complementary treatments as an adjunct to a medication-only approach. The relaxation of tension and sense of empowerment diagnosed patients gain by contributing in a positive way to their own betterment can be extremely beneficial. If symptoms of anxiety can be decreased through such non-prescription treatments, quality of life is improved, even if the underlying disorder remains. Traditional Western practitioners are becoming more receptive to and supportive of these trends as they too realize the important role of the human spirit in the healing process.

Understandably many practitioners in the field of alternative medicine do not like the term "alternative" since many of these treatments have for centuries been considered conventional in much of the world. For instance, Western medicine is a more recent form of healing than acupuncture. In Africa, ancient America, Australia, Europe, China, and India, self-healing and self-care existed long before written history.

There is a wide array of anxiety disorders that are caused by an existential crisis. It's important to explore all issues related to anxiety and panic before going for the quick fix, whether that is medication, a supplement, or a vitamin. This holds true for other mood disorders as well. A powerful nutritional supplement is not going to fill the void in one's search for meaning, nor is it likely to address some of the more significant symptoms of other mood disorder.

What if you are experiencing a life crisis of some sort or are questioning your choices in career or relationship? The first step should be to explore, perhaps with professional assistance, any immediate cause of conflict. What brought you to these feelings you're having about life, and what might have precipitated your feelings of panic or anxiety? Are there practical and rather simple ways to resolve these inner conflicts, such as talk therapy, writing, or self-exploration? If not, perhaps guided imagery or hypnosis can assist you in getting to the core of the conflict. It is often not easy, nor is it possible, to simply think your way out of your conflict because a ruminating mind, going over and over an issue in an attempt to try to figure it out, is in most cases not capable of decreasing anxiety or resolving conflict.

Guided imagery can be helpful; it is quite powerful, and it can address mind-body issues. There are a number of other mind-body approaches that are useful, such as hypnosis or interactive guided imagery. Most cities have practitioners with experience in these modalities.

Various forms of meditation, such as mantra meditation, mindfulness meditation, and transcendental meditation, are powerful anti-anxiety remedies in themselves. A focus on breathing helps most people, but some may find it more difficult than using a mantra in meditation. Mindfulness, both as a meditation technique and as a way of being in the world, can assist in focusing one's attention on the body and away from overactive thinking.

People with anxiety, especially generalized anxiety disorder, often feel trapped in the corner. Their own minds are so busy and noisy that all attempts to stop the mind seem futile. Taming the mind sometimes requires a specific technique to shift one's mental focus, which is where mindfulness meditation can be useful. As previously mentioned, meditation techniques offer ways to focus on what is happening in the moment and on the sensations in your body, which will turn attention away from future and past events, worries, and thoughts. Yoga also helps focus thoughts on one's body instead of on one's anxiety.

Jim Callner is an educational speaker and president of the Awareness Foundation for OCD. He has lived with anxiety disorder and OCD for many years and utilizes various techniques to deal with his own symptoms "OCD is a fear-based anxiety disorder. Where does anxiety live? In future thinking! I call it futurizing. It is treatable with mindfulness and focusing on the 'now' rather than the future. OCD really doesn't like those of us who live in the present moment. Mindfulness is a path to recovery, but you have to work at it, moment by moment."

As noted earlier, panic and anxiety are caused by an autonomic nervous system that is in sympathetic nervous system overdrive (fight or flight response). Meditation and yoga dampen the sympathetic nervous system and increase the activity of the parasympathetic nervous system; this sequence can encourage feelings of serenity.

A variety of natural herbs are known to help some people who suffer with anxiety. These herbs include valerian, hops, passionflower, and lemon balm. The amino acid taurine has been shown to stabilize brain function. Those who practice in the holistic medicine field have great knowledge of these herbs and supplements, and they can give advice depending on the particular situation.

Other factors that can impact mood include blood sugar (low blood sugar can make you feel anxious) and thyroid function (an overactive thyroid will cause heart palpitations and anxiety). Adrenal function contributes to stabilizing blood sugar and also produces hormones that help one cope with everyday stress, so it's important to address adrenal exhaustion. With chronic adrenal exhaustion, people become overwhelmed with simple tasks that were once part of their routines. If anxiety symptoms include hypersensitivity to loud noises, bright light, or sudden changes in movement, and if fatigue is part of the picture, adrenal exhaustion could be a culprit. The best place to start with all of these issues is a simple lab test ordered by a knowledgeable practitioner.

CHAPTER 16

TRANSCENDING SPIRITUAL PAIN

Spirituality and Other Coping Skills

> *The real glory is being knocked to your knees and then coming back. That's the real glory.*
>
> —Vince Lombardi

Some see the purpose and need of religion as a reminder of our strengths and weaknesses as human beings, and some see it as a means of providing us with tools to help us deal with problems in order to maintain a healthy outlook. Spiritual beliefs can influence a person's choices, behavior, and responses to difficult challenges and experiences. Religion and spiritual beliefs also influence our thoughts and our conclusions on the experience of distress, and the characteristics of mental health challenges. In short, religion and spirituality can provide men and women with a philosophical frame of reference and meaning for their sufferings and challenges. Spiritual beliefs have often been able to lift a person up in the face of incredible odds and arduous circumstances.

Viktor E. Frankl was mentioned in the previous book, *JUST FINE: Unmasking Concealed Chronic Illness and Pain*, but his story and observations are relevant and so vital that his experiences bear repeating. When writing about concentration camp victims, Frankl noted that survival itself required seeking and finding the meaning to life's most difficult challenges. He was talking about prisoners of Nazi concentration camps, yet his observations apply to lives besieged by mood and anxiety disorders as well.

Illness, whether physical, mental, or both, is a compelling life event that causes us to ask grand and introspective questions such as, why did this challenge come into my life? Suffering and mental disorders usually ride in tandem. Frankl wrote that "Man is not destroyed by suffering; he is destroyed by suffering without meaning." He studied the mechanisms that appeared to enable victims to transcend their suffering.

Many people coping with mental pain, despair, panic disorder, or other challenging symptoms, seek to locate meaning in their suffering. This is where spirituality plays such a critical role. It is the relationship with a greater force, whether called God, a Higher Power, a Higher Self, Buddha, Nature, Krishna, Christ Consciousness, Cosmic Intelligence, or Spirit that provides comfort. This connection gives meaning and purpose to lives despite physical or mental anguish.

For many who find themselves living with chronic mental or physical pain, fresh or renewed spiritual growth and awareness often permeate a new sense of purpose within them. However, some conclude that there is no divine purpose or meaning whatsoever to the suffering induced by any disorder. Regardless of one's beliefs, once a depression or anxiety disorder strikes, a person can grow by using what is learned to better himself and others who are facing similar circumstances and challenges.

"I don't feel that I'll awaken and my symptoms of depression and anxiety will all be gone. I pray for it!" says Karen A. "I've been struggling with depression and anxiety since I was a teen. I've been through a lot in my fifty-three years, and God knows I've been tested more than my share." For Karen prayer is her coping tool. It helps her believe that things will get better. It helps her gain strength for those difficult times. It helps her believe in miracles that might lift the struggles she endures from her shoulders. That belief in a future of relief and respite is enough to keep her going and maintain some optimism in her stride. "I keep reassuring myself that things happen for a reason, and only God has that information. I tell myself that I am human. I am worthy. I am lovable, regardless of how I feel about any particular situation. My religious beliefs have been affected by my disorder in that I pray more often and try to leave everything in the hands of my God."

For many, religion or some sort of spiritual or philosophical thought is what sustains them through life's most difficult days. Many who have found themselves in the clutches of severe mental distress or a multitude of mood shifts and discomforts have searched for answers, for a guide to lead them, and for some form of comfort. They need to make sense of their circumstances and move to a place of wisdom that offers a tangible perspective of the big picture. Through the pain of their depression, anxiety, or other symptoms, they sometimes come upon a new path offering a fresh way of looking at the world. This helps sustain them through the worst of times and feed their positive feelings about living during the best periods.

"I believe in the mind, body, and spirit connection when it comes to mental health," says Rob H., who suffers from depression. "Regardless of the pain or condition one is dealing with, having some type of spiritual practice that allows recognition of how one's life fits into the world is vital."

Rob H. relies on the practice of Nichiren Buddhism as an important part of his life to help him deal with chronic pain. "Through this practice I become more aware of the law of cause and effect: for every action there is a reaction." For Rob and others, Buddhism helps followers see that the key to happiness, despite their dark moods or anxiety, is up to them.

Others rely on the religious faith that they learned in childhood, whether Christian, Jewish, or Muslim beliefs. Lisa A.'s depression and health challenges impacted her spiritual beliefs in a profound manner. "For years I was angry with God for what I'd been given. Then there was a period during which I prayed for healing." She is now at what she feels is an amazing and more serene stage, where she has made peace with her mood disorder. "I now accept what I've been given, and I pray to God that He will give me a good day, lessen my pain, and use me to help others through my challenges."

Scherry C. suffers from anxiety, depression, and panic disorder. She feels that the disorders she's been struggling with have definitely impacted her beliefs. "I have become far more spiritual and in tune with God since I was diagnosed. I never believed God doled out pain and human suffering like candies to a trick-or-treater. I've always subscribed to the thought that God is seldom as interventional as we humans like to believe. I feel that our problems and issues are ours and ours alone to figure out. We have free choice in all things. We can derive strength and courage from God, but life, death, and the dramatic events that unfold in between those states are simply part of a great cosmic play. What we make of our time here is far more important than how long we have to act in the play. I pity those who believe God is responsible for death and suffering, for many will lose faith when their prayers for healing are not answered. I have never once asked God to take away my suffering because I know God did not give it to me. I ask for the courage to survive another day with some semblance of usefulness, grace, and dignity."

But for others who may be extremely devout, they concede that their religious fervor can diminish when their psyche is in agony. All too frequently severe episodes of these disorders can damage a long-standing religious belief. Sufferers begin to question their faith, their God, and their place in the world.

From the time Vivian was in her mid-forties, she had suffered from dysthymia (a chronic, low-grade depression) and social anxiety. To make matters worse, she could never figure out what was wrong with her. Her religious faith was unsteady at this time and she found she had little to call on for strength or perseverance. "I didn't even know that I suffered from two diagnosable and treatable disorders. I just always figured that I would someday outgrow my anxiety and blue moods. But all along my social anxiety was quite the conundrum. I had a good sense of humor, and I needed the affection of others. But I was afraid of people! Who would ever understand that?"

As so many who live with social anxiety do, Vivian began self-medicating with alcohol. Initially it appeared to lift her spirits and reduce her anxiety. But this dependence soon led to alcohol abuse, and finally to addiction. "It was only after alcoholism was added to my list of ailments that I took the time to really analyze what was going on, to really take a look at myself and at what drove me to self-destruct. What triggered my craving for alcohol? And so it turned out that social situations were high on my relapse triggers list. To a certain degree, I felt redeemed when I discovered why I kept returning to alcohol even though it had devastating consequences on my life."

Vivian discovered she suffered from depression and anxiety only after she was inadvertently treated for them with a small amount of an antidepressant, which was aimed at her alcoholism. "It was like I couldn't see what I was suffering from until I was out from under its spell. It was only after I began to feel better and was able to see the light of day, that I could grasp what I was really dealing with."

Depression and anxiety ran in Vivian's family as it does in many people's families. Her mother had a history of being anxious and despondent. "During the last few months of her life, she was so depressed she rarely left her bed. Seeing no other solution, she finally took her own life, leaving a devastated family who still mourn her . . . She lived before there were any effective medications available to help her."

For Vivian a small dose of an antidepressant made all the difference. "I noticed relief from depression within weeks of first being treated with selective serotonin reuptake inhibitors (SSRIs). It took longer for me to realize that I wasn't as anxious around people anymore and that my extreme self-consciousness was gone."

Alcoholics Anonymous works well for many but was effective for Vivian only after her anxiety and dysthymia were under control. Once she found the proper medications for her particular symptoms, her symptoms were soothed, and a once unsteady faith was renewed. Alcoholics Anonymous, along with treatment for her depression and anxiety, placed her footing on the suitable path for her particular recovery and for a return to her faith. "This spiritual twelve-step program brought me back to God and renewed my Christian faith. No matter how things are going, I now know that with Him everything will be okay."

Clearly religion can play an important role in crisis situations. However, religious attitudes can evidently change in crisis periods as well. If the climb is too steep, sometimes one's faith and belief system take a temporary or permanent tumble down the mountainside.

Judy R. was suffering with severe depression coupled with a chronic autoimmune illness that had thrown her career plans, schooling, and social life into disarray. When her preparation to rebuild her life with schooling and training had been crushed, she became depressed, and she felt defeated. As we sat and discussed her most recent ordeal with her disease, she mentioned the phrase, "God doesn't give us more than we can handle." With tears glistening in the corners of her eyes, Judy looked up at the ceiling, forced a laugh, and said, "God, I think you must be on a coffee break 'cause I don't know how much more of this I can handle." Her laughter was loud, but her smile was quiet and small. The depth of her anguish was apparent. Depression was weighing her down, and her faith no longer seemed to give her the strength she required or had hoped for, at least not in the weight of this heavy hour.

Jan W. suffered with chronic depression and anxiety. She found that not only did her religion *not* offer her the peace and comfort it once did, but she would also actually pray for release from her pain or to simply not awaken one morning. "I have no hope that I will ever get better," she shared. "In fact I usually feel it's all getting worse."

Sometimes faith is an exceptional coping mechanism. During other challenging times, however, people with severe mood or anxiety disorders may surrender a dearly held belief system. At times ongoing symptoms can test stamina, faith, and even the will to move forward. When one is at their worst—when one has hit the bottom of the ocean—seeing or remembering the sun shining above the dark waters is very difficult. When people have been dragged down too far for too long, they often cannot recall better and brighter times. It is easy for them to forget that people care about them and their well-being. Being depressed or in despair for too long induces amnesia. Sufferers forget about life's pleasures, lose a little faith, and temporarily misplace their seemingly distracted God.

Clients attending counseling sessions with a therapist may be asked about their religious or spiritual backgrounds or may be asked if they pray. If they do have a belief in a personal God, the therapist may bring the idea of God into the sessions if, for instance, issues of blame, anger, or coping are involved. Religion is a widespread and important influence on human behavior and well-being, which is likely why it is now finding its way into the therapy office and into particular practices and treatments. Religion may serve as a potentially effective method of coping for persons with mood or anxiety disorders, thus warranting its integration into psychiatric and psychological practice.

Using prayer during a session or directing a client to refer to important books of worship or spiritual reference, using religious texts to reinforce positive emotional habits, or keeping a spiritual journal are all practices that are sometimes introduced if the client makes it apparent that he is open to it and it is a part of his religious background or spiritual path.

CHAPTER 17

THE PAIN CHAIN

The Link Between Chronic Illness, Pain, and Depression

When someone is faced with a serious diagnosis or a chronic illness or condition, it is easy for depression and anxiety to slip in. Why? Any such health challenge can easily increase a person's feelings of hopelessness and helplessness, which in turn can act as triggers for depression and anxious thoughts. Since the symptoms of depression, such as stamina changes and fatigue, mimic those of chronic illness, it is easy to overlook depression as a co-diagnosis.

When people are diagnosed with major depression, they obviously have a depressed mood. But new research is showing that depression doesn't exist in a vacuum, and that the condition is associated with many other chronic health problems, from diabetes to asthma and arthritis. Being depressed actually worsens the effects of other physical illnesses. I am not referring to simply feeling down about a chronic physical problem. People with various medical problems often may feel discouraged about their condition, but they usually don't become severely depressed.

However, clinical depression may be having a negative effect on other illnesses one may also be experiencing.

"In the last eight years I've been living with multiple sclerosis," writes Montel Williams in his book *Living Well*. Multiple sclerosis is a potentially debilitating autoimmune disease that affects the brain and spinal cord. "One of the effects of my condition is that physical pain is a constant companion in my life. The feeling ranges from a constant 'dull roar' of pain that I feel all the time, 365 days a year, to episodes like the one that came close to hitting a ten on my personal Richter scale of pain, a feeling so intense that on two occasions I came very close to killing myself."[11] People cannot always see the symptoms of physical pain and illness, just as they cannot see the physical evidence of depression and anxiety. "Every single day, people walk up to me and ask me about my health. They stop me on the street and in airports, and say things like, 'Hey Montel, I heard there was something wrong with you. But you look okay.' 'Geez, Montel, you don't look sick. You look great!' Sometimes that makes me feel good, and I appreciate people giving me positive thoughts. But sometimes it cuts very deeply and it almost hurts, because I *am* sick."

"Just last week in my TV studio, a man in the audience stood up and said, 'Montel, it's really funny, man. I heard a little while ago that you used to be sick or something? You used to have something wrong with you? But you look great, so everything must be good, right?' My answer was, 'Thank you so much. I appreciate it. But believe me, I'm sick. You just can't see it, like you can't look around the room and pick out someone who has cancer. The truth of the matter is, you didn't watch me get out of bed this morning. Sometimes it takes me twenty minutes to get from my bed to the bathroom! Because ten minutes in-between is me stuck on the chair crying because my feet hurt so bad.'"[12] There are days that the pain is so excruciating that Montel Williams literally can't find his feet. He can't tell if his feet are on the floor or not. "There are times it hurts so bad that I'd go into a closet and scream my lungs out. That pain helped plunge me into spirals of depression."[13]

Physical illness can, and often does, trigger depression. One pathway may have to do with cytokines, a natural part of the body's immune response to illness. In fact when some patients are treated with a certain type of cytokine, they become depressed or even suicidal. In addition "a mood disorder can potentially affect the body's ability to fight an illness," says David Spiegel, MD, of Stanford University School of Medicine. Stress can lead to arterial spasms and heart attacks, even if one's arteries are clear. Additionally people with a history of depression are at least three times more likely to suffer from heart attacks than their non-depressed peers. In fact depression can be ranked equally with high cholesterol or family history of heart disease as a risk factor for heart disease. Depression is also associated with a poorer prognosis for a number of diseases including stroke, epilepsy, and type 2 diabetes. Bottom line: get treatment for both your physical illness and your depression.

A recent study published in the British medical journal, *The Lancet*, backs up the compounding effect of depression by suggesting that chronic illnesses become even more disabling in people who were already depressed. The authors go on to suggest that the depression itself may be more disabling than common chronic conditions such as angina, arthritis, asthma, and diabetes. Based on these and similar findings, it makes sense for primary care doctors always to consider whether their patients are depressed when evaluating them for chronic conditions.

Experts say that up to 50 percent of people who suffer from depression go undiagnosed, many of them among those who regularly see their doctors for other reasons such as asthma, heart disease, and diabetes. The patients themselves often minimize their symptoms of depression as they are struggling with so many other issues. They don't realize that depression is an illness like any other and that it's necessary to ask for help, whether it is psychotherapy, medication, or a combination of both.

People who suspect they may be experiencing depression should mention to their physician such symptoms as persistent sadness, thoughts of life being worthless, changes in sleeping patterns, changes in appetite, and less interest in the things usually enjoyed. If you are depressed, treatment won't merely improve your mood. It might also help with other health problems too.[14]

In a report that appears in the January 2008 edition of the *Archives of General Psychiatry*, researchers have shown that war veterans dealing with PTSD have an altered response to painful stimuli when compared to war veterans not affected with PTSD. The team that performed the study collected data by applying specific temperatures to subjects' hands and recording their reported levels of pain. They also measured brain activity during stimulation. As CNN reported:

> When exposed to the same temperatures, PTSD patients rated them as being less painful than did the comparison group, Dr. Elbert Geuze, from the Central Military Hospital in Utrecht, the Netherlands, and colleagues report. Similarly, the temperatures that elicited the same subjective pain rating were higher in participants with PTSD than in the others. During testing, PTSD subjects displayed increased or decreased activation of several different regions of the brain, compared with the veterans without PTSD.

Those who suffer a trauma or accident that triggers chronic pain often have PTSD as well as depression. University of Michigan researchers examined the contributions of PTSD to the pain experience, functional disability, and frequency of depressive symptoms. There were 241 patients in their study that took place in the hospital's pain rehabilitation program, all of whom reported pain that began after a traumatic injury. They were administered three different tests, including the pain disability index and post-traumatic chronic pain test.

Results revealed that depression and PTSD are significantly correlated, and both disorders are linked to perceived disability that has been ascribed to chronic pain. As a result, in cases of disabling, accident-related pain accompanied by depression, symptoms of PTSD may be critical to understanding both disorders. Increased attention to treating PTSD as a primary focus in this population of patients (who have depression along with chronic pain) is important when prior efforts for treating pain and depression only have proved to be unsuccessful.[15]

Why pain and depression appear together is not altogether clear, but it is thought that pain and depression share common brain chemicals, or neurotransmitters (serotonin and norepinephrine). These neurotransmitters assist in regulating mood states and may intensify pain when they occur at low levels in the brain. For example, the limbic portion of the brain not only regulates and receives pain signals, but is also the center of emotions. That's why, when a problem arises in the limbic area of the brain, pain can also increase as well as anxiety and feelings of sadness.

Depression, anxiety, decision-making, and sleep disturbances all can have an impact on pain levels or perceived pain, which in turn can harm the brain. Chronic pain has a widespread impact on overall brain function, which may explain some of the behavioral and cognitive challenges seen in these individuals. Additionally chronic pain may lead to permanent reorganization of the brain. That's why it's imperative to receive early, aggressive treatment to alleviate chronic pain. It may prevent associated conditions such as sleep disturbances, cognitive impairment, and depression.[16]

For instance, fibromyalgia, a chronic pain disorder, is highly unpredictable. There are days when a person will barely be able to pull himself from the couch or bed. On other days that same person may be sufficiently pain-free and have enough energy to manage a grocery shopping excursion, pick up things around the house, make dinner, or have a fun conversation with family or friends. "The typical problem that these people seem to encounter," says Dr. Shelley Slapion-Foote, "is that when they do have a good day or a good couple of hours, they are so happy that they are feeling decent that they do more than their body is actually able to handle, and then they find themselves back in bed for a few days, weeks, or months." This setback or "flare-up" as it's sometimes called, can lead to waves of depression, feelings of hopelessness and helplessness, and self questioning about whether they will ever get better. This perpetuates a downward cycle, which probably only serves to make them more focused on their preexisting pain and their inability to participate in normal life events. "Then, with these feelings, come the waves of depression that are also debilitating and help to make the person feel even worse than the physical pain is already making him feel."

This vicious cycle repeats and repeats itself, and many sufferers of similar pain conditions have a very hard time regulating how much they do at any one given time for fear it may bring on another pain cycle. For some people, the pain, fatigue, and depression of chronic illness are sufficiently debilitating that they are forced to take extended leaves of absence, and others must give up their jobs entirely. "Now," says Slapion-Foote, "added to the pain and other chronic symptoms, these people must cope with feelings of failure, uselessness, loss of work companions, and, perhaps worst of all, loss of income."

While people with fibromyalgia and other chronic disorders are considered eligible for disability payments through the Social Security Administration, the process is a long and tedious one that frequently must involve a lawyer who specializes in such cases. The entire process can take several years, which then causes the person with health challenges, as well as family members, more anxiety in waiting for it to finish.

One aspect of fibromyalgia is "fibro fog," so named because the disorder impacts one's memory, particularly short-term. Depression can and often does impact short-term memory in the same manner. It robs the person of the ability to recall what might have happened just a few minutes ago, a day ago, or weeks ago. The memory can become impaired, and things that would have been easily recalled in the past are now often forgotten. "This can come in the form of forgetting what one is doing or saying, or in the forgetting to do something that was promised yesterday," says Slapion-Foote. "In that the majority of these individuals are used to juggling many tasks at one time, this loss of the ability to manipulate as many thoughts at one time as they had been able to do in the past is most distressing. It is often one of the first things that clients will mention when they come into therapy, after they have stopped being teary or crying because they feel so terrible and think what they are feeling isn't real. These memory problems cause problems in all aspects of life including work, friends, and family, as well as in the everyday tasks of daily living."

These lapses in memory and judgment are more than an occasional misplacement of the car keys. They can range from the simplest of things like forgetting to turn off the bath, leaving pots on the stove until the water boils out and the pot burns (an obvious fire hazard), and locking oneself out of the house, to more complex tasks such as remembering lunch and doctor appointments, meeting work deadlines, or attending important meetings.

Lorna A. not only lives with depression and anxiety disorders, she also lives with the chronic pain of fibromyalgia. "If I can get a better handle on the constant pain I have with fibromyalgia, I think many of my symptoms will lessen. The combination of chronic pain and the depression and anxiety feed off of each other," says Lorna. "The more pain I have, the more down I feel. And the more anxious and depressed I get, the more pain I end up experiencing." It's a vicious cycle.

People sometimes forget that depression is an illness that includes both physical and emotional symptoms. Physical symptoms may include dizziness, gastrointestinal distress, heart palpitations, or general feelings of uneasiness or unsteadiness. People who live with depression may experience similar symptoms and complaints in regard to physical pain, limited activities, and disability as someone who has a physical illness.

Just as it can help improve one's mood, exercise can be of great assistance in improving physical well-being. Simply spending a few minutes each day (or nearly every day) performing light strengthening or stretching exercises can help control pain. Other techniques that assist with pain include massage, breathing exercises, and practices such as mindfulness meditation.

Kent Bennington, a medical and family psychologist, has found that chronic pain sufferers, who are often depressed, as well as his other emotionally distressed patients often benefit from participation in a semi-structured, eight-week, mindfulness-based stress reduction course.

Coping with anxiety, depression, and feelings of loss that often accompany ongoing pain or a chronic illness can intensify feelings of isolation and being different from others. The good news, however, is that studies show the benefits of treatment for depression may extend beyond a person's mood and actually help lower pain levels, which in turns enhances quality of life.

CHAPTER 18

THE FICKLE NATURE OF BRAIN CHEMISTRY

One of the realities about depression and anxiety disorders is that there are good days and bad days. The nature of the beast is that its course is unpredictable. You may be diligently pacing yourself, getting enough rest at night, staying away from problem circumstances that have in the past set off a bad period with your disorder, or meditating to take the edge off stress and still the bad episodes come to call.

Psychologist Cassandra Friedman feels that unpredictability is the greatest obstacle faced by those who live with a mood or anxiety disorder. "Most have conditions where what they do on a daily basis has changed drastically. First they make an attempt to go on as they once were, and they soon realize that they cannot."

Sometimes you can see a link between a particular activity and a bad episode, but at other times there seems to be neither rhyme nor reason for your plunge. During these periods, when symptoms unexpectedly ebb and flow, the only certainty is the difficulty experienced with social events, travel plans, work, or school responsibilities. Release from symptoms is an occasional gift but never a given.

Living with an ongoing mood or anxiety disorder requires coping with uncertainty. Some people have an easier time "going with the flow" than others. People who are used to feeling in control have a more difficult adjustment to their new way of being in the world. Their minds are flooded with questions that come from feelings of vulnerability and helplessness. Will they be able to take care of their children today? Will they be able to leave their house this morning? Will they be able to get through a workday tomorrow? Will they have to contend with unbearable distress, anxiety, flashbacks, or panic when they go out tonight? The list of adjustments involving family and friends, jobs and careers, child care and vacations can grow quite long very quickly.

Some people learn to pamper themselves when a difficult episode comes to call. Perhaps they crawl into bed with a book, sip some tea, or sit next to the fireplace. They may watch their favorite old film or take a long walk in nature. A sufferer's awareness of going into a difficult episode can help them deal with it effectively.

Some people beat themselves up during an episode and blame themselves for its onset. What did I do to cause it? Why can't I be like other people? What's wrong with me? Why am I so weak? We must all see ourselves as human during these times. Would the ill person berate someone who is physically ill in the same way they berate themselves? Probably not. The episodes are real, and minds have limitations. Working on honoring limitations is a worthy goal. Understanding that the patient did not cause the mood or anxiety disorder and that others are dealing with similar mood disorders is well worth remembering. A sufferer is not alone; it is possible to get beyond a difficult time.

Some people who experience frequent episodes try to accept rather than fight them. Bad periods do not become best friends, but they are part of the mind's process and need not be the enemy.

THE FICKLE NATURE OF BRAIN CHEMISTRY

There is only so much anyone can do when brain chemistry is not behaving normally. People who live with chronic mood or anxiety disorders must give themselves credit for doing the best they can with a difficult situation.

CHAPTER 19

TO SHIELD OR REVEAL

The Key to Disclosure

*Every step of the journey
is the journey.*
—Anon

Let's face it—even in twenty-first century society, mental disorders such as depression, anxiety, and panic attacks still carry a stigma. Many people still hide them like a secret or view them as a weakness. What will people think? What will they say? How will I explain it? They will never understand if I do tell them, so why don't I just keep quiet?

Those who have depression and anxiety disorders and those who seek help for these chemical imbalances often feel a sense of embarrassment. Many of psychologist Shelley Slapion-Foote's clients do not wish to be contacted at work for fear of someone finding out that they are seeing a mental health practitioner. "The biggest thing that the general public doesn't seem to understand is that psychological problems and mood disorders, specifically, are not the creation of the person who is experiencing difficulty."

We as a society need to recognize and remember that the brain is an organ just like any other. To speak unkindly about a mental disorder, or joke about it or about a person who suffers with a mood or anxiety disorder is akin to mocking someone with kidney disease, diabetes, or heart problems. Yet there remains a stigma attached to these brain malfunctions and the circus of chemicals that sometimes fall out of balance. People who live with these mood or anxiety disorders have to confront the ugly sense of shame each day, despite the fact that they are certainly not alone. Mood disorders can safely be called epidemic in today's society.

Disclosing a mood or anxiety disorder is quite different from revealing a disability that is, or will become, more obvious. After all no one ever has to know that one suffers from depression, anxiety, or panic disorder, do they? They cannot see it, and therefore it does not have to be revealed. A visible disability does not permit a choice about whom to tell, how much to tell, or when to tell. When the illness is visible, information becomes public rather than private knowledge. Surprisingly some people with a concealed mood or anxiety disorder say they would opt for a visible health condition over their concealed one. Why? So their limitations would be taken more seriously.

If you decide to tell others about your mood or anxiety disorder, whom do you tell? Do you keep it hidden from the scrutinizing eyes of coworkers, supervisors, friends, and family? Whom can you trust with this significant secret? Will your symptoms worsen if you tell others, or might they improve absent a disguise of smiles and high energy? Will you feel like a failure in the eyes of others if they see in you what you perceive as a flaw? Will they reject you? Will they doubt you? After all, you look perfectly happy and healthy to them. You *look* just fine.

If you do decide to reveal your mood or anxiety disorder and the challenges it presents, how much do you reveal? Should you remove the mask of illusion entirely, or should it remain in place?

If you do not wish to be viewed as being an "unstable" or "crazy" person, deciding whether or not to disclose your mood or anxiety disorder, or to disguise it, is very difficult. There is little doubt that opening up to potential partners about your depression or anxiety disorder can be stressful and risky. Many people who live with a concealed chronic mental disorder often have to make a choice about if, when, and to whom they disclose their illness. And they have to repeatedly make this difficult choice in each new relationship and in each new job.

In a sense revelation is akin to "coming out of the closet," and it can be challenging for several reasons, one of which is your own struggle with acceptance of your disorder. You may find it difficult to accept the limitations posed by the disorder, especially if it leaves you with a self-image of being weak, needy, unusual, or even unworthy.

However, seeing yourself as someone who stands out as different or strange can be experienced across a spectrum from uncomfortable to intolerable. You are actually projecting your own internalized biases and stereotypical beliefs about what being a person with a mental disorder means. You may fear that the same social influences that helped create these biases in you form the same negative beliefs in others and will therefore impact their perceptions of you in a negative way.

Depending on a person's situation, disclosing a mood or anxiety disorder can sometimes mean a loss of advantages such as employment, the respect of colleagues, life insurance benefits, friendship, or marriage. In truth only those who live with mood or anxiety disorders can rightfully determine what the true cost of disclosure would be to their well-being—and whether they are ready and able to handle the outcome.

"When people think of illness in general," reports one man who suffers with debilitating depression and anxiety, "they depend on seeing the results of that illness manifest in some visual way so they can compartmentalize it, justify it, and eventually accept it. Not so with depression. They can't see it, so how can they figure it out or accept it?"

"People cannot see how sad and anxious I feel," reports a woman who lives with panic disorder. "How can they believe it if they can't see it with their own eyes? How could they possibility know how deeply this knife cuts into my soul?"

"People never truly understand your limitations," says another woman, who has lived for many years with the easily concealed symptoms of her disorder. "Others may ask me to do something that is as impossible for me as walking on water. I have to keep reminding people what my limitations are. Heck, I have to keep reminding myself!"

There are some who will blame your limitations on a bad attitude or sour disposition. The most ridiculous assumption is that, because the pain is psychological and unseen, it is not real. Psychological pain is some of the most significant and intense pain a human being can endure. Attempting to will oneself out of a clinical depression or anxiety is simply an exercise in frustration.

"What they cannot see, they question as being real," says another young man who lives with severe depression. "They are less compassionate if they have never experienced the discomfort themselves. I look perfectly fine to them, so I must be. Well not so."

"How are you doing?" or "How are things going?" are two of the most difficult questions to respond to if you look healthy but are suffering with a mood or anxiety disorder and an array of concealed symptoms. How can you describe something you yourself don't truly understand and, oftentimes, are unable to acknowledge?

Once you have lived with an ongoing depression or anxiety disorder, finding the correct response is complicated and confusing. Do you really feel fine, or do you simply say that you do to avoid a delicate moment between you and a person who is, after all, asking about your well-being? You may feel that revealing depression or anxiety to someone will change or strain that relationship. You may risk feeling less in their eyes, or worse, you may be doubted and scrutinized. When you live with an easily concealed mood or anxiety disorder, "How are you?" becomes one of the most complicated questions you can be asked.

For most people, revealing their depression or anxiety disorder means facing possible rejection. If one appears serene, healthy, and happy, why would anyone believe otherwise? The dilemma of disclosing often turns into the issue of control or lack of control. Avoiding disclosure can mean maintaining distance, regulating the flow of information, and therefore preserving one's control over the entire situation. Since power and control are the very elements that diminish or are challenged when one is living with a mood or anxiety disorder, disclosing that you are depressed or anxious can further complicate the illusion of control and power. A concealed mood or anxiety disorder can cause loss of endurance and function that only a discerning eye can detect. Most people don't have such keen vision. As a result of this, family, friends, and coworkers may discount the person's disorder or fail to comprehend how it can possibly affect the sufferer. After all the person affected appears perfectly competent, clear-minded, and "okay." He looks just fine.

There are plenty of reasons to fear disclosure. Despite the feelings of dread surrounding this issue, disclosing a mood or anxiety disorder is one of the most important elements in any significant interpersonal relationship for a number of reasons. As an example, the depressed individual often turns inward and is preoccupied with his problems and mental "noise." On the outside, the sufferer of the mood disorder seems oblivious to the needs of others. If family members, friends, or partners are not aware of the mood or anxiety disorder, they make assumptions. They may assume the person is no longer interested in them, doesn't care about them, is not listening to them, or is moving away from them in heart and spirit for any number of reasons.

Trying to figure out the cause of a loved one's problems or the reason for distant or troubling behavior can cause great anxiety and depression for everyone around the sufferer. It is easy for the person with the mood or anxiety disorder to *not* disclose the illness. They may feel shame about it or have a million other reasons to hide it. However, those who orbit around the person may be imagining problems and scenarios that are much worse than the truth.

Part of the success of disclosing one's mood or anxiety disorder to others has to do with how comfortable that person is with his own disorder. The more comfortable he becomes with his symptoms, the more comfortable others will become. Strangely that is often how it works. If it is no big deal to the sufferer, it won't be a big deal to others.

CHAPTER 20

DEPRESSION AND ANXIETY IN THE WORKPLACE

Employment and Mood Disorders

Cathy W. felt as though a lack of concentration due to her clinical depression was going to be a huge hurdle in a work environment. "There always seems to be a little message in my head repeating over and over that I am just not working fast enough or well enough. I can't shut it off."

"Having to cease working because of my depression and anxiety disorders was difficult. I sometimes still struggle with it," says Jan. W. "I'll see an ad in the newspaper and know I could do the job if only I wasn't sick. I did try to go back to work briefly, before my disability status was approved, but I was only able to work about five hours per week. That in itself was very depressing!"

If you decide to do so, how do you go about revealing your mood or anxiety disorder to your supervisor without risking the security of your job or your position in the company? One suggestion is to go in and say, "You may or may not be aware that I suffer with depression. I am getting treatment for it, and I am able to control most of my symptoms. I'll make sure that my disorder doesn't become your problem. Just allow me to do my job." That's what a manager wants to hear: that you have a problem, that it is being treated, and that you will make sure it does not affect your job or become a problem for them. This is a very in-control way of saying that you have health difficulties, but you won't let them impact your job.

What if you, like many people do, choose to keep your mood or anxiety disorder secret, but you have to miss work here and there because of the symptoms? When there are frequent absences, management tends to think that the person is just not committed to the job. Under those circumstances you may want to go to your supervisor and disclose privately that you have a condition that results in some unpredictable and difficult symptoms, but they don't usually last for very long. If you are not at work for a day or two, that's probably why, and you are certainly not playing hooky.

Developing a plan for disclosure is a valuable project. This helps you determine when, how, and what information will be revealed. The decision to disclose or not disclose is a personal one. Either way involves some risk. Will you lose your boss's respect if you tell him about your mood or anxiety disorder? The other side of the coin is that you may be granted more reasonable hours and assistance with your workload. Disclosure can be a double-edged sword; arguments can easily be made for revealing or not revealing a mood or anxiety disorder in the workplace.

The first thing you need to do is understand your rights. Places such as Cornell University Law School have websites that link to every state's employment laws. Once you know where you stand, go to your supervisor and ask if you may have a candid conversation in private. People often get into trouble when they have to miss work due to their mood disorder and try to cover it with a trail of lies and tall tales. You don't need to specify whether you have a physical or mental challenge—that's your business. But share that you have some personal challenges (going into as little or as much detail as you feel comfortable with or as your state laws require).

Ask for your supervisor's discretion if you share anything specific about your disorder.

Shame and mental disorders go hand in hand when it comes to employment, providing for families, and being able to earn a living. Many people who live with severe mood or anxiety disorders are no longer able to maintain a job or career. They are living on Social Security disability income or another form of disability income, a combination of both, or having family members support them. Not only do they struggle financially, but their self-image has taken a tumble and a beating in the process of being unable to maintain a job or remain employed.

Marty W. went to school to be a licensed practical nurse but had to give that up. She then got a job working in a factory, but her pain was so bad she wound up calling in sick too often and was subsequently fired from her job. "I was terminated from my temporary job in February 2007 due to calling in sick. I have major pain issues, and I found it very hard to go to work every day. At first I felt humiliated because of getting fired and worthless because I couldn't work like 'normal' people without calling in. I had never been fired before in my life, so this was very hard for me. I am receiving unemployment benefits at this time until I can find another job or apply for disability. I have feelings of grief about my inability to fulfill my goals and aspirations I had for my life due to chronic illness. I feel like I've failed in my life. This causes a lot of grief, feelings of worthlessness, and humiliation."

Sandi H. is a wife and stepmother of two children, and volunteers at her church in her community. She struggles financially as well as emotionally and physically as a result of not being able to hold a job outside the home in a consistent manner. She shares that "our family budget is highly affected since I am unable to work. That puts a lot of stress between my husband and me. Also, with my being tired and often anxious, we often cannot do things together as a family."

Claudia G. feels a great deal of shame as a result of not being able to work, especially because she was so active and successful before her mental disorder became so intrusive and disabling. "Now that I am not able to work or go to school, there is a big hole in my self-esteem. I am having a difficult time trying to find other ways beyond work to fill the gap. When people I haven't seen in years come up to me and ask me how my graduate degree is going, and people that I have just met ask me what I am doing with myself, I always get this horrible, sick feeling in my gut, and I feel a sense of incredible shame and embarrassment. As a result I have tried to throw myself into a job or just jump back into school hoping that this time it will be different, only to fail and to feel even worse about myself as a result."

Formerly in the military, Robin T. knows this same sense of failure all too well. "I have lost my work life/career and ability to work. That part of my life is over. In some ways it is a relief because it was becoming extremely difficult for me. On the other hand, I fought against stopping because I had worked since I was sixteen (I'm fifty-eight now), and my work has always defined who I am."

Sharing this familiar feeling of failure is Lorna A. who, after twenty years of gainful employment, is unable to continue working at a job she enjoyed. "I have felt a loss in my self-confidence since I had to quit working. I had a job that I loved, and I felt financially secure in my life. That has changed. I beat myself up a lot for not being able to do what I used to do. Now I have little energy and too much pain for me to concentrate enough to hold down a job."

Pamela D. does hold down a job but has difficulty concentrating on her job duties and handling stress. This problem of relying on her mind and memory has cost her four jobs.

Martin W. lives with depression and obsessive-compulsive disorder. After he was married, his income allowed him to put his wife through law school and helped them purchase their first single-family home. "Since I grew up in New York City and always lived in apartments, this home was an amazing achievement for me." After Martin became ill with depression, however, they lost their house, and he and his wife separated. "Not working and not being able to support my family, specifically my two children, has caused me to experience many negative emotions.

I constantly fight feelings of guilt, even though my kids always tell me not to feel guilty. They constantly tell me, 'It's not your fault you became ill. It could happen to anyone.'" But Martin still experiences constant guilt and negative feelings about himself and his inability to provide for his family's financial needs. "I think to myself, I'm a failure, I'm a terrible father. I'm almost sixty, and I have absolutely no money while everyone else I know is doing great financially."

Guilt issues over not working have always been bad for Linda N., who has been out of the workplace for over twenty years. "Early in my life, it was mostly shame I felt because I didn't work. Then after working for twelve years and supporting myself, I felt totally guilty when I could no longer work." It was Linda's belief that most people felt she didn't work simply because she was lazy. They didn't know about her depression and panic disorder and how severe the symptoms were. Today she shops in thrift stores for used and recycled goods. "I have lived this way most of my life, and I think feeling guilty about not working has a lot to do with it. If I don't work, I am not worthy."

It took Jan W. two and a half years to be approved for her Social Security disability benefits, even though all of her doctors agreed she was unable to work. "It was extremely stressful, emotionally and financially. I had no income until I decided to draw from my investment accounts; I had to pay taxes and penalties on all of that. Then I was without medical insurance for over a year."

Nona L. received Social Security benefits rather easily and quickly but felt great shame that she did. She wanted to work. She didn't want to be on disability or have a mood or anxiety disorder that prevented her from working, but that was the boat she found herself in. "I used to be an information technology manager who was very industrious and creative and always believed in doing the impossible—and succeeding. It's too bad it did not last. I'm now ashamed of my disability status, and I don't like to talk about it. It made me give up my job that I cherished. I now know I don't have a career anymore, and all my past hard work and intellectual assets have been reduced to nothing. I am in a state of mind/

body meltdown, or what I call 'vocational-vacation,' and because of that, I cannot have a work life or career. Others don't give me any credit for what I am going through, and they don't understand why I cannot work or why I look good and present as being happy. They fail to see what's inside."

Not defining yourself as your mental disorder is essential. You are not your depression, just as you are not your PTSD and you are not your OCD. You do not need to describe yourself by the illness. Another person explained, "I am clinically depressed, but that is simply something I live with; and have I to be aware of my condition. It does not define the human being that I am at my core. It is simply a chemical imbalance and an illness that I must contend with."

CHAPTER 21

HOLD ON

Remaining Hopeful and Cope-ful

*When running up a hill,
it is all right to give up as many times as you wish,
as long as your feet keep moving.*

—Shama Marita, MD

Those who live with anxiety disorders and depression often have difficulty with feelings of uncertainty and confidence. Unanticipated shifts in jobs, relationships, or health often exacerbate an already difficult journey. When an unforeseen obstacle comes into the path of a person already struggling with a mood or anxiety disorder, it is easy to fold like a house of cards and feel a victim of circumstance. "Woe is me" becomes the mantra of those times. Feelings of hopelessness and helplessness set in. What can one do when the world seems to be conspiring against one?

One simple approach that seems to help during these times is to remind ourselves that whatever happens, we will handle it. Saying that over and over to oneself, to cancel out the "woe is me" mantra, is a good start at beating down the negativity that often accompanies bouts of anxiety and depression. The truth is you've handled mountains of problems in the past, and you'll handle this one too. Looking to a hero at these times is also useful. Do you have a personal hero you can picture in your mind at times of uncertainty? Gandhi? Christopher Reeve? A local philanthropist?

Coping with the Difficult Days

Contending with a chronic mood or anxiety disorder is challenging if you have family responsibilities, but what about the countless single men and women who must fend entirely for themselves and care for their own needs with no family support? How do they cope with such daily responsibilities as shopping, driving to and from therapy appointments, cleaning their homes and cooking their meals, all the while bombarded with overwhelming despair, anxiety, fatigue, and an unending parade of symptoms? Difficult days can become a full-time job.

What part of your illness can you put in the background if only for a short while? Have a visit with someone you love. For that moment you can welcome your joy to the foreground, even if only slightly. Keep inviting those inspiring, meaningful moments into your life. Most of the time, life is all about small and precious moments.

Hope springs eternal for those who suffer with mood or anxiety disorders, even when they are dog-paddling in the depths of despair. Nona L. suffers with depression, anxiety, and panic disorder. She still holds onto hope that one day she will awaken and all of her suffering will miraculously disappear, like a white rabbit in a magician's hat. "I feel that life is filled with surprises, and that one day I'll lose all my mental pain and the memory of pain and start gaining back my life, my old self, without much effort. When I do, I will do my best not to regress."

Marching through the darkness of depression and maneuvering around the maze of anxiety is not an easy expedition. Sadly it is not always possible to emerge from the march unscathed or even to escape the maze at all. The people who live with mood or anxiety disorders are soldiers who wear the uniform of normalcy, yet they wake each day to fight a personal battle of survival. They put a protective guard over their face—a mask, so that they appear calm and acceptable. They appear just fine. They appear fit and ready for combat, but within they wage a seemingly endless struggle, hoping they will pass safely through another day.

Behind the brave front lay the demons of doubt and depression. If we could see how dark and heavy these burdens truly are, we would jump back in astonishment. But the soldiers hide these heavily weighted secrets well as they can often be easily concealed from sight. To the world around them, the person with any mood or anxiety disorder seems to be confident, competent, and just fine. But the reality for these people is often quite different from their outward appearance. Their look of calm and confidence belies the pain that lies just below the surface.

Most people have experienced fleeting feelings of sadness that are often referred to as the blues or bouts of temporary woe. Such moods can gnaw around the edges of a deep depression. These short episodes of sadness, hopelessness, or helplessness often come after a bad day at work or on the heels of a curt word said at an inopportune moment. Clouds of distress can sometimes drift through our beautiful blue sky. That's life, they say.

These are the romantic notes of melancholy. Such casual sadness appears in the lyrics of a song, in lines of poetry, in the prose of a novel. It is sometimes played out in the downturned expression of an actor on film. Bouts of sadness are part of everyone's life. However, clinical depression runs deeper and stronger, pulling one under like a powerful current running beneath the outer image of tranquility, where everything and everyone appears just fine to the outside world.

Terry Wise, the author of *Waking Up,* describes the feeling behind depression in this way: "Beauty had no pleasure, music had no melody, and food had no flavor." For anyone who has experienced profound depression, these words will resonate. The malady of clinical depression can be like a fierce and frightening dip on a roller coaster. It can drop us so low we barely recognize ourselves when we come up for air. Those who are familiar with mood or anxiety disorders realize that these are serious illnesses, and that they require treatment that often includes the chaotic dance of hit-and-miss medications that tinker with brain chemistry. Depression can derail relationships, jobs, and in some cases, lives. It can paralyze us, make it impossible to speak or interact with others, immobilize us so we cannot drive down our own street, or even leave our own house . . . or room.

We may never know the reasons for many of life's mysteries or the answers to probing questions about the nature of mental illness and psychological pain. Who gets singled out for such distress and who does not never seems quite fair to a logical mind. Perhaps that's because it isn't fair. Many things in life simply are not. Nevertheless each of us needs to make peace with our state of mind and the limitations of our own psyche. We all have a wondrous, yet often flawed machine, the human mind, to take us through an entire lifetime.

Many paths lead to the same destination. In the case of chronic mental disorders and challenges, the destination or goal is not necessarily to become completely well but to learn to accept what life has handed us. It may not always be a welcome gift—this one of ongoing symptoms and unpredictable days—but rather an opportunity to learn more about our inner strength and the importance of the people in our lives. It is also a chance to use the gifts within that would have otherwise sat dormant.

Mental disorders can put us on notice that life is short; sometimes sweet and sometimes bitter. They force us to reexamine priorities and the way we spend our time. They can prompt us to take stock of friends and family and their value in our lives. Sometimes learning to be compassionate with ourselves is a far more difficult assignment than caring for others. Psychological pain can sometimes force us to care for and about ourselves in new and profound ways.

Our differences as individuals pale when compared with our shared experiences and emotions. This bond can provide extraordinary comfort to those who suffer in silence and feel isolated. Sharing experiences and feelings and eradicating the barriers that are part and parcel of depression and anxiety disorders are addressed in the final section of this book, where not only the faces but the stories of those who live with depression and anxiety disorders are candidly shared.

No one chooses to have a mood or anxiety disorder that brings pain and discomfort. When struck with severe depression or anxiety, people sometimes feel compelled to return to their past selves and rejoin their old routines. We ache for a time when life was not only comfortable but predictable. To accept a new and limited way of functioning is not very appealing. Why should a person want to live happily in a mind that feels out of order?

The good news is that despite the annoyances and various stages of grief, most sufferers eventually do learn to coexist in relative peace with their mental disorder. They ultimately learn to make space for a new reality. They learn to dance with the psychic pain using new steps. They discover what they can now do rather than what they used to do.

A long time ago, a therapist passed along this old Chinese saying to a woman who was moving through her own difficult storm: "In crisis there is both danger and opportunity." Mental anguish, although painful, can prove a pure and profitable teacher; it can challenge and guide us through periods of extraordinary change and growth.

To accept and care for our psyche as it is now, and not simply as we would like it to be, is perhaps the biggest challenge and greatest achievement we can have in this life. Mental illness, whatever its form, cannot be beaten by the power of sheer will and determination. In fact some do more harm than good when they push themselves unreasonably through a bad episode and try to imagine it away. Learning to honor limitations is a massive accomplishment, and each person has daily opportunities to attain this worthy goal.

Transformation and growth is difficult, but there is comfort in knowing that as we stumble through the process of change, so will millions of others. We must learn to pay attention to one another, to look beyond the guise and into the story that lies behind the facade. Each person and every face featured in the last section of this book has a crucial tale to tell about their journey. The reader has to peer very closely at their faces, as if looking beyond the eyes and into the soul. Read each individual's testimony and study the true story that lies behind the mask. Many feel obliged to present to their family and friends (and sometimes themselves) a pleasant, happy, and calm demeanor. Seldom, however, do facial expressions correspond to the devastation that depression and anxiety bring into one's path. A pleasing demeanor projected to the world is often in direct conflict with the chaotic and uncomfortable internal existence.

Maintaining hope and learning to trust in your strength as a human creature will help you handle whatever life hands you. Life truly is a symphony filled with towering highs and daunting lows. Learning to endure what you can, and reaching out for assistance to help you contend with what you cannot, is the most constructive and courageous way to live with an ongoing depression or anxiety disorder. The heartbeat of this proposal can be summed up in a philosophy repeated in countless twelve-step meetings across the country for a host of challenges and addictions: "Grant me the serenity to accept the things I cannot change, the courage to change the things I can, and the wisdom to know the difference."

Today there are more beneficial treatments and resources for these disorders than ever before. Support groups for specific mood or anxiety disorders meet regularly, both in person and online. Camaraderie and information are only a mouse click or a telephone call away. Numerous organizations exist for particular disorders, such as the Anxiety Disorders Association of America, Depression and Support Alliance, National Alliance on Mental Illness (NAMI), and countless others. They provide educational information and support to those with mood or anxiety disorders and to their family members. There is also a vast amount of research underway. Medical scientists and alternative health-care professionals are learning to recognize and better control the severity of episodes and symptoms of many mental disorders.

- Learn as much as possible about your disorder.
- Locate a considerate and knowledgeable mental health-care team.
- Realize that you are more than your mood or anxiety disorder.
- Use what you have learned about your disorder to assist others if you are able.
- Pay attention to your limitations and honor them.

Learning to feel hopeful is perhaps the most effective treatment for all chronic conditions. Napoleon Bonaparte once wrote, "Courage is like love; it must have hope for nourishment." Acceptance and hope are two of the most critical skills that are learned over time and often through trial by fire. The featured people on the following pages have achieved, or are in the process of building, a new level of acceptance and hope into their everyday lives. Each of these individuals is at a different stage of adjustment to a new reality. Some are newly diagnosed. Some have lived with their disorder since childhood. Each person's viewpoints and experiences are worthy of examination because each stage of adjustment is an important piece of the puzzle. All individuals must learn to adjust and cope with an ever-changing landscape of symptoms, challenges, and emotions.

Many people are continually engrossed in a mental focus that revolves around their perceived limitations due to their mood or anxiety disorder. These feelings of being restricted due to their symptoms can inhibit self-esteem and leave one feeling "less than" one's peers. "They are normal, and I am different," or so we conclude.

For other people specific circumstances may provoke episodes of mood or anxiety disorders, such as unhealthy and stressful relationships, work pressures, or travel across time zones. In these cases, episodes of mental disorders are not caused by biochemistry alone. Environmental factors can trigger an individual's genetically determined predisposition to certain symptoms, yet we often feel we should be able to will away fears, phobias, anxiety, depression, and other unpleasantness. We become extraordinarily good at blaming ourselves for our illness, even though we know that we cannot predict or control every environmental trigger or stressor or manipulate our genetic makeup. What we fail to see is that everyone (including the apparent "normal" individuals all around us) is contending with his own host of conditions or symptoms that limit his self-esteem and potential.

Here is the real story. Are you ready for it? We are all dealing with something that challenges us and often makes us feel different from or less than our peers. It could be physical, or it could be emotional. Some people are gifted at sabotaging themselves. Others are suffering from loneliness, or an inability to connect with someone from their past or gain approval from a beloved family member. Some people have diabetes and feel restricted by their diet choices. Others cannot go into a crowded store. Still others have a memory of failure from years past that determines their ability to be successful in the present. Each of us is walking around with a secret.

We are all imperfect, yet we present ourselves as flawless beings. We are all suffering in different forms. We all fall short in different areas. We are all hiding a secret that we hope no one will discover. What a different world this would be if all people walked around with their worst fear about themselves displayed on a huge sandwich sign slung over their chests. "I'm scared of rejection." "I stink at relationships." "I'm afraid you won't approve of me." "I feel worthless." "I feel terrified." "I can't enjoy a party." There would not be one sign that would not have its message repeated a hundred times over . . . perhaps a thousand times over.

It's mindboggling what some people have had to contend with in their complex and arduous existence. Life is sometimes a demanding series of tests. Most of us assume that we, and we alone, are fundamentally different from everyone else. But if we could truly see through the facades of those around us, we would realize that most people are donning a mask to conceal what they have to contend with.

The truth is most of us have some sort of scar we are trying desperately to camouflage. Some scars are psychological, and some are physical. Most go unseen, but we still feel they weigh us down, separate us, and keep us from being a whole or a significant part of the mainstream. In short all of us are not so different. We share many of the same reactions, experiences, coping mechanisms, and fears. We are all struggling, and we all want the same things for the most part: the love of others, inner peace, and successful relationships.

Every one of us is faced with extraordinary challenges in our lifetime. The men and women profiled in this book are no different. They have, at some point in their lives, found themselves immobilized, at a dead-end, or faced with a sudden bend in the road. A bit bewildered, overwhelmed, and discouraged, these courageous people have begun to cope with their challenges. Their treatment plans may vary, but their will to continue to plow ahead, to solve the puzzles, to tackle the obstacles, and to ride the waves that sometimes pull them under is their common goal.

Coping mechanisms, temporary and long-term solutions, treatment plans, stumbles and successes, emotions and experiences are all candidly discussed within this critical portion of the book. The stories of those at the start of their journey, as well as those who have developed a formula for facing their darkest days and their near-fatal fumbles, are equally vital. Every person featured may not have effective coping skills or wisdom to share just yet, but they are all on a path where they continue to learn, to struggle, and to grow. They are in their own wilderness, and they are learning the survival tools that fit their lives.

The readers of this book who find themselves contending with their own mood or anxiety disorders may likely see a part of their own story reflected in these pages. Perhaps they once had similar questions and concerns. Every viewpoint, perspective, story, and stage of coping and acceptance is worthy of exploration.

The photographs on the following pages remind the reader that a picture does not always disclose the entire story. A facial expression can offer an impression that runs contrary to the reality of an inner world of experiences and emotions. These pictures are not worth a thousand words. In fact they *require* verbiage to help tell the complete story.

I hope that those who view these photographs will take the time to read and consider the experiences, feelings, and observations that run contrary to the outward appearances depicted. Looks can be deceiving even to the most insightful and keenest eyes.

Some final words of hope:

> *Research continues on a grand scale*
> *to uncover answers for OCD*
> *and a wide spectrum of anxiety disorders.*
> *We are not alone.*
> *There are always better treatments, new tools,*
> *and many reasons to feel hopeful.*

—Jim Callner, President
Awareness Foundation for OCD

CHAPTER 22

A GLANCE BEHIND THE MASK

> *I am not afraid of storms
> for I have learned how to sail my ship.*
>
> —Louisa May Alcott

The individuals featured in this book are survivors. All have found themselves dazed and confused by their own internal challenges that often go unseen by the outside world.

In this final chapter, which is perhaps the most vital and telling portion of *But You LOOK Just Fine,* each person discusses the emotions, experiences, coping methods, and the specific challenges they've endured.

Readers may find themselves on a similar journey, contending with baffling brain chemistry and muddied confusion. Perhaps they share similar concerns, issues, and involvements. Every person's viewpoint and voyage is valid; every story deserves to be told.

The photographs on the following pages remind the reader that a picture does not always reveal the true story. One must look deeper and read further. A smile or a calm demeanor may offer an impression that runs in direct contrast to the reality hidden within. By combining the real-life stories and struggles beside the portraits, we hope to reveal a more complete and valuable account that will benefit both those sharing their tales and those reading them.

Jenni P.
Her story . . .

Generalized Anxiety Disorder (GAD), Panic Disorder, Depression

I am a freelance writer for an online resource for young women who live with chronic illness, but who strive to live a full life despite their challenges. I was diagnosed with depression and anxiety when I was twenty-two years old. However, I have been experiencing anxiety since I was a little girl and depression since I was eleven or twelve years old.

My episodes of depression start with feeling sluggish, tired, and cranky and include headaches and body aches. I begin to feel as if "I don't want to talk to anyone or go anywhere," what I call "hermiting." Nothing seems interesting, important, or urgent.

My episodes of anxiety begin when I notice I am gritting my teeth, making my face, neck, and shoulders tense up and start hurting. My heart races, my face flushes, I get a headache, and my entire body aches. I may also have abdominal and intestinal cramps, and sometimes muscle spasms. During a panic attack, my mind will start spiraling out of control, and I will start to obsess about little details and worst-case scenarios. I can't sleep, and I feel jittery. Nothing seems more important than the little thing I'm freaking out about.

Anxiety has a real impact on balancing my work life. Because I work for myself, I sometimes worry that I won't be successful or that something will go wrong, and a key source of income for my household will disappear. When I'm feeling anxious, even the smallest hint of concern can mushroom into a freak-out; therefore I try to build things into my day that remind me not to be concerned or anxious.

In the past my anxiety about income has driven me to work with undesirable clients, just because the money is good. Sometimes that wasn't even the case; the money could be really small, and still I would just take a job because I needed cash, and there wasn't anything else on my plate at the time. Decisions like that make work awful because I'm doing something that's not interesting or is frustrating, or working with someone who doesn't value me as a person or doesn't appreciate the work I do. I worked with a business coach for about a year, and during that time I learned that once I stopped accepting those crummy jobs, I would have room in my life for good jobs. It works! The more I do that, the less anxious I am, and as a result I am more productive and more profitable. So the anxiety was really holding me back professionally.

> *I encounter people who think I'm not doing anything to treat it, that I use it as an excuse ... Nothing could be further from the truth.*

It wasn't always the case, but I am now aware of how to manage my symptoms a bit better. Management may mean taking a break from work to meditate or take a bike ride. It may mean journaling, or calling a friend to talk through the issue. Because I've done a lot of work to learn my symptoms and to discern what is triggering them, I'm pretty fast to recognize when they are manifesting, and usually I can calm down quickly. Occasionally I'll still have a major panic attack, and then I will take some medication and lie down to try to calm myself with relaxation exercises.

I use a lot of coping tools to help, such as relaxation, journaling, networking with friends, exercise, humor, distraction, or medication.

Relaxation techniques such as visualization, meditation, and diaphragmatic breathing are all excellent. I took some biofeedback training, which helped me learn how to relax specific muscles or areas of my body. Writing and keeping a journal works wonders too. If I'm working through a real challenge, I'll write out all of my issues on a piece of paper and then write out the realities that seem so elusive. For example, I might agonize over the decision whether or not to take a low-paying, freelance writing job. I need the money, but the work will be awful. So I'll write out the pros and cons and then write out a few statements to remember, like "I'm worth $100 an hour, not $50 an hour," or "If I take this cruddy job, I won't be able to take the next great job that comes," or similar ideas. I might carry this paper in my pocket for a couple of days or stick it on my bulletin board so I don't forget.

I have a great network of friends, and I'm not shy about telling them that I'm anxious. Usually I can find someone to spend ten minutes with, talking through an issue. Alternatively, riding my bike or heading to the gym almost always helps. Having a good sense of humor is a great skill. I laugh a lot about silly stuff that I've done during anxiety episodes or panic attacks. My husband and friends keep me laughing about it too.

A movie, a book, or anything that will distract me from the symptoms will break the cycle, and I'll start to feel better. When things are bad, I'll take medication—not often, but occasionally. It really takes the hard edge off my anxiety, and then I can go back to the less intense self-care methods that I've already talked about.

I had all kinds of symptoms arise when I was a child, but they were a mystery to me at the time. Now I understand that they were symptoms of anxiety. I would get a sudden wave of "homesickness" although I was at home. I would get nervous before standing up in front of classmates and have to run to the bathroom with cramps, diarrhea, or vomiting. In high school I would wake up with bruises on my thighs. At first I thought someone was coming into my room at night and hurting me, which was incredibly frightening, but I was afraid to speak up. Then one night I woke up out of a bad dream and found myself curled up in a ball with my own hands gripping my legs with a ferocity I never would have imagined. I would have anxiety dreams all the time. My heart would pound so fast that I thought I was having a heart attack.

These are all incredibly frightening things for a child to experience, especially because when we are young it's hard to articulate what we're feeling. I would try to explain these experiences to my parents, but they either weren't receptive to hearing them, or they didn't understand them. Who knows? When I started having attacks shortly after college, I thought it was the first time. Yet the more I learned about anxiety, the more I understood I had experienced it from a very young age, probably as young as four or five years old.

A few people in my life have told me to "just relax" or "calm down," and that makes me furious. It is just not that simple with anxiety. Others don't seem to understand that of anything in the world, what I would often most like to do is relax and calm down, and yet my body and mind fight me. So that's incredibly frustrating.

I also encounter people who think I'm not doing anything to treat it, that I use it as an excuse or as something to fall back on when I don't want to be responsible. Nothing could be further from the truth. The fact is many of my anxiety attacks happen when I'm trying to be overly responsible, trying too hard to be perfect, to satisfy the desires of others in place of my own, to achieve everything on an unwavering schedule. So being responsible often makes the anxiety worse. If someone told me I could learn to be a little irresponsible, I would consider it! It surely would take a load off.

There have been times in my life when I thought I would never stop being anxious or depressed. During particularly difficult periods, I have felt as if my life is on hold, that I'm not able to live up to my potential, that I'm a burden to others, or that I should just go away somewhere by myself. Those are awful thoughts! I've had them a few times. Once in the cycle of self-destructive thought patterns, it can be hard to break them. My chronic pain condition is worsened by these patterns, and it also feeds them by complicating matters. So at rock bottom, I have felt as though nothing mattered, that I should just give up and go on Social Security and consider myself "disabled."

Then when I'm out of a bad cycle, and I've gotten myself out with self-care, I can see the light at the end of the tunnel and feel hopeful that I can beat it. I've stopped believing that I'll never be anxious or depressed again because that's just not realistic. I can see the possibility that my anxiety will be minimized, that my depression will be minimized, and that even when I feel awful, I have mechanisms in place to stop the cycle and get me equalized again. When I come out of a down period, and I recognize that fact, I try to write down my feelings—write about what helped so that I can turn to those steps again. And in those moments, I feel a great deal of hope, of control over my life.

John M.
His story...

Depression, Bipolar Disorder

I've been an outsider on this planet for as long as I can remember. A lot of it has to do with my depression and my propensity for thinking deeply. I can't separate the two. Back when the other boys my age were listening to Top 40 music and talking about girls, I had classical music going on in my head and was contemplating how ironic it was that Hannibal had never won a battle with his elephants. How did it feel that no one cared about Hannibal and his elephants? Well, very depressing. My mother thought I was just feeling sorry for myself.

I'm convinced there are various selective advantages to depression. Thinking deeply is one. Psychic healing is another. It's as if we're responding to an ancient imperative to crawl into our caves and lick our wounds. In time we return into the light, whole, resurrected, and able to face whatever may come our way one day at a time, and much more in touch with our humanity and divinity.

This just in: modern society makes no provision for our crawling into our caves. If we don't show up for work, mentally alert and on top of our game, we are going to become marginalized very fast. In many ways depression is the Rip Van Winkle disease. A person enters into the long sleep of depression in one world only to experience a very rude awakening in an entirely different place. The future, thought about, no longer exists. The present renders impossible any thought of a future.

Fortunately I managed to claw my way back but only because I was able to imagine an alternative reality. Trying to live a normal life in a crazy world doesn't work for me. There is no way I can hold a regular job. I need a situation that plays to my strengths and makes allowances for my vulnerabilities, one in which my time belongs to me. Oddly enough, my main strength is my ability to contemplate things like Hannibal's elephants and write about those things.

I work from home; I am self-employed. I like to joke that my boss is a cheap bastard and my employee a lazy, good-for-nothing slacker, but the two of us manage to get along. On my bad days, when my brain fails to boot up, my "boss" gives me time off. I retreat into my cave, take a walk, do something different—whatever I need to be doing to avoid becoming undone. Then I'm back doing what I love and actually getting paid for it.

Nevertheless I am living a very precarious existence. At all times I am fully aware that I am one mere crash away—mental, or physical, or economic—from my whole world caving in on me.

Mindfulness, the mind watching the mind, is my real mood stabilizer. I simply can't afford to have a depression sneak up on me from behind. Over the years I have learned to be microscopically attuned to my mood, energy, sleep, and anxiety levels. If I can spot a depression coming on early from a mile away, I can prepare for it. Sometimes I am able to nip an incipient depression in the bud. At other times I manage to pull myself into a protective crouch position.

> *I found out the hard way that the best way to get nothing done is to try to get everything done.*

These days, thanks to mindfulness, my depressions are more like the flu rather than double pneumonia. I don't kid myself. Somewhere out there, I know, this constant traveling companion that I call Fred is lying in wait for me in some dark alley. If I see him first, he will smile, wish me a nice day, and retreat back into the shadows. Should he get the drop on me, Fred will show me absolutely no mercy.

Mindfulness is also how I manage my stress levels. When I sense the world becoming a bit too much for me to handle, I'm smart enough to stop and smell the roses. I found out the hard way that the best way to get nothing done is to try to get *everything* done.

There is scientific support for the proposition that our depressions have something to do with mammalian hibernation. I certainly need to hibernate, but I also need to be out among people. In this regard, the gift of my introverted temperament—the seat of my deep thinking—is also my worst enemy. I have an unfortunate tendency to withdraw into a comforting isolation, one that invites depression in.

Yet something funny happens when I'm around people: I perk up. I laugh. I joke. Those around me mistake me for an extrovert. It's not an act. This is the real me, but what they don't know is that my psychic batteries run down very quickly. In no time a huge energy drain hits. It's like someone has pulled the plug. Often I need to retreat into a quiet corner, or I may crash right after I arrive home, which means taking at least a half day off the next day. If I have been on the road for several days, I need a good five days to fully recover.

It took me practically my whole life to figure this out. On one hand, being around people is my best antidepressant. On the other, too much stimulation invites a total system collapse. These days I know how to sync people's expectations of me to my power surges and drains. I will always be well rested going into a meeting. I will show up way early, and I will give myself plenty of time afterward for decompressing.

As you can guess, I don't exactly pack a lot into my day when I'm out in public. The person I'm meeting may be giving me one hour of her time. I'm giving her three or four hours of mine.

Loving relationships quickly blow my cover. Everyone knows about depression, but few appreciate the fanatical effort it takes to successfully avoid it. Three hours of negotiating the zoo with a date is more problematic for me than Stanley searching for Livingstone.

If I say I need to chill out with a bite to eat right now, it means right now. Any old taco stand will do. My date is thinking there's a much nicer place to eat by the gorilla enclosure that will take only a few minutes to get to. I'm thinking no one in the history of the zoo has successfully negotiated his way to the gorilla enclosure without first getting lost for twenty minutes. Twenty minutes! Each passing second exponentially raises the risk of my brain running away from me.

I am staring into the likelihood of four days of living hell; four days of walking around in a coma, pushing a rock uphill in a thunderstorm, wanting to sleep and never wake up. Already my fight-or-flight center is sending out distress signals. I am engaging in yogic breathing, trying to hold down the panic. She sees only a strange person getting upset over nothing, no fun to be around, not able to take her anywhere.

Another doomed relationship not meant to be.

Call me crazy, but this time I imagine a different planet—this one—the planet of my current residence rather than the one of my birth. This is the world of my true destiny, the one I need to come to terms with, the place where my struggles and breakthroughs will resolve into a profound healing. This time, on this planet, I see a nice lady with a blanket spread under a shade tree. From a picnic hamper, she produces Thai noodles and watermelon chunks. She beckons me . . .

Welcome home, a voice inside my head tells me. Yes, I dare to imagine.

Mysty D.
Her story . . .

Depression
My first memory of being depressed was when I was seven years old. One night I was looking at the stars from my bedroom window. Over and over again I would repeat with conviction, "I wish upon a star . . . I would die."

My childhood was more than a bit rocky. Up until I was fourteen, my dad was an alcoholic and a heroin addict. Often I would walk in on him beating my mom. We moved around a lot. There were a handful of times when my mom would pack our things and flee while my dad was still at work. As a result of my parents' instability, I attended six different elementary schools in three different cities.

My first suicide attempt was when I was eleven years old. I tried everything from overdosing on Nyquil, Advil, or just about anything I could find in the medicine cabinet to hanging myself, cutting my wrists, suffocating myself with a pillow. This behavior lasted throughout my junior high school years until the present without anyone ever finding out. The irony of all of this is I have always wanted to be very active and emotionally available to others. In high school I played sports, competed on the speech team, was captain of the dance team, and was even a peer advisor. Even now as an adult, I work as a massage therapist, a yoga teacher, and I am currently studying holistic counseling.

Dealing with depression is like having a spiritual flu. It creeps up on the sufferer, and often it's hard to shake off. For me it can last from a few weeks to six months. I isolate myself from people. I can easily sleep for ten hours a day. I emotionally eat, and after a while I begin to fantasize about dying. It is still a mystery to me why I continue to deal with severe depression when I consider myself to be a highly evolved human being. Yes, my past was hard and painful. That's true. Yet I am very much aware on a conscious level that my parents did the best they could.

One of my teachers told me that my biggest challenge would be offering my gift of healing to others. With that in mind, I now perceive depression as a gift for I have experienced the full spectrum of emotions and continue to live to tell the tale. Depression is not an easy disease to live with, but each time I overcome and move through it, I feel stronger and more empowered.

Studying holistic medicine has taught me alternative solutions to taking medicines, which I'm against. I have been using essential oils and Bach Flower Essences, and I see a counselor every week. We focus on releasing admonitions, which are negative imprints that she and I feel I inherited from my parents. I am very conscious about what I eat, and I make certain that I get plenty of alkalizing foods. I do yoga on a daily basis and play the didgeridoo and crystal singing bowls to help balance my mood.

> *... dealing with depression is like having a spiritual flu.*

Innately I have always been a positive person. I try to spread love and light wherever I go. Whenever I share my experience with depression, most people are surprised that someone like me is even capable of feeling sullen. It is not always easy to stay positive. Sometimes I feel as if I'm crawling through the day, and all I want to do is stay in bed. Often I cry for no reason or scream as loud as I can while driving my car. What really gets me through is simply taking one day at a time and reminding myself that, no matter what, I love and accept myself totally and completely.

Janaya G.
Her story . . .

Obsessive-Compulsive Disorder (OCD), Social Anxiety Disorder, Depression, Eating Disorder

I was diagnosed with obsessive-compulsive disorder and social anxiety when I was eighteen years old, and I've lived with my symptoms for more than twenty years. With OCD, my primary symptoms are an obsession with cleanliness. I can't go to bed at night until everything in the house is clean, and everything is in its proper place. I clean everything as I go and get upset with others if they don't do the same.

I also have an obsession with time. I feel the need to start or stop doing activities at the beginning of an hour or the half-hour (like brushing my teeth at exactly 11 p.m., watching TV from 2:30 p.m. until 3:00 p.m., etc.). I do certain things in sets of threes, such as taking three bites of food before taking a drink, or rinsing my mouth out and spitting in sets of threes. I also have intrusive, obsessive thoughts about deep issues like death, and I question reality and my own existence. My psychiatrist has referred to this as "deep end-of-the-ocean" thinking.

With social anxiety disorder, my primary symptoms include anxiety about being in public places and having to interact with others. I often rehearse what I'm going to say to the checkout person in a store before I approach her, and I often feel awkward and nervous. I also avoid eye contact with others and even struggle with going out with friends. I spend a lot of time isolating myself from others.

I was always an anxious, nervous child, and when I was five years old, I started obsessing about germs and disease. As I got a little older, I developed a number of phobias such as the fear of spiders, fear of fire, and fear of getting fat. I also began obsessing about deep issues like death and the nature of reality.

When I was thirteen years old, I began to obsess about my weight and food and exercise. I was diagnosed with anorexia nervosa at the age of sixteen. I also developed depression around the same time as the eating disorder, and the depression seemed to get worse when I was in a period of recovery. When the anorexia was treated and in remission, the old obsessions with germs and the deep, obsessive thoughts reemerged. A cycle began, which alternated between the obsession with weight and the OCD symptoms. This cycle lasted until I was twenty-one, when the anorexia was in recovery for about four years.

The social anxiety disorder started when I was in high school, and it worsened as I spent more and more time in hospitals and institutions because of my eating disorder. I had always been a shy kid, but the institutionalizations transformed my shyness into a phobia of being around others, including friends at times.

> *I try to take pride in small accomplishments that I'm able to manage and to recognize them as steps toward independence.*

When I was nineteen years old, a psychiatrist told me that medicine couldn't do anything more for me and that I would likely spend the rest of my life in institutions. I believed what he told me, and I truly felt I had no future to look forward to. One day a nurse came to check on me and asked, "Don't you think it's a beautiful day outside? How can you be so sad when there is so much to be thankful for?"

Over the years that I've struggled with my illness, I've heard this kind of thing from nurses, doctors, friends, and family. I think the problem is people simply don't understand how different reality is to a person who is struggling with a mental illness. We have a tendency to compare other people to ourselves and to assume they see the world the same way we do. This is simply not true. For a number of reasons (medical, genetic, circumstantial, chemical, etc.), my mind simply was not able to see the positive side of things. I wasn't sad because I didn't realize the sun was beautiful or that I didn't realize I was fortunate to be in good health or to have plenty to eat. It was because of something much deeper that I most certainly could not simply "snap out of." I fell into a deep depression and even attempted suicide.

With OCD and social phobia, I often feel like I'm trapped in a cage that I built myself. I can see others going about their lives and I want to take part, but I can't figure out how to open the door. Sometimes I get a taste of what it's like to be a part of that world, but something always seems to push me back inside. There is a sense of security and familiarity in this cage, but it comes at a great cost; my social life has become very minimal.

Even though I'd been a shy person most of my life, I enjoyed being with friends. Now I find it difficult to even be with them. When friends invite me to go out with them, I usually accept and then make up an excuse at the last minute so I can pull out of it. It has put a lot of strain on relationships I've had, and I've lost good friends and potential relationships as a result. Now I try to be more honest about how I'm feeling, and that seems to help. Being honest also makes me more likely to go out with them, since I know they'll understand if I have to leave. I've also told myself that I know I'm safe with friends, and nothing terrible is going to happen if I don't eat at exactly 6:00 p.m., so doing so isn't really part of my illness. This kind of self-talk is, of course, just me rationalizing about my behavior, which is indeed disordered.

I have never been in a serious relationship, and I often worry that I am simply not able to be intimate with anyone. My illnesses have certainly had a major impact on my sex drive and my ability to form intimate relationships. Over the years I've been with a number of incredible people, but the relationships were very short-lived and painful. After just a couple of days of seeing someone, I felt an incredible sense of panic and dread, and I would break up with that person. At the time I couldn't understand where those feelings were coming from, but they were so strong I felt the need to end the relationship. I've realized a lot of the feeling of panic I experienced stems from a fear of intimacy, both sexual and emotional.

I don't like being this way, but I often feel that the anxiety of letting anyone too close would be overwhelming. I'm a loner, but I don't want to be one. I'm afraid that someone won't want to be with me after seeing me at my worst. I don't think it was ever in my nature to be this way, but these illnesses have pushed me in that direction; and I often feel it is impossible to change. A big part of me still believes I'm a freak, and I'm afraid that others won't accept me.

I also have difficulty acting on compulsions when I'm with another person, so I often see the person as an intrusion. However, there is a part of me that longs to be with someone and to know what it's like to be intimate with someone. I see couples walking together, and I feel a tremendous longing. I feel like there is a big gap in my soul that wants to be filled, but there is so much fear and guilt blocking the way that I can't seem to let anyone in. There are many times when I can't even stand being with me, so I have a hard time believing someone else would want to be with me. This has probably been the most difficult consequence of my illness and the area I still have the most trouble working on.

When people I haven't seen in years come up and ask me how my graduate degree is going or when people I've just met ask me what I'm doing with myself, I always get this horrible, sick feeling in my gut, and I feel a sense of incredible shame and embarrassment. The fact that I'm not working or going to school is causing me a great deal of guilt and shame, and I really struggle with it on a daily basis. Before the symptoms of my illness became extremely intrusive and disabling, I was a very active and successful person.

As a result I have tried to throw myself into a job or just jump back into school, hoping "this time will be different," only to fail and feel even worse about myself as a result. I am, however, working on this issue, and I am beginning to accept my circumstances so that I can move forward, step-by-step, toward finding a job or school in which I can be successful in spite of my struggles.

One of the major things I've learned through all of this is the importance of not being too quick to judge someone. When I was growing up, a family member struggled with post-traumatic stress disorder and generalized anxiety disorder, and I can remember being frustrated at how that person was acting. I thought the person was simply crazy, and I never really tried to figure out what would cause a person to be so anxious over what I considered to be simple things. My view has certainly changed over these past years, not only in regard to mental illness but also in reference to the way people act in general. It has made me a much less judgmental person, and I'm grateful for having the opportunity to learn this.

My struggles have also made me more aware of what is really important to me in life, and I no longer take precious things like health, family, spirituality, and even life itself for granted. My priorities have made a major shift—certainly for the better. I had become so consumed with trying to be perfect and being such a high achiever (in everything from school to sports to work) that I had allowed these other things to fall by the wayside.

I find the most effective thing I can do to help myself through a tough time is to talk to someone about it. Embarrassment and shame have often caused me to try to hide my true feelings, but I've learned that talking to someone when I have symptoms can really help. Talking about it to someone, as opposed to letting thoughts run crazy in my mind, often helps me to get grounded and to feel less overwhelmed by what's happening. It also allows me to feel more comfortable around others, knowing I can be open and honest with them about how I'm feeling instead of wearing the "everything-is-fine" mask. It takes some practice to get used to talking with other people, but I've found it has really paid off in the end.

As a result of my illnesses, I've become very dependent on others (especially my parents and health-care professionals) for my basic needs. The thought of living on my own and taking care of myself financially is pretty overwhelming at the moment, so I've decided to take things a step at a time. If I look at the big picture down the road, I start to panic, and I'm filled with a terrible sense of dread and helplessness. I've learned this is not helpful to me in any way, so I try to stay away from that kind of thinking as much as I can and stay focused on what I can do here and now by taking things step-by-step.

I try to take pride in small accomplishments that I'm able to manage and to recognize them as steps toward independence. For example, I've been looking into renting an apartment in order to gain a sense of self-reliance. I am also seeing a career counselor in order to find work and, hopefully, education that I will be able to succeed at despite my struggles. It takes a lot of time and patience, but it's given me a direction and goals that I can work on and succeed at. Slowly but surely, I am creating a new future for myself.

Today I see my illnesses as coping mechanisms. I've had some pretty stressful events in my life, and even though I can see how my illnesses have helped me to survive at the time, they have now become more of a burden. I have experienced a lot of pain and loss as a result of my illnesses, but I believe I'm alive because of them.

Fortunately a lot has changed, and although I still worry about my future and what kind of a life I'm going to be able to live with these conditions, I believe I will have a life worth living. I have also learned a lot of important lessons along the way, and I've gained self-awareness and insights that can only come with the kind of experiences I've had. My illnesses are both a gift and a curse, and my feelings about them change depending on what is happening to me at the time. They are a part of me, and I wouldn't be the person I am today if I hadn't experienced all of it—the pain and the joy.

Jim C.
His story . . .

Obsessive Compulsive Disorder (OCD), Anxiety

Who knew? It's a phrase my Jewish relatives frequently used decades ago.

Who knew that spirituality would be the strongest most lasting medicine for my disorder? Who knew that reclaiming and cultivating the damaged spirit within me would calm the trauma of anxiety, panic and depression?

In 1982, at age twenty-nine, my OCD and anxiety symptoms became quite severe. I had a devastating nervous breakdown and was hospitalized in a psychiatric ward for six weeks. I became fearful of living. In short, it was a terrifying time for me.

My OCD symptoms included repeatedly washing my hands, complicated bathroom rituals, showering formalities that took hours, and performing checking and counting rituals. My primary symptom, however, was the phobia of germs and contamination. I wouldn't let anyone touch me for fear of passing or receiving germs.

Recovery began with anti-anxiety medication so I could begin the long process of Exposure and Response Prevention Therapy (ERPT). However, now that I was able to lean on ERPT to help me manage my symptoms, what was there to help me balance my emotional life? What was there to bring serenity back into a daily existence of stress and fear? What I found was a big surprise to this nice Jewish boy from Wisconsin. I was about to enter a particular realm of spirituality.

The spirituality I am talking about is not of a religious nature. It does not come from any religious denomination or sect. It is a spirituality that is about reclaiming one's own damaged spirit. At this point in time, my spirit definitely needed mending.

It all started when my psychiatrist suggested that I surround myself with individuals who share the same sorts of challenges and disorders. He recommended going to a 12-Step group meeting.

At the time, groups such as *Obsessive-Compulsive Anonymous* were virtually nonexistent in my area. My psychiatrist suggested I attend Al-Anon instead. "Now wait just a minute," I said to him. "I don't think so. There's nobody in my family that is an alcoholic! Why are you suggesting Al-Anon? After all, I have OCD."

He informed me that the first step in all 12-Step programs reads the same except for one word. For instance, in Alcoholics Anonymous it will read, "*We admitted we were powerless over alcohol, that our lives had become unmanageable.*" In Codependence Anonymous it will read, "*We admitted we were powerless over others and that our lives had become unmanageable.*" Then he looked at me and asked, "Jim, what are you powerless over at this time in your life?" Of course I knew the answer. I was powerless over my fears and my OCD. The doctor agreed and continued to ask me questions. "At any point has your life become unmanageable or out of control?" I thought for a few moments. Bang! It all made sense. I had no control over my fears from OCD and my life was a mess because of it. He then asked the crucial question, "Jim, in that first step in the 12-Step program, do you think you could replace the single word of what you are powerless over with the word *fear?*" The answer was yes.

> *When you let go of control, you get control.*

On a Wednesday evening I attended my first 12-Step meeting. In the beginning I found myself internally having fights with the program. All their slogans and ideas made absolutely no sense to me. *Let go, let God?* What the hell was that suppose to mean?

I went back to my psychiatrist and asked him what *Let go and let God* meant? He replied with words that I carry to this day. He said, "All it means is stop trying to figure it out."

But what about the God or higher power part? Apparently, that was up to me. I could replace God with: Source, the Universe, the ocean, the wiser part in me. It was my choice.

For the first time in my life I became very quiet. The noisy "committee" in my mind stopped arguing. Something finally made sense. I had been trying to dissect and figure out life for decades rather than simply living it.

Suddenly my brain snapped back into judgment mode. This sort of "let it go" approach seemed too simplistic for a person to combat such severe phobias and fears. I became defensive with my doctor. "Stop trying to figure it out? And then what?" He replied with another life-changing spiritual concept. "Let go of controlling all your feelings and fears. Have them. Own them. Feel them. Life is about feeling all feelings, including fear, but it's not about trying to control them."

There is a very strange paradox about control that is learned when you begin spiritual work, whether it is through 12-Step programs or books and recordings on spirituality from authors like Melody Beattie, Wayne Dyer or Deepak Chopra. The paradox is this: When you let go of control and stop trying to figure it all out, you get control. That's right. *When you let go of control, you get control.* Isn't that strange? I found it unbelievable, but I tried it. It worked and continues to work for me in my life.

In one particular 12-Step meeting there was an elderly lady sitting in the corner. She never spoke, she just listened. She looked a little like Mayberry's Aunt Bea character from The Andy Griffith Show! She sat in the same chair in every meeting week after week. In one particular meeting, I began sharing with the group about the bad day I was having. I was filled with anxieties, rituals and obsessions. I was exhausted, mad, frustrated and full of anger. The elderly lady quietly lifted her hand to speak. It was the first time in months she had done so.

She spoke softly but I listened hard. "You know, you can start your day anytime you want." The room went very quiet for a few moments. Then, my thoughts started to judge her statement, as I had been judging her silence for months. How can you start your day anytime you want? I didn't understand. Then all of a sudden, I did. Aunt Bea wasn't Aunt Bea anymore. She was like some sort of wise guru who had just offered a life lesson that would stay with me for a very long time. A lifetime.

That was the day I started to understand gratitude. I had a horrible day but I could make the conscious decision to start the day over no matter what time it was. I could choose in that moment to be grateful to the universe or God or myself for having even one minute or one hour of a good day. I could then build on that gratitude. Maybe next time I would have two or three hours by simply altering my attitude to gratitude. Start my day over at any given moment? What a concept. Take back my power and decide to feel the feelings of anxiety and let them pass at any given moment? Yes, I could do that.

Adding spirituality to my treatment and recovery from obsessive-compulsive disorder has changed my life. It was the missing treatment modality that I needed. It has given me a toolbox for living. I wish I had been able to take a class in "spiritual compassion" in the third grade. Most of us were never taught spirituality without organized religion being attached to it. Learning how to look at my life from the inside out has been a powerful tool.

I have continued treatments for my OCD through cognitive behavior therapy, ERPT, medication, 12-Step programs, spiritual books, and by "giving back" in the form of offering lectures on OCD recovery. I believe that we all need to teach what we learn, and that is what I am doing now. All of these tools have helped me to reclaim my life, which is a good life. I now want to pass along to others what has become valuable in my own life.

At first, spirituality seemed to me like "New Age" thinking. It's actually "old age" thinking in many ways. It's based on philosophies that are centuries old that are now made understandable for those of us who took awhile to locate and truly absorb the concepts.

My favorite spiritual saying is this: *When the student is ready, the teacher will appear.* When I became willing and open to healing, new concepts arrived and my symptoms of OCD started improving.

Spirituality. Who knew?

Elizabeth C.
Her story . . .

Post-Traumatic Stress Disorder (PTSD), Depression

I've lived with my symptoms of post-traumatic stress disorder for thirty-six years. It causes extreme emotional numbness, panic attacks, and an inability to get along with people or to work with others. I no longer work and was recently put on both Social Security and veteran disability benefits.

My symptoms began after being gang-raped in the military at age twenty-four. I covered up the incident and did not discuss it for twenty-five years. This contributed to very low self-esteem over my lifetime. My behavior has become clearer to me after attending a military sexual trauma inpatient program for a couple of months.

I have no intimacy in my life or sex drive. I try to control most situations that I'm in, and I have little tolerance for others who appear inept or incompetent. I get irritated with others very quickly. Most people cannot tolerate me for very long, as I am too intense and controlling. I inflict my personality on others, I suppose. For some reason I have little tolerance for others. I have almost zero compassion for others. I can only relate logically and try to do things to fix problems on a matter-of-fact level, not an emotional level.

I actually was pretty good at recognizing that I had a problem. When I'm in the midst of an episode, I feel sheer panic. Everything is magnified and exaggerated. The depression sometimes makes me feel like I'm going nowhere in my life; I just plod along from one day to the next. I have few friends, and I have trouble getting along with the friends I have. I have no relationship with my two siblings or their families. I often just go off on trips by myself, but that doesn't really bother me. I have accepted loneliness as my norm. I feel lonely but try to compensate by having my cat nearby to soothe me and doing some regular reading, decorating my house, and always trying to get organized, which is extremely difficult for me.

My coping tools seem to be doing yoga, water aerobic classes, going to the gym, using Transcendental Meditation practice and guided imagery CDs, and taking anti-anxiety medication if I am in significant stress. The support group for panic disorder that I attended through the Veterans Administration was very helpful. I can't imagine what being "cured" would feel like at this point since I have been this way for over thirty years.

I would not know what being symptom-free would be like, as this has been going on too long. I have become accustomed to the way I am and my modes of operation as they are now. Life does not hold the zest and exuberance it once did.

> *I must now seek new goals and ways to enjoy the remainder of my life, which means taking my limitations into consideration.*

I feel helpless because I have to find a new path for myself now that I'm unable to work. I feel like I don't know how to go forward now that I cannot work. I got fired from every job I ever held. It is astonishing that somehow I've been able to have a good standard of living along the way with so many job losses. I have some sort of a talent for survival. It baffles many of my friends! They can't figure out how I get by financially. I have some sixth sense on how to survive, and I survive well.

I am not religious, although I do believe in a higher power, but I'm not sure what that means to me. I hope to learn to cope with my condition and must now seek new goals and ways to enjoy the remainder of my life, which means taking my limitations into consideration.

Don K.
His story . . .

Depression, Generalized Anxiety Disorder (GAD)

I can trace my journey through depression and anxiety back to a single event in my early life when I was six and just starting first grade. My parents moved us during that year to a new house and neighborhood. Until then my memories are pleasant and what I would deem "normal." I had friends on my street, and I only remember fun activities and encounters. After the move I have memories of feeling different from the rest of the kids.

I was the new one in school among students who seemed to know each other. I became very anxious each morning, and I would become nervous and vomit almost every morning on the way to school. Finally my mother had to walk me up to the school gate because I felt so totally alone and scared.

Instead of playing with friends after school, I'd walk home alone, sit and watch TV, and eat. And I'd eat. And I'd eat some more. At age six I began gaining weight, which only served to isolate me even more. At a time when most kids were thin, a fat kid was the object of much ridicule and taunting. I remember the feeling of never knowing when a verbal attack would come. I could be anywhere, and the word "fatso" being shouted at me from an anonymous stranger would hit me like a random bullet.

As a result of this, I withdrew and ate more, which seemed to give me a sort of comfort. This pattern continued throughout twelve grades of school. I became more anxious and depressed with each passing year. The anxiety was so pronounced that I had an absolute mortal fear of having any kind of attention directed toward me. Oral reports were like standing in front of a firing squad, and each kid in class had two guns as eyes, pointed right at me.

The physical reactions to this anxiety were so intense that I could not get past them. I opted to take an F grade rather than experience those terrible feelings. Depression walked hand in hand with anxiety, and together, they stopped me from seeing ways to improve my lot in life. I basically wanted to lie down and let life walk all over me.

> *Anxiety holds me back from saying what I really want to say to the people I care for the most.*

Social anxiety always impacts my friendships and relationships. The physical discomfort that came from having any attention paid to me was so overpowering that I would avoid any kind of closeness, even though closeness was the only thing I wanted. Anxiety holds me back from saying what I really want to say to the people I care for the most. It leaves me tongue-tied and silent. It stops me from joining in and becoming a part of a group of people. It forces me to be an outsider and creates inner conflict when all I want is to join in and feel included. The depression episodes drive me deep into myself and make me very moody and uncommunicative. I am not a pleasant person to be around when I'm depressed.

Depression is a sneaky beast. While in a state of depression, I try to act light and upbeat. It takes a lot of energy to do this, and this creates an inner conflict in me. I desperately want help and comfort. I insist the people around me who care about me will intuitively know I'm hurting inside, grab me, hold me, and make me feel better. If they don't provide this attention because they are convinced I am okay, since I am presenting myself as okay, I begin to feel terrific resentment toward them.

Most people do not see my depression because I try so hard to cover it up. I don't want it to be there, so I work extra hard to appear happy and positive, even if I'm not. Maybe this is an effort to counteract my disorder, and perhaps this lessens my depression a bit. However, it also can be a form of denial and can set me up for resentments toward others. I feel I'm trying so hard, and nobody really takes notice of the Herculean effort I think I am making!

The anxiety is tougher sometimes. I find that by accepting that people generally give others the benefit of the doubt and don't judge me as harshly as I judge myself, I start to release the idea that I'm thought of as the failure my anxiety tries to convince me I am. I am usually aware of the anxiety because it is so immediate and manifests with physical symptoms. The symptoms come on suddenly—heart pounding and hot flush to the face, especially my ears. The depression is not as evident. Because it seems to come on gradually over a longer period, I get used to the depression and seem to adjust to it. Other people usually notice it before I do. I become quieter than usual, and I become more hesitant to do things. I become more negative and quick to anger. Being an alcoholic (now in recovery), I feel a strong urge to medicate. I find myself seeking relief from the oppressive mood by any means, regardless of the cost to others.

This avoidance of unpleasant feelings logically led in time to my acceptance of chemicals, which could momentarily relieve the unpleasantness. Alcohol was a perfect choice in my early teens. The "noise" from the other kids and their unkind comments was shut down, and I could breathe for a moment. Of course this is a shortsighted fix, and it led to a multitude of other problems. For a brief time, I felt right with the world. It did not change my personality to one more outgoing, but it made the noise in my head less. This grace period did not last long. Within a year I was a full-blown alcoholic, requiring the substance each and every day. It stopped lifting the pain, and it created much more pain and depression than it ever masked.

Having to deal with addiction has been the key to treating the underlying problems. I've had to dig deep into my memories and behaviors to see what delivered me to that dark place. In doing so, I've been able to come to terms with many of the anxiety-producing thoughts and find various ways to short-circuit them. They are still there, whispering to me, telling me I'll fail, that horrible things will happen, and that I won't be able to handle problems as they arise. However, with some attention, I can make the choice not to engage those feelings. When I allow some time to pass between the onset of these feelings and my taking action to run away from them, they usually evaporate or quiet down.

The AA program has helped me immensely. By treating my alcoholism, it, in turn, treats my depression. The skill of acceptance is very important in depression. My depression seems to feed on an extreme sense of discontent and on a feeling I am missing out and should have more in my life. For me depression is an extreme fog of frustration, of being immobilized and helpless against the forces of life. How can I have a positive, hopeful attitude when deep down I feel a random angry sea called "life" batters me around.

When faced with this feeling of helplessness, I become frustrated. When the frustration is allowed to cook for a long time, a heavy cloak of grey depression settles in. When I accept life for what it is and stop judging situations as good or bad, I am no longer looking for things that are lacking. I can allow life to flow where it will without trying to control it. This seems to circumvent frustration, which in turn stops leading me to the path of depression.

I can't remember a time in my life when anxiety and, to a lesser degree, depression did not have some effect on my life. As a child I was overly concerned with how I was perceived by others. I always thought others thought of me as inferior or different. This outlook caused me to withdraw inward and build a wall against the perceived threat. The more distant I became, the more I found proof that I was indeed different. It was a self-fulfilling prophecy. I felt different, so I acted differently. As a result I was treated as being different. I truly believed that life was for someone else but not for me. This fueled the depression and was a downward spiral.

The anxiety drives my behavior in almost every area of my life. It stops me from joining in with other people in activities. It convinces me I can never have what I want or deserve. It creates fear and worst-case scenarios. I've tried medication for both depression and anxiety, but for me it was not the answer. It's too easy for me to think that an outside force can fix me. But that very thought is what led me to alcohol and drugs in the first place. I wanted to find the root, the seed that caused this negative thought in the first place. Taking a medication to change my circumstances does not get at the source. Everyone's reason for a particular disorder is unique, and I believe some are caused solely by chemical imbalance and the right meds can correct that. I know in my case, these conditions are situational and behavioral. My path to recovery is one of digging deep, identifying patterns, learning new skills in thought management, and taking steps to change the patterns. I accept the fact that once these behaviors are established, anxiety, depression, addiction are there forever. I cannot expect to be "cured" of them.

The most I can attain is remission. I am at peace with that. I've learned there are many blessings that come from the inner struggle. I feel the process of dealing with these demons has made me a stronger, more compassionate person. The path of recovery is teaching me to get out of myself as much as possible, so that by lifting up and helping others up, I am lifting up and helping myself.

Robin T.
Her story . . .

Post-Traumatic Stress Disorder (PTSD)

I've come to dread the words, "You look great!" Something inside me just wants to scream, "I'm *not* great! Everything hurts—my mind, my body, my soul!" Looking great means that nobody really knows my suffering. It requires me to act as though nothing is bothering me. I am forced to choose between becoming someone I am not or isolating myself because I no longer have the energy required to act the part.

I've been a fake, performing the part of the witty, bubbly person I once was. That was prior to an incident that occurred during my service in the Army that changed my life and my world. I buried it for thirty years until it all bubbled up to the surface several years ago, and I suddenly found myself in crisis.

Post-traumatic stress disorder (PTSD) is a disease of [repetitive], painful memories, with a side order of surrendered personal dreams. In between waves of suicidal ideation, PTSD interferes with sleep and causes depression and a sense of loss and yearning for "the way it was prior to the incident." The numerous medications I take on a daily basis have their own side effects and remind me that I am not the person I once was.

Sometimes I feel numb, and yet I experience periods of deep depression. There's no place to hide anymore since I opened my Pandora's box and faced the problem head on. I'm now working with a wonderful psychiatrist at the Veterans Administration clinic. However, doing this has produced more complications for me, and I sometimes wonder if

I did the right thing in bringing it to the surface, where it has to be dealt with.

In addition I was diagnosed with fibromyalgia in 2005. The diagnosis helped to alleviate fears that I was becoming a hypochondriac with my constant complaints of various ailments. Episodes of pain, fatigue from simple tasks such as getting dressed, and the infamous "fibro fog" continue to plague me. Feeling alone and confused increases my depression. Sleepless nights add to my exhaustion and make me even more confused. Some days I simply can't get out of bed. Stress is a factor that increases the likelihood of occurrences, commonly called "fibro flares," and then I get caught up in the vicious cycle of sleeplessness, depression, and confusion.

I have become isolated and withdrawn. My friends eventually backed off when I didn't return their attempts to see or contact me. I feel relieved that I don't have to put up a facade for their benefit, as that was too demanding for me. My world is smaller now. My family and best friend of fifty-five years understand my limitations and place fewer demands on me.

> *Something inside me just wants to scream, "I'm NOT great! Everything hurts— my mind, my body, my soul!"*

Thoughts of how quickly my life has changed haunt me, and I yearn for the days when I could do the things I love. I no longer work, and being on a fixed income has been most difficult because, for many of us, our work validates us as productive human beings. My days feel unproductive and wasted for the most part, but I am blessed. I have a wonderful husband, a great dog, and a home of our own, when many others have lost their homes to foreclosure.

I still can't say whether my glass is half full or half empty, and I don't know what tomorrow will bring, but in the words of an old song, "I'm Still Here!"

Chuck P.
His story . . .

Depression

I was sixteen years old when I was diagnosed with depression. I've been living with depression for fourteen years. I experience feelings of worthlessness, suicidal thoughts, and pain. Despite the depression I still like to read, watch movies, and cook for my partner.

Many days my depression feels like a black horse that has been let loose and is taking away all the joy in my life, leaving only pain behind. When I'm deep in my depression, I just want to lie in bed and do nothing but sleep. I am unable to work because there are too many days that I don't want to get out of bed. I feel as though I'm worthless, and doing anything at all is pointless and a waste of everyone else's time.

Depression makes me feel as though it's my fault that I have this problem; I simply need to try harder to be happy. Then I can be "normal" and feel the same way everyone else does.

I can remember a time when I felt good and had many happy days and times. Only later, in my teens, did my depression become an issue . . . and it never left. I always have some degree of depression, but some days are worse than others. I sometimes go months without feeling a deep depression, just unhappiness. Then one day I'll wake up and feel I have no real reason to live any more. The feeling usually lasts anywhere from three to five days, sometimes longer. It always goes back to just unhappiness. It never stays with the desperate loneliness that the really bad times bring.

I often try to appear happier than I am, trying to hide how much I hurt, so no one sees the extent of my pain. Maybe people can't see it anyway, and I just feel it. When I have a low period, I feel as though there's no reason for me to be alive. All the happiness and joy in the world are gone, and I don't have any real reason to go on. I just want the hurting to stop.

Trying to look and appear happy has always posed a challenge because it's a lie that has to be kept up all the time, unless I'm alone. A depressed person has to smile and laugh while inside are hurt and tears. Trying to make everyone think that everything is okay when it's really not just adds to the pain. When I attempted suicide, the first thing that people said was, "Why? He seemed so happy! Like nothing was wrong!" Yet in reality my world was nothing but pain and despair. I felt like I had nothing to live for, and I just couldn't take the hurt any more. I wanted to stop being in pain.

In my head I was convinced that everyone would understand if I killed myself, and they wouldn't mind because they really didn't care. I wanted to stop lying to everyone I knew, making them think that everything was fine and nothing was wrong, when in reality I was in severe pain.

> *Trying to look and appear happy always posed a challenge because it's a lie that has to be kept up all the time, unless I'm alone.*

My depression keeps me from doing things with my family and friends because I either don't feel like it, or I'm unable to muster the energy to bring myself to participate. Many people do not understand how debilitating depression can be and how much it can really impact a person's life.

Obtaining Social Security benefits was extremely difficult, simply because so many people assume that depression is simply "all in your head," and all you have to do to get better is to try harder to be normal and happy. It has taken more than a year for me to get as far as I have, and I have my partner and family to thank for giving me the strength to stick with my efforts to make progress.

Sex has felt nonexistent on more than one occasion. Either I felt as though I was ugly and not worth the effort, or that people didn't love me or want to be with me, but they just couldn't find anyone else willing to be with them.

With the help of my current medication and the love of my partner, I have come to terms with my illness. Without him I wouldn't be alive today or motivated to take my medications. Medication has greatly improved my symptoms. Since I have been taking medication, I have few symptoms and am able to live a relatively normal life. I worry that in time my medication may not control my depression, and the feelings of worthlessness and pain may come back. Right now, however, my symptoms are under control, and I hope they stay that way for a long time. I know at some point I may have to have a stronger or different medication to control my depression, but I'll do whatever it takes to continue to have the kind of life that I deserve.

Linda N.
Her story . . .

Generalized Anxiety Disorder, Depression, Panic Disorder, Seasonal Affective Disorder (SAD)

I am sixty years old, and my illnesses forced me out of the workplace more than twenty years ago. I currently live a rural lifestyle, and I spend most of my days gardening and being an artist of sorts. I feel at peace in nature more than anywhere else, and I tend to avoid all things that might cause me stress.

There are times I feel lost in a fog or as if I'm hiding in the shadows. Sometimes I feel like my "on" button has been switched to "off." I have lived with my symptoms for my entire life but was only diagnosed twenty-five years ago. During this time I have experienced depressive moods in which I find myself totally dysfunctional. I will literally stare at walls unless someone drags me away. If someone were to ask the question, "What would make you the happiest right now?," I would have absolutely no answer. My disorders have caused me to lose all interest in almost everything, leaving me feeling like a blob of nothingness.

My panic attacks have caused me periods of great anxiety and stress attacks in which I could not breathe. At one point I experienced many irrational fears; I was certain I was dying, hardly able to swallow, and had absolutely no appetite. I even became deathly afraid of the dark, not wanting to die in the dark. I realized later on that these were unreasonable feelings, but I had no control over them.

Because of my generalized anxiety disorder, I have an extremely low tolerance of stress. Sometimes I feel my whole life has been stressful, when in truth, it has not been. I have been able to overcome some of the fears, but many remain with me. As a child I was described as being "nervous," terrified of flushing the toilet, plugging or unplugging an electrical outlet, having my photo taken, and using the restroom in my grade school. Consequently my childhood was a bit of a nightmare because I suffered from so many more irrational fears I did not understand; yet intuitively I knew that I was different. Eventually I was diagnosed with an avoidance personality. I avoided that which I was afraid of and still do to a certain extent.

As a teen I used to bang my head against the wall in the hope that my brain would start working better. At one point I felt shaky all the time, which turned out to be panic attacks. I could neither sleep nor eat. I could barely swallow. I was having chest palpitations all the time. Friends and family avoided me because they did not know what to do. I knew I was dying and was basically just waiting for it to happen. I just wanted to be Linda again, but I feared that she was gone, and this horribly terrified, panicked person had taken her place. I remember at one point I told myself that I had to get out, and I should get out of bed and get on with life. If I were going to die, I would just die.

> *I don't like the idea of having to "maintain" my condition. I just want it to go away.*

When I finally received a diagnosis and information about my disorder, things became much clearer to me. I used to blame myself for everything, and I was pretty hard on myself because I just didn't understand why I couldn't do what others seemed to be able to do so easily. I'm sure many of my family members and friends doubt my diagnosis because they just can't understand it without having experiences such as mine. They can't see the invisible.

With the help of medications and a diagnosis, I slowly came back to life. This was one of the worst anxiety times of my life. I still have a dread and fear that the panic attacks will return. I also worry that my medications are not as effective as they once were. I don't like the idea of having to "maintain" my condition. I just want it to go away. I no longer doubt my diagnosis because, in a sense, it "lets me off the hook." It's not an excuse, but it's a reason.

Initially it was very difficult for me to make the decision to try medication for my depression. I had always been anti-drug. I tried many different medications to get me through my panic attacks. I knew I needed immediate help but never thought of using drugs long-term. I was totally afraid of becoming addicted to anything, so I used drugs very sparingly. Then at one point I was referred to a therapist who basically told me, "Your insurance will only cover five sessions with me, group therapy, or medications." That's when I decided to try medication.

At times I almost lost faith that medication could even help me. The side effects from some of these medications were difficult, and I wasn't prepared to live with them. It's like fixing one thing, then breaking another. Eventually I finally found a medication that worked for me without bad side effects, and I had my first taste of what life could be like. It was a great high for me, but I still struggled with having to be on meds. Finally I decided if this is what it takes to have a happy life, what choice do I have? Unfortunately the high wears off, and now I just get by— certainly better than I was but not as good as I wanted to be.

I do not work, have a career, or maintain any goals toward employment. I lived with my parents and was supported by them until I was twenty-seven years old. I was afraid to face the world because of my disorders, never believing I could fit in. When I finally did go to work, my sister had to literally take me by the hand and drag me off to a restaurant where she was working to get me a job. The stress nearly destroyed me. My pains and nervous tension would become unbearable. My working career lasted a total of twelve years. Before I finally quit, I had been working only part-time for a few years.

Guilt issues over not working have always been bad for me. Early in my life I felt mostly shame because I didn't work. Then, after working for twelve years and supporting myself, I felt totally guilty when I could no longer work. I was feeling that most people just thought I was lazy or something. Today my lifestyle includes wearing thrift store clothing and shopping for used and recycled items. I deny myself anything that might be considered a luxury, and I very seldom buy anything new for myself. I have lived this way most of my life, and I think feeling guilty about not working has a lot to do with it. If I don't work, I am not worthy.

I was taking antidepressants, and they helped a lot. For a while so many things were going right that I thought I was cured. However, one cannot totally avoid stress. Life's events seemed to trigger symptoms again, or perhaps my antidepressant treatment became less effective over time.

At any rate I don't seem to have coping abilities when stresses build up. Now I just tell myself, "Here 'it' comes again." I have found that being aware of what happens makes it easier to deal with. Sometimes I try hard to talk myself out of it, or I go for a walk, or do something more physical. Other times I just spiral down to the bottom, knowing that sooner or later I will come back up to the surface.

People don't understand that I have no control over my disorders. They tell me, "Just do it!" This doesn't work for me. Or they'll say, "Just try it!" There always seems to be a wall between what I believe I should be doing and actually making myself do it. No one can understand this. It's a feeling of cowardliness and shame, and it has haunted me all my life.

I have definitely had times of bliss in my life, such as finding the man of my dreams and living a lifestyle I had always dreamed of. I have a loving relationship with my husband but absolutely no sexual desire. I pretty much blame this on my antidepressants. Still our relationship survives and works well.

My husband and I have very similar disorders, although he denies his. Much of the time we are no help to each other as far as encouraging each other to move through our problems. He dislikes having to make all the phone calls. I understand his fears, but if I call him on them, he gets very defensive. Despite all that we feel "safe" with each other because neither of us puts too many demands on the other, and we understand and accept each other's limitations.

Today, among other things, I still have a fear of making phone calls. I know that my disorders keep me from pursuing or maintaining relationships with friends. I am shy and uncomfortable in most social settings, although medication has helped this part of my disorder quite a lot.

I guess my family just writes me off as being a weirdo—weird Linda. I do not communicate with my family as often as I should, and I wait for them to contact me. As mentioned before I do not like to use the phone. This fear has allowed many relationships to slip away. I am also not one to plan outings or get-togethers with people, and instead I rely on others to coordinate events. I do, however, enjoy social situations much more than I used to, but I seldom initiate them. I feel exhausted because I've been dealing with these fears and feelings all of my life, afraid I would never be me again.

How do I cope? I fake it or just avoid it. Over time I have developed a sense of humor that I use to make everything seem all right. Having a sense of humor and avoiding things that cause me great stress help me to survive. I have tried meditation but haven't had much success with it. I read through volumes of self-help books at one time, and I did learn quite a bit about my inferiority complexes and such, but one just can't make the feeling go away by reading about it. Sometimes I feel my whole life has been one of avoidance, a pattern that I learned very early on.

I always have a dream that I'll be "normal" someday. I will never stop hoping to be well. If I am well, then I can be more of who I am rather than what my disorder makes me.

Larry F.
His story . . .

Post-Traumatic Stress Disorder (PTSD), Depression

I am retired now from my own private investigative business. Prior to that I was a security consultant and a producer/director of video, both on the local and international level. I was also a Detroit police officer for ten years. All the while I suffered with the symptoms of post-traumatic stress disorder.

I often take steps to appear the very opposite of how I am truly feeling inside, and since I am a good actor, it really doesn't take much effort to appear different from how I am really feeling. I have always been able to get through difficult periods without a breakdown, especially in front of other people. I breathe deeply and try to relax as much as possible to cope with my symptoms.

My symptoms can range from deep rage and anger to flashbacks, depression, sleeplessness, strange and rather intensive dreams, difficulty in relationships, and infrequent erectile dysfunction. My symptoms can come and go. I am very sensitive to the sound of gunfire. For instance, the sound of a gunshot, if it comes suddenly from seemingly nowhere, can jump-start me right into an angry place very quickly. Reading about a tragedy, especially involving children, can take me into a deep, dark mood. My symptoms make me feel as though I inhabit a world totally alone with no one to relate to. However, there is still a much more accomplished person locked away somewhere inside of me.

My anger issues have greatly impacted my family life. I would often blow up at nothing at all, which did a very successful job of scaring my young daughters and upsetting my wife. When I want solitude, which is quite often, my family understands and seems to give me the space I need.

All of these inner demons have led me to a very solitary life. I don't go out to parties or bars or other public places. I can't stand small talk and am not good at it. Most people don't seem to understand the unpredictable nature of my PTSD symptoms, which is why I only have one or two good friends who I talk with on a regular basis. They understand where I have been and what I have been through.

I know exactly where and when these disorders took root. It was when I came home from Vietnam. I couldn't and didn't want to tell anyone about my experiences because I knew most people couldn't relate. Some of the experiences I went through were so horrible. I kept them bottled up inside me and denied their existence. The symptoms began to express themselves without my volition in dreams, fits of anger, and an undeniable need for solitude.

> *... the challenges I face may seem insurmountable, but they are not.*

I often feel different and isolated from others because of this disorder and because my experiences in life have been so different from the norm. My closeness to violence for ten years and the things I have seen and done, all set me apart from others. At least that's how it feels. The fact that I suffer from extreme memories, and guilt and anger at who I allowed myself to become, even though it is useless and counter-productive to do so, sets me apart from others.

I take medications for depression and have for many years. I have also used meditation to reduce my symptoms. When I get into a regular routine of meditation, I feel much more relaxed and open. However, it is difficult to maintain such a regimen because after awhile it feels just like work! For some reason anything that I "must" do becomes something that I don't want to do.

I have learned to control my anger through the use of stress/mood cards. By holding the stress cards and breathing deeply, I learned to change the color from black (angry) to blue/green (calm) rather quickly. I now use this technique when I feel myself getting upset.

I have come to terms with my mood disorder and, for the most part, have eliminated my PTSD symptoms through my spiritual pursuits. About thirty years ago, I discovered astrology, which gave me an entirely new perspective on life. Having been an agnostic, I saw that there was a higher intelligence at work, putting me on a spiritual path. That path has served me amazingly well over the years. My faith, which has been severely tested, has brought me through those tests whole and still hopeful.

My spiritual perspective also helps me when I start to feel down, disorganized, or even sorrowful. I think of the experiences that have happened in my life, the angel who rests lightly on my shoulder, and my refusal to back down from the challenges presented, knowing that I am here for a purpose. That purpose keeps me going. I now understand that the challenges I face may seem insurmountable, but they are not. I am in a hopeful mood most of the time now. I have accepted my limitations and spend most of my time trying to help other people smile, either through my writing or by personal contact.

Nancy G.
Her story...

Depression

In everyone's life, there are defining moments, a time of experiencing something that changes a person forever. For me that moment came in 1992 when I was in a car accident. The accident not only left me with chronic pain, but it also caused a change in my personality and brain function. My best friend noticed how much of who I was had changed, and it was not in a positive way. I lost my sense of humor, and I became clinically depressed for the first time in my life.

I believe something in my central nervous system was damaged, and it caused me to experience a type of depression I had never experienced prior to the accident. Simple decisions became difficult to make, and I forgot things much more easily than ever before. The daily stress of my situation was compounded by continuous battles with sleep deprivation and being surrounded by people who couldn't relate to how I felt. Others often doubted the pain I was experiencing, whether it was physical or mental. My body didn't exhibit any noticeable physical injury or handicap, which makes my condition seem invisible to everyone around me. This left me feeling lonely and isolated.

My entire world that I had known before and felt comfortable in was now shattered; it was as if someone had turned off a switch that made life happy and worth living. Suddenly I was thrown into a sea of pain and depression. It swallowed me up, but no one could see it! Because I looked fine, no one could truly understand the depth of my grief and depression over losing my previous "self," a happy, optimistic person with a life mission to help others. (I was a counselor.) Now it seemed I couldn't even help myself, and that became even more depressing.

I now understand how difficult it can be to pull oneself out of a depression and how dark and lonely it can be. I felt helpless and, at times, ashamed that I couldn't just "pull myself up by my bootstraps." The compassion I felt for my clients who suffered with depression grew deeper. I don't think I would have had that without going through my own depression.

I spent the next six years after my car accident trying to manage my pain and depression while continuing to work. I no longer could concentrate, and my sleep was always disturbed and non-restorative. I no longer trusted my own judgment. Once the social butterfly, I now no longer wanted to go out of the house. I started to hibernate at home and avoid social opportunities. That really scared me because in the past I was an extremely extroverted person and never had a problem with such activities.

> *Suddenly I was thrown into a sea of pain and depression. It swallowed me up, but no one could see it!*

I tried everything I could think of to keep working and functioning, but I finally got to a point where I had to surrender to the reality I could no longer work. Then I become further depressed. I felt I had to make a major change in my life or kill myself, as I could not imagine living like this for another forty to fifty years. Giving up was not in my vocabulary. Yet here I was, choosing to live or to take my own life. It was surreal and shocking because this kind of depression had never been part of my experience prior to the car accident. I didn't recognize who I had become.

One of the most devastating things I experienced was the loss of a sense of purpose, of not being able to be of service to others. My self-esteem was at an all-time low. I was fortunate to have a caring sister in whom I confided how much pain I was in physically and mentally, and who offered to help me. We made a plan for me to stop working and apply for disability. I moved to California, where the rest of our family lived. Family support and finding the right antidepressant were two of the three ingredients I needed for a recipe to make lemonade out of lemons and to begin a new life.

But the third ingredient for my recipe came almost a year later after going on disability. This third ingredient helped my depression immensely. I discovered a rare breed of dog called a Xoloitzcuintli, commonly known as the Mexican hairless (Xolos). Xolos are ancient dogs that were used by the Aztecs 3,500 years ago as heating pads for muscle and joint pain because they are hairless and therefore warm to the skin. When I heard about their history, I had to get one of these toy-size Xolos and put her around my neck where most of my physical pain was located. I called her Toaster, as she was quite toasty on my neck.

Little did I know that the amazing healing benefits of Toaster went way beyond pain relief. Toaster helped me so much more than just as my 24/7 hot neck wrap. Xolos are extremely intuitive and sensitive to their owner's needs and moods. One of the first things I taught Toaster was to sing with me. When I am having a bad day, we sing together, and I am quickly lifted out of a blue mood.

Secondary conditions such as depression often accompany physical conditions such as pain. Toaster revitalized my will to live and got me back to exercising because I had to walk her every day. I was responsible for her. I couldn't let her down. She helped me so much that I decided to train her as a service dog through a two-year service dog training program, during which I had to take her to training class weekly, so this got me out in the world again. Toaster graduated as a certified service dog. Then Toaster took me by the leash and led me down an even greater path: she inspired me to help others again, thereby helping my depression.

I had no idea when I got Toaster how much more she could help me in addition to being a "hot dog" neck wrap. But when she was three-and-a-half months old, she posed for my first greeting card from the comfort cards and gift line of *Paws for Comfort*. These greeting cards, inspired by

Toaster, led me to find a positive expression of my personal struggle with pain and depression, and my wish to share the potential healing a small service dog can bring.

I combined my professional experience and skill as a therapist with my personal experience of having an invisible, chronic illness, and depression. I resurfaced with a new mission: to help people bridge relationships affected by illness and disability, by providing avenues of communication through inspirational greeting cards and gifts.

Such an innovative use of dogs and such a heartwarming story captured the attention of the TV channel Animal Planet, which filmed a half-hour show entitled "Toaster" on their series "That's My Baby." Toaster's story on Animal Planet inspired so many others to want a Xolo that I ultimately founded a nonprofit organization to help others afford and train Xolos as service dogs. Having purpose again has definitely lifted my spirits.

Fred H.
His story . . .

Depression, Seasonal Affective Disorder (SAD)

My depression makes me feel as though I'm locked in a car on an unbearably hot and humid day. The windows are rolled shut, and the doors lack handles. I can't get out, and every breath of humid air makes me feel weaker. At some point I give up trying to get out of the car. That's what my depression is like.

My occupation was a psychiatric social worker. I had a job that paid well, but it was incredibly stressful. It paid more than any job I've ever had. However, between the stress and conflicts among workers at the job, I became unable to function. I was so drained from the job that I began to fall asleep at my desk at work.

I have become very isolative and find social contact anxiety-provoking. I have difficulty finding motivation to do anything, and I experience low energy levels and sadness on a continual basis. I avoid contact with people when I'm feeling acutely depressed; then a vicious cycle emerges of having less contact with people who might be supportive and helpful because talking to them feels too difficult. My appetite grows, and I often gain weight. I sometimes have trouble getting to sleep and staying there once I fall asleep.

One of the most difficult aspects about having seasonal affective disorder for the better part of my life is the repeated setback. For most of my adult life, I have had surges in which I make progress followed by periods when I slip backward. With seasonal affective disorder, I usually lose weight during warmer months and gain it back during the winter. I may exercise for as much as eight or nine months per year, and then I stop during the winter.

I was a very sensitive kid, although I don't think I started to feel any symptoms of depression until I was about eleven or twelve years old. I did well in school without trying, until around the time I hit sixth grade. School became much more difficult at that time, and the stress level increased exponentially. This was my introduction to how stress can create a kindling effect for depression. I began to experience psychological signs of stress at that age, such as headaches and a strange burning sensation on my back.

After being shifted to an academic program that had a slower pace, I improved. Similarly, when I have been in jobs that were not fast-paced and stressful, I've done much better. Depression has been an unwanted companion throughout most of my life. There have been times, however, when I've managed better than others. As a result I have come to realize that I can't accept just any job. I have to be careful about stress levels as well as the pace and the level of conflict among coworkers. It's not a matter of lacking the social skills to deal with other people; I know how to do that if it comes up on occasion. If high stress is part of the job on a daily basis, I take it home with me and dread going back the next day. It becomes overbearing and overwhelming.

> *Depression has been an unwanted companion throughout most of my life.*

Therapy has helped me identify and look for objective signs that I am becoming depressed. One of the ways therapy has helped me is to recognize the signs that I am slipping into a depressive episode. Strange though this may sound, one step is for me to note how often I floss and brush my teeth. When I'm doing badly, that hygiene happens less often. When I'm doing well, I give my toothbrush at least one daily workout.

Ignorance may be bliss, though, because sometimes when I see the signs that I'm slipping,—such as eating more, becoming more isolative, etc.—I am not always able to do anything to intervene and help myself up and out. It is especially heartbreaking to know I'm beginning to do worse and to be unable to stop it.

In cognitive behavioral therapy, which I utilize, one learns about the role of the thinking process in depression and anxiety; in addition, one also learns to look for ways to help the self. If cognitive behavioral therapy is not being taught as a portable, self-administered technique, it's not being taught correctly.

I've recently experienced some problems when trying some new, fairly adventurous things. Learning from those episodes, I tried to view them as successful insofar as they compromised my comfort level and were activities I'd not tried before. While not raging successes, they were not utter failures because I got myself somewhere, and at least I tried.

At an audition for a play, I had a flash of panic. I almost said from the stage, "I'm sorry. This was a terrible mistake." I countered that urge by saying to myself, "You're here. Finish what you started." After a few deep breaths, I soldiered on. In retrospect I'm glad I did. Doubting myself is dangerous, and unfortunately, it's often part and parcel of being depressed. It's frustrating to think about undertaking something that requires sustained effort and then to doubt my ability to stick with it. At my worst I may avoid taking tasks on because I worry that I'll end up quitting.

It would be wonderful to have a good year. I want to think that, between my own efforts and the help I get from a psychologist and psychiatrist, it will happen. I plan on getting a light box device to help me with my seasonal affective disorder this coming fall and winter. Staying better would be wonderful! I'd do anything to have that happen.

Many people don't understand depression. There isn't a uniform depressive experience that all people have. Having read a magazine article about depression doesn't give one the knowledge to understand what it's like on the inside. It would help me for interested people to dare to ask questions and really listen. Then those interested may come out on the other side with a greater degree of closeness. Ask me questions, and I won't break. Caring people simply have to listen—really, really listen—to my responses.

Jewel G.
Her story . . .

Depression, Generalized and Social Anxiety Disorder, Panic Disorder

I am a licensed practical nurse, and I have experienced depression, chronic anxiety, and social anxiety for thirty-two years. I was diagnosed at the age of sixteen. I feel as if I am under a dark, heavy cloud when my illness is at its worst. It follows me everywhere, and there is no getting out from under it.

I have experienced chronic anxiety with severe social anxiety most of my life. I also suffer from chronic depression, which, again, I have dealt with for most of my life. I cannot remember a time when I was totally free of those things.

I also deal with agoraphobia and the feelings of extreme panic when I am in crowds, outdoors, or in a large open space of any kind. In addition I have the problem of rarely wanting to leave my home. This makes working very difficult as I will explain. I have been diagnosed with severe clinical depression at times, which will basically confine me to my bed. These instances have occurred mostly in my past, before I gained the knowledge I have now. I have more of a dysthymic depression now. It is chronic and feels like a dark cloud, but it is pretty well managed with antidepressants. My anxiety is helped by anti-anxiety medications, although for me, this is the hardest problem to treat.

I find that I am much more irritable and withdrawn when I am depressed, and in turn I experience increased pain. Because of my severe social anxiety, it is difficult enough to interact with others on a good day. I tend to go into my room and either sleep or read when I am down. If the anxiety is accompanied by more pain, the little social life I may now have becomes nonexistent. I have missed many family gatherings and social invitations as a result of these disorders. My life basically revolves around my boyfriend and future husband, whom I live with, and my daughter and granddaughter plus, of course, my computer. About 80 percent of my social interacting is done online. This limits the social anxiety, as I can neither be seen nor judged, and it is much easier to take control of my social life when it is limited by the constraints of the computer. I don't think I would have any social interaction at this point without it.

I am pretty much unable to work at this time. I work *per diem* or "as needed" at a local nursing home one or two days a week. I have tried many different jobs in my life, and I would have to say that work life is the area most affected by my illnesses. I have never been able to maintain steady employment. Either the anxiety or depression levels become so great that I quit or am fired, or I have to reduce my hours to the extent that I often barely scrape by. I was also a single mother for about seventeen years, and this was nightmarish at times.

> *I feel like I am being followed by the proverbial dark cloud, and then I hear from others, "But you LOOK so good!"*

I am not so stressed by my current relationship, since my partner is gone five days a week, eight to ten hours a day. I only work about sixteen hours a week. Therefore I am alone a lot. I am usually exhausted the day after I work. It takes so much for me to put on a "front" and pretend to be normal that it just drains me. My inability to maintain that front for any lengthy period of time took so much out of me when I worked full time. People, quite frankly, get on my nerves. That is not as negative a statement as it sounds. I just cannot relax around others, especially those whom I do not know well, and it is very stressful to keep up the front. I try to pretend that everything is OK, that I am OK, and that nothing gets to me when, in fact, everything gets to me.

I receive a low-income health plan from the county. It only goes so far. That is why I continue to work and to function at all. I don't think I will ever be able to stop taking antidepressants and anti-anxiety medicine or the many pain meds and muscle relaxants I now take to get through the day.

I am pretty much always depressed and anxious to some degree. However, there have been occasional times when I felt and looked and acted better. This led one doctor to become convinced that I was bipolar. I disagreed with him. Having lived with these symptoms all of my life, I knew what feeling normal was—the way most people feel most days of their lives. I was fairly stress-free, felt confident, usually lost weight because I had more energy to work and exercise, and took better care of my appearance. It was wonderful while it lasted. Then the dark cloud of depression and severe anxiety would descend, and the struggle to survive would begin all over again.

My disorders are "invisible illnesses"; they are not easily seen or understood. I can be in severe pain, have the weight of the world on my shoulders, and feel like I am being followed by the proverbial dark cloud; and then I hear from others, "But you look so good!" It is very discouraging, to say the least. How does one explain pain or fear or inexorable sadness? It is almost impossible as these are subjective things, unlike objective things such as cancer, a broken leg, or an amputation. I can feel emptiness in my soul worse than any phantom limb pain, and no one will know. I can feel fear and despair, and again, who would know? It is not apparent in my appearance. I put on my false front, which has taken many, many years to develop. Even so, I can keep up the front for just so long. I feel tears beginning to form as I write this part, as even my most intimate friend, my boyfriend, does not completely understand what it is I experience. He cannot, although to his credit, he does try.

I am happy to say that I am a much more compassionate nurse than I might have been without all the suffering, both physical and mental, that I have endured. I know what it is like to hurt and feel fear, anxiety, and helplessness. I am able to be more empathetic toward my patients, family, and friends when they are feeling as I often feel. My difficulties have made me a stronger and kinder person. I made the choice to be compassionate, and it wasn't easy, let me tell you. I still fight anger and self-pity; I just don't let such negative feelings get a foothold on me. I do plenty of self-talk.

I have developed a deep spirituality from these disorders and the lack of control I have over them. Acceptance has been a big key, along with my faith in God. I believe that He has given me these experiences to "grow me" and teach me more about life and the gift of health, family, and friends, however limited. I appreciate so much more things such as the sounds of the late summer while I read out in our camper on the "back forty" and the gift of a beautiful voice that I may not be able to share very often, but when I do, it truly is a gift. I appreciate listening to another gifted individual or the joys of loving and being loved, something I was unable to do when caught up in self-pity and anger. In my acceptance of my illnesses and limitations and in my continued faith, I have found a measure of peace. "What doesn't kill me, will make me stronger" and "If God brings me to it, He'll bring me through it," for you see, He has already.

Lisa A.
Her story . . .

Depression

My depression often feels like I'm secluded in my own internal world, which seems to be a far cry from reality. My emotions are numb, and my life seems dim. My symptoms of depression usually show up as fatigue, irritability, and loss of interest in almost everything. I feel different and isolated at times, which results in deeper depression, withdrawal, anger, and frustration. I stay at home more now. I was previously a licensed nurse but had to quit due to multiple health conditions.

My depression strongly impacts my friendships and social life as well as all of my relationships. When I have flare-ups of physical chronic pain, I am thrown into periods of even deeper depression. I am irritable and very withdrawn from all of life's activities. There are days when it is extremely hard for me to pull myself out of bed. My friends and family have had a very hard time adjusting to the ups and downs of my depression. When I withdraw because of increased periods of depression, my husband has to increase his activity and workload within the family. At one time this caused resentment. We have learned through the last five years of marriage, however, how to cope and communicate more effectively through these low periods.

Although I have been battling depression for over a decade, I have now learned the steps I need to take when my symptoms become problematic. When my symptoms grow, my anger does too. It's then that I usually spend time alone, whether it's in bed or in a long, warm bath to collect my feelings and try to get back on track. My other coping tools include visualization, music, aromatherapy, sleep, chocolate, the comfort of my pets, and using my spa sounds machine. I have also used nutrition, such as supplements and different diet plans. I have additionally tried relaxation, massage therapy, and physical therapy to ease my symptoms. However, none of these has made a huge impact on the degree of depression I experience.

Most people are unable to understand the cycle of my depression. It is difficult to understand unless the observer has suffered similarly. My depression greatly impacts my intimacy and sex life with my husband. There are times that I don't even want to be touched in any way. That can put a huge stress on our marriage. We are getting better at coping with this though.

I know, without a doubt, that I would spend most of my days in bed either sleeping or crying if I didn't have my medication for depression. Some people look down upon others for taking antidepressants, but for me, I must. I cannot see living my life without being on medication. It has saved my quality of life. Medication has been a true lifesaver for my mood disorder. I have had to try several different antidepressants over the years because of the side effects and a buildup of tolerance, and I admit the times I go through the trial and error of new medications are the hardest periods in my life. I feel lost, as though things are spiraling downward.

> *My depression has impacted my personal growth positively. It has increased my self-respect and my respect for others who live with these disorders.*

When people make insensitive statements about my depression, it hurts. I realize that I cannot spend the precious energy, whether physical or emotional, on people in my life who do not understand my condition. I have had to completely eliminate contact with people who are insensitive to my mood disorder, and focus only on those who empathize with what I am going through and are willing to learn about it. This has saved my sanity.

My depression and health challenges have impacted my spiritual beliefs greatly. For years I was angry with God for what I've been given. Then there was a period that I prayed for healing. I am now at a point where I feel amazing improvement. I now accept what I've been given and pray to be given a good day with less pain. I ask God to use me to help others through their challenges.

My depression has actually impacted my personal growth positively. It has increased my self-respect and my respect for others who live with these same disorders. I have a strong desire to begin a support group so that I can help others cope with illness like mine.

Learning all I could about my disorder has made a tremendous difference. There are still times when I struggle, but I realize the sun will shine again. It is up to me, through my knowledge, coping techniques, and acceptance, to find my way out of the dark during these difficult times. After many years of hopelessness, I now feel hopeful when I think of my future. As long as I'm fulfilling my personal growth through knowledge of this disorder, I feel that the potential of my future is limitless.

Lorna A.
Her story . . .

Depression, Panic Disorder (Agoraphobia), Generalized Anxiety Disorder (GAD), Obsessive-Compulsive Disorder (OCD)

I have had problems with depression since I was in high school. Sometimes I will suddenly, and for no apparent reason, feel like a heavy wave of depression has come over me. I actually feel the sensation of being enveloped by it.

I worked as a hospital systems analyst for twenty-five years before I became disabled. I still am something of a nerd, and I spend a lot of time at my computer. I'm interested in drawing and painting and in doing other types of arts and crafts; however, I have difficulty scheduling time to do many of these things since I get terribly confused and have difficulty concentrating.

I'm now fifty-nine years old. I have problems with anxiety too, but the panic and anxiety became very severe about twenty years ago after I got clean and sober. I had just gone through the Betty Ford Center's program after many years of abusing alcohol and drugs. I know one of the reasons I drank was to cover up and self-medicate what I realize now was agoraphobia and social phobia. After I stopped drinking and using drugs inappropriately, I began having severe panic attacks whenever I went to places where there were crowds, or sometimes even when I was part of small groups of people at work or in social situations. A couple of years ago, I began seeing a new psychologist and was diagnosed with OCD and adult attention-deficit disorder.

When I start having a panic attack, it is as though I just realized where I am, but at the same time, I feel I am not connected. I almost don't remember how I got wherever I am, and so I am startled to realize that I am in a situation with people with whom I should be interacting. I start to get very shaky and lightheaded, and feel as though I have to get out of the situation immediately or I will pass out. I am not able to stand in a line without being afraid that I will have a panic attack, and of course, the more fear I feel about having one, the more likely it is that I actually will.

Most people who don't really know me think I am a very laid-back person because I hold a lot of the anxiety inside. I usually try to stay away from people as much as possible when I am in a severe state of depression. If being around others is unavoidable, I do my best to act as if there is nothing wrong. I really don't want others, except for close friends, to know I'm depressed. It's the same with my panic and anxiety disorders. I don't want anyone except good friends to know about them.

I don't have much of a social life anymore. I never know when I am going to feel like going somewhere, so I don't like to even schedule anything. I especially won't go somewhere that may trigger a panic attack if I am with someone who doesn't know I have that problem. I will try going places as long as my partner is with me, because I know she will help me out of a situation if I become uncomfortable. I have missed out on concerts, parties, and other social events because of my phobias. Since I love movies so much, I can go to them if I know I will be able to get a seat on the aisle in case I feel a need to leave. I don't even like talking on the phone to friends or family, so I often have to force myself to make contact with others. I would much rather send an e-mail than make a call!

Most people who don't really know me think I am a very laid-back person because I hold a lot of the anxiety inside.

All of my disorders affect my family life. I feel as though I have placed an extra burden on my partner, but she doesn't complain. She's in the medical field, so she knows something about my conditions from a medical point of view. I feel that since I don't have a job, I should be able to take care of things at home, but I am unable to do the grocery shopping because of my fear of having panic attacks while standing in a line. Anywhere I need to go where there are lines—the post office, bank, department of motor vehicles, airport—will often trigger a panic attack if I have to stand in a line for any length of time.

Having mental disorders has directly impacted my work history. It was difficult for me to find a job where I wouldn't have direct contact with others, but I was able to do graphic art for a while. I started working at a hospital where I learned about computers and hospital information systems. I was a systems analyst for more than twenty years before I had to quit working altogether. Some of my job duties included meeting and training the employees, and that often led to panic attacks. Often I had to cancel training sessions or meetings because of the possibility of an attack.

I haven't worked for the past three years. I loved my last job but just couldn't do it any longer. When I filed for disability, my claim was ultimately approved for my psychiatric disorders. I miss my job and the sense of self-worth I got from it. My self-esteem has gone way down since I stopped working. Additionally, since I have been unable to work because of my disorders, our household finances have changed. We had to move to a less expensive neighborhood and watch our spending very closely.

There have been times that I've thought that I no longer needed to take my medication, and that is a dangerous thought for me. I have tried it before, and I got so low and disconnected that it took a considerable amount of time to get back to feeling "normal" once I went back on the meds. For me it takes medication as well as love and support from my family and friends. There are times, however, that all of these things simply do not prevent my having a panic attack or a period of depression anyway.

I have pretty much accepted the fact that I will likely be on medication for the rest of my life. I hope my symptoms don't get worse than they are now. I have been hospitalized, and I have a fear of having to do that again. I think about how fortunate I am in having the home and family that I do. I try to focus on those things and to keep things in perspective. When I think about others who have a lot more to deal with than I do,

I know I can handle my problems. I am more encouraged now than I have been in the past.

In addition to taking medication, I see a psychologist on a regular basis as well as listen to music, watch movies, and cozy up with our two dogs to help calm me down. These actions make me feel better when I am depressed or anxious. However, sometimes the depression is so bad that I cannot stay focused long enough to follow a story in a film or in a book. Listening to music helps and can calm me or perk me up, depending on the type of music I am listening to at the time.

I can hardly remember when I wasn't experiencing some depression. I feel these disorders all the time. I am not always deeply depressed, but I can still feel a bit of the "overcast" of depression most of the time. The degree of depression goes up and down, but it seems it has always been there. I don't recall having a panic attack before I was in my late twenties. I did a lot of self-medicating from there on until I stopped drinking around age forty. Now my psychiatric medications have helped me feel better for the most part, but the chronic pain I live with is very difficult to deal with.

The OCD causes me problems on a daily basis. I make lists and lists of things that I need or want to do, but I have a really hard time getting the tasks on the list accomplished. I believe that I should be able to get the things on the list completed, but I get stuck thinking about each part of the task over and over, until I am unable to make any decisions about what I need to do to complete something. I end up getting very anxious and disappointed in myself.

Since I have been dealing with these disorders for so long, I can usually tell if I am getting worse. That doesn't necessarily mean I am going to be able to stop it though. There are times that my partner recognizes changes in my behavior before I do. If I can remember that I always pull out of a bad period, I can hold onto staying positive. I'm fortunate to have a partner who continues to remind me that things will get better, no matter how I am feeling at the time.

Dana A.
Her story . . .

Post-Traumatic Stress Disorder (PTSD), Phobias, Generalized Anxiety Disorder (GAD)

My depression began at age twelve, and as I got older, the other disorders came along. I also had headaches and intestinal problems that I was told were "all in my head." Later in life I was involved in one bad relationship after another and became pregnant with a son, who is now grown.

I hate going into elevators, crowded areas, or any small places. My symptoms feel different every day. Sometimes I feel as though I have the world on my back, and I'm trying to carry it around. It's so heavy my body feels like it's going to fold in half. Other days it is black all around me, and I get so scared that I can't find a way out. Those are the days I stay in bed and can't seem to get up. Sometimes I hate my life! I hate the way I feel or how I cry about everything all the time. Why am I so scared? What am I scared of? Why can't I get out of bed? Why is it I had to drink in order to accomplish things in my life? And now I can't drink, and my life is supposed to be better. I haven't had a drink in thirteen years. Great! But why is life still so hard?

I can't seem to close my bedroom door or my bathroom door. Closed doors are an issue for me. And forget about going to concerts. There are way too many people, and I have to sit in the very last row of seats in the movie theater or someone might stab me! I also don't like people to be too close or behind me. Having them breathing down my back is awful. I can't seem to get over these phobias and anxieties.

What people don't understand about these disorders is . . . oh let's see . . . everything! I don't think some people out there, unless they experience similar problems themselves, understand or can even begin to comprehend what I go through or feel. It's hard for me to explain to an outsider how my mind is always in chaos. It's so hard to calm down to go to sleep without the aid of medication. I also need medication to function during the day. It's a never-ending balancing act with body and mind, and I get so tired of it.

The trial and error of medication has impacted me quite a bit. I've had to go on and off medications so many times. When I was on Paxil for about thirteen years, if there was a day or two that I forgot to take my pill . . . uh-oh, hold on tight! I was a loose time bomb on the days I wasn't medicated.

> *What people don't understand about these disorders is . . . oh, let's see . . . everything!*

All of this impacts intimacy with a partner. I have been married for more than eight years, and for the past four years, we haven't had sex! I'm going to be fifty years old. He's my fourth husband. What does that tell you?

Living with these issues for so many years makes it very hard to retrain one's brain. I used to be an alcoholic. I have now been sober thirteen years. I really didn't realize how bad my anxiety or phobias were until I got sober. Wow! What an eye-opener.

Vivian E.
Her story . . .

Depression, Generalized Anxiety Disorder (GAD)

I suffered from dysthymia (a chronic low-grade depression) and social anxiety from as far back as I can remember until my mid-forties. To make matters worse, I could never figure out what was wrong with me. I didn't even know that I suffered from two diagnosable and treatable disorders. I just always figured that I would someday outgrow my anxiety and blue moods. But all along my social anxiety was quite the conundrum. I had a good sense of humor and needed the affection of others. Afraid of people? Who would ever understand that?

When I came of age, I found a solution (or so I thought) to my problems. Self-medicating with alcohol seemed to lift my spirits and reduce my anxiety. However, this dependence soon led to abuse and finally to addiction. It was only after alcoholism was added to my list of ailments that I took the time to really analyze what was going on, to really take a look at what drove me to self-destruct. What triggered my craving for alcohol? And so it turned out that social situations were high on my relapse triggers list. To a certain degree, I felt redeemed when I discovered *why* I kept returning to alcohol, even though it had devastating consequences for my life.

I figured out I suffered from depression and anxiety only after I was inadvertently treated for them with medications aimed at my alcoholism. It was like I couldn't see what I was suffering from until I was out from under the spell of my true illnesses. It was only after I began to feel better and was able to see the light of day that I could grasp what I was *really* dealing with.

When I first stopped drinking, it was suggested that I take up journaling, and writing filled a void for me. It was where I submerged myself when I needed comfort, therapy, or to just sort things out. Writing helped me heal so that I could help others recover, and everything I had learned in life formed the foundation of my book, *Recovering Me, Discovering Joy*.

Again, while being treated for alcoholism, I was encouraged to look at my past, and I remembered my mother's story. Depression and anxiety runs in families, and it certainly did in mine. My mom had a history of anxiety and despondency. During the last few months of her life, she was so depressed she rarely left her bed. Seeing no other solution, she finally took her own life, leaving a devastated family who still mourns her. She lived before there were any effective medications available to help her. There were medicines prescribed, but they surely didn't help her any.

> *... a small dose of an antidepressant has made all the difference for me.*

There are ongoing studies regarding the benefits and the downsides of prescribed medications, but all I can say is a small dose of an antidepressant has made all the difference for me. I noticed relief from depression within weeks of first being treated with selective serotonin reuptake inhibitors (SSRIs). It took longer for me to realize that I wasn't as anxious around people anymore and that my extreme self-consciousness was gone.

Alcoholics Anonymous, which works so well for many, was effective for me only after my anxiety and dysthymia were under control. Now I enjoy twelve-step meetings. The group support is awesome, and the coping skills offered come in handy every day. This spiritual twelve-step program brought me back to God and renewed my faith. No matter how things are going, I now know that with my strong spiritual beliefs everything will be all right.

I feel so much gratitude for my miraculous recovery that it would be unconscionable not to share my experience, strength, and hope with others. It is my mission to raise awareness regarding the strong correlation between depression, anxiety, and alcoholism, one of society's most baffling problems. Today I not only am hoping to help others but I'm also like a kid again, excited about the unfolding mysteries of life.

Carol W.
Her story . . .

Depression, Panic Disorder, Generalized Anxiety Disorder (GAD), Obsessive-Compulsive Disorder (OCD), Seasonal Affective Disorder (SAD)

I have severe feelings of sadness, mental fog, withdrawal from people and activities, and an overall loss of interest in life. When stressed I become frustrated and anxious to the point of tears. I avoid large crowds and situations where I know I will be under pressure or stress.

Although I am on antidepressants as a regular part of my medical treatment, there are times when they just don't work, and my disorders limit my social activities when I have a breakthrough episode. I know and can recognize when my depression isn't being controlled by the medication. I identify the symptoms fairly easily now, and I typically add an anti-anxiety medication to my normal medicine routine. I also take care to reduce my social activities until I am feeling stronger. I have learned that I have to protect myself from stress, especially when I am having a depressive episode.

I am not sure if my children truly realize that I suffer with depression because I have never talked to them about it. My sisters, on the other hand, understand because they too have all suffered with depression at one time or another.

My husband doesn't fully comprehend my depression, but he is supportive of me when I become depressed. I try to keep signs of my depression from him because I know it upsets him deeply when he sees me depressed. There is no intimacy or sex drive when I am in a depressive episode. I feel withdrawn, and all I want is to be left alone.

Most people think depression is brought on by worry or by unhappiness. They think it is something that I can just "get over." I know my mother suffered from depression over the years, but when I said anything to her about my own depression, she would always say, "You have nothing to be depressed about." She'd then go on to list all the positive things in my life, as though that was supposed to pull me out of my depression. In actuality all it did was make me even more isolated and depressed because she didn't understand that it wasn't about the "things" in my life.

The medications I am taking have made a huge difference in the quality of my life. My depressive episodes are much less frequent and easier to manage now. I know what life is like without antidepressant medications, and I much prefer life with the medications. I have had to change antidepressants a couple of times when they stopped being effective. Then it's a very difficult time for me, waiting for the new medication to build up in my system and wondering how long this one will take to work before I have to change yet again. Also the cost of some of the antidepressants can be prohibitive.

> *While I don't appear to be disabled, I am. People don't realize that depression is caused by a chemical imbalance with very real physical ailments.*

While I don't appear to be disabled, I am. People don't realize that depression is actually caused by a chemical imbalance with very real physical ailments. I believe it should be viewed as any other physical impairment that's corrected by medication, such as high blood pressure or arthritis, but it's not. I tell people that depression isn't something one can snap into or out of. Having someone tell me to do things like "pull yourself together" just makes me feel sadder, because these people aren't trying to help me at all.

At times I have a really hard time dealing with my inner desire to work, yet I have to face the fact that I am no longer physically or mentally up to the task. I think it's my inner desire to be the way I used to be: whole, completely functional, and able to do anything I wanted to, whenever I wanted to. It's an adjustment issue that keeps coming up over and over again. I used to have an excellent memory and top-notch business skills, but that was before I became disabled. Now I wouldn't be capable of performing the simplest job in an office.

I've been on Social Security disability since May 1989, and it took me thirteen months to be approved to receive it. I hired an attorney before I filed my claim with Social Security, as I needed help with the application. I couldn't work, and I couldn't afford to make any mistakes in the application process. I have since had follow-up letters and psychological examinations, which provoked episodes of severe anxiety and depression. Dealing with the Social Security Administration is one of the most intimidating, emotionally disturbing, and draining experiences I have had to do since I became disabled.

Some of the coping techniques I have found useful that influence my mood in a positive way when I am facing a rather difficult state include pampering myself with soaks in the tub, resting, sleeping, or just lying in bed and reading. If I'm up to it, I go out and rent a good movie with an ending that will be sure to make me cry. I have found that having a good cry does help, since it releases the pressure somehow. Walking and using a headset with a book on tape is also beneficial.

I have pretty much come to terms with my depression. While it is not as bad as it used to be, I think that it is a result of becoming more vigilant in watching for signs that my medication is no longer working properly. I am also very hopeful about the future. I believe that everything in this life happens for a reason and that we are here to learn how to live and to love others. I have come to understand that we learn through our experiences, even when they are painful.

My disorders have also impacted my perception of life in that they have made me more introspective. They have made me think about life and what people have to go through. I think we all deal with some physical problem or other; that's just the nature of our existence. Over the years I have learned to look at my depression and moods as a source for learning about who I am, how my body functions, and what lessons life is trying to teach me.

Tracy M.
Her story . . .

Depression, Generalized Anxiety Disorder (GAD), Social Anxiety Disorder, Obsessive-Compulsive Disorder (OCD), Panic Attacks, Seasonal Affective Disorder (SAD)

I was officially diagnosed at the age of twenty-two with generalized and social anxiety disorder. When I do have a panic attack in public, I am unable to breathe, I get severely nauseous and shaky, and I need to leave the area as quickly as possible.

During an attack it seems as though I can't leave the room I'm in fast enough. Having a panic attack in public makes me feel like the whole world is looking at me and laughing because they know just how frightened and stupid I feel. On top of that, it can take me anywhere from five minutes to three hours to completely recover. I find that the attack passes more quickly if I admit I am having an attack and let myself feel what my body is doing to itself, rather than trying to appear the opposite of what I am experiencing.

My anxiety started when I was about ten years old, so I really don't have very many memories of being a carefree child. What I remember most is always being anxious, scared, or worried about something. Anything new terrified me, and I was always afraid of doing something to embarrass myself. I felt as if I stuck out like a sore thumb and that everyone was always watching me. Of course, back then I had no idea what anxiety disorders or panic attacks were. I just felt like I was a weird kid.

I'm not really certain when my depression started. I had always been a moody child and oversensitive to things other people said to me. What stands out in my mind the most is that I always felt I was different from the other kids.

Having an anxiety disorder along with depression makes me different from the majority of the population, but I'm okay with that. It is a part of my daily life, and I know now how to live with it. I don't feel isolated from others because of my disorder, but I choose to spend the majority of my time at home by myself. That is where I'm the most comfortable, relaxed, and happy.

The lowest point I ever felt with my anxiety disorder was before I was officially diagnosed. Here I was, feeling panicky and anxious in normal, everyday situations. My heart would race, I would have trouble breathing, and I felt shaky and nauseous. I knew this was not normal, but I had no idea what was wrong with me. I felt like I was going crazy, but at the same time, I was too embarrassed to tell anyone what I was experiencing. The symptoms finally got so bad that I had no choice but to consult a doctor.

> *If they understood my condition, they would know that a person can't just "snap out of it" or "pull it together" at will.*

I have never doubted or denied my illnesses, but getting the diagnosis really helped me. It made me realize there was a physical problem and that it could be helped with therapy and medication. It was also a relief to know I wasn't going crazy. Most of the people I am closest to in my family know about my disorders. They understand when I get "overloaded" and need to take a time-out from all the activity that is happening around me. Unfortunately my dad is unable to handle the fact that his daughter suffers from a mental illness. I don't know if he doubts my diagnosis, but I do know that he denies it.

It really used to bother me when people would tell me to "snap out of it" or to "pull yourself together." I felt they had no idea what I was going through and no empathy for my situation. Then I realized that they *didn't* have any idea what I was going through. If they understood my condition, they would know that a person can't "just snap out of it" or "pull it together" at will. Once I realized these people were ignorant of my illnesses, their comments no longer bothered me.

Unless a person has experienced anxiety and depression personally, or has a close friend or family member who suffers from these disorders, I don't think anyone can truly understand them. It is very difficult to explain to others how these illnesses affect one physically and mentally. First-hand knowledge is required in order to even begin to grasp the concept of how these disorders affect a person's life. I've had to deal with these symptoms and illnesses for so long that I really don't remember what it's like to live a "healthy" life.

I have never tried to "will myself better" or to become "cured" because I know that doesn't work in these instances. These diseases are permanent, like diabetes or heart disease. Medication can help ease the symptoms and the severity of the disease, but it cannot cure the disease. Now that I'm on medication, both the anxiety and depression are pretty much controlled all the time. If there's a lot of stress in my life, the anxiety will flare up badly from days to weeks at a time until things start to calm down. The depression doesn't flare up very often anymore. In fact the last time it flared, there had been a death in the family. The length of a depression flare varies based on the cause of the flare.

Medication and talk therapy *have* impacted my symptoms and my everyday life. Medication keeps all of my symptoms under control and manageable. After six years of talk therapy, I recently stopped seeing my therapist on a monthly basis. Having a nonjudgmental third party to discuss issues with and to be completely honest with was a huge help. Being able to honestly admit what I was thinking and feeling helped me to learn how to handle those thoughts and feelings in a constructive and positive manner. I learned about myself and discovered ways to cope with my illness. I also learned that a big part of being mentally ill relates to attitude. A person doesn't choose to be sick, but the ill person can choose how to react to various situations.

The trial and error of new medication definitely has impacted me. I hate going off medication. I have to wean off all medications slowly, or I suffer horrible withdrawals such as severe nausea, headaches, and "wide" mood swings. Going off meds can often make me so sick that I'm bedridden for days. Trying new medications is very scary. I have to start on the lowest possible dose and work my way up. New medications often cause the same side effects as going off old medications. It can take weeks until I'm feeling "normal" again.

I am on several medications whose side effects include decreased libido. Combining all these medications in one body results in a sex drive of zero. It's very frustrating. I know I am missing out on what should be a great experience in my adulthood.

Being approved for my Social Security disability benefits was a very long and frustrating experience. I had to fill out endless forms, hire a lawyer, and see many different doctors. Some of these doctors made me feel like I was lying about my condition. They also made me feel as though I was lazy and asking for a handout for doing nothing. It was a very demeaning experience. I have hope that someday researchers and doctors will learn what actually causes anxiety and depression. Once this happens I believe doctors will be better equipped to help those of us who suffer from mood disorders, including finding medications with fewer side effects.

When I first went on disability, I felt very guilty. I had worked since I was old enough to babysit, and I was used to making my own way. At first, accepting disability felt like taking a handout for doing nothing. I also felt very negative about myself. When I was working, I made very good money; now my disability payments are rather low. Additionally I felt like I had reduced my family's standard of living. The longer I've been on disability, the more these feelings have lessened though. I realize

I am entitled to these benefits because I paid into this very same system when I was working.

Sadly I don't cope well with the depression at all. Most of the time I give in to it, knowing that with time it will go away as it always has in the past. I'm still looking for a coping tool to help me deal with the depression.

One coping tool I use when the anxiety flares up and causes a panic attack is trying to refocus my attention on something else. I have found that doing crossword puzzles and word searches often calms me down and helps reduce the severity and length of the attack. I've read some self-help books, and they've given me some insight into my illnesses. Most of the time I've used the Internet to gather information. What relaxes me the most is a massage. I feel very calm and sleepy after a massage, but unfortunately they are expensive, and insurance doesn't cover them. I'd love to be able to get a massage on a monthly or semi-monthly basis.

I don't worry about the future. I feel my symptoms are well under control most of the time. If that changes I know there are other medications I can try, and I always have the option of returning to therapy.

Sharon T.
Her story . . .

Post-Traumatic Stress Disorder (PTSD), Depression

I am an artist and illustrator. However, right now I am not healthy enough to do much of my art or to teach art as I have previously done, so I work part-time as an office administrator. I experience frequent intense nightmares and memories, hypervigilance, flashbacks and some irritability, and I overreact to stress. I am sensitive to loud noises and sometimes feel numb. I have had these symptoms for at least seventeen years. Sometimes, when I'm in the midst of symptoms of my PTSD, I feel like my outer self, my skin has been stripped away, and all that's left is my raw nerves and organs. I feel completely vulnerable and only half myself.

My doctors are not yet certain if my PTSD began in my adolescence due to violence and trauma I experienced then, or if it began later after several violent attacks, including being stalked and raped at knifepoint when I was twenty. Perhaps the trauma in childhood made me more susceptible to PTSD when I experienced trauma later in life. I was originally diagnosed after my rape, when I was experiencing depression and classic PTSD symptoms. Very recently I was rediagnosed with PTSD by a therapist and biofeedback specialist. Initially the rediagnosis surprised me, but after talking about it and thinking about it a great deal, I realize that I had just grown very accustomed to my symptoms and coping strategies.

I'm still examining things to try to see connections and to understand which of my feelings, behaviors, or stresses are actually caused by the PTSD. It's hard to tell what "normal" truly is. Sometimes I feel like I'm taking off a pair of really distorted sunglasses and trying to squint into the light to see what's really there, and to determine what the reality of the situation truly is. It's quite bizarre; I've always felt that I am an intelligent and thoughtful person and am capable of seeing life clearly. With PTSD it's not always that simple.

I certainly can remember a very happy time, idyllic even, in my early childhood. I still had some recurring nightmares then, but otherwise I think I was very healthy and felt very safe, secure, and loved. When I was twelve or thirteen, things got progressively worse at home. After this period I am not sure exactly when the PTSD started.

> *I have found talk therapy and support groups to be tremendously helpful. They helped me to realize I was not as alone or as isolated as I felt.*

I am only beginning to examine how my struggle with PTSD is affecting intimacy and sex drive. I know that I find it very difficult to want to be with a partner; for the last ten years that person has been my husband, who isn't supportive or understanding about my past or current symptoms. What almost seems worse sometimes is having my partner not be at all interested in knowing about these things. Like many women I feel that emotional intimacy needs to be there prior to sexual intimacy. Otherwise I feel really distant and uninterested.

I feel furious, frustrated, and immensely sad when people tell me to "just get over it." Where is the compassion? I have worked so hard and have been so proactive in trying to recover my life, to live well, and not to let my past or the PTSD control me, I feel it's a flippant and uncaring thing for another person to say to me. It's not remotely helpful. Very few people in my life have ever put much or any effort into trying to learn about and understand PTSD and the events that caused me to have it. It makes me feel so sad and unimportant. I always go out of my way to be supportive of others and to educate myself as much as possible about what they're dealing with. I don't see why I can't expect the same caring and respect from other people. I think initially it was really disillusioning and quite devastating to find that lack in others. Now I think I expect less from other people in order not to feel so hurt.

I have not used any medication specifically for the PTSD. Years ago, when I wasn't sleeping well after my rape, I was offered sleeping pills but declined. Recently my doctor had me try an antidepressant, but I had severe side effects and could not continue taking it. Now I've begun thyroid replacement therapy, and my doctors don't want to try any new medications until my thyroid levels have stabilized. In general I prefer not to take prescriptions because I tend to react strongly to them.

Instead I have recently begun to see a biofeedback specialist to try different relaxation techniques. So far I have been working with progressive muscle relaxation. I also just purchased a "white noise" machine to lure me to sleep when I travel. I've found the relaxing and refreshing settings to be quite valuable to me, especially after a night of bad dreams. Using the machine keeps me from carrying around the memories of the nightmares all day, and it seems to help "program" me to handle stress in a better way.

I have found talk therapy and support groups to be tremendously useful. They made me realize I was not as alone or as isolated as I felt. That was a great comfort to me, and it still is. I also find that talking though things in my own mind can help me deal with certain situations. It is beneficial to simply let all these memories, thoughts, feelings, and concerns out, but it also has been helpful to begin seeing things a bit differently. It has also meant a great deal to have the terrible things I've experienced in my past acknowledged now in a meaningful way by another person. I feel lighter after my sessions.

There are several techniques I use that influence my mood positively when I'm in a deep and difficult state: music, exercise, escaping into a good book, writing in my journal, or doing art. My art has been valuable, both as a means of temporary escape and reprieve, and as a way of working through things that are hard to put into words. Often I will give myself a block of time in which to "let it out," and then I "put it away" and resolutely do something that will usually help me feel better. Doing things that give me pleasure helps create some balance for me as well.

I have attended support groups in the past, mainly during the months leading up to the anniversary of my rape, when my PTSD symptoms are at their most extreme. Generally I prefer to be alone, at least initially, until I feel more balanced. Otherwise I feel great pressure to pretend everything is OK, and that makes me feel even more different and isolated. Perhaps I have been very lucky with the groups I have joined, but I have always found them to be really helpful. Part of my successful release is having a safe space where I can really be entirely who I am, where I can let out all the pain, anxiety, and messiness, where I can be understood and not judged. Having that safety enables me to get through my "regular" life during the rest of the week. When things come to my mind, I do not have to dwell on them so much because I now can discuss them openly at the next group session.

I hope that one day I'll wake up and feel wonderful and whole—physically, emotionally, and mentally. Since I hadn't realized until recently that I was still suffering from PTSD (I thought I had "kicked it" years ago), I'm not quite sure what it would feel like not to have my PTSD symptoms. I'm not sure if it's realistic to believe that I will ever be completely PTSD free. I think I have tried to disconnect from what my body-mind has been trying to tell me for a long time. As the years go by, it becomes more difficult to imagine feeling any different. I'm actually a little shocked as I write this because I'm such an optimistic, "glass half-full" kind of person that I wouldn't have thought I would feel so fatalistic about this.

I am just beginning to understand my disorder. I have always thought of it as temporary, the way I felt directly after my rape. To find out now that I am still suffering from PTSD is both comforting and unnerving. It's comforting because it explains so much of the pain and distress that I've dealt with, and unnerving because I've been so unaware that I still had this disorder. I'm also trying to shake my feelings of failure. I've worked so hard with therapy, support groups, and on my own that now I feel as though I was unsuccessful in coping with the trauma effectively. At the same time, there is a part of me that almost feels relieved and vindicated that my experiences were truly terrible and important, despite how my friends and family minimized them. I am trying to tell myself that having PTSD is not a sign of my weakness or inability to deal with stress. It's my psyche desperately trying to work through some very difficult and painful experiences.

Marilyn M.
Her story . . .

Generalized Anxiety Disorder (GAD), Panic Disorder

When my anxiety disorder first surfaced, I'd feel a rush of adrenalin pour over my entire body, and my heart would begin to race. Later numerous symptoms began to develop, and I felt an overwhelming sense that I was having a serious health problem. I was unable to concentrate, had heart palpitations, felt weak, nauseous, and sometimes thought I was going to pass out. A couple of times I called 911 and went to the ER, where all tests were negative except for high blood pressure and a rapid heartbeat. I eventually learned to relax and control the anxiety symptoms most of the time, and now, after several minutes, the symptoms slowly subside.

I started working at an early age and at one point raised my family as a single mom. I kept up my home, pursued interests, took classes, and led an active social life. My condition forced me to retire, which was a personal blow to me, physically, mentally, and financially.

My panic disorder began to limit my ability to do the things I loved to do. I started to feel unsafe in certain environments. I was apprehensive about going to movies because I felt closed in. When I did venture out to a movie, I always had to sit in an aisle seat with one foot partially in the aisle so I could "make a break for it" if I became overwhelmed. I had to have anti-anxiety medication with me at all times, and if I forgot to put it into my purse, I felt anxious. I also didn't like to be out of the sight line of my family, and I felt uncomfortable being around people who didn't know me. I spent months trying to evaluate what places, times, and things would set off an attack, but they were too random, so I was frustrated in my attempts to avoid situations.

I tried to hide my anxiety, which caused more anxiety. I felt people would not understand what I was going through, and I didn't want anyone to see me when I felt out of control. I therefore limited my exposure to people and avoided going to places I would normally go.

Certain unusual body sensations caused me to panic and to think that something terrible was going wrong. When I was symptom-free for a period of time, I'd begin to feel safe and convince myself the symptoms were gone for good; but then I'd have another attack, and the cycle kept repeating itself. I liken the anxiety and panic experience to having a stalker; I never knew when or where he would sneak up on me.

In times of despair, I hoped the nightmare would end and that I could function normally again, as I perceived everyone around me was able to do. The doctors offered little hope. They attributed my symptoms to stress and offered me medication but never explained what was happening to me. Somehow I was able to function at work, but sometimes I would have attacks that I felt I had to cover up and take medication to relieve.

> *I tried to hide my anxiety, which caused more anxiety.*

There were long stretches of time when I was nearly symptom-free. These were times when I was not under heavy stress. I tolerate everyday stresses of life very well, but when I am under stress from several sources at once, my coping mechanisms seem to break down. If a family member or I has health-related problems or if I'm faced with several medical procedures, my symptoms are exacerbated. I have noticed I'm slow to recover from procedures that require anesthesia; my symptoms get worse, and it takes a long time to feel healthy again.

Alternative methods of coping with my condition have been helpful. Biofeedback helped me get through the immediate nature of the attacks.

Guided imagery had a calming effect, and I could quietly practice it when I was away from home and starting to feel anxious about a situation. I would imagine that I was in one of my favorite places—by a lake, or a waterfall, or anywhere quiet and beautiful. I've tried swimming and yoga. Everything provided temporary relief without medication. I didn't have much success with nutritional supplements, as most of them produced side effects I couldn't tolerate.

The unpredictable nature of my disorder has affected my everyday life. There have been times when it was difficult, if not impossible, to attend social events. I would accept and then break invitations because I had an irrational fear that I would have an attack. I was also unable to explain my behavior to people who were unaware of my situation. I remember going on a home tour with a friend. There was a long line of people waiting to get in, and I became overwhelmed. I had to get away from the crowd. I told my friend I was feeling ill and that I wanted to go and rest in her car. I wanted her to be able to continue and not have to take me home, so I sat in her car until she finished the tour.

Prior to my anxiety and panic attacks, I loved to entertain. After the attacks started, even the thought of entertaining a group of people was too upsetting. For a period of time, the attacks were so severe that when I was alone and trying to deal with them, I would have to breathe into a brown paper bag to get my oxygen level back to normal. This seems foreign to me now, but at the time it helped me get through the process.

The trial and error of new medications has definitely affected me. I have learned that I am sensitive to many drugs. Through the years my doctors prescribed several different medications, and most had side effects I was unable to tolerate. I was on a roller-coaster ride: having a side effect, then going off the drug, then having more side effects, and ending up with my original problem. This cycle was anxiety producing, and I developed a fear of trying new medications. I would down the first pill and wait for one of the reactions that I'd read about, one that might send me to the hospital emergency room.

I've been fortunate to have the support of my children and the full support of my husband, who has a lot of empathy for my condition. I'm also fortunate to be part of a support group, which is an important part of my life and a source of knowledge and comfort. I have *not* been as fortunate with some of the personnel in the medical system, however. Although most are kind and understanding, some are quick to judge and to place blame for too many things on a broad term of "anxiety." I believe individuals know their own bodies and have to be their own advocates. When a patient feels the diagnosis is improper or inappropriate, it is time to be diligent in seeking answers.

Now that I better understand my condition, I feel I have more control over my life. I take proactive steps to minimize any discomfort without using many medications. A turning point came in my condition when I was diagnosed with high blood pressure. After trying a variety of drugs that I could not tolerate, I was put on a medication that tapered off my anxiety attacks after a few months until I was nearly symptom-free. While doing research I learned the medication was also an anti-anxiety drug, a fact my doctor failed to mention. It slowed down my nervous system and my metabolism. One undesirable side effect is weight gain though. I'm hungry most of the time, and if I don't eat often, I feel as though I'm having a low-sugar reaction. Since I tolerate this medication, I just buy larger clothes!

When I saw a cardiologist for the first time, he found I had five severe blockages that could have ended my life. I had two coronary artery stents and two renal stents implanted, and I went through a lot of rehabilitation. Now doctors caution that anxiety can be a warning sign of heart disease, especially in women. My condition didn't occur overnight, so anxiety might have been an early clue that pointed to a more serious condition.

I survive by turning to my sense of humor, which I inherited from my father, and to my many Internet friends who help me keep a positive outlook. My friends are funny and fun, and we share our difficult times in humorous ways. Laughter is the best medicine!

My mood is also influenced in other positive ways. My husband and I enjoy eating out with friends, and we attend monthly luncheon meetings with my support group. Like my father I'm a nocturnal reader; I read almost every night. Sometimes I wake up with a book clenched in my hand, or from the loud noise the book makes when it crashes to the floor as my hand goes limp. Lucky for me, my husband can sleep with the light on!

My poetry has been a great outlet for expressing my feelings, and my wish list includes self-publishing a book of my poetry. It's important for my well-being to set goals, but they have to be realistic goals.

Amber W.
Her story . . .

Generalized Anxiety Disorder (GAD), Panic Disorder

I was diagnosed at the age of twenty-nine with anxiety and panic disorder, and I have lived with my symptoms for eight years. My primary symptoms are shakiness, sweats, and an overall feeling of thinking something terrible will happen. My anxiety and panic make me feel like a caged animal with no way out!

I try to appear normal for as long as I can. At times that doesn't work, so I will revert to taking a tranquilizer to calm me down. I was doing fine until my boyfriend started working nights. Now I find I have to take something most nights. I hate being dependent on medications. It just makes me more depressed.

I can remember my younger years and how different my life was. I was never home, and I loved to go out. I can remember when I was normal like everyone else. I remember when I used to love, and laugh, and live—and now I don't! My symptoms affect my behavior and my activities with others insofar as I never seem to enjoy myself. I'm always thinking about my anxiety and wondering if I look foolish to others. I definitely have trouble with outings, trips, and day-to-day activities.

In the last few years, I've become a recluse. Now I find it difficult to go to functions, and I don't want anyone coming over to my house. My best friend has not been here in years because of my anxiety. I would love to entertain more, but I never feel well enough.

My boyfriend has tried to be patient with me, but even he is losing control. Now he just gets really upset when I tell him I have to take medication. He feels I shouldn't be taking it and that it's doing more harm than good. The antidepressant medication I am on has killed my sex drive. My boyfriend and I rarely have sex anymore. He tries to get close to me, and I push him away. This has really affected our relationship.

I also feel bad because my son and boyfriend both want to go to different events, and I never feel like it. We barely go out, and when we do, I feel sick. There are times when I just push myself for their benefit. I even had to push myself to go to my son's eighth-grade graduation. I felt so out of place and stupid that I had to take a tranquilizer.

> *It's hard for people who lead a panic-free life to understand how I can't just do what everyone else is doing.*

People don't understand my symptoms and how I feel. They tell me I am strong and an adult and I should just get over it. The words "suck it up!" have been used. I think to myself, "Yeah, it's easy for you to say, 'You're fine.'" It's hard for people who lead a normal, panic-free life to understand why I can't just do what everyone else is doing. I wish I was on some kind of disability, but I'm not.

I have negative emotions surrounding the job issue. I constantly feel guilty because my boyfriend works so hard to support us. I actually may be in line for a collaboration job soon, and I just hope I can put in the hours required. However, with my symptoms, it's almost impossible to work outside the home. And when I tell people I don't work outside the home, they look at me as if I'm an alien. When I look around and see everyone else working and making money, I become depressed as well.

I just want to be able to contribute some money, especially when funds are low. We have been in this position more than once. I am truly hoping that my writing career starts to pick up. I seem to get offers, but then the client just disappears for some reason. I've been told how good my work is, but getting the projects is hard. I've done everything to try to promote my book, and myself, especially through my website.

I always have some anxiety just below the surface. It just takes something to bring it to full-blown panic. I am in therapy, and it has helped over the years. Other than therapy I have really not tried anything else except some yoga and Pilates. Therapy, for the most part, has helped.

I think medication makes me feel worse at times. It makes me tired and drowsy, and I have no energy to do anything. I have been on only one medication, but the dosage has changed, and that may be affecting me. I have had trouble sleeping and seem to drift in and out of sleep. I really don't know what symptom-free would feel like because I have had this disorder for so long.

There are days when I feel good, and that is a hopeful period for me. When I wake up and the sun is shining, I think there is hope for a better future. My disorder has made me more empathetic to others, and I have gained more knowledge about it through reading.

There are many low periods in my anxiety disorder. Sometimes I feel as though it all is so useless, and I can't go on. I have even thought about suicide at times. But I would never do that. I would never leave my son without a mother, but those are the truly low points. I don't think I will ever come to terms with my disorder. I struggle with it every day.

I sometimes feel isolated from others because of my disorder, and this just makes me feel more depressed. I really don't talk to my family, so I rely solely on my boyfriend and my son. I try to feel hopeful, but mostly I feel weak and helpless. I just wish I were stronger.

I have read about a number of different coping tools. What has helped me most are exercise, meditation, and deep breathing. Once in a while, I try to "will" myself to get better. I tell myself that nothing is wrong. However, in the end, this tactic doesn't always help me.

I think getting out and taking a walk is a good thing. Spending time with my family makes me happy. Since my passion is my writing, I try to get my feelings down on paper.

Lately I've thought that someday I'll get better and stay better. I have been so depressed that I'm holding my partner back from achieving his goals. I have been praying and asking God for help to get through all this. I hope someday I will get better and stay better. That would be a miracle to me.

Layla A.
Her story . . .

Postpartum Depression, Generalized Anxiety Disorder (GAD)

I'm a tax preparer and a homeschooler, and I have lived with my symptoms for more than twenty-six years. My disorders make me feel like the terrorized bleached blonde in a bad horror movie. Something always seems to be after me, and I keep tripping in my heels!

During the bad times, I alienate myself from those I love by becoming impatient and moody. I scream and yell a lot, and I have very little time to listen or find a way to positively react to those around me. Trying to block my disabling thoughts takes up all of my energy, and when I'm interrupted by other stressful feelings such as tension from a whining child or the condescending undertones of a customer service representative, I react in a harsh manner. I might say things like "What do you want now?" or "Listen, you insignificant little man, why don't you just take the dress back?" As a result I try to remove myself from the rest of humanity. I ask my husband to take the kids out for the day. I tend to reject any invitations to engagements that involve a crowd, and I drown myself in TV, a book, or anything that will help me get past this bad spell.

The most regrettable part of this disorder is that the best part of me is often hidden from my husband and kids. I have a hard time being happy because I feel that happiness is a prerequisite to death and doom. Watching my children play in the sprinkler, cuddling on the couch with my hubby, and eating at the table with the family are difficult because these activities involve contentment and joy, so I avoid them. My husband

and children beg me to become more involved, so I try to overcome instinctual aversion to these "Norman Rockwell moments" and join in.

I am blessed with a supportive husband, who understands when I need extra help and who drove me weekly to the therapist; then he'd wait in the car with the children until my appointment was complete. The therapist helped me with identification and coping techniques to get me through each episode. I now know the subtle clues when I am nearing an anxiety episode, and I've learned how to avoid them. The first clue is twitching. Usually my right index finger or eyelid will twitch. At the first sign of either of these clues, I pull out all the stops. I make my husband aware, and he clears the house (or at least my bedroom); and I sleep, exercise, meditate, or do anything that keeps me feeling sane. The twitching may stay for a while, but once it's gone (absent any other symptoms), I know I'm okay and not getting worse.

> *Yes, I look fine on the outside, but on the inside my mind is racing...*

It is fruitless to deny anything about my disorder. Everything about it feels too real. My heart races, my chest hurts, my stomach burns, and my muscles constantly contract to the point of exhaustion. My disorder is just there, and I better deal with it, or it will take over. My husband and my four best friends have helped me climb out of what I call my "personal pit of despair," and they continue to be there through my struggles. Other relatives have not been so accommodating. They think I'm just being dramatic or not able to deal with life's ups and downs. I've heard it all: "You just need to tough it out," or "You have so much, and you are still not happy."

My best coping tools are my friends. I have four of the best women friends in the world. They've cried with me, laughed with me, stayed up with me in the middle of the night, and constantly reassured me I was going to be okay. We relate to each other in a way that makes me feel like I'm human again. After talking with them, I usually feel better because I feel okay with being a little selfish: Selfish enough to get in my car and drive to the beach and just watch the waves. Selfish enough to announce to my husband, "You've got to get out of this house and take your kids with you." And then I sit and read my latest novel or watch a chick flick. I need quiet when my mind is racing. I need to be able to walk around without any demands. The quieter it gets, the quieter the thoughts become.

I was surprised to learn at the time of my initial diagnosis that I'd been struggling with anxiety since early childhood. As I recounted my experiences, I realized I was around eight years old when my symptoms first appeared. My father had kidnapped me, and I found myself in the middle of a custody battle. During that time I saw my father suffering from third-degree burns all over his back (my mother's little thank-you note for taking her two daughters). I was pawned off on my grandmother and my uncle (both of whom were wonderful to me) and then placed with a woman I didn't know, who went on to abuse my sister and me. That was the beginning of a difficult childhood of abuse, impoverishment, and molestations.

When I was old enough to escape, my disorder was already ingrained. I was a young woman starting her career at a Fortune 500 company, and I was deeply involved in developing and maintaining an Islamic life. By all accounts I had it together, but I was falling apart inside—still afraid all of the time, still having obsessive thoughts about dying. I hid it all well, and during all those years I never verbalized my symptoms to anyone.

My symptoms come in phases, and their intensity depends on my ability to address them effectively. My symptoms begin to appear once I'm agitated by a stressful event, such as an illness or death in the family or problems around the house or with money. The warnings may start with a nervous feeling, the way people feel when they're about to take a test. I may start getting to sleep later and sleeping less because I can't relax. My finger or eye will start to twitch, and then CLICK! An obsessive thought will enter my head. The thought is usually about pain or death. A phrase like "You're going to die!" begins to play over and over in my head. Then I stop sleeping, and I experience heart palpitations, difficulty breathing, and chest tightness or pain. I feel like a trapped animal on alert, seeing danger everywhere.

What most people do not understand about my disorders is how devastating they can be. Yes, I look fine on the outside, but on the inside my mind is racing with the words "You're going to die" every minute of every day. The anxiety is constant with no relief, even when I'm sleeping. I become vigilant and apprehensive, like I have to fight my way out of a corner. Yet there is no corner. And what all these people see is only me being the modern-day wife and mother. They see the confident woman who will not back down from anyone. They do not see a person afraid to close her eyes in the middle of the night, so they brush me off as another bored housewife, ungrateful for her blessings.

I have learned not to communicate my disorder with just anyone, giving me the opportunity to escape callousness. I discuss my condition only with a few people, including my husband and a few friends. I shut the rest of the world out.

The lowest periods of my postpartum disorder occurred following the deaths of my mother and grandmother and after the birth of my first son. The stress of death and pregnancy was just too much, and I spiraled down into a deep anxiety episode. It clicked on right after my son was born: "You're going to die." At first I thought the anxiety would fade just like the other times, but it lasted for four months. I was exhausted from lack of sleep. I was taking care of two children under the age of two and sleeping only two hours at a time. I was constantly crying, and my house looked as bad on the outside as I felt inside.

I still don't know how I took care of my children because I was such a mess. I was so tired that I'd walk into walls. I left things on the stove to burn until my husband ordered me not to cook unless he was home. He would often cook for the kids and me before he left for work. I would feed, change, and dress the children and then sit them down in a closed-off room with me, lying on the floor because I was too tired to do anything else. My mind and my heart were always racing and I couldn't sit still, but I was too exhausted to really function. I finally looked at my husband across the table one day during lunch and announced, "I think I'm going crazy! I need help before I lose my mind."

A hopeful period came when I was expecting my second son, and I dreaded going into another anxiety and postpartum depressive episode. It had taken me over a year to get relief from my obsessive thoughts and anxieties. What if everything came back? What if I ended up where it all started? Thankfully it didn't happen. I gave birth, and then I did something I hadn't done before: I focused on myself. I told the nurses to feed my son a bottle at night, and I nursed him during the day. So I got to sleep more than I had in previous years. My husband took a week off from work, and when the new baby and I got home, we both went straight to my bedroom, and I closed the door behind me. No visitors were allowed, and my husband had to take care of the older children. It wasn't until the baby was three months old that I realized I hadn't had an obsessive thought, and I was sleeping pretty well. Even though I was overwhelmed, I was not having any major anxiety episodes. I realized I could monitor my disorder and take the necessary precautions to prevent my symptoms from getting worse. I felt more empowered and less helpless.

I have learned to give myself a break. I know I'm not perfect, and neither is life. Things will happen, and the way I react to them will affect my disorder. I have to mellow and roll with the punches. I have to submit to whatever Allah wills. I am better at it on some days than on other days. I have also come to realize that no one ever knows what people are carrying with them. My own disorder was not apparent, but my negative attitude because of it certainly was. People can't make that distinction just by looking at someone, but I can because I know what is inside of me. So now, when dealing with people who are a little "attitudinal," I cut them some slack because they could be hurting the way I was on the inside. As corny as it sounds, I feel better when I handle it this way.

My anxiety disorder will be with me for the rest of my life. The only thing I can do is to manage the symptoms to the best of my abilities. I think the things that work best in stabilizing my mood are working out at the gym and spending quiet time with myself, either reading or watching a movie that no one else in the house would appreciate except me. It has taken me awhile, but I have found that exercising really helps when I'm having an anxiety episode. Exercise stabilizes my mood and makes me feel better.

I feel I've gained some power in managing my disorder. I also think I have gained a level of control in preventing major episodes. If I take care of my emotional well-being and myself, I can remain symptom-free for months at a time. Although I'm aware this disorder can get worse if left unchecked, I think I was diagnosed before my symptoms progressed beyond my control.

This gives me hope that someday I will allow myself to fully enjoy my family and life, without having a sense of dread that I'll once again feel like climbing the walls.

Trudy C.
Her story . . .

Depression, Generalized Anxiety Disorder (GAD)

I am a sixty-three-year-old retired teacher, principal, and former business owner. I was officially diagnosed with anxiety and depression over a decade ago.

My symptoms make it difficult for me to relax and meditate. Sometimes I'm a perfectionist. I'm also a people-pleaser. I grew up in a traditional, postwar, poverty generation, born to a German father and a woman he dominated, just as his mother had dominated him. My father had four brothers, and he was the first to marry. His mother was never kind to me or to my mother or my brothers. I lived in constant anxiety about how to keep the peace, and I was on alert for any signs of my daddy's mood changes.

I remember two "escapes" (an amusement park and a trip to Nanna's) where I got extremely sick from anxiety. I was afraid of getting lost, making mistakes, feeling emotions, doing anything Daddy would not like. His approval never came. He gave me the determination to succeed though, and I never moved back home after I went to college, except when I returned during the summers to work.

I started getting severe headaches when I was fifteen years old. We had just moved away from Nanna, and my mom had just had heart surgery. I have taken a muscle relaxant ever since I was in my early twenties. I've tried every alternative therapy out there, and I have been in talk therapy three times.

My symptoms have impacted my behavior and my activities with others. My husband is very protective and nurturing. I worry that he worries about me! Many of my friends have a partial understanding of my physical disorders, but I had never discussed depression or anxiety with friends, except when my mom died. I'm sure they see it though. They accept me as doing the best I can. They know I try to do one big thing a day, and they're okay with this. They love me; I'm lucky. I know I am a good person, a fantastic friend, and lots of fun. I pick and choose activities carefully and when to spend time with my friends because I tire easily.

There are several things that have a positive impact on my symptoms: my attitude, lots of sleep, exercise, journaling, "ocean" time, creative work, being with people I love, humor, being with my husband, watching TV, yoga, going out for lunch, coffee or tea, a good meal, a healing touch, acupuncture, massage, meditating, reading, and photography. My anxiety and depression do not seem to impact my sex drive at all. I have always enjoyed sex, and I think it makes me feel better.

> *Knowing that my symptoms are not life threatening and that I can get better helps me to cope.*

I used to have difficulty planning and carrying through on activities such as trips and social outings. I used to say "no" in case I couldn't do certain things. Now I say "yes," unless I really feel it's too much or I don't want to participate. Knowing that my symptoms are not life threatening and that I can get better helps me to cope. I want to play, not write lists and spend my life trying to fix myself.

Claudia G.
Her story . . .

Generalized Anxiety Disorder (GAD), Depression

My depression makes me feel like I am isolated in a glass bubble that is moving very slowly. I can see the rest of the world outside my bubble. It is full of happy, healthy people who are accomplishing so much, but I remain trapped in the bubble.

Since early adulthood I have been an athlete. The term "athlete" would be in the top descriptors I would use to define myself, along with wife, mother, professional, and volunteer. My husband and I met playing coed softball more than twenty years ago. We've played indoor and sand volleyball, enjoyed rock climbing, and are both certified in scuba. We snow ski and play tennis.

Subtle, progressive changes are difficult to detect until there is an impact on a major component of life, such as in a relationship or in a career. The impact was the loss of my ability to work and my inability to participate in sports on the high level to which I was accustomed. Once the reality set in that my life would not be as active as it once was, I started grieving for who I once was. During that period it was easy to assume that soon I would spontaneously recover to normal, because I had not fully accepted my diagnosis.

I still hold on to the idea that someone will discover an underlying curable medical problem, and that once I receive the proper diagnosis and treatment, I will be perfectly okay again. This would be magical for me. Then reality creeps in, and I realize that, at best, I may recover after many years, but by then I'll be too old to accomplish anything of importance. I am afraid to allow myself to visualize full recovery, because the disappointment I would experience when recovery never comes would be worse than learning to cope. I grieve for my loss of career, wasted higher education, and my bubbly old self.

I still travel and attend social outings, and I have good and bad days during those times. If I'm planning to attend a party, but I am not feeling particularly social, I make a deal with myself to leave early if I'm really not enjoying myself. I find this helps to ease the anxiety of going, and once I'm there, I will have a great time.

I have probably always been somewhat of an overachiever in search of recognition from authority figures. I often excelled, and I was used to being considered an asset. Because of my illnesses and my inability to work at a traditional job, I do my best to feel accomplished. I try to be as productive as I can be, either in simply keeping the house clean, cooking, doing laundry and paying bills, or in creating artwork. I guess I'm just learning to lower my bar.

> *I have learned that it is okay to take a break without announcing the fact and that taking time for myself is not a bad thing.*

I find meeting new people the most difficult situation because, inevitably, I will be asked, "What do you do?" I don't want to get into a discussion about my illnesses with strangers, and I'm not old enough to say I'm retired without getting looks of disbelief. I don't have small children to take care of, so people are left wondering and sometimes ask why I don't work. Some people respond by saying they wish they didn't have to work, and then they list all the fun things they would do with their extra time. I know they mean well, but the comment indicates to me that either I haven't been clear enough in describing the debilitating effects of what I have to live with, or they are just insensitive idiots. Some people will comment that I look so healthy and ask, "What do you do to stay in such great shape?" Needless to say, this question causes me anxiety and grief.

I long for the day when I can put my talents to use and offer something to my community. It's not that I don't make good use of my good days. I volunteer for the Lymphoma Society and the American Heart Association. I help and support my family as much as possible. I do some writing and other small administrative jobs from home, and in the last year, I have learned to paint. By all accounts my life should be considered "full," but without earning a steady income for my contributions or reporting to a job every day from eight to five, I just feel less capable than most other people.

My current daily accomplishments don't tell people that I have a degree in psychology and a graduate degree in communication disorders, specializing in audiology, or that I have worked with the deaf culture, know American Sign Language, and can dispense hearing aids. My small accomplishments don't let people know I have training and experience in writing and giving presentations. They don't say that I have training in gastrointestinal and cardiovascular health. In my daily activities, there is no hint of the fact that I still have so much to offer to society—if only I had the energy.

Since being diagnosed with anxiety and depression, I have been on Social Security disability. I had been an audiologist for eight years prior to working as a representative for one of the top five pharmaceutical companies. I overworked myself, striving to excel. After three years I was nominated as representative of the year. I competed for and won a regional recognition award and was on my way to a national competition when I became sick. The company allowed me four weeks of short-term disability but made it clear that neither chronic fatigue nor chronic pain were strong enough diagnoses for their long-term disability plan. A diagnosis of depression would qualify me, but I was well aware I'd then be labeled and therefore would not be considered the asset I once was for that company.

Fighting for my rights was draining what little energy I had left in me, so I resigned on the anniversary of my third year with that company. I had, however, applied for long-term disability before I resigned. I was also required to apply for Social Security disability but had no intention of collecting from Social Security at the time because I thought I would only be ill for a month or two. I didn't want to be on disability because it conjured up notions of long-term illness, laziness, and giving up.

I fully expected a denial letter, but the response from Social Security came swiftly and in a very small envelope. I remember seeing it in the bundle of mail my husband brought in while we were entertaining close friends. I opened it right then, thinking that because of its size, it must be a decline of my application. The letter stated that I'd been approved for disability income for three years. I was shocked and saddened and brought to tears by an unexpected blow to my self-identity. From that moment I would not be the same person I once was. Although the monthly income was necessary, I felt like I sold my soul to the illnesses, and they sold it to Social Security.

I have always considered myself sensitive and empathetic to others, and I've always chosen careers that allowed me to help others. Having chronic illnesses has allowed me to realize that even though there is always someone who has things worse, ironically, for someone else I may very well be that person who has it worse.

In terms of growth and self-knowledge, I'm in the process of learning that I sell myself short all too often and expect too much from myself. I have been my own worst enemy. I have learned that people take short cuts and are better than I at being able to determine how much is enough to do. I have learned that it is okay to take a break without announcing the fact, and that taking time for myself is not a bad thing. I have learned that my happiness comes from being a little selfish. I have learned that I am a very talented and creative being, but to tap into that creativity, I *must* take time for myself. In doing this I can benefit others through my art. If I had not become ill and been forced not to work, I most likely would not have taken the risk to create.

Karen E.
Her story . . .

Depression, Generalized Anxiety Disorder (GAD), Post-Traumatic Stress Disorder (PTSD), Panic Disorder

I am a single woman, and I live alone with my two pet companions and another companion called depression. Living alone with my disorders has been exceptionally hard and continuously challenging.

My depression often makes me feel as if I have been pushed into a pool of dark water with no bottom to it. When I'm in the worst of my depression and anxiety, I pull things from my "tool box" of coping methods and techniques for managing during difficult times. I live alone, so I must take responsibility for keeping myself on track.

Over the years I have learned many ways to help myself live a comfortable life. Some of these techniques include keeping my environment in a cloistered mode, in that I do not seek any visitors. I politely turn down any offers to go out with friends. I do this as a managing technique to conserve my energy and lessen my pain. The physical presence of people drains so much energy from me that I simply cannot afford the pleasure of their company.

What else do I do? I limit conversations with friends. The confusion I experience is very stressful for me because I often can't remember the conversations after I have them. In the past my friends were accustomed to me remembering even the smallest details of our talks. I have always remembered to call and ask how a friend is after someone has shared some difficulty. Now I am unable to do this. I have not found a way to explain the changes in myself that does not sound like an excuse rather than a reason.

My coping tools also include prayer, meditation, walking, exercise, eating nutritious food, getting plenty of sunshine, listening to positive affirmation and relaxation CDs, feeding seeds to the birds, caring for and playing with my other pets, dancing around the house while listening to the radio, watching TV offerings of comedy and information shows, and continuing to write up a list of blessings in my life as a constant reminder. Of all these tools, the most important is getting plenty of sunshine.

> *I set a timer for 15-minutes and make myself sit in silence for the entire time, feeling terribly sorry for myself. It has successfully cut down the time I feel sorry for myself because I give it a specific window of allowable time.*

When feeling sorry for myself, I set a timer for fifteen minutes and make myself sit in silence for the entire time, feeling terribly sorry for myself. It has become an agonizing ritual, but it has successfully cut down the time I feel sorry for myself because I give it a specific window of allowable time.

I use the telephone etiquette technique of smiling while talking on the phone in an effort to sound better to the other person. This technique also makes me feel better about myself. I am certain that it works because the person I am talking to has often commented that I sound much better! It's funny, but I feel better when I smile while talking on the telephone.

I have quite a battle sometimes to keep myself from falling into the "nobody cares" trap. On my last birthday, none of my family members remembered my special occasion. My close friend was out of town with her family. I knew this was a sure setup for a pity session. I took hold of the situation before it set in on me though. I went outside several times during the day to get plenty of sunshine. I took a nice, refreshing shower, and then painted my toenails and fingernails. I watched some TV and DVDs. I turned on a classical radio station and played conductor to several pieces I was familiar with. I meditated several times, instilling peace within and a calm atmosphere in my home. I thought about the two loving and caring parents who adopted and raised both my wonderful big brother and me.

I have been on Social Security disability since 1986 due to my depression and anxiety disorders. Prior to that I had worked from the age of nine. I enjoyed working. I was a diligent and dependable worker with a high work ethic. Even though I have tried working in the years since 1986, I have not been able to work full time. This has left me feeling unproductive because I wasn't contributing to society. I felt I was nothing. I felt useless. I had lost my identity somewhere along the line. My work environment had been my main method of being in contact with people.

My feelings of guilt over being unable to work were very intense for the first few years. I was only thirty-eight years old when I became unable to contribute to society. I felt shame over not being able to work. When I came across someone I had worked with previously, and there were many, I felt dread from the inevitable question that followed the normal greetings: "Where are you working now?" I felt physically ill when I had to answer, "I am not working at the moment." In time the answer has become more honest: "I am not able to work any longer." It took years for me to be able to answer that question without my heart beating rapidly, my mouth going dry, and my voice cracking under the strain.

I would feel anger after such an encounter. Guilt and shame altered my world, but it was anger that was my greatest challenge. I did not know how to express my anger, as I had never recognized the feeling before. In retrospect I think that there were situations that made me angry, but being raised as a female in a male-dominated world, I learned the only response that seemed acceptable was to be quiet and obedient.

The frustration that this hidden anger caused me was painful, and it was an issue I did not want to explore. I feared that if I opened up and cried, I would never stop. At thirty-eight, I had already had two hospitalizations in a mental institution for nervous breakdowns. The first was when I was twelve years old. All of these experiences carried their own abuses and neglect that I had stuffed deep down. I was terrified that if I acknowledged these painful experiences, I would not be a good person. My self-esteem plummeted when I did start digging up these abuses in therapy. I felt that only a bad person would be treated so terribly; therefore I must be a bad person. My self-worth was nearly extinguished.

My depression and anxiety disorders since age twelve imploded. I was defeated and depleted. I went into a catatonic state that I nearly did not emerge from. I can't recall how long I remained in this state, but I do remember the terrible confusion I experienced when I did finally come out of it. It was, after all, of these experiences that I finally defined what my work was to be. That work was to heal and seek out ways to enrich my life and the lives of others around me.

I am a very accomplished woman with many talents that I share freely with the people in my life. I am a very loving, empathetic, intelligent, and quick-witted lady. I love my life, and I see many joys and wonders in the simple things in life, from the wonder of the inside world of a strawberry as viewed when cut in half to the individual beauty of the leaves on my plants. I came out of darkness into the light.

Polly M.
Her story . . .

Panic, Generalized Anxiety Disorder (GAD), Depression

I work with my husband in the medical field, and I am also a publisher. I have been experiencing symptoms of anxiety, panic attacks, and depression for about fifty-five years, beginning when I was only seven years old. I have feelings of anxiety and fear, shakes, instant diarrhea, upset stomach, obsessive thinking about symptoms, dry mouth, cold sweats, a need to get to a safe place, and I worry about upsetting others.

For the first thirty years or so, I tried to hide my condition, and I was very ingenious about that. If I had something to do, I might tell my husband I was feeling ill so that later I would have an excuse. I would make sure I could escape by taking my car or motor home, and I would park close enough so that I could escape quickly. If I thought I might get sick or have diarrhea, I would be able to get out fast. I sat on end seats, close to the exits, and never got stuck in lines. I didn't eat much because I was worried the full feeling would make me feel sick. I chewed gum or sucked Lifesavers to keep the action going down, not up. I would arrive at the last minute. I would work only if I felt safe.

In college I actually stopped writing to my best friend from childhood because I didn't want to let her down by not being able to come see her in Chicago. Dating was a struggle, although in my teen years, I would go places if they were not more than fifteen minutes from my home. I didn't go to camp, and I hated riding buses. Every time I started school, I would have to go through the anxiety all over again, even when Christmas or Easter break ended. I went to the restroom on nearly every break. I made up all kinds of excuses. I wouldn't play sports because I might have to travel. I felt comfortable staying at only a few friends' houses. I would never spend the night with my boyfriend in college. I had rules about staying up too late or drinking because those behaviors would bring on the symptoms.

My family life was impacted greatly. Taking my children anywhere had to conform to my anxieties. My husband bought a motor home so I could shop for the family or do anything with them. I cooked every meal so I wouldn't have to go out. If I worked, it had to fit into my requirements. I didn't socialize, except when I knew I could escape. My husband finally left me because his life was too restricted.

> *For the first thirty years or so, I tried to hide my condition, and I was very ingenious about that.*

I never became a doctor because I knew my fears would prevent me from completing my education. I did go to college, but I had to plan the time of classes, how many to take, and to consider how I could escape if I needed to. I lived one block from campus because I felt I could get to a safe place fast. I am probably the only successful real estate agent I know who never took a client in my car; I was very creative. For the first few years, I worked with my husband in the clinic. I drove my motor home, even out to lunch with the staff.

I became aware of the problem when I was very young, but no one knew what it was in those days. I'm a very good judge of my symptoms, but I often made up stories or excuses so others wouldn't know. I don't deny or doubt my diagnosis. I'm an expert in the field now, so I am very aware. I can oftentimes spot a person or patient with a similar problem without their saying a word.

To cope I always used to carry gum and Lifesavers and a seasickness bag, and I never went anywhere without my motor home. When I felt better, I drove a van with a portable toilet and a place to lie down. I carried anti-anxiety medication in my purse at all times, and I had a backup supply in the car and travel bag.

I never thought I would wake up from this and be better. At my worst I used to pray that I would pass out and be taken to an institution where they would keep me away from all the obligations of normal life. I also thought about living off the land and never having to have contact with the world, so the chances of a panic attack would be lessened. I hated the attacks, which were much better if no one was around. I was always concerned that I would upset others.

Today, having discovered a huge piece to the anxiety puzzle for myself, I do everything in my power to help others overcome their own symptoms of anxiety. Today I love waking up every day. Even though I am not perfect, I am so happy to feel as good as I do.

Keith M.
His story . . .

Depression, Social Anxiety, Obsessive-Compulsive Disorder (OCD)

My OCD was diagnosed when I was about ten years old, but it started when I was five years old. I have to align items, and they have to be perfect—nothing out of place, not just my things but also other people's things. I once was told I had to leave a museum because I moved a painting that was crooked on the wall.

My depression makes me frustrated; it makes me want to cry ... and sometimes I do. I feel like all my efforts are in vain. I feel worthless and moody. I get tired and my body actually feels sore when I'm depressed. It often causes me to feel alone and unwanted when the depression hits. I feel like I'm made from all these rejected parts that nobody else wanted. I sometimes think I was put on the earth to suffer for something or for someone else's mistakes, and that no matter how hard I try, I'll never be able to get out from being "damaged."

I try to never let others know if I'm feeling sad or depressed. Usually I'll say that I'm not feeling well and go to my bedroom if I can. That's where I let my feelings out. When I'm really upset and I'm at a social event, I'll say I'm sick.

My social anxiety manifests in nervousness when I'm in a social situation and there are many people around. I panic and get frustrated. I even hyperventilate sometimes.

I don't really have many friends. I try to keep people in my life more on an acquaintance basis than on a close-friend basis. I'd love to have lots of friends and do things, but I don't want to make anyone else have a bad time or feel sorry for me. Everyone has his or her own problems. I don't need my instabilities dragging them down too. I cannot have a social life outside of my significant other. I feel unwanted, unworthy, and just too much of a personal burden to others. I want to, but I just can't. I've tried, but I just panic and want to retreat to the safety of my home, where everything is where it should be: nothing is new or different or out of place.

I never know when I'm going to "freak out," as I call it. It just happens. Sometimes its gradual; sometimes it's in an instant. I don't like not being able to go too far from home or to be someplace where it's awkward to leave when I feel an episode coming on. Yet, on the other hand, I don't want to be limited. I want to experience life and not just have it "happen" to me.

My family life has certainly suffered because of my disorders. I'm now on my third marriage. I know it's partially because I don't express my feelings until they are so bundled up that they explode in a fit of rage and crying and just plain ugliness. All of my previous relationships have ended because of unfaithful actions by my partners, but I can't blame anyone but myself. I'm a broken man. Why would any woman want a man who is not a whole man?

> *I don't like not being able to go too far from home or to be someplace where it's awkward to leave when I feel an episode coming on.*

My sex drive is failing slowly, more and more every day. I'm just not interested, and I ask myself why my partner should be interested in me. I'm more hassle than I'm worth. Why be intimate since I'm not going to be happy anyway? What's the point?

I take medication, but I feel like it makes me less me. I don't want to be sad or depressed or angry or scared. However, I don't want to be a lifeless robot with no emotions either. Sometimes I think taking the medication makes me feel worse, because I see others around me not having to take it or pop pills all the time. Plus the medications cost money, so I'm always broke. It's a cascading negative effect.

I used to work at the second-largest advertising agency in the Midwest, one of the top 10 in the world. I had an awesome job, great pay, fun atmosphere, and it was one of the things that was good in my life. It was taken away from me. Everything I went to school for and worked hard for and wanted out of my life was suddenly gone. I felt as though what I did was who I was, and it was all gone. Now I cannot provide for my family, let alone myself. I had a good job, and it could have gone even farther. There were doors yet to be opened, and now they are gone, locked up, and never to be opened again.

Sometimes I know when I'm going to become depressed, angry, or nervous. It's as though I can feel it slowly getting worse and worse. Other times it's like a car crash. Bam! It just hits me. No warning.

Other than using medication to cope, I try to focus on something good that happened to me in my past or on a pleasant smell of something around me. This preoccupies my mind so I do not concentrate so intensely on my mood situation. I draw a lot, and sketching does seem to help. I can unload my worries, anger, and fears on a piece of paper, a canvas, or on something else that takes concentration off my feelings.

I have learned to control my OCD. To some extent I have gotten better on the "just let it go" part of things. I still have my personal items organized by color, size, and a certain angle, but I have made some progress in learning to control fixing other people's stuff. Sometimes I'm fine; at other times I get so panic-stricken. If I find a person and talk about a subject that highly interests me, I can forget about the other people around me and avoid a panic attack. As for the depression though . . . I'm always depressed.

I struggle with my disorders on a daily, if not hourly, basis. I always feel like my depression or anxiety is there. I can't deny it. I can't "fix" it.

I can just struggle with it and take it day-by-day. I try to simply will myself to get better. I do it a lot.

My grandmother was a strong woman. She had experienced ten strokes by the time she died at age seventy-six. She refused to use a walker. She would go outside in the summer and mow the lawn with a push mower a couple of days after having had a stroke! She was my hero. I try to be like her.

Things have to be done. I don't have time to feel bad or worry about me. If I don't do it, it won't get done; and if it does get done, it won't get done right, and I'll have to do it anyway. My mind is stronger than my body, and if there is a will there is a way.

Jannine P.
Her story . . .

Depression, Panic Disorder, Post-Traumatic Stress Disorder (PTSD)

I am a published author who was diagnosed with major depressive disorder in my early forties. I've been living with these symptoms for about forty years. My primary symptoms include sweating, graying vision, fainting, claustrophobia, irritability, and feeling out of control. When I am out in public, I feel as if my world is getting smaller, and everything suffocates me; I start getting tunnel vision.

I am usually aware of what is going on around me, although sometimes I'm in a fog. I try to smile to hide my depression or panic attacks, but inside I am frantic and fearful. My friends understand my disorder. However, my social life is nonexistent. I don't like new situations—too many people and strangers I don't know. I usually don't put myself into those situations unless my husband or daughters are with me. Even then I can't mingle socially for long. There's an awful feeling of everything and everyone closing in on me.

My family understands my disorder and works around it. I have to rely on my husband, daughters, or sons-in-law to get me places outside my comfort zone of driving. Before I was put on medications, I was virtually a prisoner in my home. I seldom ventured outside the house except to get the mail or to garden. I cannot work outside the home. I'm a published author, but I cannot do all the promotions other authors do because I am not comfortable being the focus of book signings and writer's group meetings. Just the thought of working in public places makes it difficult for me to breathe.

Until recently I had no particular method of dealing with my disorders. I would just stay home and not go anywhere. A therapist showed me methods to help relieve anxiety. One was tapping my hands, one and then the other, against my thighs or on the seat around me to calm me down. She also showed me how to put awful thoughts inside imaginary boxes. Both of these techniques have helped me to cope.

I was having panic attacks as far back as my teen years. I didn't realize it until I was put on medication and saw a therapist in my forties. Things I had done, such as walking in a wide circle around a group of people, hiding in bathrooms, and not daring to look anyone in the eye, were all part of my teen years, and they carried on into my adulthood. I have no recollection of my early childhood, with the exception of visiting my grandparents in New York.

Prior to taking medications, I experienced many episodes of panic attacks. If I took my kids to soccer or gymnastics practice, there were times I would hide in the bathroom and not be able to come out. I would have to call my husband to come and get me.

> *The diagnosis shocked me. I thought PTSD was a soldier's disorder. I didn't think I'd gone through something as horrendous as going off to war.*

The medications have helped tremendously, but they are not a cure. My symptoms are less, but they are not gone. I always seemed to know when a panic attack would strike. I would begin to sweat, my outer vision grayed, and I couldn't breathe.

I could always tell when my depression was getting worse because I not only felt sad, I was self-loathing, self-destructive, and suicidal. I believe I was depressed for most of my life, starting in my teens.

There are times when I will not leave the house to go shopping, even within my comfort zone of driving. I simply cannot face other people or handle the responsibility of driving a car. I'll be terrified of getting into an accident. I'll be fearful of what other people might do: attack me, shoot me, or try to confront me in a bad way. I will not go into a bank because I'm afraid it will get robbed while I'm there. I will not put gas in my car because I'm afraid the pumps will explode. I will not get into an airplane because I'm afraid it will crash. Often I will plan on going on a picnic or going to an amusement park with the family, or to a concert, but I usually cancel at the last minute. I make up one excuse or another. Nighttime is the worst. I don't drive at night, and when I'm in the car with my husband, I imagine all kinds of things (people, animals, the unknown) jumping in front of the car.

When I first started taking medications in my early forties, I felt as if I had gotten my life back. It was amazing how alive I felt and how much I looked forward to each new day. My comfort zone spread out, and I even drove the freeway short distances. I went shopping by myself too. While the overall symptoms eased, I knew the medications would not cure my disorders, and I would need ongoing treatment. Seeing a therapist had its advantages. I was able to voice my thoughts aloud without worrying what my family or friends would think. Therapy opened my eyes to see that I was not the only person going through what I was feeling. While the medications helped to take the edge off, the therapy showed me that I have a lot to offer, and I don't have to dig a hole and never come out again.

Work is a sensitive issue for me. I tried to work early in my marriage, long before being diagnosed with depression, but I never stayed at a job for more than a year. I couldn't face people, I suppose. So my husband's income was, and still is, all we have to live on. To this day, even though I'm a grandmother, I still feel guilty for not contributing financially, especially because we have a lot of debt and can't seem to get out from under it. My husband never pressured me to work. It was I who put the pressure on myself. My daughters loved having me as a stay-at-home mom. So did my husband. But I can't let go of the guilty feeling that I could have made our lives much easier financially.

I'll never forget my oldest sister telling me, "You have to snap out of it." She told me to get over whatever it was I thought I had. My family never really understood what was going on; they never really cared enough to know, I suppose, with the exception of my mother (who had two nervous breakdowns) and my husband and kids. I have heard other people say that what I am experiencing is just a phase.

One of the times I had a severe emotional breakdown was a few years after my mother passed away. I discovered that my father had a whole other family. I couldn't stomach the woman, twenty-two years his junior, with whom he'd been carrying on a double life. I'd had a falling out with my father by phone, and I lost all hope of living. I grabbed a kitchen knife and held it to my wrist. I remained that way, crying and fighting against slicing open my wrist. My daughter called my husband home from work. He called my therapist, who wanted him to take me to the hospital. I refused and curled up in bed, wishing I could end my life.

A hopeful period would be about two weeks after I began taking medications for the disorders. I was an entirely different person. I felt as if the cell door was thrown open, and I was set free. It gave me hope that I did not have to feel as trapped or frightened as I had almost all my life. My comfort zone widened. I was able to drive on the freeway for short trips. I wasn't having panic attacks any longer, and I felt an inner calm, not the turmoil that had seemed to plague me constantly.

I feel good if I'm driving and listening to my favorite music. When I'm out shopping, I will hide in the bathroom for a few minutes if I feel overwhelmed with other shoppers. In doctors' offices I will pace until I'm called in. These are all coping methods for me, and the fact that I can pull myself out of a phobia makes me feel good about myself. I have my four dogs at home. I love dogs, and I love being surrounded by them. If I'm sad I'll sit down, and they'll all come around me. We'll sit together for an hour, maybe watching TV, and I'll usually feel much better. I also have three grown daughters with whom I can talk about my fears or what's worrying me. Two of my daughters are on antidepressant medication as well. So we understand each other, and the four of us are good friends. In fact they're my only friends.

I had been depressed for so long, I feared that was all I had to look forward to. It was a vicious cycle, a merry-go-around of self-loathing and feeling sorry for myself. Now I look forward to the future. I'm in a place that is peaceful and enjoyable. I still struggle with a few of my phobias: fear of flying, fear of heights, and fear of fire. I realize there will be things I cannot overcome, and I look for other opportunities. I've used Amtrak to visit my daughters and have traveled out of town or out of state. I avoid putting myself in situations that will feed one of my fears.

After many visits to my therapist, I was finally diagnosed a couple of years ago with major depressive disorder. My husband lost his job in 2010. It was a difficult time, but the support of our daughters has helped. At the time of my major depressive disorder diagnosis, I was also diagnosed with PTSD. The cause was the surgery and chemotherapy I went through when I was thirty-two. That entire year was filled with blood tests, chemo, and sleeping. I lost a whole year out of my life. I can't even remember how much of a mother and wife I was during that time.

The diagnosis shocked me. I thought PTSD was a soldier's disorder. I didn't think I'd gone through something as horrendous as going off to war. I've come to hate even-numbered years (I was diagnosed in 1984). In stores I'll go to an uneven-numbered checkout. If I can't, I start to feel shaky, and I lose sight of my surroundings. I also think that the year I had chemotherapy traumatized me. If I see anything associated with chemo, I start tasting the meds in my throat. I had to take all my meds intravenously because I was allergic to the pills and broke out in sores all over my head and in my throat. As the med was released into my vein, I got an awful taste in my mouth as well as feeling the liquid in my throat.

These are just a few of my behavior patterns since 1984. I haven't had the chance to see my therapist to learn how to combat this disorder because of lack of funds. So I continue to suffer, and I try to make the best of my days any way that I can.

I don't worry about the future because I know there will always be medication to help me. When I'm used to one medication and it becomes ineffective, there will be another to take its place. My disorders will never be gone, but I am confident that they will always be under control to a degree, and I can carry on my life as normally as possible.

Kim B.
Her story . . .

Seasonal Affective Disorder (SAD)

Fall and winter are when I suffer the most with my symptoms of SAD. The days are shorter, sunlight is absent for days at a time, and the cooler temperatures cause me to slow down. I am drained, stiff, and lethargic. Like a grumpy old bear, I want to hibernate in my warm, cozy bed until springtime.

Often I have just enough energy to do what is required to get ready for the day, keep my house in order, and plan and prepare dinner. I'm grateful for the ability to accomplish one task a day in addition to my other routines. On the other hand, spring and summer cause me to feel hopeful, energized, and alive. The sunlight is my friend! I love the brilliance reflecting off the swimming pool and the warming rays on my shoulders. I experience physical and emotional freedom, and I find I have more energy to embrace each new day.

When the days are longer, I have the stamina to make it through. Like a brown, dry bulb planted in the earth in autumn, I bloom when the warmth of springtime dawns, and I open to the life-giving rays of the sunshine.

SAD impacts my family whether I like it or not. While I was lying in bed and battling the flu one day, my youngest daughter entered my room upon returning from school. "Mom, are you still in bed? You were there yesterday too!" Then she told me, "Today I thought, 'Yep, summer is almost over, so Mom's going to be sleeping more.'" Upon hearing her words, my heart sank.

My daughter knows me only this way, and there's really not too much I can do to make it any different. I know she sometimes is saddened by my lack of energy and my mushy, forgetful brain. This alone is reason for me to take care of myself and maximize every opportunity, particularly as it relates to spending time and investing in her and in the rest of the family.

Household chores have become more of a group effort. Prior to realizing I was living with SAD, I was one woman who could do it all and do it all myself. I managed my home, family, business, and numerous volunteer and leadership responsibilities. Not any longer.

Now, with my husband's coaxing, I have a housekeeper; my son helps with the grocery shopping, my daughter does the laundry, and my dear husband pitches in everywhere else. His understanding and acceptance have been crucial to my learning to cope, accepting my limitations, and giving myself permission to rest.

Like a brown, dry bulb planted in the earth in autumn, I bloom when the warmth of springtime dawns ...

I challenge myself to think from another perspective. For instance, just last winter after weeks of dreary, rainy days, it dawned on me how important rain is to the human existence. It is not just a messy inconvenience, interrupting places to go and things to do. Our very livelihood depends on the daily consumption of water.

This new viewpoint helped me get through the remainder of the rainy season last year. I assume it will help again this year. Winter just seems like such a dead season to me. I've learned that every living thing needs seasons of rest, down time, inactivity. Our society today is addicted to busy-ness, and I think that contributes greatly to many illnesses. I am learning to give myself permission to sit and read a book, watch the flames in my fireplace, sip a cup of tea. I'm finding new things to appreciate about the months I'm most impacted by SAD. In fact just looking at the acronym SAD can be depressing! How about calling it HAPPY? It would stand for "Have a Positive Perspective, You." I'll make a mental note to remember *that* acronym as the seasons change!

Greg G.
His story . . .

Post-Traumatic Stress Disorder (PTSD)

I was diagnosed in 1990 with post-traumatic stress disorder at the age of thirty-two. My symptoms include severe anxiety, heightened startle reflex, claustrophobia, increased heart rate and blood pressure, mood swings, insomnia, and depression.

At times, something as simple as a bug flying by will startle me into a fight-or-flight feeling. Or I'll become afraid to go anywhere or to be around anyone. A trip to see the doctor or to go to the grocery store can become a white-knuckle, heart-pounding nightmare. What people don't seem to understand is although I looked okay on the outside, in reality I felt horrible inside. I can and do become stressed out over the smallest things.

There was a time when PTSD was not part of my everyday life. I was a healthy, happily married, family man with three kids before the accident. Life was pretty good. All that was shattered when a truck rear-ended me at high speed. The vehicle I was in was crushed, and the man I used to be ceased to exist.

At first I attempted to cope on my own. I was afraid to tell the doctors I had issues with my fears. Instead of addressing the problem, doctors started telling me to take "drugs" to mask the symptoms. I hated it. Some of the prescriptions were for heavy narcotics, and I felt out of it, drugged-up, tired, and lethargic. I was taking ten different medications, and my problems seemed bigger than ever. I was finally able to stop taking nine out of the ten drugs by taking a natural remedy over a two-week time period.

I have tried medication, physical therapy, meditation, relaxation techniques, self-help, self-talk, motivational recordings, and psychotherapy. I'm sure they all helped in some way or another. What I found helped the most was getting the proper vitamins, minerals, and antioxidants in my body so it could heal itself.

I know the doctors I saw did the best they could in an attempt to balance positive side effects with the negatives. I became sensitive to some of the medications, and I ended up in the emergency room several times. That didn't help reduce stress! It wasn't pleasant hoping that the next new drug would help, only to find out it actually caused more bad things than good things.

The unpredictable nature of my disorder made it hard to schedule much of anything, because I never knew how I was going to feel when the time came.

I've had amazing results using minerals and other natural remedies. They have reduced pain and inflammation, boosted my immune system, and given me back a relatively normal life, considering all the issues I've suffered from. I believe one has to give the body what it needs to heal on its own, and giving the body the nutrients it needs offers a fighting chance.

I'm hopeful I can keep feeling good by taking natural products and staying away from the damage of synthetic medications. My comparison is to a car: While driving around town, if the oil light comes on, a good driver pulls over. Taking a drug is like cutting the wire to the oil light and continuing to drive on. I'd rather refill my nutrient reservoir, just like refilling my car with more oil, instead of continuing to hurt myself by avoiding or covering up the symptoms.

PTSD has definitely impacted my friendships and my family life. I've lost most of my friends over time because they didn't understand the stress and pain I was going through. I believe they thought it was all in my head until they heard the "official" diagnosis and could accept that. I think people mistook my anxiety as rejection, and we became distant. It was difficult to explain how a barking dog or a phone ringing could make my heart race as if I was in a life-or-death situation. My family didn't understand the pain I felt inside and out. I feel they would rather avoid contact than deal with the radical changes I go through from moment to moment.

The unpredictable nature of my disorder made it hard to schedule much of anything, because I never knew how I was going to feel when the time came. I would get highly stressed over things I had planned, and I could not make commitments to carry through. I choose to be alone a lot because I don't like a lot of noise and disruption. A quiet evening with my sweetheart beats a night out, in my opinion.

I used to work in office equipment repair and in law enforcement. I found work impossible to perform. Just the thought of driving a car made my heart race and my hands sweat. I shook from fear. I could not fathom coming across as a paid professional in any field because of the anxiety I had. I felt devastated that I couldn't work. I was supposed to be the breadwinner of the family, and now I felt utterly useless. With my lawyers I fought for five years to obtain Social Security disability.

My hobbies are gardening, target shooting, and motorcycle riding. I've kept pushing my comfort zone until I was able to go skydiving to conquer many of my fears. Life is about the journey, not the destination, and I hope everyone enjoys every minute of the journey—stress-free and pain-free. Listening to music, playing guitar, taking a walk, or getting some other exercise are some things I like to do to cope and relieve a little stress.

My experiences with PTSD have definitely broadened my self-knowledge. I surely got an education in what others might be going through with hidden problems, and I have a lot more compassion for people than I did before.

I now know I cannot control things as I would like to. This attitude has shown me I can let go of some of my anxiety and go with the flow instead of fighting it. Some days are just going to unfold as they do, and I can't always change that—but I can change the way I react to it all.

Iris K.
Her story . . .

Depression

I'm a ninety-four-year-old woman who was diagnosed with depression in 1993 at the age of seventy-seven. At the time I was diagnosed, my depression felt as if I were in a glass cage, unable to communicate with those around me. I felt completely closed in.

Depression hit me in a strange way. I had always been happy and upbeat, but I woke up one morning feeling shaky, as if my innards were quivering. I had no appetite whatsoever for food. Since I was feeling so strange, my husband insisted we visit our family doctor. After I had answered a few of the doctor's questions, he said, "I think she's depressed."

We had recently moved to a new location (our retirement home), and I had not had time to make new friends or connections. I worried about what I would do in a strange environment if I should lose my husband. I felt isolated and insecure. Sometimes I felt as though I was in an isolation booth, unable to communicate with people or feel my world around me. I'd hear some astounding news on the TV, and I'd think, "So what?"

The doctor prescribed antidepressant medication, which helped. The real help came when I met a group of ladies from our mobile home park at our clubhouse, where I was invited to join them at a weekly card party. They called themselves "The Huggy Bunch," as they all embraced each other. They made me feel at home with their warm welcome. I never felt weird or alone after that, and the weight of the depression gently lifted.

I can't say I was depressed after my husband died, although I was terribly sad and lonely. He hadn't been in the best of health for some time, but it was still difficult to care for him at home. Having that hospital bed in the living room, with an oxygen machine running constantly, was a warning of sorts. I got up several times in the night to replace the oxygen tube that he kept pulling out. One morning I found it dangling over the side of his bed and noted no movement in his chest. No rise and fall of breath. He was gone. My love was gone.

> *I felt as though I was in an isolation booth, unable to communicate with people or feel my world around me. I'd hear some astounding news on the TV, and I'd think, "So what?"*

I take steps to appear the opposite of what I'm feeling. I just pretend all is well with me. The coping tools that work for me are my religion, being with people, and playing cards with friends. I also enjoy listening to music.

When I got depressed, other people worried about me. When people said things such as "Just snap out of it" or "Pull yourself together," they didn't understand how I felt. I couldn't just turn it off and on.

Depression affected my spiritual beliefs in that it made me more prayerful. I experienced an overwhelming sense of loss when my husband died. I have come to terms with his loss, and the pain is less. I still miss him every day, and I always will. I often tell myself, "Be grateful instead of pitiful, or as I like to say, pity-full."

Holli M.
Her story . . .

Post-Traumatic Stress Disorder (PTSD), Generalized Anxiety Disorder, Panic Disorder, Social Phobias

My primary symptoms include insomnia, moderate to severe anxiety, anger, feeling alone, nightmares, flashbacks, chronic pain, migraines and frequent headaches, chest tightening and shortness of breath. I often feel as if I am in the middle of a large lake; my boat has drifted quite a distance away, my body is cold and tired of treading water, and I can see no land. I am wearing no life jacket, and I am not always sure if I'm going to make my way out of this situation.

I was brought up in an extremely dysfunctional family. Whenever something was going on within the family, we were told to act as though things were normal. I don't know how we knew what "normal" was, but it was not carrying on or saying anything to anyone. I feel very vulnerable and uncomfortable with my feelings. I have had experiences where people find out things about my life or diagnosis that cause them to no longer want contact with me. I feel it is because of their lack of understanding or just not knowing how to be around me. I just want to be treated normally, but I seem more accepted if I don't let on that I'm having a really rough day! I believe that it takes a lot of energy to pretend.

My disorders are very hard on my family. When I get an invitation to something, I feel incredible trepidation about going, and I start to get an anxiety attack. It is only when I am at the event that I feel okay. I often don't like making appointments and engagements for fear that I may have to cancel and disappoint people. My husband has to talk to me and cheer me on, making sure I feel comfortable enough to get to locations I may or may not have been to before. He has to deal with my anxiety and frustrations that can, at times, come easily to the surface. He has had to work from home on days that I am having extreme symptoms.

For the most part, I am aware of my symptoms probably 90 percent of the time. I have been utilizing cognitive behavioral therapy for more than fourteen years. During this time I cope by myself, or I will talk to my husband, to a friend, or to my psychologist. Occasionally, when I am in the middle of a storm, it will require my husband's slowing me down and telling me that it seems as if I am having a difficult time. We will usually problem-solve at that point, so I can take a realistic approach to what I can "take off my plate." Then I will usually do something for myself, such as take a hot bath or take a nap with relaxation recordings to start my day over again.

I don't have a bruise, and I am not bleeding, but I have this amazing amount of pain. Things that people cannot see seem less credible to them.

I've noticed that guided imagery and relaxation CDs have helped me most. Acupuncture and chiropractic treatments have also been helpful. Just taking time out to "breathe," to do things that I enjoy, helps me a lot. Playing a game with my son or cuddling up to watch a movie can be very healing, and it doesn't require a lot of "body" work. I try to use self-talk as well, but it is a little trickier to master.

I don't recall having anxiety as a child. I know now that I did, but I don't recall it or how it felt because that was simply the way everyday life was. I remember being sick a lot, having stomach problems and headaches; but I didn't know what that was, and I thought everyone must feel this way. I didn't know any better. When I was diagnosed with PTSD, I was really confused. Okay, now I have a name for my symptoms, but what is this? It made sense once I was able to get my head around it, and I couldn't believe that not everyone lived as I did. I felt cheated and very sad about my lost childhood.

I am always feeling one symptom or another somewhere throughout my body, either from the PTSD or anxiety. In daily life, I struggle with things going on around me, such as people, places, and the world. It seems all these things are constantly changing. If I'm not dealing with anxiety, I might be dealing with some other symptoms. I like it best, and function better, when things are my life are relatively stable.

My anticipatory anxiety often causes me to want to avoid situations that I perceive to be stressful. Ironically many of these situations turn out to be very beneficial to me. Examples would include spending time with friends, going for any of my appointments, or going to a new place.

Most people cannot see or relate to my disorder. For example, I don't have a bruise, and I am not bleeding, but I have this amazing amount of pain. Things that people cannot see seem less credible to them. A person with a broken arm in a cast signals to people what has to be endured. What if the body is broken but doesn't require a cast? There is nothing anyone can do, and no one sees or understands. I look like any other American mom in her mid-thirties, so people cannot relate to my experience, and they cannot see that I struggle.

It would be great if I could take something and be "all better." It would be great if they could really put Humpty Dumpty back together again without a crack or two showing. Yet that, to me, isn't reality. I would rather have the knowledge and understanding of what I am dealing with and go from there trying to improve my life. Medication has all sorts of goofy side effects. I may take something for my anxiety, but when I take enough to reach a comfortable point, I might be so tired that I can't function. I have a life and a family that I want to live for, not sleep through.

It is incredibly difficult to be disabled, and I find a lot of shame attached to it. I understand that it is the way it is, but I long for the glory days of working in my career, talking with others who work, and being able to relate with others on that level. I can't relate to a group of people when they are talking about careers and coworkers, etc. I don't live in that world, and they do not live in mine. I've had people make comments such as, "It would be great to just stay home and get paid." What an ignorant comment! It's awful, and it's not as if the pay is really great either! It's another form of isolation. I don't know that I will ever feel comfortable with my disabilities, but then again, it is what it is. It does me no good to be hard on myself, which I tend to be. At times I feel as though I'm not contributing to society.

Sometimes simple tasks like taking a bath or shower seem huge, and because I'm slightly agoraphobic, I sometimes fear leaving the house. Luckily caring for my son requires me to move every day or to leave the house for reasons associated with him. I also feel safer in numbers. Before the birth of my son, I might have needed my husband to stay home with me. I would be like a zombie, isolating myself or picking at my feet until they would bleed without realizing that I was doing that. This would happen because I was disassociated. All of this improved when my son came along. I now have so much more going on in my life that requires my full attention; it's actually difficult to disassociate.

I feel very different because of my disorder, and this makes me feel as though I want to isolate, as if I just don't belong. It makes me feel sad, it makes me feel like things are unfair, and it makes me wonder why I have so many things on my plate already. It is up to me to get myself through those feelings and feel worthy, as if I matter too, as if I can breathe and take up some space on this earth simply because I am who I am.

I like to think that I have come to terms with my disorder for the most part. I believe that we are all constantly working on ourselves. The journey does not end until death. Therefore I will not end my healing journey. I will not give up on myself even though it takes all my strength to keep going. My body is sometimes filled with anxiety, nightmares, sweats, flashbacks, or irritability, and it takes over everything. But I will not let my sufferings win when there is something I can do about them. I am a survivor, and I will continue to thrive. I am a realist. I know that there will always be a struggle with something; everyone has that. It's what we do with the struggle that counts.

My anxiety hasn't necessarily impacted my religious or spiritual beliefs. However, the abuse I endured as a child, being diagnosed with a chronic pain disorder, and being in so much agony because of it has changed my spiritual beliefs to agnostic. I was brought up Catholic, but I don't know that God exists. I feel like He's left me alone. I feel many of the same ways that Holocaust survivors feel: where is God? God is gone. I once read a quote from a Holocaust survivor who said, "When I get up to heaven, God will have to get down on His knees and beg my forgiveness." This statement rings true for me.

Ira Z.
His story . . .

Depression, Generalized Anxiety Disorder (GAD)

I believe I have suffered with low-level depression for most of my life. I've also had bouts of anxiety so severe that functioning was difficult. I was diagnosed in my early- to mid-twenties, and in my mid-thirties I suffered through my first major depressive episode. So far I've endured two or three major periods of depression in my life.

My depression is like living in a bleak, dark world with no way out. It's like having a heavy load on my shoulders that I can no longer carry around. My primary depression symptom was a feeling of deep despair, with everything appearing black and hopeless. I would wake up with a terrible feeling in the pit of my stomach. Anything I looked at or experienced caused me to feel more depressed. I'd visit my parents, who lived in a nice, spacious apartment, and I'd look at the building and think, "This is all life has to offer? Ending up in a small box they call an apartment?"

I went to law school after Army basic training and advanced individual training in the National Guard. While I was training, the woman I was very involved with broke up with me. It took me years to get over her. I left law school after one year, partly because I was still so incredibly depressed over the breakup. Years later I began obsessing about her, and the obsession controlled my life. At the time I was married with two children. I believe the obsessing was part of my depression, and the depression was controlling how deeply I was feeling about her. It also fed into feelings of dissatisfaction with my life and how little control I felt I had over the direction it was going.

I'm disabled, and I have not worked in ten years. I was self-employed and ran a small computer consulting company. I love films, and I love to read. I maintain my equilibrium by watching films, including many documentaries, and by taking care of my two children. Before I became disabled, I loved playing sports—specifically basketball and tennis. I would play ball at least three times a week; it helped reduce stress and made me feel good about myself.

I have always taken steps to appear the opposite of what I'm feeling. When I was working, no one was able to tell I was suffering through a severe depression. People would often remark to me that I seemed like the kind of person who never had a sad day in his entire life. I was still working when I experienced two or three major bouts of depression. My job was high-pressure and stressful, but my depression never got in the way of my performance, nor was anyone able to detect how I was really feeling.

> *...no one was able to tell I was suffering through a severe depression. People would often remark that I seemed like the kind of person who never had a sad day in his entire life.*

I went to law school after graduating from college, but I took a leave of absence after a year. It wasn't that I couldn't do the work; rather my inability to deal with my feelings of depression caused me to leave. I remember taking a criminal law midterm and freezing up during the test. Criminal law was my favorite subject, but I was unable to think, and I had a severe panic attack.

Many times I would not attend social events or go out with friends because of my mood disorders. My moods affected every aspect of my life. I went to my friend's son's wedding, and I couldn't talk to anyone, even though I'd known all the people there for many years. I've isolated myself and sometimes thought of driving into a brick wall, even though I knew I wouldn't actually do it. The anxiety caused me to feel as though I was coming out of my skin. I felt as though I was going crazy, and it was the worst feeling I'd ever had. My anxiety makes me feel as if I'm drowning, and I'm in a panic, desperately trying to reach the surface.

The trial and error of new medications has had a tremendous impact on my life. I have been on many, many different medications. I often feel like a guinea pig being experimented on by the medical profession. Since no one can predict how a particular medicine will affect an individual, it is truly a trial-and-error proposition. I've experienced a number of side effects while being treated with different medications. I've had an eighty-pound weight increase, enormous problems with fatigue, and short-term memory difficulties. My anxiety level greatly increased, and some of the medication side effects felt as though I was jumping out of my skin. My mind would race, and I would feel the need to change my environment quickly. Some medications made me feel as though I was going crazy.

I cannot remember a time when my disorder was not part of my everyday life. When I was younger, I used to think everyone felt, to some extent, like I did. It wasn't until things got worse and I entered therapy that I came to realize many people did not experience what I felt. It was an incredible revelation to me, and it made me feel even more depressed and anxious. I then came to understand how much depression and anxiety had become part of my life and how my actions were guided and controlled by my mood.

The fact that I have not been able to work for at least ten years has caused major problems for me. I had always worked and derived my identity from my career. Although I left law school and bounced around for years, I finally found a career that was emotionally fulfilling and economically rewarding. I trained as a computer programmer and after a number of years went into computer consulting and began my own small consulting company. I used to have a partner, but after a while he left, and I ran the company myself. I also started another company with five coworkers. I was an aggressive entrepreneur and a successful one. I felt incredibly fulfilled!

After I got married, my income allowed me to put my wife through law school, and it helped us purchase our first single-family home. Since I grew up in New York City and always lived in apartments, this home was an amazing achievement for me. After I became ill, we lost our house, and my wife and I separated. Not working and not being able to support my family, and specifically my two children, has caused me to experience many negative emotions. I constantly fight feelings of guilt, even though my kids always tell me not to feel guilty. "It's not your fault you became ill. It could happen to anyone," they tell me.

I still experience constant guilt and negative feelings about myself. I think, "I'm a failure. I'm a terrible father. I am almost sixty years old, and I have absolutely no money while everyone else I know is doing wonderfully financially."

I currently receive Social Security disability and private disability insurance. The process of getting disability was arduous, but luckily my best friend is an attorney, so a lot of the pressure was diminished because of him. It still was difficult, and the private disability was very hard to obtain. Insurers put deserving people through the mill; things become very difficult, and there are roadblocks every step of the way.

It makes me frustrated and angry when people say things like "Just snap out of it" or "Pull yourself together." Many people just do not understand what it's like to suffer from clinical depression and major anxiety. Those who do are few and far between. I've had a number of discussions with individuals who also suffer as I do, and we are continually amazed at the lack of empathy and sympathy from so many people.

I've often said I'd rather lose a limb than suffer from depression and anxiety. There is still a stigma attached to these illnesses and an incredible lack of compassion and understanding, even within the medical profession. People will talk about having "a bad day" and their solutions for dealing with it, but they really don't get it. Depression is not like having a bad day.

I worry about the future all of the time. I think about those periods when I suffered through major depressive episodes, and they scare me. Right now my deep depression is under control, but I'm so fearful I'll slip back at some point. The medicine I'm taking keeps me from slipping, but I always think about those previous episodes and how scary they were. Everything was bleak and dark, and I was controlled by the depression. It felt emotions for me, and it spoke for me. I did not have control over my life, and I never thought I would come out of it. Nothing has ever affected me like those episodes, and I wonder if I would be able to survive more of them.

Marty W.
Her story . . .

Generalized Anxiety Disorder (GAD), Depression, Obsessive-Compulsive Disorder (OCD)

I've lived with my symptoms for approximately thirty-three years; I was diagnosed at the age of twelve or thirteen. I went to school to be a licensed practical nurse, but I'm unable to do that anymore. I got a job working in a factory, but I was terminated because I called in sick too often.

Often my depression feels like I'm in a deep, black, soundless pit with darkness so dense that light cannot penetrate it. I envision myself feeling along the walls of the pit, searching for a way out. The walls are made of concrete, and they are cold, damp, and impenetrable. There is no way out whatsoever.

My disorders have definitely impacted my friendships and my social life. I have isolated myself from others, and I find it difficult to keep and maintain offline friendships. I spend most of my time at home and rarely talk on the phone to the very few friends I have.

I have established friendships with people on message boards that I frequent. When online friends from the message boards want to call and talk to me on the phone, I make up excuses not to speak on the phone. I get invited to different social events; I usually find a reason not to go. Most times I just want to stay at home where I feel comfortable and safe. People stop inviting me to some social events because I rarely show up.

Because of my anxiety, OCD, and depression, I find myself spending less time with my family. We don't talk on the telephone as much as we used to, but that could be related to busy work, family, social and school schedules. When we do get together, I become irritable and find myself watching the time so I can go home. For some reason there's always some kind of dispute going on that leaves people upset or with ill feelings. I don't like a lot of drama or arguments because such contention makes me feel uncomfortable and anxious. I love my family, but I just can't deal with some of the emotional stressors that come up.

Back in the 1990s, I qualified for Social Security disability, but I didn't want to be on disability for the rest of my life, so I began working again after two years. Ever since I have returned to work, my depression and anxiety have been very problematic. It's hard to work when I feel so depressed that I want to die or crawl under a rock. My coworkers would sometimes notice something was wrong with me, and I usually made up some other excuses to hide the real reason why I didn't feel good. Also when given new tasks at work, I found myself panicking and becoming very anxious. I was afraid I wouldn't be able to do the tasks because of my memory problems and because I'd never previously done what they asked me to do.

> *What's it like to be genuinely happy? Where do other people find the energy and motivation too do the things they do?*

I was terminated from a temporary job in February 2007 for calling in sick too often. I found it very hard to go to work every day. At first when I got fired, I felt humiliated and worthless because I couldn't work like "normal" people. I had never been fired before in my life, so this was very hard for me

I don't have the self-confidence I used to have when I was younger. I find that change is hard for me most times too. Fear of the unknown is scary now, and it wasn't always that way. When I was younger, I welcomed and embraced change, and I felt it was better to try new things than to stagnate with the status quo. Not anymore.

I'm very aware when my symptoms become problematic. I withdraw and isolate myself from people; I become quiet, and I will become irritable if approached by others. I try to warn people when I'm not feeling good, and I don't want to be bothered. When I'm having a particularly bad day, there's nothing that can get me out of the depression. I go through the motions of trying to live my life on a daily basis like a robot. There is so much emotional pain, anger, and negativity that others know when I'm not feeling good, even though I try to hide it. The only thing that helps in this situation is rest and when I can get a decent night's sleep. It may take a day or two to get a good night's sleep, but sleep does help.

Depression has been a part of my life since I was diagnosed with it as a kid. There were times when it wasn't so dominant, but it's always been with me. When I did have periods of happiness, I'd feel as though I didn't deserve them, as if I was unworthy of happiness. When I was in my twenties, I was able to work full time, attend school full time, raise my kids, and occasionally socialize with friends. We'd go to a happy hour to meet people, and I'd often go out with my coworkers after work.

I've had my moments of severe depression and problems with rage, but the depression wasn't the way it is now. The rage is controlled better now than it was back then, but I still have problems with it, so I'm seeing a psychologist.

A lot of times my mood does play a role in my sex drive, or lack thereof. When I feel very depressed, the last thing on my mind is sex. My medication also has a major impact on my sex drive. Many medications list decreased libido as a side effect. I have sex anyway because it wouldn't be fair to my fiancé to have to pay the price for my lack of sex drive. If I wait until my libido increases, I might never have sex again. Even though the desire is not there, I like the closeness and the feel of another person's body close to mine.

I'm receiving unemployment benefits until I can find another job or until I apply for disability. I don't feel guilty about being unemployed; I've worked hard and paid into the system for years. Now that I have health problems, I think I should be able to get some help. I have feelings of grief about my inability to fulfill the goals and aspirations I had for my life. I feel as though I've failed in my life, and this causes a lot of grief and feelings of worthlessness.

I feel very different and isolated from others. It seems as if other people are genuinely happy. They go to social events, plays, concerts, and art galleries. They have unbounded energy, are able-bodied, have successful careers, loving relationships, and wonderful friendships. They have great support from their family; they are positive and upbeat. They're "normal," able to deal with life better and look forward to the future. Other people don't seem to have a care in the world, and I can't figure out how they're able to do all these things. How can they be genuinely happy? What's it like to be genuinely happy? Where do other people find the energy and motivation to do the things they do?

Because of my depression, I cannot imagine what it's like to be genuinely happy and have "normal" relationships. I can't fathom what it's like to go out and attend social events or do fun things. All of this is foreign to me. I'd rather stay home alone and isolate myself from others. At home I feel safe and have a measure of comfort. I wish I knew what it was like to be genuinely happy without the specter of depression looming over my shoulder, to make friendships and keep them and without pushing people away. Not being able to do this just adds to my depression and feelings of isolation.

India M.
Her story . . .

Depression, Anxiety

My depression and anxiety issues started becoming extremely difficult when I went through puberty. I found myself feeling so incredibly sad for no apparent reason. It caused me to believe that my life just wasn't worth living anymore. Everything during this period of time in my life seemed to be either black or white, with no shades of gray. Even today shades of gray are often difficult to come by.

As a child I never had the courage to tell my parents how depressed I was feeling, because back in the 1960s, the only emotions that seemed to be acceptable were anger, fear, or a total lack of affect. However, something that did have a profound effect on me was when I was labeled by my parents as the "emotional one." Obviously I took it to be a bad thing, figuring that if one's parents were singling me out as "one" of anything, it had to be bad, right? How could I explain to them that I found myself crying for no apparent reason, or why I had actual physical symptoms in my gut?

I didn't know it then, but depression and anxiety disorders are on both sides of my family. However, it wasn't something that was openly discussed. In the 1960s there wasn't the same knowledge of brain chemistry that there is today. Back then being depressed for no apparent reason meant one had a weak personality and that the person should just snap out of it! My mother shared these same sentiments, yet she too grew up with a plethora of problems, including problems with my grandmother who, I later discovered, suffered from some sort of mental illness.

Most of what I have discovered about myself later in life has been through my own research on depression and anxiety disorders. As a little girl, I grew up knowing and finally believing that I was overly emotional and that there was something inherently wrong in my being that way. I used to tell people close to me that I was like the little girl in the fairytale "The Princess and the Pea." This story made me feel as though there must be something good about being "the emotional one," since this story was about a sensitive little girl who was also a princess! As I grew up, I discovered that this was actually true! My sensitivity allowed me to feel immense joy and pleasure just as it could make me feel intense pain and despair.

How could I explain to them that I found myself crying for no apparent reason . . . ?

In many of my romantic relationships, I would try to stay as emotionally disconnected as possible in order to not get hurt. That didn't always work, as I would fall in love with some partner. Then when it was over, it would be as though my world had ended. I wouldn't be able to eat, or I would eat too much. Or I'd smoke too much. For some reason I don't particularly like the feeling of being out of control, so I never drank too much. During these low periods, I would also find it difficult to concentrate or to sleep. I would spend many nights lying awake or sitting up watching television, anything to occupy my mind.

I went through a divorce in my mid-twenties, but the thought of divorcing the man I still loved, despite all his shortcomings, plunged me into the depths of depression. This severe depression forced me to move back home to live with my parents. To have to move back in with my parents when I was twenty-five years old was humiliating.

Occupying my time and mind with work and school at this time did little to help my emotional state. So I decided to take on some additional classes, this time in psychology, to see if I could figure out what I could do independently about my depression and to try to heal what was wrong with me. It was during these courses that I discovered that a person could be depressed for a reason as well as for no reason at all. I also came to understand that I wasn't the only one in the world that had ever experienced an anxiety attack.

When I came to realize and accept that it wasn't my fault that my marriage turned out to be such a disaster, despite all my attempts to make it better, I felt wonderful. So through my life, I have experienced both periods of feeling great and then periods of deep depression. Some periods of depression were situational in nature, such as the divorce or the loss of a pet, while other periods were not.

After the divorce I did something I thought I would never be able to do: I applied and got hired as a police officer. My new husband, whom I had met in college and dated for two years, had also become an officer and encouraged me to try. I had interned for the detective bureau and got to know some of the officers, but I wasn't entirely sure I could do the job.

I did take all the tests and interviews, and I did get hired. The time I spent in the police academy was, without a doubt, the most stressful part of that career. I spent fifteen years as a police officer, and I really loved the work. Yes, at times it was scary, but the training I had received had given me skills I had never had before. I learned to put myself "out there" and try new things, even if I was afraid of them.

I continued to work, but it was beginning to wear me down. I would lie in bed late at night and tell my husband of the fear that I had of quitting the job I loved so much. He would tell me everything would be okay, but I knew that it wouldn't be. I knew that I would fall into a major depressive episode once my work was taken away.

Me? Not work anymore? I couldn't imagine it! I couldn't imagine not being a cop any longer—not doing the job that gave back to me emotionally so much more than I could ever give, and boy did I give! It was the best feeling in the world to offer compassion to someone who had gone through a terrible experience of some sort, instead of the television-stereotyped "just the facts ma'am" that people have been taught to expect. My career gave me a sense of purpose in the world at long last, but now this illness was threatening all of that.

For a while I was able to get a work assignment, taking me off patrol, which wasn't as emotionally or physically draining on me, but after September 11, 2001, everything in the police department changed. The police chief and mayor decided that pretty much every officer that could work had to get back onto the street and back onto patrol. No one at that time knew what was going to happen next.

I knew then that I was in trouble. I purposely didn't tell many people about my depression, anxiety, or pain. The last thing one wants to do, when working on the police force, is admit any limitations. I remember saying that I'd be lucky if I made it on the street six months, and in July of 2002, my worst fears materialized. I had to go to my command officers and inform them that I was just too ill to continue working.

I spent the summer of 2002 in bed much of the time, and this is where I began to think about suicide. I couldn't think of any reason to live if I had to live with this continual pain and depression, had to give up the job I loved, be a burden on my husband, and depend on him for survival. I felt trapped.

During all of this time, I barely spoke of my depression to anyone besides my husband. My husband isn't the type to talk about topics like this to anyone either, so only he really knew how bad things were with my situation and me. Obviously though, my talk of suicide had him really scared. While scaring him wasn't my intent, I only thought it was fair to let him know in advance that I might not be around much longer. I felt that I had to be honest and share with him that it was *that* bad for me. Bad enough for me to want to permanently "check out" . . . as in forever.

Despite all my attempts to explain to my doctor what little relief I was getting from any of the medications, my prescriptions remained the same. He would sometimes say to me how he was going to change the medications, and I would say, "Great! Let's do it!" But later on I began to think he was just trying to test me and see if I was just a drug seeker. That was the last thing I wanted!

A therapist began to show me how my own negative thoughts could lead me down the path of depression. I began to learn that I could take feelings that were bothering me and continue to think about them to the point of making them far worse in my mind than they really were. He taught me that I had to learn to "think my own thoughts" as crazy as that sounds. I had to actually learn to not let my thoughts wander to the negative, where they could easily begin to control my emotions.

I knew I had upset many people in my family by not attending various functions over the years because of my depression, but the problem was that I just couldn't because of the way I was feeling that day. I guess they thought I was just being inconsiderate. They couldn't *see* my depression.

Now I know that I will do what I can, *when I can do it*, and that's the end of it. Sometimes my husband is forced to attend these functions by himself, where he has to explain over and over again that I have an illness, and I can't always make every family event. I think they are slowly starting to understand, but I also now know this disorder will affect what I can and cannot do for the rest of my life.

John B.
His story . . .

Depression

I was diagnosed in 1990 with a chronic type of depression called dysthymia. At that time I was frequently sad, restless, and angry. I would often arrive home after a long day's work and not know how to occupy my time. In other words I was having a hard time enjoying life's simple pleasures. I became anxious in response to mere thoughts of difficulties and even more so when confronted with life's inevitable problems. I was crying a lot and feeling that life is a series of onerous tasks with little or no reward, a dreary existence without respite from a sadness that wouldn't leave me the hell alone.

I'm certain that I have been depressed since I was a child of six years old or so. Throughout my years I was frequently unable to control my negative thoughts, which would come upon me sporadically, and at the most inconvenient and inappropriate times. I might be sitting in a business meeting and start thinking to myself how lonely I felt and how happy everyone around me seemed. I was easily peeved and irked by any hint of disrespect. I felt like a failure at the game of life, no matter how hard I tried to win.

I take steps to appear the opposite of what I am feeling when I am in a severe state of my depression. I don't want to burden anyone else with my sadness, nor do I want to share it. Much of my depression derived from having survived an extremely hard childhood replete with routine emotional abuse, physical abuse, alcohol-fueled parental rages, extreme criticism, and reflexive blaming and disrespect. As an adult I continued to endure the ridicule, deprecation, sneakiness, and downright dishonesty of two very difficult parents. Both my parents think nothing of insulting their grown children, all of whom have grown into productive and well-adjusted adults. My parents could not have asked for children who are more thoughtful, self-reliant, and entirely free of the kind of problems that plague many dysfunctional families: divorce(s), financial difficulties, alcoholism, promiscuity, addiction to gambling, and the inability to build a successful career. And yet nothing is ever good enough for them. Coming to realize how poisonous these parental traits were to us as children has been one of the keys to coming to terms with the underlying causes of my depression.

> *My experiences with depression have impacted my social relationships in a very positive way. I'm extremely selective about my friends, and yet I tend to be very, very close with those who make the grade.*

Fortunately, through the years following my diagnosis, I was able to get my depression under control with medication, psychotherapy, self-appraisal, the normal process of maturing emotionally, and other means. I still cope with depression on an occasional and unpredictable basis, and so I've developed specific techniques for dealing with incipient episodes. By recognizing the sadness that I am beginning to feel, by acknowledging that it is not rational or beneficial for me to harbor negative and self-critical thoughts, and by taking immediate steps to gain control of those ugly and hurtful thoughts and feelings, I've been able to avoid the chronic episodes of depression that I endured in 1990.

My symptoms include sadness, helplessness, feelings of being a maladjusted failure, helplessness in improving my situation, anger at my parents for their abuse, anger at myself for having put up with their abuse for as long as I did, anger that my mother is still abusive and cruel. Fortunately my father has mellowed as he has grown older, and he has apologized for much of the meanness that he directed toward my siblings and me as children and young adults. That makes me feel grateful, as well as vindicated.

Notice that I just wrote that I'm angry at myself for having endured parental abuse, when it is absolutely clear that children do not have the means, much less the worldly perspective, to push back at abusive parents. Depression is irrational in many ways. Why on earth should I be angry at myself for enduring hideous behaviors that were directed toward me as a child by maligning adults, and thus entirely beyond my control? I still am though.

Oddly enough, my experiences with depression have impacted my social relationships in a very positive way. I'm extremely selective about my friends, and yet I tend to be very, very close with those who make the grade. I refuse to tolerate shabby behavior, either on my part or by others. I've endured quite enough of that already, thank you.

Over the years I have discovered how to cultivate my own emotional intelligence. I've learned to calm myself down when things are going badly, to respond effectively when others are behaving swinishly, and to persevere when I'm failing and desperately want to succeed. I've learned how to forgive others and to forgive myself. I've learned to laugh out loud at life's ironies, to keep things in perspective when I'm tempted to react in ways that are detrimental to my own well-being, and to keep moving forward in my own life, come what may.

As we've grown older, my two older siblings and I have worked hard to recall as much about our background as we can, and to offer one another mutual support and comfort. I am very fortunate that my two older siblings remember so much that I have either forgotten or failed to notice about our family life as children. On the other hand,

I remember a lot that they do not, so we help each other as we struggle to be happy and self-aware. I'm certain that my oldest sibling suffers from some form of depression; the next oldest has been hospitalized with depression. Therefore a serious and determined examination of our childhood experiences is a necessary and ongoing endeavor. Learning and remembering what happened to us has been extremely helpful.

Although I've never doubted my diagnosis for a minute, I was clueless for many years about my depression. Looking back, I'm certain that it caused me problems in high school and college. I suppose I wasn't a very good judge of how serious my depression actually was.

Positive steps that I take include getting plenty of exercise, eating well, moderating alcohol consumption, and getting plenty of rest. Watching funny movies helps, as does enjoying a good meal or meeting with friends. I also remind myself that I have no logical reason to be depressed, that the ugly experiences of the past remain in the past, and that I have done extraordinarily well at creating a "safe," comfortable, and productive life for myself. Finally I remind myself that I have much to be grateful for and that I am truly a survivor of experiences that would have destroyed most people emotionally and psychologically.

I suppose that most people who know me would be surprised to learn that I have been treated for clinical depression. I'm the most relentlessly cheerful person I know, and that's because I constantly work at being so. Anyone who has ever been depressed knows how frightening a sudden and unexpected descent from contentment to despair can be.

Vicki T.
Her story . . .

Generalized Anxiety Disorder (GAD), Panic Disorder, Bipolar I

I write dramatic women's fiction with strong, unforgettable women characters in real-life situations. I was diagnosed with generalized anxiety disorder and panic disorder when I was forty-one years old. I cycle from manic to depressive to stable on an irregular basis. There is no predicting when I will have the next cycle. I also have severe anxiety. I get very anxious and nervous, tend to overeat, and clench my jaw. When in a panic, my mind loses focus, I breathe very shallowly, my heart races, and I get very intense. I can't concentrate on anything except the thoughts or words that are repeating in my head, feeding my panic.

Living with my mood disorder makes me feel as though I'm an alien among the rest of the human population. I react differently to various situations. I don't feel as if I have the same emotions as others. What makes some people cry or laugh doesn't do it for me. I know a lot of it is because of the medications I'm on. I no longer view the world through the same window as other people do.

I definitely hide my feelings and reactions when I'm around other people. I'm very careful to make sure I'm not ever in a situation where something might occur, so it's very rare for me to end up in a severe state around others. My husband is very good at helping me recognize when an episode starts, and he'll help me by being proactive. He can tell sometimes before I can when it would be time to take an anti-anxiety pill to head off a more severe reaction.

Only a very few select people know the depth to which my illness carries me. Some friends know that I have an anxiety disorder and that I am not always comfortable outside of my normal comfort zone, like my house. I rarely accept invitations for social functions because I'm afraid I'll have an episode while socializing. Mostly the episodes start before the function begins. I get anxious just thinking about going. Even among the few people who are my confidants, I don't think anyone knows I'm bipolar. I have a few online friends who know that I'm bipolar and whom I consider my support group. I'm not ashamed of it. I just don't think people truly understand the illness. Early on when I was diagnosed, I didn't think I was capable of explaining it to people. Now it's just become habit not to say anything. I guess the longer I don't tell others, the harder it is to say, "Look, I've had this illness for all these years, and I never told you."

No one has ever asked me outright what is wrong, so I guess I'm pretty good at disguising my moods.

I used to be a technical writer, and I was also working as a tech-writing consultant before I became ill. The stress was too much for me, and in order to maintain a certain level of "saneness," I had to give up my job. It wasn't all that bad because I had always dreamed about being an author, and this was a perfect opportunity for me to start working toward that goal.

Being a creative person, I wrote quickly during my manic stages of bipolar. The ideas flowed, and I only had to write them down as fast as they'd appear in my mind. Mania doesn't last forever, and at times, it cycles into depression. It's difficult to write when I'm depressed. I can't connect with my characters or with the story. I don't feel the desire to put words to paper. My doctor uses my writing as a "barometer" to determine where I am in my cycles. If I'm not writing, then we make adjustments to my medication to get me back to it. Sometimes the depression cycles last for quite a while. I go through months of no writing, which is very frustrating and difficult for me. I want to write, but the desire to write and the creative forces behind my writing aren't there.

As part of my medical treatments, my doctor would like to see as few manic episodes as possible. However, I miss those episodes because I felt like I could really harness my writing spirit and capture the ideas that would burst in my mind. I've learned to make sure to capture those ideas and write them down before they're lost forever. I keep binders full of ideas that I've thought about while manic. That way when the mania goes away, I still have ideas to help me during my "normal" (stable) times. I have episodes of normalcy where I can write effectively and with passion. I've learned to harness my other writing talent to coincide with my bipolar cycles. If I'm not in the mood to write, I work on other parts of my writing career such as promotion and public relations.

Generalized anxiety disorder and panic disorder don't have as much impact on my writing as a bipolar cycle does, but they can interrupt my writing temporarily. Most of the time when this occurs, I can distract myself with reading or watching a movie, taking anti-anxiety medication, and waiting for the crisis to wind itself down. Then I can get back to writing. One thing that does affect my writing career is being too anxious to hold book signings or to speak at events about my writing. It takes a lot of courage and determination to build up to a speaking event. I don't do them often because of the effect they have on me.

My anxiety level can increase dramatically to the point where even medication is unable to calm me down and handle the panic attacks. It's strange, though, that once I'm at the event and activities have started, my anxiety slowly ebbs to a more manageable level. However, getting me to that point can seem insurmountable.

With the medications I'm on, I don't have significant mood changes that negatively affect my behavior. I am pretty much stable. When I cycle into a depressive mood, I become more housebound and less active with my friends. I may disappear for a while, but I'm not sure how much my absence really affects others. I come back eventually, and when I rejoin activities, people are happy to see me. At least it seems that way to me. No one has asked me outright what is wrong, so I guess I'm pretty good at disguising my moods.

It has never occurred to me to doubt my diagnosis. It explains so much in my life. My past is littered with uncontrollable manic episodes and deep depressive cycles. Reading back through my journals, I can see the events clearly. I think my husband doubts my diagnosis at times, only because I tend to be stable most of the time. He wasn't with me during my past "out-of-control" life. He sees me now with only mild swings as compared to the way I was before medication. If I ever went off my medication, he might then see the other side of me. I hope I never do that though. With health insurance the way it is, there's always the chance that I might not be able to afford all the medications I'm on. I don't even want to think about that.

Anti-anxiety medication has become my friend, and I don't mean that in a bad way. It has given me the ability to function. So have the other bipolar medications I'm on. Outside of medication I use the distraction technique to help get through anxiety or panic attacks. If I'm having a panic attack while my husband and I are on a long driving trip, he'll have me read to him. This distracts me from the traffic. At home if I'm getting anxious, I'll turn on a movie or read a book. This tends to distract me from what was making me anxious in the first place.

I went through some depressive cycles as a teenager. I thought it was typical teenage angst. I did have thoughts of suicide then, but I never expressed them verbally or otherwise. They scared me.

I'm always aware of my illness, but there are many times when I'm stable and go about my life knowing that I am a capable, productive part of society. I go to the grocery store, get my hair styled, take my dog to the vet, and do other normal everyday activities. I think all of those places have been extended into my comfort zone. However, being aware of my illness, I know there are places or activities that I just won't venture into because I don't want to trigger an episode.

My mood cycles don't follow the calendar. I can't predict that next month I'm going to be depressed; it just happens. There really is neither rhyme nor reason for them. I have a bit more control over my anxiety and panic. I just don't put myself in situations where an episode might occur. There are occasions when panic still happens. I use one of my coping techniques, take an anti-anxiety medication, and wait for the threatened episode to go away.

I think eating healthier, taking care of myself, and getting physical exercise all help. I take vitamins and supplements every day as well as my medications. I think that they've helped me maintain a level of stability that I wouldn't have otherwise. They've given my body the extra boost it needs to deal with my illness. Stress, bad eating habits, too much sugar and caffeine, and irregular schedules can all wreak havoc on my illness. By watching what I eat, avoiding caffeine, and getting enough sleep, I know I'm taking steps to lessen my chances of an anxiety episode.

I tend to stay home more and make excuses to avoid potential events that might trigger an episode. I walk my dog down to the end of our street, but going past our road makes me uncomfortable and anxious, so I don't. I turn down most invitations to go somewhere with others, especially if I have to go alone. If I'm with my husband, I'm more likely to go, even though the anxiety is still there—it's just below the surface.

When my husband and I plan a trip, I have to have plenty of notice ahead of time so that I can "worry" about it and prepare for it. Most times with enough notice, I can worry through my anxiety, and this helps me get prepared. The same is true with any trips outside the house. I don't do anything very spontaneous anymore. I have to prepare for it so that I can look forward to it. I'm very lucky that I can work from home. I think the stress of having to commute and work with other people and project deadlines would be too much for me to handle. Being able to write when I can and in my own time schedule works best for me.

Taking my medications has enabled me to live a more stable life. Without them I'd be out of control. Who knows how much money I've saved just by being on my medications? I was a horrible compulsive shopper, but now I have more control over my spending habits as well as my eating habits. I used to be a big emotional eater. I still am to a degree, but with my medications I can control it better. I've lost sixty pounds since going on my medications.

Taking new medications has always been a major issue with me, as I am very sensitive to any changes in my medications. Right now I'm in the middle of a medication change, and the side effects were initially quite debilitating. I had to get more adjustments because I couldn't handle the changes. One of the antidepressants I'm on has a tendency to lose its effectiveness after a while, so the doctor slowly stops me from taking it, lets my body readjust to not having the medication in my system, then slowly reintroduces the medication back into my system, making it think it's new. That is rough on me as it takes around six weeks to do this—a very long six weeks!

I feel isolated because I don't tell people I meet every day what kind of illnesses I have. Mostly I don't think it's any of their business. Furthermore, I don't want to have to explain myself all the time. And deep, deep down, I'm worried that they will think less of me, that they'll look back into our past and think, "Was that a moment when she was having an episode?" I'm lonelier without my friends, but I've found a whole new set of friends on the Internet among the forums and support groups. I feel that they don't judge me. They didn't know me "back then"; they know me only after I've been on my medications. This is the "me" I want people to see. I don't know if I can get back together with old friends and get them to want to be with the new "me." I can't be that old "me" anymore. Maybe they won't like the new "me."

Sometimes I look back on my life and wish I could be the person I was who wasn't afraid, who didn't panic over the little things, who had a full schedule of work, projects, friends, and a life. I think about how I was back then, and I know that even though I may not have all those things now, I'm better because I'm on my meds and stable. Being stable is more important than stretching myself thin across multiple projects that have the potential to blow up in my face. Another way I deal with my illness is to stay in control of as many situations in my life as I can. Being in control over as much as possible helps me when anxiety or panic throws me out of control.

Kurt F.
His story . . .

Generalized Anxiety Disorder (GAD), Depression

I have been an expressive art therapist and holistic minister for people living with developmental disabilities for nearly twenty-five years. This enriches my life because I am mentoring people who live with other types of disabilities, and I am accepted. I experience fatigue, muscle pain, cognitive impairment, and coordination challenges with my depression. The fatigue feels as if I am walking through water. The anxiety includes a sense of everything being on overdrive. This affects my ability to read or keep my attention on something written. The depression reflects a sense of not feeling content or of not reaching my aspirations.

I have become more honest with people and no longer apologize when I can't do something I had made plans for. Once I explain to my friends what I'm going through, most understand. I don't do this for sympathy but rather for empathy. I start planning three or four days in advance for any obligation that is a major priority. I will rest more, maybe increase my medication, and let go of other things that can wait. I have learned how to prioritize through a life with chronic pain. I have a very understanding partner. My disorder has impacted intimacy, but this is my hang-up. I am learning that love can be expressed in simple action; for instance, my partner always has my favorite beverage in the fridge. It is his way of demonstrating his love and acceptance.

Dealing with these symptoms is a lifelong process, and so I am aware of when they become problematic. I am blessed with an employer who is empathetic to my life. I work for an agency that reflects compassion in the lives of nearly six hundred young and older adults living with disabilities. I have been with the same physician and the same job for sixteen years. This mirrors safety and reassurance for me; therefore I don't feel that others doubt my diagnosis.

When I was younger, I felt isolated. I realized that I would have to become my own advocate. I have come to terms with my disorder. I feel I am who I am. I just have to treat myself with unconditional acceptance as I am supposed to do with others. Watching metaphysical movies, especially *The Wizard of Oz*, has a positive impact on my mood. Other methods include chiropractic, massage, and daily self-inventory methods. I never feel helpless; I am a survivor.

> *I facilitated a workshop called Erase the Pain. I directed people to write about their pain experience on magic slates and then to lift the film to let it go.*

I have always experienced symptoms. This is who I am, and from this I have grown. I have learned what really matters, and I remind myself of the contract I have with myself on those challenging days. I am a spiritual being having a physical experience. I am always in some level of pain. I do, however, keep the stress in check or at least try. Stress for me can cause a flare-up. I continue to use guided imagery, painting, and poetry to enable me to witness the creative self, which has allowed me to adapt to living with a life of challenges. I have also come to understand that the way I feel can be expressed, giving life to my art.

Medication, in my case, is something that is required. I see it all as a pie with many slices that make up the whole "me." I feel that one has to find what medications work. I am always up-to-date with new medications, and I believe continued education about them is fundamental.

To cope with symptoms, I use my own creative tools such as art making, journaling, poetry, and giving conferences on this very topic.

I was a presenter at the National Expressive Therapy (Association) conference. I facilitated a workshop called "Erase the Pain." I directed people to write about their pain experience on magic slates and then to lift the film to let it go. I am always trying to connect with like-minded people who are traveling a similar path through life. I also never allow people to tell me to "snap out of it." If they do, I will call them on it. I feel I need to be perfect, and when fatigue is high, I feel low. I wouldn't expect people to understand my disorder. Each person is unique. I would expect empathy as I see this as what binds us together.

Knowledge is the key to living a self-productive life. I don't find structured support groups helpful, and thus I do not attend. I got tired of hearing people talking about who hurts the most. I find my support group outside the traditional support group.

I do not try to "will" myself to get better. I will enable myself to see the world in a neutral way. I remind myself that I am the one who gives someone or a situation power. I hope for better ways to improve my quality of life. I do not want to be viewed as a victim. I see myself as a survivor. I view this condition as my life, and I try to do something productive. I feel most hopeful when I use my art. My spiritual beliefs have been strengthened. I don't blame God as this would serve no purpose. I don't see my creator as a judge or one to hand out illness to certain people.

At times I worry about the future; however, I have no control over the future. I live life as positively as I am able to.

Lawrence J.
His story . . .

Post-Traumatic Stress Disorder (PTSD), Depression, Generalized Anxiety Disorder, Panic Disorder

I am a retired Air Force master sergeant. After retirement I was a self-employed residential contractor doing high-end remodeling. In 1999, I was in a serious auto accident in which I suffered a concussion and subsequent severe depression. Recovering from that led to my recalling all the horrors of my wartime service. I like to work with wood and make things to enhance our home. I buy the materials I need early and then start my projects but seldom finish any of them because of my depression. For years I was able to accomplish creative improvements to others' homes, and now I cannot do the same for myself. I bought a 1955 pickup truck to restore, only to have it sit untouched for five years before selling it. That was hard for me.

I have been living with PTSD, anxiety disorder with panic attacks, and clinical depression for approximately forty years. Looking back, I realize I've been affected by these problems since returning from Vietnam in 1968 when I was twenty-five years old. I remained undiagnosed until 2001, when I talked to my family doctor and told her that I needed some help dealing with what I felt was a mental breakdown. She sent me to see a psychologist, who revealed that I indeed had a problem dealing with past issues and needed to see a psychiatrist. I saw a psychiatrist who identified that I had unresolved issues from the war in Vietnam. After working with me for a while, and after prescribing numerous drugs and combinations of drugs, she suggested that I see a psychiatrist at the VA.

I began to see the psychiatrist at the VA clinic. He soon diagnosed me with PTSD and encouraged me to join his Vietnam PTSD focus group. That did not help me at all. The things I had experienced, the ones that were at the root of my problem, seemed trivial compared to the others; but they were, and still are, traumatic for me.

My feelings of aggression and worthlessness were causing me problems in my work as a contractor. I always felt I wasn't performing at my best even though I received many compliments on my work. I prided myself on being a perfectionist, and regardless of what I had accomplished, I just did not assimilate that into my feeling of well-being. Many people tried to make me realize all the good I had accomplished in my life, but I would always measure my successes by my failures. It was as if I was never satisfied with what I did. Almost all of my symptoms are under control now due to psychotropic drugs, counseling, medication monitoring and management. It's been a long, hard road to achieve the control that I needed to function as well as I do now.

> *Some people say I seem so normal ... and that the symptoms are all fabricated in order to gain sympathy or money. I usually respond by telling them to walk in my shoes ...*

When I returned from Vietnam, I felt no fear of dying. I had the utmost concern for the people who were under my supervision. I would try to protect them from all types of problems, even at my own jeopardy. I had recurring flashbacks but did not recognize them as such. I thought a flashback was like watching a tape on a VCR. Little did I know that the strong emotional feelings I had when I thought about the war or saw some news on TV were setting me up for disaster. Sometimes a word or image would send me over the brink and into complete despair.

Several years ago, I visited a friend who is a doctor in Kansas City. I was in his study reading my e-mails on his computer when he called me into the great room and wanted me to enjoy the fireworks show visible from his hilltop home. I watched for less than a minute when I excused myself and went and sat down. He again called me over to see the fireworks show before he realized that I was sobbing and shaking. After some prodding, I admitted that the fireworks had triggered a flashback so severe that I was shaking, crying, and very pale. I confided in him what had happened in Vietnam. He said that I had never discussed what went on over there, and he had no idea what I had gone through. I did not elaborate on all the gruesome details of wartime service, but I told him enough so he understood that watching the fireworks was like being back in the war and having rockets and mortars exploding around me.

After my return from Vietnam in 1968, I was usually angry and moody. I never thought there was an underlying problem that was the cause of my aggressive attitude. In the military I usually worked the night shift, where I was subjected to very little pressure and very little interaction with others. This allowed me to excel in my duties and achieve promotions, despite my open hostility toward others. I did ask a more senior NCO who had been stationed in Vietnam with me about this inability to get along with my peers and supervisors. I told him that I was thinking of seeking the services of a mental health doctor. He advised me that as soon as I sought help in that venue, I would lose my security clearance and be discharged from the Air Force and into the medical care of the VA. His advice for me was to put all the memories and feelings in a little box, store it in the recesses of my mind, and then not go there. That worked for the next thirty-one years until the accident in 1999 shattered my little box and released all the horrors of war back into my consciousness.

There is no magic bullet that I can take when I am depressed and nonfunctional. Of course there are medications that I take when I feel depressed, but they don't work very fast. I take twice the recommended daily dose of mood stabilizer as prescribed, and that seems to be the best medication for me.

When I feel that I am getting depressed, I can take steps to resolve this mood either by reading, lying down, or doing a crossword puzzle—just about anything to distract me from having a meltdown. There are, however, times when others ask me why I am so difficult to live with or to be around. When this happens I usually assess my inner feelings to understand why I feel this way. Is it from a lack of sleep, a day when I am in acute pain because of weather changes, or am I just feeling poorly? I need to assess my feelings and make some changes, such as taking a nap, calming down by doing something else, or just being alone for a while.

There is no doubt in my mind that my PTSD stems from my service in Vietnam. I thought I had dealt with those war memories long ago. I did ask the VA psychiatrist if I would ever be cured. He did not answer me directly but said they could control the symptoms. I saw my civilian psychiatrist yesterday about my medicine and asked whether I will be taking it for the rest of my life. She replied, "Probably so." I did tell her that although my PTSD was under control, I had missed my medicines for two or three days, and I was right back where I was years ago. Getting back onto my medication routine seemed to readjust my symptoms and put me back in control.

Some people say I seem so normal that I cannot be considered disabled and that the symptoms are all fabricated in order to gain sympathy or money. I usually respond by telling them to walk in my shoes for a couple of days to see what I am going through on a daily basis.

There are two methods I use in dealing with depression. First I reread the book *Psycho-Cybernetics* by Dr. Maxwell Maltz. I can relate to so many of the topics and exercises he presents in his book. Reading it helps me gain a better perspective of myself. If that fails I go into total withdrawal from everything until the anxiety passes.

As much as I would love to be rid of this millstone from around my neck, I cannot erase it from my conscious mind. Even during my best days, I feel I am under enormous pressure to become the man I was when I was stationed in Vietnam. Several people have told me that I am not the same as I was before going to war, that I am more morose and unable to relate to the things going on around me. At times I display an attitude that all is right in my world, where nothing is bothering me, but I know that is just a facade to mask the inner turmoil that is wrenching the guts inside me. I can and do put on a happy face to enjoy some comfort from my friends. Unknown triggers seem to blast away at my false front and result in my falling into the depths of depression. Of course there are times that I feel symptom-free, and I am seemingly quite happy. These are times that I can indulge in the simple pleasures of being a nice person to be around. However, I am never more than a word, sight, smell, or sound away from regressing to the person I was when I first asked for help from my doctor—in fact from the person I was upon my return from Vietnam.

Few people understand what really goes on during wartime. Sure, they see the images on television, but they miss the fear, anxiety, and horror that war entails. The realization that someone is intent on injuring or killing you numbs the senses and makes the thought of killing another human justified. At the time this was going on with me, I did not rationalize that killing was against all the principles I was ever taught. It was a matter of survival and necessary at the time. Still the horror of seeing the corpses of fellow servicemen, the noise and confusion of being under attack, the smell of death, the stench of rotting human remains, all were so traumatic that the result was, and still is, the price of my wartime service.

Talk therapy helped me after many sessions over five years. I was able to see that the problems I was having were understandable and manageable. In one of the sessions, the therapist asked me if I had ever thought about suicide. I responded, "Doesn't everyone?" She replied, "No, Lawrence, not everyone thinks about killing themselves." That gave me something to think about. Was I so wacky that thoughts of suicide seemed normal to me? I admitted that I not only thought about it, but I had a plan. That was the day when all my guns were taken away and the privilege of driving was severely restricted.

Drug therapy would give me some hope of controlling my symptoms, only to have the medications' efficacy fade in several months. Inpatient care at three different hospitals brought me little relief. I was kept under sedation much of the time, but that did not stop my attempts at self-mutilation. At times I was so overmedicated that I was not functioning at any level other than taking care of my most basic needs. My life was going by without me in it. I was told that PTSD was not curable but was controllable with medications. I felt that I had enough trials on medicines and that I was ready to quit. Urged on by my doctors and my wife, I agreed to continue trying different drug cocktails. It was during one of these trials that my psychiatrist hit on the drug that seemed to really help me. I have been taking a mood stabilizer for more than two years, and it is still working well.

When I was working for myself, I made it a practice to always arrive at the customer's home at the exact time I promised, a trait from my years in the service. After my accident and subsequently until I ceased working, I would not care if I was on time for an appointment or even show up at all. I realized that I could no longer run my business, or my life for that matter, so I just quit. I applied for Social Security disability and VA disability at the same time. Social Security was approved within ninety days, citing my thorough documentation.

Confinement at three psychiatric hospitals was insightful at one, traumatic at another, and downright hellish at the last. The first one was at a medical university mental health facility, where I received counseling, medication management, and testing. This proved helpful for a while, and I came home feeling hopeful about the future. That feeling lasted for about nine months before I was sent to the VA hospital for treatment. I could relate to some of the other patients and got along well with them. Of course my caregivers tried different drug regimes, which left me confused and sort of out of touch with reality. After one week I was sent home with a list of medications that the VA psychiatrist could use for my therapy.

Eight or nine months later, I was so depressed that I was sent to a charter hospital for evaluation and medicine trials. That hospital made me feel unimportant and overmedicated. That hospital is where, in a desperate attempt to get some help, I cut a three-inch slash on my forearm. That got some attention, all right. I was restricted even more than before and labeled a troublemaker and given even more sedating drugs. That place did more harm than good. There was no counseling and no activities, save for watching TV or sleeping all day. After six days I started to refuse my medications and threw them away. Cognitive thought returned, and I insisted that I should be allowed to leave because I was a self-admitted patient. After a loud and threatening confrontation, I was allowed to go. I would do anything, anything at all, to keep from going back to a place like that.

When a particular medication had a very positive effect on me, I would revel in a very positive way. Trivial irritants would not bother me, my restorative sleep would refresh me, and I would appear as a very upbeat persona. However, for every step up I took, I would have further to fall when the next depressive episode hit. This is something that I have had to get used to—to know when things seem to be going well, there is always the risk of a crash. I have read and studied all the aspects of PTSD and have had to admit to myself that I am enmeshed in a futile struggle to rid myself of this terrible burden, a burden that I never asked to carry but nevertheless endure.

Sherry J.
Her story . . .

Generalized Anxiety Disorder (GAD), Depression

I'm a fifty-two-year-old retired RN, happily married, with two grown children and three grandkids. My children and grandchildren live in California, and I live in Georgia with my husband, several cats, and two dogs. I have lived with my symptoms for over thirty years; I was officially diagnosed in 1996. I have only the depressive side of symptoms with occasional anxiety. I am tired most of the time, have pain in my neck, my back, my joints, and my head, and I lack the motivation I used to have. I am not as upbeat and happy as I used to be, missing the positive outlook on life that I had in the past.

I was fired from my last nursing job two years ago, and I have not returned to nursing since, causing me a great deal of pain. I truly think my depression had a role in my getting fired from my last job, but I'm just not sure. I had worked at that job for over three years with good reviews. I was a good nurse when it came to dealing with the emotional side of illness, and I believe my disorders have given me the ability to be more empathetic with my patients. It wasn't until three months before being fired that I started screwing up. I was also in a depression at the time. However, I no longer experience guilt or other negative emotions surrounding my career. I put in twenty-five years as a nurse, despite the pain and the disorders I suffered, so I feel I did my best with what I had to work with.

I have been in and out of doubting my diagnosis ever since the diagnosis was made. Sometimes I realize when I am in a depression, but sometimes my husband has to point it out to me. When I start doing less than I usually do, that's a pretty good clue I am about to go into a depression. My poor husband has had to deal with my snappiness at times. While I'm not always like that, when I am I tend to dole out a lot of apologies later. I also have problems feeling sexual and pretty when my anxiety or depression is getting the best of me.

Depression for me is akin to being in a deep well where the water is almost up to my nose. I get anxiety thinking the water is going to drown me, but it never quite gets to my nostrils. Depression makes me feel that I am a bit different from "normies," which is what I call normal people. As a result of my disorders, I have lost many friendships. I don't have a best friend, with the exception of my husband. When I was a child, I had tons of best friends, but I just don't do well with people now except on a surface level, yet I don't feel isolated as I have a great family of "fur" children...my household pets...and a wonderful husband.

The unpredictable nature of my disorder means I just don't plan ahead of time.

The unpredictable nature of my disorder means I just don't plan ahead of time. I have learned throughout my years of coping and trial and error what works for me so I won't have to worry. If I absolutely have to plan something ahead, I continue with it as planned, no matter what, ignoring the signs and symptoms, and I go on with life. I look for projects to take my mind to something else instead of getting caught up in the mood. I force myself to make sure I make my bed and keep the house clean so no one thinks I am in depression. I also force myself to take walks with the dogs. I force myself to continue to do what I normally do so I am not "caught." Eventually the project does take me away from the mood.

I have come to terms with my disorder, but I am not completely satisfied that there is nothing else I can do about curing it. I have tried to force myself to get better, and I've also tried self-talk and nutritional therapy. I want to awaken feeling refreshed, pain-free, and happy to start another day. I believe if I keep seeking ways to fix my disorder, eventually something will work, and I'll be free of this ball and chain.

I can remember a time when my disorder was not part of my everyday life. It was in my childhood, prior to finding myself pregnant at the age of thirteen. I woke up every morning refreshed, pain-free, and eager to start the day and hang with my buddies. It was heaven. I loved my life so much then.

A hopeful period in my life came when a doctor put me on a medication that helped me after three days. I woke up pain-free for the first time in twenty years, and I cried my eyes out in true, elated happiness. I thought this was going to cure me of anxiety and depression. I know now that was irrational thinking, but it did give me some solid hope. It was short-lived, however, because I had a bad reaction to the medication, and I had to stop taking it. Following that letdown, I first went into an anxiety state and then a deep depression.

One deeply low period I remember is the time I was awake for one week straight because of anxiety. I was so upset that everyone in the house except me was sleeping. I envied them. I worried so much that I was going to die from lack of sleep that the worry kept me up.

Last year I found a ten-day-old Pomeranian who has become a great therapy for me! He has inspired me to open an online store and sell dog clothes. He is the "owner," and I am his hired hand. He is also the main focus, along with the doggie clothes. I have found that having him in my life has really made a positive change in my happiness level.

My home business has really inspired me to be creative and to learn some new things I otherwise would not have bothered with. To influence my mood in a positive way when I'm in a difficult state, I will go to my website and make improvements to it, which actually makes improvements in my mood! I have learned to make my own fancy website with Flash, and I learned HTML. I know that may not be a big deal for some, but for me it's a great accomplishment. If it weren't for my new occupation, I'd still be lying around in bed or hypnotized by the TV.

I definitely feel hopeful about the future, although I know I have a struggle to deal with. I feel as long as I am alive that I have hope for my future. I'm hopeful that I'll fix my illnesses before I die. If I don't, at least I tried. Maybe in my next life I will have these things licked.

I always thought that life is what one makes it, and one can be one's own worst enemy or best friend. I chose to be my best friend after being my enemy for too many years. I used to worry about the future, but I have wisdom now to know that the future is not in my hands, so there is no use worrying about things I cannot control or change.

Cindi J.
Her story . . .

Seasonal Affective Disorder (SAD)

I was diagnosed with seasonal affective disorder at the age of thirty-one. My primary symptoms include fatigue, sleeping too much and too often, weight gain, and hopelessness. I sometimes try to explain SAD by comparing it to asthma. I look just like everybody else, but I'm battling this terrible sickness that threatens to suffocate me.

I didn't have seasonal affective disorder for most of my life. Maybe that's partly why it makes me so angry now, because I still see and remember myself as a healthy person. Growing up in Southern California, I never liked the rain or cool weather much, but winters there are short and very mild. Before moving to the Pacific Northwest, I had only experienced the occasional rainy-day blahs when a tennis date got rained out.

It's too bad that the acronym for seasonal affective disorder is SAD. Sometimes people say it just like the word "sad." People make it seem so simple, like "lonely" or "scared," as if it's simply an emotion that I should be able to regulate. I don't want to call it a disease, but there's no denying the biological factors. People don't realize how bad it can become and that it can be life threatening. I surely didn't.

One thing that defines seasonal affective disorder is that the depression follows a seasonal pattern, usually related to sunlight. I tend to start feeling bad in October or November, around when daylight saving time (DST) ends, and I start to feel better when things get brighter outside. We get an "extra" hour of light when DST starts in April, but because of the rainy weather here in the Pacific Northwest, sometimes I don't feel 100 percent until May or even June. I'm back to my happy optimistic self once the weather is good.

The last couple of winters have been really difficult, and I had thoughts of killing myself. I could no longer write off the previous four winters as coincidences. I would get so hopeless that I felt as if I'd never be happy again. I just couldn't envision the end of the winter. I really didn't want to die, but since I was already on antidepressants and was using a bright therapy light, I couldn't see a way out. I eventually realized I was getting depressed every year for several months at a time (maybe even up to six months), and that added up to half of my life! That really made me feel like all the effort of trying to hang on wasn't worth the reward of being normal the other half of the time.

> *It's too bad that the acronym for seasonal affective disorder is SAD. Sometimes people say it just like the word 'sad.' People make it seem so simple . . . as if it's simply an emotion that I should be able to regulate.*

This disorder has almost ruined my marriage. I blamed my husband for moving us to a crummy place and then for not being willing to move away to somewhere sunny so I would feel hopeful. Never mind that I had originally agreed on the move! I felt as if he was more concerned with his career than with my mental health. I decided I would be brave enough to go live by myself somewhere nice, rather than curl up and die here, so I tried to leave during the last two winters.

The first time I went to Arizona, until my husband got a job in another city that got thirty inches less rain a year than the Pacific Northwest. Even though this new city turned out to be better and absolutely beautiful, I still had a "winter freak-out" and moved back to Southern California for five months. Fortunately we had some couples' counseling in the fall, which probably helped us enough that I agreed to come back to our shared life in June. I don't know if we will start a family though. The past six years have been so hard. I am determined not to have kids if I'm not a whole, healthy woman.

This is currently a hopeful time for me, and I'm really focused on prevention right now. I am happy, back in school, my marriage is good, and I love who I am. Now I'm establishing relationships with a counselor, a primary care doctor, and a psychiatrist. I'm on a new antidepressant shown to help prevent the onset of SAD, and I'm using a new therapy light (much bigger and brighter than my old one) on a regular schedule.

Even if I were to get depressed, I've got a puppy now, and she sure as heck won't let me stay in bed! Although I'm hopeful, I'm trying to be prepared, and I do get scared about what might be coming. I've started being pretty honest with friends about what's been going on, and I ask them to help look out for me, by noticing signs that things aren't right. I look at it as a kind of early-warning system, just in case.

Spence K.
His story . . .

Depression

My depression was diagnosed when I was thirty-four, after I sought therapy a decade earlier for what I thought was as form of Peggy Lee condition: *"Is that all there is?"* Things felt dull and unexciting. I was experiencing career success but also experiencing feelings of incompleteness.

My symptoms included feeling melancholy, having sensations of being "stuck," and finding myself withdrawing from life and from others when my symptoms deepened.

I usually have some sort of physical regimen going on in my life. Right now I'm into running and hiking. I've been a rather athletic person throughout most of my life, but I find that my depression makes me feel as if I'm caught flat-footed. When I'm not in the worst of my depression and I'm running or in motion, I am generally pretty fluid and quick, but when I'm feeling locked into a depression, I am slow on the uptake. Everything seems to emotionally overwhelm me.

When my symptoms first began, I was working at a life insurance company where I provided video recordings, photography, and sound work for sales promotion and travel support. Five years later I began studies in a seminary. I initially ministered to formerly homeless veterans and did that for one year. Then I ministered in various churches for the next fifteen years. Last year I began studying for a master's degree in counseling.

I'm a pretty calm person most of the time, and having grown up around a manic-depressive dad, I think I found good reason to display a calm exterior. I've seen ups and downs. I want to be or at least appear even-keeled. The personal quiet that I present creates a sort of mask. I'm low-drama and understated anyway, so if I feel down, I simply withdraw to an even greater extent and keep to myself.

My entry into therapy at age thirty-three was the beginning of my self-knowledge. I've always attempted to be conscious of my thoughts, my actions and my affects; but from that point forward, I began to become aware of aspects of myself that at that time were beyond my perception. Becoming more aware of my behavior and reasons for it has been very worthwhile.

I feel my depression has contributed to not having established a family of my own. I'm wary of what I bring to the table. In the years since my previous relationship, it's become relatively common to have a date or two, but I've only been able to sustain a relationship for a month.

The ebb and flow of my symptoms impacts my social life. When I'm not feeling positive about myself, I initiate fewer new things, causing me to meet very few new people. I tend to make relatively close friendships with a small group of people rather than having numerous low-investment relationships.

> *My depression has exaggerated an already-present tendency to be self-deprecating. I tend to discount my strengths and contributions.*

After fifteen years in ministry work, where one has some responsibility for the people one is working with and mixing with, I found that this career was not an easy dynamic for my temperament or mood. Having to move a lot as part of my job compounded the anxiety and mismatch of my mood disorder with my lifestyle.

My depression has exaggerated an already-present tendency to be self-deprecating. I tend to discount my strengths and contributions. In some ways, however, the insight offered to me by my mood disorder helped me to empathetically work with others. For instance, I could empathize with the anxiety of folks having to be in front of cameras. I could relate to the anxiety of having to be "on" so we had *that* in common!

I'm an introvert by nature, but because of the experience of my own chemistry and awareness of my father's chemistry, and of the mental disorders of other family members, I've made a persistent and conscious effort to always temper my judgment of others around me.

When I found myself having responsibility for a community that had some unhealthy dynamics, I felt particularly isolated. This led to a deeper depression, which I ultimately chose to help with a combination of antidepressant medication and talk therapy. The medication helped me to temper what was becoming profound self-doubt in a toxic work atmosphere. I had self-medicated with alcohol but later found that taking antidepressant medication was much more effective.

Sometimes I just leap into a circumstance that generates anxiety, trusting that my instincts will eventually kick in. Sometimes I listen to my mood and let myself withdraw for a short period. I've considered myself fortunate that the nature of my work has helped propel me from being inaction, my more comfortable state, to a more active role. There are things that need to be done, whether it involves schedules that must be met, people who must be visited in hospitals, or meetings that must be attended, so I let those events and activities spur me into action...even if I feel rigid or unable to move forward.

Meditation has been very helpful to me, much of it in devotional practice. Spiritual direction has also helped. Along the way a particular nun introduced me to some Buddhist traditions. Ultimately I determined my involvement in my previous ministry was diminishing my sense of the divine, which had sustained me through a lot of chaos. Now I'm free to trust my intuition once again, free of loyalty to some determined orthodoxy of faith practice. Learning rules isn't what spirituality is about for me. Rather it's about deep meditation, behaving with integrity, and contributing to good, which helps and encourages others.

Right now I study with folks younger than me and, after thirteen months, have not made social connections because I'm not very social.

Surely there's a component of depression expressed in this type of uneasiness and isolation .

I guess I don't expect many people to understand me. I'm happily surprised when someone embraces me with a minimum of knowledge about my background. I've recently realized that I've sort of "checked out" in certain key moments of intimacy and sex, as I find it overwhelming. As for my sex drive, it's often there, but getting to fulfillment seems a chasm I don't manage to cross.

When people suggest I simply "snap out of it," it doesn't feel helpful at all; it just suggests my circumstances are coming from a lack of will or execution on my part. Nothing could be further from the truth.

Rob H.
His story . . .

Depression

I have struggled with depression for most of my life without understanding that I was depressed.

For the most part, my childhood was idyllic; however, I found myself alone quite a bit. I was the youngest of four brothers, and the other three were at least a decade older than me. As a result I grew up feeling as if I was an only child, even though I wasn't. There was a structure to my life that mapped my days: school, sports, homework, and time with Mom and Dad at the dinner table. This routine served me well into my teenage years.

I started to notice a shift in my mood during my years in junior high school. This new school had a larger and more diverse group of kids. I began to notice that I wasn't like some of them, and I certainly wasn't as outgoing or social as most of them appeared to be. I excelled at my classes in school. I enjoyed learning new things, and my classmates soon referred to me as "the brain," though I wasn't quite sure how to handle that label and I began to question what it meant. I tried not to dwell on it, but I noticed that when I did dwell on it, I grew dark and introspective. From that time on, I preferred "me time" rather than shared time with others.

When the pressure of doing well on a test or working on a group project became too much for me, I would either become angry, thereby eliciting comments that I wasn't "playing nice," or turn inward and withdraw from the activity.

It was around my junior year of high school that I began to deal with the schoolyard ridicule and exclusion by looking to the future. I felt there was a larger world that I wanted to experience, and I began to think about how I would get there. In my high school years, still not calling myself depressed, I took solace in the few friends I did have, and I began to plot a course for leaving my current life behind.

For me it was normal to feel "down" on a daily basis. It was normal to be excluded from group activities because I had developed a reputation as a hothead, someone who couldn't take the ribbing that was a normal part of friendship. As that reputation for lack of a sense of humor grew, my circle of friends became smaller and smaller. My desire to belong to the "in group" also began to change. It went from wanting to belong to a strong desire to get as far away from that environment as I could.

> *Having a therapist available as a sounding board and being offered guidance when I strayed too far helped immensely.*

By my last year of high school, I was ready to get out. My time was not spent with the "popular" kids, and I was already looking to a future away from my current life. I still hadn't put the label of depression on my frame of mind, but I was feeling the effects of four years of sensing the talk behind my back, exclusion by others, and embarrassment. That was back in the 1980s. Today it is probably labeled shame or maybe a lack of confidence.

During these same high school years, not only was I struggling to fit in at school, but I was also becoming quite embarrassed by my parents. They were old enough to be my grandparents. That led to a definite generation gap in how they raised me.

My parents were no help in the battle to understand myself, understand other people, and particularly how to interact in a now fast-changing world with those same people. My parents' methods of coping became my methods of coping. That involved little communication about what problems I encountered and how they could be dealt with, and a lot of "there, there, don't worry everything is going to be fine," sugar-coated bull. I was on my own emotionally as I was heading out into the world. That was quite frightening, although I didn't understand that at the time.

Although I was struggling to understand myself and my world during my mid- to late teens, I still wasn't calling myself depressed. I was feeling the anxiety of new surroundings, new challenges, and the typical angst of being a teenager. I had this underlying lack of feeling connected to anything. My remedy for dealing with the present was to imagine a better life away from the now. I was beginning to run away from my life, rather than running toward a better life. It wasn't until years later that I realized what a big, big impact this way of thinking had on my life then.

After high school, my college years and early work life were lived in this constant forward-looking anxiety, always focused on tomorrow. Away from my high school reputation and parents, I began to relax a little . . . with the help of alcohol. During high school I really didn't drink or party. I was too scared of what my parents would do if they caught me. I knew my dad's father had died of complications of alcoholism, but as was the norm with my parents, this was never discussed openly. Now, away at college and living on my own, I began to drink and party (attending class in-between). Drinking gave me the confidence I lacked in high school. It helped me fit in with this new crowd and lessened my fear of rejection. It opened up the world a little more. I had developed a way of living that limited who I allowed to get close to me in order to prevent the past from repeating itself—the ridicule and embarrassment. I didn't let people get close to me.

It was also my first experience with being truly depressed. Those periods were typically short-lived, a few days or so. They occurred after a hard night or two of partying. I began to question this emotion more and more. I was running away. Running from my problems during this time by looking forward to the next party was enough to keep things in check outwardly. I had become a social drinker and was getting good at hiding my anxieties about the future.

Until recently much of my post-college adult life was spent in a frustrating cycle of work at a job where I found little satisfaction in what I was doing, and then I would get more frustrated when additional responsibility and money didn't come my way. Living for tomorrow wasn't panning out. Running away from everything was starting to catch up with me.

Looking back on my life now that I'm in my mid-forties, I understand that much of my life to the present time has been colored by depression, never drastic or long lasting, except for a year or so in my mid-thirties. I was able to function at an emotional level that kept me engaged in activity. My work required much travel, and that fit nicely with the "running theme" I had based my life on.

In the early part of the new millennium, it all caught up with me—the running away, the looking for something other than what I had, and the dissatisfaction I felt with my life. I was laid off from my job, and I was away from my wife for six weeks. She was staying with a friend who was dying of cancer. She was with her friend for moral support for her and her family, but she wasn't there for me. The combination literally pushed me over the edge of fear and anxiety into depression.

I had been seeing a psychologist for about a decade prior to this time to help get some type of handle on what I was experiencing. That was my first (and only) experience with antidepressants. For me the medications worked. I was on them for about a year, which was enough time to get me through the agonizing job search, the interview process for new positions, and the "good" stress of starting a new job. The medications evened out my days, unclouded my outlook on finding a new job, and boosted my confidence a little.

Ten years removed from that experience of using antidepressants, I don't regret taking them. The combination of meds and talk therapy is what did it for me. I would suggest therapy to anyone. It's worked for me because I have discovered that I am a searcher. Having a therapist available as a sounding board and being offered guidance when I strayed too far helped immensely. I was willing to put in the work to get to the root of my problems.

In the end, I realize that life is a journey. My entire life—up until a few years ago when I came to this realization—was spent trying to reach a specific place. The struggles to get to that place without enjoying the "ride" to get there are what caused my depression. In the last few years, whenever I've lost sight of the journey, I've tried to stop and ask myself what it is that I value. My answer lies in how I am spending my time and whether I am enjoying my journey.

Diego S.
His story . . .

Clinical Depression

On October 1, 2002, at one in the morning, I entered the world of recurrent clinical depression. I had already read a number of academic studies on depression and social support, but the truth was that before October 1, I could never have imagined that depression could be so horrific. I had a friend who suffered from chronic depression, but I never took the time to ask her to help me understand this disorder.

Here is a complex and confusing phenomenon I've experienced many times: I may be feeling quite wretched the entire morning, often immobilized on the sofa or floor, yet with a surprise visit from a friend or during a scheduled appointment with my psychiatrist, my brain chemistry may dramatically change; suddenly I will feel "normal," perhaps even euphoric and animated, and often quite communicative. During one such episode, one psychiatrist, failing to use a diagnostic instrument covering the past twenty-four hours, actually stated, "Why, I don't think you're depressed." Following this session and back in my car, my brain chemistry again altered dramatically, leaving me in such a state of paralysis that I could not drive home.

When I see the typical list of symptoms on an Internet site, I often feel quite perplexed; who is being informed . . . the sufferer or someone interested in learning about depression? "Sadness" is a common symptom across Internet sites. It isn't that "sadness" and "despair" are not real symptoms of depression, but for a chronic sufferer, the voice within rebels, "Don't talk to me about the rain, when I'm being hit by a *tsunami!*"

I always walk into my psychiatrist's office with typed notes for him or her, including my symptoms since our last visit. With nearly nine years of visitation notes, "sadness" is not on any one of them. I tell my closest friends, "Think of the last time you suffered from the most wicked flu; now multiply that by three." Sadness and despair are real! But these feelings are overwhelming during episodes of depression. These episodes are characterized by real "physical pain" that emanates from deep within the body, the nervous system, and the frontal cortex of the brain. No chance to get into one's sadness when overcome with a feeling that death might be close, when every breath requires tremendous effort, when, lacking oxygen, the body gasps for air. When visiting my psychotherapist on a weekly, sometimes bi-weekly basis, I bring my despair, my hopelessness, and my confusion. I bring it all into the room, some of it on pieces of paper or in my journal writing, but most of it I share through tears and in my own familiar voice of anguish.

> *For some people with chronic depression, there is a bizarre connection between suffering a nearly unbearable anguish and an energizing passion. In that amalgamation, one can find great creativity.*

I have learned to live with the ebb and flow of clinical depression and the dizzying array of medications. Complaints regarding symptoms made to my psychiatrist often translated into additional medications. Depression does not stop me from mentoring my students, nor does it stop me from loving those I have loved for years. It did not stop me from becoming involved in two romantic relationships, each involving a divorcée and a beautiful boy, where marriage was clearly something we had hoped would happen. It did not stop me from traveling and presenting at national and regional conferences, or from accepting invitations to give key-note addresses at two important seminars.

In the summer of 2007, I began reading the medical literature on yoga, yogic breathing, and depression. I found a yoga studio in Pasadena and began my yoga practice. After reading the foremost book on yoga and depression by Amy Weintraub, RYT, I contacted her and explained my history. Immediately after the call, I booked a flight to Austin, Texas, and took a five-day workshop with her and twenty-seven women yoga teachers and psychotherapists. In the fall of 2007, I left for an intensive two-month training stint at a well-known yoga center in the Berkshires of Massachusetts. I returned with my first-level certificate as a registered yoga teacher, with a specialty in depressive and anxiety disorders. I began teaching yogic breathing at my church. My hatha yoga practice, when regular, keeps my depression in check, away from the most debilitating episodes. But hatha yoga classes are expensive, and most studios make little effort to attract an age-diversified clientele.

I do not wish to romanticize clinical depression in any way. It is a hellish disorder, and one that does not captivate and induce family and friends to rally around. Besides depression there is unbearable loneliness—and by definition, no one sees my loneliness. For some people with chronic depression, there is a bizarre connection between suffering a nearly unbearable anguish and an energizing passion. In that amalgamation, one can find great creativity.

I am a writer, teacher, and researcher, and I live with recurrent clinical depression. At any moment I may find myself lying in the corner of my carpeted bedroom floor in a fetal position, trying to withstand the crashing and painful blows of a psychic tsunami. This very same person can also write with passion, fly halfway across the globe to Taiwan to lecture for three days, withstand the legal battle of a lifetime, and love someone as deeply as anyone can. I, who suffers from depression, continue to mentor my former students (now assistant professors) and inspire them, all the while helping them develop coping strategies that will empower them in the face of the racism or sexism they may face in their careers. I, who suffers from depression, can show up for a level II yoga class and, along with twenty-five other students who are, on average, twenty-eight years younger than I am, can proceed through ninety minutes of yoga poses without a problem.

So where do I go from here at age fifty-five, with nine years of depression behind me and with my academic career at a critical juncture? At this point in time, I acknowledge that my depression has blessed me with the authority and experience of being a teacher, a counselor, and an advocate for all who suffer with this illness called depression.

NOTES

[1] People Magazine, May 17, 2010, page 80.
[2] Excerpt from *Down Came the Rain* by Brooke Shields:
(New York: Hyperion Books, 2006).
http://www.ppdsupportpage.com/brookeshields.html
[3] "A 'Visual Diary' of Depression" by Marvi Lacar;
CNN © 2010 Cable News Network:
http://cnnphotos.blogs.cnn.com/2012/02/06/a-visual-diary-of-depression/
[4] "Strategies for Coping with OCD in the Workplace,"
co-authored by Michael McKee, PhD, Clinical Psychologist:
http://www.michaelmckeephd.com/workplace_ocd.htm
[5] Archives of General Psychiatry, January 2004.
[6] Newsweek, Dec 11, 2006, page 62.
[7] "Stress and Exercise: Look Better, Feel Better,"
by Elizabeth Scott, MS; About.com:
http://stress.about.com/od/programsandpractices/a/exercise.htm
[8] Excerpt from *Against Happiness* by Eric G. Wilson.
(Sarah Crichton Books, New York: a division of Farrar, Straus and Giroux, LLC, 2008)
[9] *Living Well* by Montel Williams and William Doyle
(New York: New American Library, division of Penguin Group USA Inc., 2008), page 17.

[10] *Living Well* by Montel Williams and William Doyle, (New York: New American Library, division of Penguin Group USA Inc., 2008), page 19.
[11] *Living Well*, page 4
[12] *Living Well*, page 5
[13] *Living Well*, page 15
[14] Medscape Medical News, Feb. 6, 2008
[15] "PTSD Influences Levels of Depression and Pain" (American Pain Society, July 22, 2008).
[16] Excerpt from "The One-Two Punch of Major Depression" (Johns Hopkins University, 2007).

Made in the USA
Charleston, SC
08 February 2013